MUSSOLINI, ARCHITECT: PROPAGANDA AND URBAN LANDSCAPE IN FASCIST ITALY

MUSSOLINI ARCHITETTO: PROPAGANDA E PAESAGGIO URBANO NELL'ITALIA FASCISTA

MUSSOLINI, ARCHITECT
Propaganda and Urban Landscape in Fascist Italy

MUSSOLINI ARCHITETTO
Propaganda e paesaggio urbano nell'Italia fascista

PAOLO NICOLOSO

Translated by Sylvia Notini

UNIVERSITY OF TORONTO PRESS

Toronto Buffalo London

Edizione originale:
© 2008 e 2011 Giulio Einaudi editore s.p.a., Torino
Prima edizione <Einaudi Storia>
www.einaudi.it

English-language edition:
© University of Toronto Press 2022
Toronto Buffalo London
utorontopress.com
Printed in the U.S.A.

ISBN 978-1-4426-3104-5 (cloth)   ISBN 978-1-4426-3100-7 (EPUB)
     ISBN 978-1-4426-3099-4 (PDF)

Toronto Italian Studies

Library and Archives Canada Cataloguing in Publication

Title: Mussolini, Architect : propaganda and urban landscape in fascist Italy =
    Mussolini architetto : propaganda e paesaggio urbano nell'Italia fascista / Paolo
    Nicoloso ; translated by Sylvia Notini.
Other titles: Mussolini architetto : propaganda e paesaggio urbano nell'Italia
    fascista
Names: Nicoloso, Paolo, 1957– author.
Series: Toronto Italian studies.
Description: English-language edition. | Series statement: Toronto Italian
    studies | Translation of: Mussolini architetto : propaganda e paesaggio urbano
    nell'Italia fascista. | Includes bibliographical references and index.
Identifiers: Canadiana (print) 20220222908 | Canadiana (ebook) 20220222983 |
    ISBN 9781442631045 (cloth) | ISBN 9781442631007 (EPUB) |
    ISBN 9781442630994 (PDF)
Subjects: LCSH: Mussolini, Benito, 1883–1945. | LCSH: Fascism and
    architecture – Italy. | LCSH: Fascist propaganda – Italy. | LCSH: Architecture –
    Italy – History – 20th century. | LCSH: Fascism – Italy – History. | LCSH: Italy – Cultural
    policy – History – 20th century.
Classification: LCC NA1118.5.F28 N5413 2022 | DDC 720.945/09043 – dc23

The translation of this book was made possible thanks to a grant from the Graham
Foundation for Advanced Studies in the Fine Arts.

Graham Foundation

We wish to acknowledge the land on which the University of Toronto Press operates. This
land is the traditional territory of the Wendat, the Anishnaabeg, the Haudenosaunee, the
Métis, and the Mississaugas of the Credit First Nation.

University of Toronto Press acknowledges the financial support of the Government of
Canada, the Canada Council for the Arts, and the Ontario Arts Council, an agency of the
Government of Ontario, for its publishing activities.

Canada Council   Conseil des Arts
for the Arts   du Canada

ONTARIO ARTS COUNCIL
CONSEIL DES ARTS DE L'ONTARIO
an Ontario government agency
un organisme du gouvernement de l'Ontario

Funded by the Financé par le
Government gouvernement
of Canada   du Canada

Contents

Illustrations

Foreword

Paolo Nicoloso's subtle book with a provocative thesis will intrigue scholars and general readers interested in the complex relationship between art and politics during the twentieth century. Originally published in Italian by Giulio Einaudi Editore in 2008, this critically acclaimed study was reprinted in 2011 due to the high volume of sales. Not incidentally, Einaudi, one of Italy's premier publishers, was established in 1933 in Turin in defiance of fascism, which made it a fitting publisher of the book. The thesis of Nicoloso's highly anticipated English-language translation goes as follows: From the mid-1930s onward, Mussolini – who was not trained as an architect despite what the title of Nicoloso's book seems to imply – began to demand a modern and monumental architecture that was explicitly classical as a means to educate and thus rally the masses more effectively to fascism. This explains why Rome, Italy's politically charged capital, became the site of Mussolini' propagandistic agenda, culminating in the E42 (Esposizione Universale Roma) neighbourhood, executed under his leadership with the contributions of architect Marcello Piacentini and several others. Nicoloso argues his case for Mussolini's gradual shift in approach (one that the dictator himself astutely sought to conceal), which unfolded following the 1936 annexation of Ethiopia, through carefully crafted chapters that are selectively illustrated (with rare period photos) that reveal the different facets of this compelling story. Most importantly, the episodes described throughout the book make abundantly clear Mussolini's almost daily involvement with architecture and architects.

The engaging and scholarly quality of Nicoloso's writing directly counters the hyperbolic tone of the propaganda produced during fascism and more recently in Italy by pundits who continue to celebrate the multifaceted "accomplishments" of Benito Mussolini while ignoring the repressive politics that enabled him to achieve them. The seemingly unbiased approach is reassuring insofar as one is inclined to believe that this historian does not have an overtly political agenda of his own. Nicoloso is on the faculty of the Department of Engineering and Architecture of the University of Trieste, which is housed in a monumental building realized under fascism. He is far enough from Rome to foster a certain critical distance while patiently focusing his scholarly work on the "inter-war years" (that is, fascism between 1922 and 1943) in Italy. While Nicoloso is an architectural historian (trained at the prestigious IUAV University of Venice with Giorgio Ciucci, Manfredo Tafuri, and Georges Teyssot), his *Mussolini, Architect* is as much architectural as cultural and social history. Among Italian histories of Fascism that have been translated into English, cited here with admiration is Emilio Gentile's book entitled *The Sacralization of Politics in Fascist Italy* (Harvard University Press, 1996). Like Gentile, Nicoloso makes extensive use of archival material to support his carefully argued thesis.

In the pages that follow English-language readers now finally have the opportunity to discover for themselves what Nicoloso makes of Mussolini's strategic exploitation of architecture as a tool for propaganda.

Michelangelo Sabatino
Inaugural John Vinci Distinguished Research Fellow
Professor and Director, PhD Program in Architecture,
College of Architecture, Illinois Institute of Technology

Sabatino's award-winning study *Pride in Modesty:
Modernist Architecture and the Vernacular Tradition in Italy* (2010)
was also published by the University of Toronto Press.

Acknowledgments

This book is based on research for several previous studies I undertook on the relationship between architecture and politics during the fascist regime. In the spring of 2001 I turned to focus more on the figure of Mussolini and the role he played. I was able to develop and discuss the themes presented in this book during the two-year courses I taught at the Graduate School of Art History at the University of Udine. I was offered an early opportunity to discuss my research with Massimo Martignoni, Jeffery T. Schnapp, and Marida Talamona at a seminar entitled "Architettura e politica negli anni del fascismo," held at the School of Architecture in Trieste in May 2003. I was later able to analyse Mussolini and the Città Universitaria in a paper that, on Giuliana Mazzi's invitation, I presented at a conference entitled "L'università e la città," held in Padua in December 2003. In March 2004, I was invited by Giorgio Ciucci to hold a seminar for the European Masters in History of Architecture at the University of Rome Tre on some of the topics discussed in this book.

I have been helped by many people while conducting my research; they include Marina Gianetto of the Central State Archive in Rome, Gianna Frosali of the Piacentini Archive in Florence, Paola Pettenella and Carlo Prosser of MART in Trento and Rovereto, Chiara Campagnolo, Gianguido Folena, Paolo Mungiovino, and Marta Petrin. I am especially grateful to Ferruccio Luppi of the Portaluppi Foundation for the iconographic research as well as for his great help in so many ways. I express my gratitude to the other scholars for their help with the endnotes.

I am also grateful to those who read, partly or completely, the draft manuscript, and discussed both doubts and ideas for exploration; these interlocutors include Donata Battilotti, Cristina Bianchetti, Massimo De Sabbata, Roberto Dulio, Vilma Fasoli, Flavio Fergonzi, Michelangelo Sabatino, and Marida Talamona. I also wish to thank Marida for her hospitality while I was in Rome. Heartfelt thanks to Sergio Luzzato for having believed in this research and for his precious contributions in the form of criticism, suggestions, and annotations. Naturally, the responsibility for the final text is mine alone.

The translation of this book was made possible thanks to a grant from the Graham Foundation for Advanced Studies in the Fine Arts. I am indebted to Michelangelo Sabatino for having invited me to translate into English the story that is told here, and for his countless, invaluable suggestions. I am also grateful to Jean-Louis Cohen and Kurt W. Forster, who both supported this project. Lastly, heartfelt thanks to Sylvia Notini for her competence, commitment, and the passion she dedicated to the translation of this volume.

This book is dedicated to Laura.

Abbreviations

AEG	Allgemeine Elektricitäts-Gesellschaft
AGIP	Azienda Generale Italiana Petroli
E42	Esposizione Universale Roma
GIL	Gioventù italiana del littorio
GUR	Gruppo Urbanisti Romani
INA	Istituto Nazionale Assicurazioni
INCIS	Istituto Nazionale Case per Impiegati dello Stato
INFAIL	Istituto Nazionale Fascista Assicurazioni Infortuni sul Lavoro
INFPS	Istituto Nazionale Fascista di Previdenza Sociale
LUCE	L'Unione Cinematografia Educativa
ONB	Opera Nazionale Balilla
ONC	Opera Nazionale Combattenti
PNF	Partito Nazionale Fascista
RAS	Riunione Adriatica di Sicurtà
SCIA	Società Costruzioni Italo Americana

MUSSOLINI, ARCHITECT: PROPAGANDA AND URBAN
LANDSCAPE IN FASCIST ITALY

MUSSOLINI ARCHITETTO: PROPAGANDA E
PAESAGGIO URBANO NELL'ITALIA FASCISTA

Introduction

In the first half of the twentieth century, there was no other country as politically invested in public architecture as fascist Italy. Over the course of the 1920s, and even more so during the 1930s, Italy produced a vast architectural output, exceeding that of many other countries. The regime left its mark on the country by raising hundreds of structures and developments: Case del Fascio (Fascist Party Meeting Houses), schools, government buildings, post offices, ministry headquarters, courthouses, railway stations, Opera Nazionale Balilla (Fascist Party youth group) headquarters, local government office buildings, swimming pools, state-controlled institutions, urban renewal projects for old town centres, and even whole new cities. Even when compared with Nazi Germany, whose regime launched a more ambitious and comprehensive program, fascist Italy was more successful, because the works were actually completed. In 1941, in his analysis of this architectural production, Marcello Piacentini wrote that Italy had built much more than "any other people in the same period had ever even imagined doing." The evocative image of a country viewed from above and turned into one huge smoking building site, an image that the fascist propaganda relentlessly promoted, enthralled the masses then and continues to capture the public imagination today.

In those years in Italy, architecture and politics enjoyed a close alliance. Architecture became an instrument for the government to obtain the consensus of the masses. The regime pointed to new public buildings as examples of fascist architecture it had built for the people. Everything displayed the emblems of the Fascist Party. Though it had always been an *instrumentum regni* (instrument for the purpose of ruling), architecture became an extraordinary tool through which the dictatorship could demonstrate and consolidate its power. As in preceding historical eras, which it deliberately invoked, architecture was extensively used to celebrate the regime and its dictator. Architecture's efficacy as a means of communication and its results at a political level were plain to see. It was not just that the subjugated masses were awed by the buildings' massive dimensions, the splendour of their forms, the richness of the materials: the buildings' physical concreteness, their social impact, and their functional connotations also won the support of people who were indifferent to politics, and the sheer number of buildings erected contributed to defusing the dissent of the regime's critics.

Up until now, the scholarly literature has almost always stressed that the regime, during a particular phase of its existence, used architecture primarily as a means to achieve political consensus. This book aims to move one step further and show how the regime also turned architecture into a tool to educate the masses, and, indeed, show how Mussolini's stance vis-à-vis architecture changed over time. His attitude towards architecture at the beginning of the 1930s was different from what it was by the end of that decade. We need to acknowledge this discontinuity if we are to avoid falling into the trap of the usual simplifications, and if we are to fully understand the novelty of Mussolini's relationship with architecture. In short, while at first the dictator used architecture to earn the support of the masses, he later made architecture a part of the process of the totalitarianization of society, aimed at transforming the character, habits, and mindset of the Italian people. The thesis put forward here is that architecture became an essential tool in the totalitarian turnaround of the regime.

Mussolini used architecture to educate the masses in a fascist sense; he exploited its symbolic prowess. Italian fascism distinguished itself through its mass politics based on myth. We see this in the way it drew a link between Rome's imperial past and its revolutionary present, the way it coalesced the people and consolidated them in the figure of the leader, and, lastly, the way it promoted the model of the "new man," who was both warrior and builder. The "arcane power" of architecture – as Piacentini aptly described it – was a formidable tool to make those myths visible, to root them in the masses, to transform the mindset of an entire people, and to fuel their self-consciousness. In other words, architecture could be used to convert people to fascism. In the 1930s, as though Italy itself were an enormous stage, countless buildings went up across the entire country, and they could instantly be recognized by the people as the works of the Duce. Architecture played a crucial role in the enactment of fascist policies. These buildings were not superfluous props or marginal manoeuvres in the overall economy; rather, they were real symbols of the regime, essential to the dissemination of Mussolini's secular religion.

Architecture has always been key to the process of forging identity. The architectural monument has the ability to convey meanings that can reach an entire community, which, in turn, identifies with it. In the mid-1930s, fascism doubled down on this tried and tested identity-forming device in order to determine, with greater clarity, the unifying and distinctive elements of a people's sense of belonging, as well as to give a clearer material form to the myths needed to forge the character of the Italian people. This led to the transition from architecture used as a means to achieve political consensus, to architecture used as an educational tool, which also led to a change in attitude towards style. Whereas at the beginning of the decade Mussolini's support swung indifferently between traditionalist and modernist styles, the mid-1930s marked an important change. The regime established a preference for architecture that was modern, but classicist as well, as was the case for the buildings of the E42. The E42 was a universal exposition intended to showcase an unparalleled vastness and splendour, to take on the weight of a global political event to establish fascism's hegemony. The paradoxical paradigm of a dictatorship with a liberal approach to the arts only survived until the mid-1930s. The years following the 1935–6 Ethiopian War saw a dramatic rise in totalitarianism, with a clear move by the state towards greater intervention in architecture and other artistic forms.

Architecture that could educate the masses needed clear forms, shapes that everyone could understand. Hence, a style had to be "invented," one that, without abandoning the characteristics of modernity, would speak to the collective memory of the nation. This type of architecture would exemplify traditional, classical architecture, whose original splendour dated back to ancient Rome. It would reawaken a sense of belonging and national pride; it would nurture, in the collective imagination, the idea of a country that was once again powerful and invested with a civilizing mission. By recalling the eternal classicist order, such a style could act as a reassuring talisman against all the chaos, alienation, and angst that came with the rise of modernity. Between 1937 and 1940, the E42 became a huge building site where this new architectural language could be developed, a language capable of shaping the myths of imperial fascism. The E42 was an architectural model for all the other building sites established throughout the country at that time.

However, Mussolini did not wish to impose a "fascist style" from above. The new style had to be achieved through a much finer strategy – a complex, participatory, and gradual process. The new style had to appear spontaneous, it had to be an earnest, confident manifestation of all architectural culture, cohesive in its search for a "unity of direction" shared in full by the masses. In other words, it had to seem as though it respected the "general will" of the people. This way of configuring architecture, by making it seem as though no rules were being imposed – but rather that it emerged as though the architects themselves were naturally finding harmony among themselves, almost in unison, progressing towards a unity of direction, in the direct expression of a popular need – was one of the new and distinctive features of Italian fascism. As we shall see, Mussolini governed these choices without appearing, at least publicly, to be injunctive. But behind the scenes, Mussolini did intervene, he directed fascism towards a particular style: he wanted to forge the identity of a people, so that being Italian and being fascist would come to mean one and the same thing.

During those years, Italy saw a large-scale political effort to use architecture to manipulate the consciences of individuals in order to control the people's code of identity. The language of this architecture could not at all be "international," because that was synonymous with "plutocracy and socialism"; rather, it had to be identifiable as national. It also had to be modern, because fascist Italy was marching towards the future, and because fascism was a revolution, albeit one linked to the classical tradition of "arches and columns," or in any case elements that were easily recognized by the people. Such a language had to be able to unite all Italians, not only in the present, but also from a historical perspective. Thus, echoes of the classical age, characteristic of Italian art in general, served to enhance architecture's eternal nature and universal mission.

As had been done in the distant past, Mussolini was seeking to use architecture to establish the supremacy of Italian civilization. The deep, centuries-old crisis that had marked Italian history – that of a country with a great tradition of civilization and culture, which it never balanced, except in ancient Rome, with a similar manifestation of political power – now finally appeared to have been reinstated and to have found its seal in the close alliance between fascism and architecture. Alongside fascism, which, after many centuries, had finally restored Italy's role as a great country, here was a type of architecture capable of rising to the occasion in representing the "leader of civilization." The powerful metaphor of rebirth intimately connected fascism to architecture. Architecture, more than the other arts, offered the fascist revolution the historical depth it needed to legitimize its ambition to dominate. Fascism's mission, that of spreading its "superior" order to the rest of the world, found essential support in this particular genre, which had already produced lasting monuments, both in ancient Rome and during the Renaissance, and was now being reborn. It was no coincidence that at the Olympics of Civilizations, that is, at the E42, the idea was for different countries to compete in the field of architecture. The regime, in order to achieve its ultimate goal of creating the new fascist civilization, gradually found architecture to be an extraordinary ally, one it could not do without.

While it is true that, when the regime fell, the ambitious project of exporting its architecture abroad failed miserably, its architectural program had a huge impact on Italy itself. Nationally speaking, it achieved undeniable results in terms of political consensus, even though it may not have fared as well in terms of its educational purpose. Nevertheless, we need to consider that the educational function of architecture had broader repercussions, and that results were not always immediately perceived. Architecture did not only involve those who lived under Mussolini's rule, but future generations as well. They too were involved in the process of creating an identity. The buildings the regime raised were destined to become the heritage of the country as a whole. They were extensions of the glorious heritage of the past, on which fate had bestowed the task of defying time, and they formed the new basis for the Italian people's historical memory. Fascism did not just seek to colonize history, realigning national identity heritage along an arbitrary temporal arc aimed at celebrating the splendours of the present. Through the enduring nature of architecture, fascism aimed to influence posterity as well, for decades and even centuries to come. In other words, Mussolini fully intended for those works to continue carrying meanings, even when fascism no longer existed. He knew that the anthropological transformation of the Italian people would take a long time. He therefore chose architecture over the other arts because it was made of stone, and it would endure.

Mussolini himself was the leading actor in the regime's achitecture program. "I am an expert on architecture," he confided to the art critic Ugo Ojetti during a visit to the Venice Biennale in June 1934. How should we interpret this statement? Was the Duce really well versed in architecture? Or was it an empty brag? Were his words simply a way to hide his self-confessed difficulty understanding the art on display at the exhibition? Or did it reveal something else? In the mid-1920s, Margherita Sarfatti, his first biographer, wrote that "architecture interests him the way it once interested the Latin people, for its usefulness, for the work it entails, and because it is a sign of a flourishing state and the expression of a nation's greatness."[1] But however indicative this passage may be of the high profile the Duce assigned to architecture, as well as its author's intention to place the dictator within the myth of ancient Roman tradition, is it sufficient to convey the complexity of the relationship between Mussolini and architecture? Could it not be said that, during the 1930s, the Duce established a more multiform, participatory, ambitious, and essential political project centring on architecture? The historical analysis presented here tries to answer these very questions.

This book documents numerous encounters between Mussolini and architecture. They are not limited to formal events, pre-established rituals, or episodes of conspicuous and deceptive fascist hagiography. Mussolini did not always wear a mask; his behaviour was not always histrionic.

He was also genuinely interested in architecture. The documents examined here reveal Mussolini's skill in dealing with architectural issues and his desire for architects to involve him in their work. Not only was he concerned about the type of marble used to clad a palace, he was also involved in some far more important issues, such as a monument's placement and its shape. Not everything was about propaganda, and indeed the term seems reductive in explaining what actually happened, which was more serious and complex. Contrary to what has been commonly believed until now, Mussolini played an important role in many of the fundamental events in the history of Italian architecture through his influence and the decisions he imposed. In the extravagant project to build a new fascist civilization, one that could, through strength, dominate the new European order, architecture had the educational role of representing and reviving that myth in the marble itself. The charismatic figure of the leader who swaggeringly led the Italian people towards the future, towards a new civilization, needed the support of an architecture that was equally charismatic in form, capable of designing scenarios that could reassure its citizens, who were being asked to have faith and believe in their own glorious future. The widespread idea that the fascist dictatorship did not have its own policy with regard to architecture must therefore, at least in part, be reassessed, at least as concerns the period after 1936.

And yet, such a significant and in many ways extremely evident reality – newspapers regularly reported Mussolini's frequent visits to building sites, and Istituto LUCE newsreels often featured images of inaugurations of public buildings – has never been adequately studied by historians of fascism. The clearest example of this can be found in the work of the most important scholar of that period in Italy history. In his monumental and extraordinary work on Mussolini, Renzo De Felice entirely overlooked the issue of architecture. In the almost 4,000 pages dedicated to the Duce, from his rise to power in October 1922 to the events of July 1943, the word "architecture" never appears.[2] There is one reference to the E42, an important one no doubt, but only as concerns the regime's plan to use it to fund the war. It seems strange and hard to explain how a historian as brilliant and attentive as De Felice could have overlooked Mussolini's involvement in architecture; how the significance of the dictator's activism in the sector, which was far from marginal, did not deserve even a few lines in his massive opus.

By contrast, the most enlightening contribution is the one made by Emilio Gentile. His research, itself inspired by research George Mosse carried out on Germany, demonstrated for the first time and with undeniable efficacy that the secular religion of fascism exploited architecture to celebrate the cult of the "Littorio," and to impress a political faith upon the people.[3] Gentile's most recent book dedicated to Rome and its myth also discusses the regime's desire to influence the destiny of Italians through the construction of monuments.[4] Architecture historians, for their part, have dealt with the relationship between fascism and architecture in many works, using different approaches and achieving different results.[5] In the mid-1970s, Giorgio Ciucci wrote about the ideological support provided by urban architectural culture to the regime's anti-urban policy. Antonio Cederna extensively documented Mussolini's involvement in the demolition of Rome's historical centre in the name of the restoration of the myth of imperial Rome and the newfound splendour of fascism. Diane Ghirardo underlined the contribution of young Rationalist architects in the celebration of the regime. More recently, Jeffery Schnapp examined the Exhibition of the Fascist Revolution and its unexpected political success.[6] However, despite these individual contributions, the role of architecture in the Duce's strategy of consensus has yet to be deeply and broadly analysed. Studies have paid even less attention to the educational effect of architecture, and its essential role in fascism.

Generally speaking, historians and architecture historians have underestimated architecture's role in fascism, at least in part. It is safe to say that while the former have supported the notion of the absence of a fascist policy in the field of architecture, the latter, encouraged by this thesis, have claimed that architecture was substantially separate from politics. Hence, this research on a grey area that has not yet been sufficiently studied, bounded by these two disciplines and based on the documents collected, suggests a different historiographical thesis: that is, that Mussolini did indeed have a strategy for architecture, one that, over time, changed its physiognomy and expressed itself in contradictory ways, eventually coming to fill a central role in the general political scheme.

One of the reasons for the difficulties in studying the role that architecture played in the 1930s is the attitude of the architects themselves in the postwar period. Those who had played a leading role in fascist Italy tended to try to erase that part of their past, their party membership, their ideology, and their relationships with the regime all the way up to the highest echelons. They successfully managed to redefine the role they had played in that period. They distanced themselves from the regime, they refused to take responsibility, they denied any collaborations they may have had, or else they made them seem less important than they actually were. They disentangled themselves from a compromising political past. Above all, they claimed the discipline's resistance to politics. Their reasons are evident, and perhaps even understandable, as they mostly wished to resume work when the war was over.

The same cannot be said for the complicity of many historical studies, recent ones as well, unfortunately, concerning architecture in that period. Worse still, they have worked and are still working on a "de-fascistization" of the historical context, minimizing or deliberately avoiding any analysis of the relationship between architects and fascism, or directly with Mussolini, dissociating the work of such architects from the political framework in which they were active. And without ever asking themselves about the purpose of the buildings that were built. Hence, they flatten history, make its protagonists unrecognizable, its values indistinct. As if designing a public building to represent Mussolini's dictatorship or postwar democratic Italy were the exact same thing.

The first part of this book focuses on one of the most evident manifestations of the political use of architecture for the purpose of creating political consensus: the inaugurations of buildings that Mussolini attended during his travels through Italy. Those events, treated with the utmost importance by the press and the newsreels, functioned as an extraordinary showcase both for the Duce and for architecture. Especially during the 1930s, Mussolini travelled extensively across Italy in order to put his "signature" on architectural works. Dozens of architects accompanied him on what resembled pilgrimages. In so doing, not only did Mussolini become acquainted with the leading names in the field of architecture, but he also acquired a direct, albeit superficial, awareness of of Italy's vast architectural output, an awareness which probably surpassed that of many experts. His trips were carefully planned and, most of the time, the buildings themselves determined the itinerary. Funding for these works was granted in preparation for Mussolini's visit, for the purpose of making his appearance seem even more "triumphal." Propaganda magnified those events in order to present the image of a country marching, with the utmost determination, towards modernization and fascistization. Wherever Mussolini travelled, new building sites were opened, scaffolding was put up, and buildings were inaugurated.

Although Mussolini travelled extensively outside of Rome, he was unquestionably more concerned with architecture in the capital. Rome was the city where his architectural policies were focused. It was in the capital that, from the outset, the encounter between politics and architecture was openly expressed. In Rome the Duce could monitor works directly, from the planning phase to their realization, as documented by his numerous inspections of building sites. For the dictator, the city was one huge, open building site. He assiduously pursued a strategy aimed at leaving a Mussolinian mark on the city, at building the Third Rome, which would take its place alongside the Rome of antiquity and the Renaissance.

The trips examined in this book took place between 1929 and 1940. The year 1929 coincides with the Lateran Pacts and the Plebiscite, both of which marked a phase during which the regime managed to consolidate consensus, as well as the passage to an evident fascistization of the country and the establishment of the cult of Mussolini. By contrast, the year 1940 saw the outbreak of war, which led to a crisis for the regime, although some signs of disaffection had already begun to emerge.[7] During that period, there was hardly a region that Mussolini did not visit, and only a few of the provinces were excluded from his itineraries. He viewed hundreds of works. All things considered, these trips offer a general idea of the vastness of the program and of the importance the regime assigned to architectural works. They also reveal the mechanisms that fuelled the myth of Mussolini as a builder of cities, and that enhanced the cohesive function of architecture. The work of thousands of people was embodied in the image of a single figure, the Duce himself. He communicated with the masses through architecture, which became the emblem of a political pact between the dictator and his people, and a powerful bond based on loyalty and obedience. Architectural works, therefore, acted as the nation's unifying emblem: symbols made of stone, designed to endure so that the glory of fascism could be handed down to posterity. No less powerful than the means of modern mass communication used by the regime, such as cinema and radio, this ancient art confirmed its effectiveness in producing powerful collective imaginaries among contemporary Italians. In modern times as well, its "arcane power" continues to affect the masses, consolidating and coalescing them around a cultural icon.

Nonetheless, at this time, buildings made with Mussolini's support were very different from each other. There were works by both traditionalist and Rationalist architects, such as Armando Brasini and Ignazio Gardella, Ugo Giovannozzi and Giuseppe Vaccaro, Cesare Bazzani and Giuseppe Pagano. A building in the classical style might casually follow one in a Rationalist style. This represents another, more complex, order of problems, one which constitutes a basic issue raised in this book. Which choices were Mussolini's? Did he take a stance with regard to contrasting styles? Did he express preferences, or did he remain neutral?

The rare statements he publicly made about the matter do not help. The dictator kept his judgments to himself; and when he did make statements, they were ambiguous or contradictory. Between 1925 and 1934, some of the statements and decisions he made bear this out. However, the situation changed in the second half of the 1930s after the war in Ethiopia, and Mussolini's position became somewhat clearer. The final part of this study focuses on this change, which emerged at the same time as the regime's enforcement of its totalitarian policy.

While Mussolini officially had little to say about architecture, he did have a great many ties to architects. Some of them wrote to him, others sent him books, and others still gave him ideas. Some of these architects were even invited to Palazzo Venezia. Drawings were unrolled on Mussolini's desk, photographs of the models were spread out, notebooks with budgets were laid open, so that all could be discussed with Mussolini – but without a true exchange of ideas, as the Duce did not like to be contradicted – and the architects could prove the worth of their proposals. The idea was to convince him that their particular style of architecture offered the best possible interpretation of the regime's policies. According to archival records, around fifty architects were welcomed to Palazzo Venezia. On some occasions, it was Mussolini himself who summoned them to the Sala del Mappamondo (Map Room). Only a few words were exchanged face to face, to emphasize an idea that he cared about, or to provide motivation. Knowing that one's work was being monitored directly by the dictator – that he had personally examined the drawings and that he had spoken well of the ideas put forward – was an extraordinary source of pride and inspiration. One can sense the Duce's preference for Giovanni Muzio, Mario Palanti, and Luigi Moretti, his courtesy towards Francesco Leoni, and his satisfaction with Brasini. However, what stands out especially is his relationship with Piacentini.

On the whole, between his travels and his audiences at Palazzo Venezia, Mussolini came into contact with hundreds of architects. Mussolini met with the majority of the most active, most talented Italian architects, such as Piero Portaluppi, Vaccaro, Adalberto Libera, Arnaldo Foschini, Giuseppe Terragni, Gio Ponti, Giovanni Greppi, Giuseppe Samonà, Luigi Figini, Gino Pollini, Mario Ridolfi, Luigi Piccinato, Pietro Lingeri, Pietro Aschieri, and Mario de Renzi. In the 1930s, Mussolini became a privileged interlocutor for broad sectors of architectural culture. Often, during meetings or journeys, he was asked to approve projects. In some cases it was only a formality. However, Mussolini demanded to be kept informed on the progress of all the major works, and he also wanted to intervene so that his signature would always be on the projects. The simple gestures of claiming a project, examining it, signing it, all implied that he at least shared those ideas. They conveyed to the public that it was the Duce himself who wanted that particular work to be built, that he had examined the project and was watching over its realization. From this set of facts a decidedly centralizing Mussolini emerges.

However, Mussolini did not limit himself to examining and approving the projects. The dictator himself sometimes picked up a pencil and suggested changes. In some cases, these were minor. In other cases, however, he became involved in fundamental decisions. It is this point that we wish to focus on here. Perhaps, unlike Hitler, Mussolini did not aspire to be an architect but, towards the mid-1930s, he had begun to acknowledge the important role that architecture could have in the political and educational process of building a "new civilization." Hence, he supervised it even more closely in order to influence its direction.

Among the architects who worked with Mussolini, Piacentini was certainly the most productive and important. From his proposal to relocate government headquarters to the Campidoglio, just a few months before the March on Rome in 1922, to his commission to create a tomb for Mussolini's son Bruno in the summer of 1941, Piacentini was the most trusted of the dictator's advisers in the 1930s. Their relationship further reveals the major role Mussolini played in architecture. It was thanks to his collaboration with Piacentini that Mussolini could test an architectural policy that implied specific choices in style. This mainly occurred in two projects for Rome: the Città Universitaria and the E42.

The Città Universitaria (1932–5), besides being an important academic building, also served as a workshop to demonstrate, to the public both in Italy and abroad, after the bitter controversies that had arisen between the Rationalists and the traditionalists, that architecture in Italy now followed a uniform path. The involvement of about a dozen architects from different parts of Italy, all coordinated by Piacentini, was meant to emphasize the project's uniform nature, and demonstrate that a "unity of style" could indeed be achieved, therefore also reflecting the country's cohesion. Mussolini frequently asked Piacentini to submit the drawings to him, and he rejected a first plan because he deemed it too decorative.

The project for the E42 (1937–43) was unquestionably more important, as it meant designing a new satellite city outside Rome. The founding principle of the Città Universitaria was applied on a broader scale, involving about fifty of Italy's best architects. When Mussolini was with Piacentini, who was the superintendent of architecture at the time, the dictator was neither a spectator nor an administrator. It was Mussolini himself, in fact, who laid down the guidelines. For the E42, not only did the architectural style have to draw on "classical and monumental sentiment," it needed to outline the ultimate style of the age of Mussolini as well. All of the works had to be approved by him, and some of the projects, the most important ones, were modified according to his wishes.

Mussolini's ever-growing presence in the field of architecture went hand in hand with the country's totalitarianization, and with the acceleration in the creation of the "new man."[8] The War in Ethiopia (1935–6) was one manifestation of the imperative to forge the warrior man. And along with war, architecture acquired an increasingly important role in the creation of the new Italian. In Mussolini's view, building and fighting were parallel actions, the two pillars on which political action was founded. As in Germany, although in a distinctly "Italian" way, fascism counted on both war and architecture to shape the nature of the Italian people. The E42 represented a challenge at the highest level within this totalitarian experiment. It should come as no surprise that, in 1939, Mussolini called for a national mobilization, as was traditionally done in case of war: "every Italian has to consider himself, from now on, personally engaged" in the fight to exploit architecture in order to make fascist civilization number one in the world.

After establishing the "empire," as correctly pointed out by De Felice, there was a fundamental change in Mussolini's political action and in his psychology: from a rationale of "enduring," he moved to one of "daring."[9] The change also involved architecture. The initial desire to leave an enduring impression of himself via public buildings now shifted towards a more active, incisive function of the genre that, in this later phase, was adapted to the totalitarian project, one in which architecture was invested in as an essential tool to shape the conscience of the Italian people. Architecture would have to be able to interact with the political myths adopted by fascism in order to accelerate history. The most important of these was the myth of ancient Rome; it was used prolifically in promoting the nationalization of the masses, in offering a collective identity in which they could sink their roots. Now architecture no longer indifferently oscillated between the abstract and the traditional. On the contrary, it was stylistically characterized by a language that recalled that glorious past, while, at the same time, authentically reflected its own time. It had to be figuratively intelligible to the masses. The epitome of this turning point was the E42, which was meant to serve as the showcase for the new civilization. The E42 was conceived not simply as a temporary backdrop for the exposition, but rather as a real city with a "new population," with impressive marble buildings that interacted with the images the dictator evoked about the glorious fate of the descendants of ancient Rome. Above all, it was a work capable of transforming those ideas into deeply rooted and long-lasting beliefs.

Mussolini was well aware of the challenges that might delay the forging of a "new man." He wanted to accelerate the process by creating an architectural context that could catalyse the transformation. It was a change that gradually marginalized modern architecture, considered unsuitable due to its cosmopolitan and unstable language. Modern architecture was too influenced by foreign models and, therefore, not Italian enough to produce fruitful correlatives with the Roman myth of the warrior man, the conqueror of empires. The E42 was part of a broader context, and became a model for Mussolini's new imperial Rome. Via della Conciliazione, Corso del Rinascimento, Largo Augusto, Termini Station, and the Palazzo del Littorio were all part of this plan. Mussolini personally assessed drawings for each of these. This was also the case for Moretti's grand design for the Foro Mussolini, the next step after the E42, and the 1941 Variante (Variant) to the city's Piano Regolatore (urban redevelopment plan).

Mussolini's actions did not just influence the architecture of the capital. Something similar took place in Milan as well. The dictator directly supervised major building projects, from Piazza Duomo to Piazza San Babila, from Piazza Diaz to Piazza Cavour, from Piazza degli Affari to Piazza San Fedele. If examined all together, those projects were aimed at bestowing imperial Milan with a "uniform character." Mussolini demanded numerous changes, so many, in fact, that it would not be incorrect to consider him one of the co-designers of the city's urban redevelopment plan.

Such activities were not limited to Rome and Milan. All of Italy was involved in the plan to reshape the country's architecture, and the most important works required Mussolini's approval. Plans involving almost a dozen cities, such as Bologna, Naples, Bolzano, Genoa, Livorno, and Trieste were entrusted – either directly or for expert advice – to Piacentini. And Mussolini was well aware of all of the plans. In these interventions one can glimpse the signs of a gradual – not linear or polyhedric – process aimed at extending these uniform architectural styles on a national scale. In this process, Rome represented a reference model and the E42 its origin. This was an endeavour that would require several decades, and that would be interrupted by historical events. However, its significance cannot be underestimated, especially if we consider that, in the early 1930s, the fascist regime was not expected to fall, and certainly not as quickly or as dramatically as it did. Many expected Italy's participation in World War II to be short and victorious, not much more than a hiatus, and in any case not enough to disrupt the country's ambitious architectural plans.

The part of this project that was interrupted reveals Mussolini's clear desire for architecture to participate in the totalitarian experiment. To educate the people in this greater representativeness, to involve them in this new myth, the architectural symbols of fascism's secular religion had to share common linguistic features. Consequently, architectural uniformity would serve as the clearest demonstration of the desire of a people – transformed into a compact mass – to believe in its own mission. It was because of its newly found uniformity of architectural style that Italy would be able to take part in this "great appointment with history." After the initial victorious phase of the war, Italy would face an important challenge with emerging nations – first and foremost, Adolf Hitler's Germany – with which it would have to compete in order to affirm the "new fascist civilization" worldwide. This challenge would primarily involve architecture, which would once again exert a unifying effect, just as it had in the great ancient Roman and Renaissance eras, when Italian civilization spread to the rest of the world. Architecture in the age of fascism presented itself as the legitimate heir to that tradition, to that same "dynasty," and therefore as the bearer of universal values. Italy believed itself to be entitled, again in its own right, to lead other countries, in terms of both architecture and civilization.

It is important to emphasize that this quest for a uniform architectural style did not correspond to a rigid scheme or follow some openly declared plan; rather, it proceeded with pragmatic and intuitive action, taking into account the diverse situations. At this venture's core, there was Palazzo Venezia and a series of – not always official – meetings with architects, where dozens of projects were examined. A complex strategy thus emerged that involved the skilful political manipulation of architecture, without losing sight of the ultimate goal: not the destiny of the discipline, despite its increasingly close association with the regime, but rather the construction of the "new civilization" and of the "new fascist man" to stake their claim in the Western world.

1 Travelling to See the Buildings

1 The Myth of the Duce as Inaugurator

The more or less active and consensual support accorded to fascism by the Italian population in the late 1920s was consolidated, albeit in varying ways, over the course of the 1930s. Investments in public works, and the resulting massive rise in employment, represented a key aspect in a broader political strategy to move towards the people. Mussolini travelled extensively throughout Italy, thus directly participating in the celebration of the government's involvement in public works, and reaping the rewards of its wide-ranging and multifaceted activity. These journeys became a tool by means of which to consolidate popular support for the regime, thanks to the monopolization of the media and an efficient propaganda machine – initially supervised by Mussolini's press office and later by the Ministry of Popular Culture. Most importantly, these trips reinforced popular support for Mussolini himself, generously fuelling the myth of the Duce.

As Renzo De Felice pointed out, a peculiar aspect of the consensus towards fascism was the lack of "real and informed involvement." The regime was embraced by the masses in a rather "irrational and religious" manner.[1] A full-fledged lay religion was created around Mussolini. The myth of the Duce, along with that of ancient Rome, the empire, and the new Italian, was the expression of a political strategy that sought popular consensus based on an emotional and totally uncritical approach. And within this context aesthetics played an important role. On many occasions the Duce would say that "the cult of beauty and strength are the underlying principles of the fascist ideal."[2] In the religion of fascist politics, beauty was considered indispensable to conquer the trust and the devotion of the crowds, to get them emotionally involved. Following in the footsteps of Gustave Le Bon, Mussolini thought that governing a people meant appealing to their imagination; it meant creating or evoking powerful, seductive images. Architecture was considered an art that possessed this strength, being capable of conveying deep, evocative impressions to the masses. "If I were leading a group of Jews, I would rebuild the Temple of Solomon," Le Bon wrote in a book that was of "capital" importance to Mussolini, and that he had read several times.[3] And if we take into account the increasingly important role he assigned to architecture, then we can clearly see that he kept these words in mind. Mussolini himself would later declare he had been inspired by the work of the French sociologist to "build the incumbent regime in Italy."[4]

The trips Mussolini took across Italy were thus an important chapter in this political creed founded on image. During these pilgrimages, which became almost ritualistic in nature – the celebration of the Duce's arrival, the gathering of teeming masses, the "historic" speech, the promise to return – one feature prevailed: the testimonial of progress marked by architectural objects. And what could be more effective than architecture – a school, a Casa del Fascio, a bathing establishment for the members of the Fascist Party's youth group – to demonstrate the regime's industriousness, its desire to both politically and socially integrate the masses, those who up until then had been excluded from real citizenship? Every single piece of architecture thus became the enforcement of one of Mussolini's key slogans, which was to "move towards the people."[5] Every single work was a piece in the construction of a great mosaic of consensus, it was an object by which to compare the current fascist regime and the previous liberal government. In the collective imagination, even the smallest building was a brick that could be added to the construction of the modern Italian fascist nation. Every building was a sign of fascism, to be handed down to posterity. It was proof of the appearance of the regime on a mythicized historical horizon, which transformed the perception of everyday life into something remarkable and unique. On the whole, there was real constructive activity going on. Alongside it, however, there was an impressive, insistent, and modern network of mass communication, through which the crowds could be moulded as well. It is worth noting that the populace was considered a passive subject, both "irresponsible" and "colloidal," one that needed to be shaped.[6]

During the inauguration rituals, when the masterpiece was officially handed over to the people, it was Mussolini himself who really took possession of the proceedings. The constructions that were "offered" to the people became "his." The epiphanic gesture, one that he repeated dozens of times, of taking a trowel, spreading the mortar, and placing a brick atop a wall under construction, became a ritual, acquiring symbolic strength over time. In the eyes of the masses, Mussolini became the great, singular maker of the nation that he himself had transformed into a unique, bustling, "smoking building site." The crowds identified with him alone. All the other actors – the politicians and the local entrepreneurs, the bricklayers, artisans, and architects – were swallowed up by his iconic power. Mussolini would use this ruse to appear as the original and true creator of the new Italy. He used architecture to develop and hold together his own myth. As a careful reader of Le Bon, he knew that "only history can immortalize myths."[7]

The works that were inaugurated during these journeys demonstrate just how much architecture contributed to the establishment of this mythical image. In broader terms, these buildings brought out the active participation of the architects in the creation of a consensus with respect to the regime. However, as we shall see, these architectural itineraries involved buildings that were rather different from each other. Some of them, in fact, celebrated modernity, whereas others were more traditional, and the architects who collaborated on this great venture pursued different and at times contrasting ideas. At this level of analysis, there is no direct connection between Mussolini's trips and the style of "his" buildings. In other words, he indifferently used buildings that featured a variety of styles for his propaganda strategy.

Between 1929 and 1939, when public consensus was strong, Mussolini travelled to all the Italian regions, and visited seventy out of eighty-nine provincial capitals. This included all the cities located in southern Italy and the islands, while some northern towns, such as Varese, Sondrio, Como, and Bergamo, were excluded. During the period of time analysed here, Mussolini inspected over three hundred and twenty locations. Evidently, his plan was to impose his presence systematically, and to do so even in the smallest towns in the most far-flung provinces of Italy, like Tricarico in Basilicata, Cogne in Valle d'Aosta, or Grottacalda in Sicily. This physical embrace of the crowds was a very modern approach and characteristic of Mussolini's politics, and it denoted a sharp difference with the previous, much-maligned liberal tradition.

Messaging around Mussolini's activity as inaugurator was repeated incessantly. In nearly every town or city he visited he placed the first stone, he inaugurated a building, he visited a construction site or one that had just recently been finished. He visited certain cities many times. He went to Florence six times, to Milan and Naples five times each, to Venice four, to Turin three. The Romagna region, his birthplace, was a case apart. Predappio, his hometown, Rocca delle Caminate, where he had a second home, and the Adriatic Riviera, a favourite spot for holidays, were all frequent destinations. He went to Forlì seventeen times and to Riccione nineteen. Another area he visited frequently was the Pontine Marshes, the chief target of the regime's vaunted farmland improvement policies. Above all, it was the place where reclamation had achieved the best results. Mussolini went to Littoria, currently Latina, at least eight times to reinvent the myth of the "founder of cities." He followed its development step by step, from the laying of the first stone to the completion of the sugar refinery, the railway station, the Palazzo di Giustizia (Palace of Justice).

On almost every occasion, Mussolini's visits coincided with the dates that marked the fascist calendar and the revived anniversaries of the country's key historical events: 23 March, the founding of the fasces; 21 April, the birth of Rome; 9 May, the founding of the empire; 24 May, the day Italy joined World War I; 28 October, the March on Rome; 4 November, the victorious end of World War I. Through their inauguration on these dates, their inclusion in the commemorative rituals, the buildings fulfilled the needs of fascist ideology.

All the works that Mussolini touched in his travels strengthened their political connotation, or acquired one if they did not already have any. They were identified with the presence of the dictator; they were recognizably in his image. They were there to ensure that future generations would remember the historical, legendary event. However fleeting it may have been, Mussolini's presence bestowed on these buildings an aura of sacredness. They became local and sometimes national symbols of a collective memory around which the fascist party wanted to build a long-lasting Italian identity. In 26 October 1926 Mussolini declared, "my rallying cry is a verb: to endure! To endure, day after day, month after month, and year after year."[8] To endure meant "to strengthen the regime more and more, to multiply its 'creations,' to fascistize Italians as much as possible."[9] And to endure also meant fervently creating architecture that would last for decades, leaving the mark of fascism for posterity. When possible, marble was a preferred building material, one that both Hitler and Mussolini favoured.

2 Building and Fighting

In 1932, the regime planned to celebrate its first decade in power by displaying the exhilarating bulk of its accomplishments thus far. The works that had been finished or were still under way at the time were supposed to "consecrate" the progress made by this "hard-working nation." Mussolini alternated inaugurations with political speeches, thus breathing life into a sort of imaginary relationship with the masses.[10] The crowds that he addressed directly in the form of a simulated dialogue followed him enthusiastically. Short questions and choral monosyllabic answers transformed the disorganized tide into a compact mass, and thus into a consistent political force. The crowd was mesmerized by

Mussolini's oratorial skills, by his plain-spoken, determined, and direct eloquence, by the powerful images he evoked. The crowd was euphorically drawn into the illusion of being, together with its leader, a protagonist of its time, a time that was perceived as a mythical continuation of a glorious history. From the speeches delivered to crowded squares during inaugurations to concrete initiatives, from building sites to built works, all were clear indications of a political strategy that paradoxically sought to appear both anti-ideological and pragmatic.

Let us begin with Mussolini's visit to Turin on 23 October. In the morning, in Piazza Castello, Mussolini stressed the "ancient Roman roots" of the city "rebuilt" by Julius Caesar, and currently – though he did not actually say it, it was clear to all – being rebuilt by another "Roman dux." An unrivalled play-actor, Mussolini mocked the opponents of fascism who "had invented" a people in order to "mystify" it and to impose "imaginary needs" onto it. In this city of blue-collar workers he praised the sacrifices made by the working classes, who "bore upon their shoulders the inevitable burden," who were "dutiful in times of crisis." Not only was every social "controversy" viewed as an attack on the fascist government, it was also seen as a danger to the whole nation, a "betrayal" of the country.[11]

In the following days, Mussolini visited numerous building sites. He went to the fruit and vegetable market designed by Umberto Cuzzi, to the stadium by Raffaello Fagnoni, to the Cassa di Risparmio building by Giovanni Chevalley.[12] Through the meticulous organization of his visit, he aimed to demonstrate that only through the social "contract" forcibly imposed by fascism could people enjoy the benefits of hard work. The stadiums, markets, and schools acted as counterparts of a political ideology. "Walking and building" – along with "fighting and winning" – were the buzzwords for the new decade that he entrusted to the "people of Turin" upon taking his leave. Two days later, in Milan, he started over again and extolled the theme of "concord," of the relationship that tied a leader to his people, of the "unitarian force" that persuaded the Italian people to support the regime in order to become, at last, "protagonists of their own history." Before the crowds gathered in Piazza Duomo, Mussolini prophesized that this "would be the century of fascism." Fiercely, he announced his grandiose and warmongering ambitions: "In a decade, all of Europe will be fascist or fascistized."[13]

Mussolini spent the morning of 1 November in Brescia, where he visited the new town centre designed by Piacentini (figure 1). The main square in Brescia was the crown jewel of the regime's construction works. From the balcony in Piazza della Vittoria, with the architect at his side, Mussolini was deliberately laconic, in order to allow the architecture itself – which was much more effective than any pedantic speech – to take centre stage: here was a far more immediate way to identify fascism

1. Marcello Piacentini, Piazza della Vittoria in Brescia, 1929–32. With Piacentini at his side, on the day of the inauguration Mussolini said no words could describe the façades of such "superb buildings."

with the work itself; to turn it into a symbol, not so much of a political elite as of the "regime of the people," the very same people he had deprived of its freedom, but whose consensus he sought. Ultimately, those buildings were just another way, perhaps the best one, to once again talk about himself. Before the "superb buildings of this square," the dictator cleverly remarked that "words are superficial, because it's the facts that talk."[14] The dictator was well aware that more than his speech, the crowd would remember the ritual, his statue-like figure, and the architectural frame where the event took place.

From Brescia Mussolini headed to Gardone, where he was a guest of Gabriele D'Annunzio. In a certain sense, the visit was almost obligatory. In its appeal to the masses, Mussolini's style owed much to D'Annunzio's Fiume adventure, which inspired "the commander" to develop the forms of a new political liturgy dependent on myth and symbol. The Roman salute, the structure of the dialogue with the crowd, the speech from the balcony, and the Christian symbolism applied to secular reality all drew upon the aesthetics of D'Annunzio, a writer who recognized the crucial importance of architecture.[15] Giancarlo Maroni escorted the dictator through the crowded chaos of the Vittoriale, whose construction, mostly financed by the government, had yet to be completed. Even the golden retreat of Gardone had resulted from the "moral and material" corruption that Mussolini had enacted in order to obtain the political "silence" of the much-feared poet.[16] On 3 November Mussolini arrived in Ancona, where he inaugurated the Monumento ai Caduti (War Memorial) by Guido Cirilli, praising the architect's work. The following afternoon he was back in Rome to inaugurate several other new works. These will be discussed further on.

In Brescia, Mussolini had Piacentini at his side, in Gardone, Maroni, in Ancona, Cirilli. Although not all of these encounters can be documented – the rare press reports almost always focus entirely on Mussolini, while photographs and newsreels simply show who attended the events – it is almost certain that during these visits Mussolini was always accompanied by the architect of the work in question. For the architect, being introduced by the head of state, walking up to the stage at his side, answering his questions, and receiving his praise meant earning public acknowledgment as a participant in the historic plan devised by the country's leader. Over the course of a decade, Mussolini's trips involved dozens of architects, whose designs were used with remarkable effectiveness to prop up the great forge of consensus that fascism was building.[17]

In 1933, Mussolini embarked on a drastically reduced itinerary, limited to Venice, Riccione, and the Pontine Marshes. In September 1934, he visited Puglia. It was 8 a.m. sharp when the ship *Aurora* sailed into the port of Bari. From there Mussolini headed to the stadium designed by Vincenzo Fasolo, then to the new Palazzo delle Poste (Post Office Building) by Roberto Narducci, which he admired; he then strolled along the Nazario Sauro shoreline, where, with a view of the Mediterranean, rising up before him was the new Bari that was built during the dictator's time. From there, the procession moved on to the Comando Aereo (Air Command) headquarters designed by Saverio Dioguardi, the police barracks by Bazzani, the Palazzo dei Lavori Pubblici (Public Works Building) by Carlo Vannoni, and then Mussolini presided over the quick ceremony to inaugurate the Palazzo della Provincia by Luigi Baffa. Early that afternoon, having returned to Piazza Vittorio Emanuele, Mussolini appeared at the balcony of the Palazzo del Governo (Government Palace) to deliver a speech in which he stressed the ancient roots of the people of Italy and of the Mediterranean Sea that had witnessed the birth of the greatest civilizations and of the Roman Empire. By contrast – against the backdrop of the crisis in relations with Hitler's Germany after the Führer's attempted *putsch* against the Austrian government – he derided Nazi race theories: "Thirty centuries of history allow us to look with sovereign compassion at some of the theories coming from across the Alps."[18] In his words you could already hear the signs of a more marked political choice in the years to come, the attempt to turn the debate with his most powerful and corrupt ally towards the theme of civilization.

The following day, Mussolini inaugurated the Casa del Balilla (Fascist Party Youth House) in Lecce, and Brasini's Palazzo del Governo in Taranto, whose purpose was to emulate the magnificence of Rome.[19] In Brindisi, Mussolini examined the design and then laid the first stone of the Collegio Navale (Naval College) by Gaetano Minnucci. Afterwards, the dictator crossed the port on a speedboat, moored it to the dock where the Monumento al Marinaio (Monument to the Sailor) by Luigi Brunati stood tall, and climbed all the way up to the stone helm. He had followed all the architectural problems that had been involved in this work, and rejected the previous megalomaniacal proposal that had been made by the podestà, Serafino Giannelli.[20] In Foggia, he cut the ribbon for Bazzani's Palazzo del Governo, and visited the building site of Brasini's Palazzo del Podestà, whose plans he had already been able to see. Finally, he went to the Palazzo degli Studi by Piacentini. In this case as well, Mussolini had stepped in to put a halt to a proposal by Piacentini which he felt was excessively lavish.[21]

In June 1935, Mussolini went to Sardinia, and in August he travelled through the provinces of Bolzano and Trento. While in Alto Adige he visited a new building designed by Piacentini, the headquarters of the Comando del Corpo d'Armata (Army Corps Barracks). Finally, he was personally able to admire the Arco della Vittoria (Victory Arch), whose planning, as we shall discuss further on, he had followed closely.[22] In Trento, Mussolini had Ettore Fagiuoli accompany him to the monument to Cesare Battisti on the hills of Doss Trento, a mausoleum that had been inaugurated shortly before, and whose design and related events were already familiar to him.[23] The main purpose of the trip to the Venezia Tridentina was, however, to check on the military training that was being conducted in the province of Bolzano. Before an audience of one hundred thousand soldiers, their leader announced that the size of the army would be increased to a million.[24] The fascist military attack on Ethiopia, which was perfectly consistent with the regime's policies, was imminent. "Building" but also "fighting," lest they forget, would be the buzzwords for the new decade: two actions that were not at all incompatible and, actually, complementary in Mussolini's ideology. This could also be seen in the way he alternated his visits to the building sites with his inspections of the troops. Nonetheless, this political program would soon find itself limited by inadequate funding. Mussolini needed the war to consolidate his popular support as well as to increase his personal power, which also extended to his role as military chief. He did not want to risk failure. In order to make sure he had an overwhelming superiority of men and means, Mussolini looted the state coffers. The Ethiopian enterprise cost 40 billion lire, with a 20–25 per cent increase in total national expenditure, and with negative consequences on the financing of public works, which were just as necessary in fuelling the consensus, and in creating the "new man."[25]

A few months later, while the Ethiopian War still raged, Mussolini inaugurated Pontinia, the third new city after Littoria and Sabaudia, in the Pontine Marshes. Many buildings had not as yet been completed. It was 18 December and the inauguration of the new town deliberately and significantly coincided with the Day of the Wedding Ring (Giornata della Fede). On that day, in cities, towns, and villages, the women of Italy offered their wedding rings to the country in response to the economic sanctions, deemed be unfair, that the League of Nations had levied against the country in response to the attack on the African nation. The introduction of this extraordinary, powerful mass ritual, a celebration of the communality of fascism and the idea of the fatherland, was a brilliant propaganda move. The regime notably asked women, specifically, to perform an act of devotion, a "gesture of complete submission," the donation to their country of the object that was "perhaps closest to their hearts."[26] It had to be clear to all that in fascist Italy women were on the front lines helping to fund the war their sons and husbands were fighting and risking their lives for. In Pontinia, with the new rural buildings in the background, Mussolini explained to the settlers, who had mostly come from Veneto to flee from poverty, that the war in Ethiopia was "the war of the poor people, of the disadvantaged, of the proletarians."[27] If that was their war, those would be their houses. Just a few simple words – fighting and building – to help the people understand that those two things were on the same level, that they were the parallel actions of fascist pedagogy.

3 Buildings Built to "Endure"

On the eve of 9 May 1936, from the balcony of Palazzo Venezia, Mussolini announced the "empire's reappearance on the fateful hills of Rome." The gathering of people, who were listening to the speech via radio in the city and town squares of Italy, was a powerful one. Mussolini's ability to move crowds and direct their collective imagination was extraordinary. He was unreservedly proud of his success. As he himself recalled, he was able to produce "the greatest vibration of the collective soul of the Italian people." A people who, in his own intentions, had to be willing to believe and obey, and who "could not afford the luxury of wasting time in search of the truth."[28]

The campaign aimed at shaping the Italian people continued, moving from the war front to the travel front, highlighting the reciprocal relationship between foreign and domestic policy. Popular consensus was a necessary condition to the pursuit of an aggressive international policy, while the comfort of military success was a prerequisite for the radicalization of the "reclamation" of the masses in a fascist sense. After Ethiopia had been conquered, Mussolini's trips became more frequent and more meticulously organized. Moreover, cities awaiting their leader's arrival received more funding of public works. The dictator's itineraries traced a single, imaginary, architectural route. However, it is worth noting that the series of constructions the dictator visited and raised to the glory of fascism hardly reflected a unified architectural agenda and the monolithic forms suited to the politics of a totalitarian regime. Most of them still reflected a rationale of "endurance," not the incentive of "daring" that marked Mussolini's policies after the Ethiopian enterprise. The crucial turning point, when architecture truly entered the fray to educate the masses, only happened with the E42, in mid-1937. Even after that, however, stylistic unity emerged gradually and not without contradictions. Once he had founded the empire, in the fall of 1936, Mussolini travelled through the Marches and Romagna. In Corridonia he inaugurated the town hall; in Macerata he signed the project of the new Casa del Mutilato for wounded veterans designed by Bazzani. He then headed up to Bologna, where he visited Vaccaro's School of Engineering, spending time with the architect. He crossed Via Roma and enquired about the new projects under way. He solemnly opened Alberto Legnani and Luciano Petrucci's Palazzo del Gas to the public; he visited the houses on Via Pier Crescenzi and the Villaggio della Rivoluzione by Francesco Santini. And when he had finished, he sped away by car to Imola to inaugurate Adriano Marabini's Casa del Fascio.[29]

In March 1937, Mussolini crossed the Mediterranean and sailed to Libya. During this journey he announced his support for the mass colonization of the North African region, and he stressed the centrality of colonial expansion in the Mediterranean.[30] According to the memoirs of Ugo Ojetti, who was a member of the Duce's entourage, the splendour of the Roman ruins of Leptis Magna and Sabratha influenced some important future decisions affecting the fate of architecture. Indeed, those were the months that saw the launch of the E42 project. The leader's preferences increasingly leaned towards a revival of Roman traditions. In those amazing monuments across the sea Mussolini perceived the beauty of a mysterious force, and saw a further architectural confirmation of the new nation's imperial vocation.

After returning from Libya, Mussolini headed to Predappio to carefully inspect the new Casa del Fascio by Arnaldo Fuzzi, a former loyalist referred to as "Rachele Mussolini's engineer" (Rachele was Mussolini's wife).[31] In August Mussolini travelled all around Sicily. In Messina he laid the first stone for the Stazione Centrale e Marittima (Central and Maritime Station) by Angiolo Mazzoni. He inspected the model, which, among other things, was incomplete, and he ordered that the work should begin even if it still had not received a safety clearance from the authorities.[32] In Catania he laid the first stone of the Palazzo di Giustizia by Francesco Fichera (figure 2). In Syracuse he inaugurated the Pantheon (War Memorial) designed by both Ernesto and Gaetano Rapisardi. In Ragusa he inaugurated Ernesto La Padula's new Casa del Fascio. In Pergusa he officially presented fifty new houses. During a stop in Gela, the man known for his statuesque poses and inscrutable facial expression revealed his "ability to change disguises in the manner of Leopoldo Fregoli." As Bottai noted in his diary, on the round terrace of a bathing establishment, to the sounds of a small orchestra, "he gazed at the 'more common' girls, the ones whose features were the least fine, who were stocky and overweight. He danced and swung back and forth with them, all the time with that strange, controlled smile of his."[33] In the following days, a directive put a stop to the publication of this piece of news.[34]

In Enna Mussolini reminded the crowd that he was the first member of the government to visit since 1860: the truth of the matter was that the city had only been a provincial capital for a decade. While he was there, he inspected the models of the new city centre by Salvatore Caronia Roberti.[35] In Agrigento he inaugurated the building site of the new Casa della Madre e del Bambino (Home for the Mother and Child). In Palermo he was the first to enter the new Banco di Sicilia building, also by Caronia Roberti. He then inspected the building site of the Palazzo di Giustizia by the Rapisardi brothers, he officially launched the works of the Casa del Mutilato (Home for the War Wounded) by Giuseppe Spatrisano, and he inaugurated the fire station by Antonino Pollaci and the Casa della Madre e del Bambino in that city as well. Before leaving Palermo, Mussolini spoke at the Foro Italico from atop a 15-metre-tall platform. He claimed that Sicily and fascism represented "a perfect identity," and he promised that the "foundation of the second Roman Empire" would be for the island the beginning of "one of the happiest moments" in its long history. Then, with his mind on the annual military operation that had taken place a few days earlier in Trapani, he prophesized: "Here [in Sicily] no one will ever land, not a single soldier."[36]

2. Francesco Fichera, project for the Palazzo di Giustizia in Catania, model, 1937. During his visit to the city, Mussolini inspected the model and personally congratulated the architect.

It was a lovely sunny day when, shortly after his meeting with Hitler in Rome, Mussolini reached Genoa from the sea. A throng of people welcomed him in Piazza della Vittoria, which was dominated by Piacentini's Arch: the Roman architect was also the architectural consultant for the entire complex (figure 3). In the city's new fascist forum, Mussolini extolled his recent meeting with Hitler and the beginning of a stable and long-lasting alliance with Germany. He criticized the foreign policies of France and Great Britain, and warned that in the "fight between nations and continents one cannot hesitate: he who hesitates is lost." He reassured the crowd that Hitler "does not want peace in Europe any less ardently than we do. But for peace to be ensured, [Germany] must be armed."[37]

The following day Mussolini inaugurated some local Case del Fascio, and in Sturla (Genoa) the Gaslini Pediatric Institute by Angelo Crippa. Even though the Gaslini had been privately funded and was not directly sponsored by the regime, Mussolini took credit for it all the same.[38] He then went back to Piazza della Vittoria and opened the new Palazzo dell' INFPS by Piacentini. Only four days earlier, they had met on the building site of the future Via della Conciliazione. The architect stood behind Mussolini the way his most loyal officials did. From Piazza della Vittoria, Mussolini reached Viale Duca d'Aosta, where he presided over the opening of the Casa Madre dei Mutilati (Amputees Headquarters) by Eugenio Fuselli, one of the closest collaborators with Piacentini's architectural firm.[39] Once the ceremony was over, Mussolini headed to Piazza Dante to admire the skyscraper that was being built there, another work by Piacentini, and the Palazzo INA by Gino

3. Mussolini on the podium in Piazza della Vittoria in Genoa, 14 May 1938.

Cipriani, the powerful engineer at the helm of the insurance company's real estate sector. The entire afternoon was devoted to the Riviera di Levante. The stops he made along the way, while speeding from one place to another by car, included Rapallo, to see the building site of the Casa del Fascio by Luigi Vietti, Chiavari, where he visited the PNF bathing establishment by Camillo Nardi Greco, and Sestri Levante, where he inaugurated the Casa del Fascio by Beniamino Bellati. On the last day of his exhausting trip he visited the mountain colony in Savignone, the Gioventù Italiana del Littorio (GIL) School by Camillo Nardi Greco on Corso Monte Grappa, and the new Casa del Fascio in Prà (Genoa) by Mirco Dapelo and Raffaele Bruno. Some of these party headquarters, sanctuaries of the leader's political religion, were part of a greater program that, between 1938 and 1940 alone, involved the building of more than 950 Fascist Party headquarters in some 8,000 cities and towns across Italy.[40] When submitted to Mussolini, this astonishing and unprecedented list of projects represented one of the clearest demonstrations of the widespread process of the fascistization of the Italian people. This process, launched by the regime in the second half of the 1930s, has been exhaustively studied by Emilio Gentile.[41]

In September, Mussolini travelled to the northeast of the country. As in Genoa, Mussolini's appearance in Trieste called for a grand entrance by sea. Climbing up to the podium in Piazza Unità, Mussolini announced his support for Nazi Germany's policy of aggression against Czechoslovakia. Another topic he dealt with, a "burning issue" in a city that had one of the largest Jewish communities in Italy, was the Jewish question. Mussolini described world Judaism as "an irreconcilable enemy of fascism." He claimed that fascism's racial policy was based on the idea of "more evident superiority," and he announced the adoption of impending "necessary solutions." By imitating the Nuremberg Laws of 1935, which discriminated against Jews, he demonstrated his loyalty to Hitler. But with regard to the exclusion of Jews from schools he went even further than the German leader. Mussolini believed that antisemitism upheld the features of a national identity, and was therefore a necessary step towards the realization of the fascist revolution and the new civilization.[42]

In the following days, Mussolini engaged in the usual hectic yet carefully planned inaugurations. Enrico Paolo Salem, the Jewish podestà and the person behind the new fascist face of Trieste, a city that Mussolini now hastened to celebrate and identify with himself, had been removed from his office a few days earlier. At Mussolini's side during those days was the minister of public works Giuseppe Cobolli Gigli, a native of Trieste, and someone whom Piacentini did not like: "He is terribly ignorant, and well worthy of Trieste, this Mr. Minister of my boots."[43] In Trieste, Mussolini officially opened the building sites of the Casa del Fascio by Raffaello Battigelli and Ferruccio Spangaro, the Casa della GIL by Umberto Nordio in Piazza Oberdan, and the new university, also designed by Nordio along with Fagnoni. Consistent with the dictator's new political approach, his "triumphal" itinerary through the city avoided the new Assicurazioni Generali building by Piacentini, and the RAS, by Nordio, as both companies were run by Jews.[44] He officiated at the inaugural rites of war memorials in Redipuglia, which had not yet been finished, and in Caporetto, both designed by Greppi and Giannino Castiglioni. He also inaugurated the one in Oslavia by Ghino Venturi. In those places that had witnessed the war and its massacres, Mussolini said to the mothers who lined the road with their children that "today's children will be tomorrow's soldiers, and Italian soldiers will always be victorious." In Udine he inaugurated the Casa della GIL by Ermes Midena, and the Tempio Ossario by Provino Valle and Alessandro Limongelli.[45] In the town hall, Pier Arrigo Barnaba, the podestà, showed him a model of the Cassa di Risparmio, whose purpose was to leave a fascist mark on the new town. The building's architects were Foschini and Cesare Pascoletti, the latter of whom worked in Piacentini's firm.

In Torviscosa, the newly founded city designed by Giuseppe del Min, Mussolini revved up the new machinery for the production of cellulose. From Treviso he flew back to Rome to celebrate the end of the year of Emperor Augustus, 1938, presenting the restoration of the Ara Pacis, installed in the pavilion and designed by Vittorio Morpurgo. The next day he was once again in the Veneto, to visit Padua, Belluno, Vicenza, Verona, and a number of smaller towns. Then he made a quick trip to the capital not only to demonstrate his omnipresence, but, above all, to affirm that the link between the heart of Italy and the regions located all around it lay under the sign of Rome. And that it was he, because of one of those "marvellous ebbs and flows" of history willed by God, who travelled those lands like a new Augustus. Meanwhile, in the cities of the Veneto, labourers and peasants repeatedly rehearsed parades before a "pretend Duce."[46]

In Piazza Bra, Verona, in a farewell speech to the people of the Veneto, as the fighting on the border between Germany and Czechoslovakia seemed to intensify, Mussolini stressed the need for a peaceful solution, and insisted that he wanted to avoid a war between the European countries. He also warned, however, that the time would come "when the nature of the conflict will involve us directly. And then there will not be nor will we allow for any hesitation." At that moment, in September 1938, what he needed was peace, a war to expand the empire and "educate the Italians" not yet on board with the program. After that speech, the dictator informed his German allies that "he needs to prepare his people. And that is exactly what he is doing doing, meticulously and scrupulously," remarked Joseph Goebbels, the Nazi Party's minister for popular enlightenment and propaganda, and a skilled controller of crowds and manipulator of consciences. The geometric configuration of the crowds at the mass public events of those days was yet another sign of the escalation of the regime's totalitarian policy, both domestic and foreign, and of Mussolini's desire to mould the unwarriorlike nature of his people.[47] A good example of this was the public event of the GIL in the arena of Verona. A few months later, in December, Mussolini arrived in Sardinia from the sea to inaugurate Carbonia, a new town designed by Cesare Valle, Ignazio Guidi, and Eugenio Montuori.[48]

In late March 1939, Mussolini travelled through Calabria. In mid-May he was in Piedmont and Valle d'Aosta. Between those two trips, Italy continued its policy of aggression, and in April it invaded Albania. Mussolini emulated Hitler, who had invaded Czechoslovakia in March. "Albania is the Bohemia of the Balkans," the Italian dictator declared.[49] During a visit to Reggio Calabria, Mussolini decided to spend two million lire to complete the National Museum of Magna Grecia designed by Piacentini, whose works had come to a halt due to a lack of funding. Mussolini developed plans for the areas, and he talked about the need to create "two brand new cities [in Calabria], connected by two motorways between Naples and Reggio Calabria."[50] In southern Italy, however, public works were slow to get off the ground. The architectural influence of the regime was much more visible in northern Italy. In Turin, the itinerary began with the huge villa belonging to Riccardo Gualino. Gualino was a textile entrepreneur and a patron of the arts who had suffered bankruptcy and had been exiled. His villa had therefore been "given back to the people," and turned into a youth sun therapy colony by Mario Passanti and Paolo Perona. The itinerary also included the headquarters of the Gruppo Rionale Fascista "Porcu," also designed by Passanti and Persona, the Casa dello Studente by Ferruccio Grassi, and Ettore Sottsass's Autarchy Exhibition. Mussolini then continued on his way to see the Casa Littoria (Fascist Party Meeting House) designed by Ottorino Aloisio in Asti, and the anti-tuberculosis dispensary designed by Gardella in Alessandria.

In Piazza Vittorio Veneto, Turin, the dictator recalled the rallying cries he had raised in that same city the last time he had visited it, and he proudly claimed he had kept his promises. Italy, in the past seven years, had "built, fought, and won." Comforted by these successes, the dictator confirmed his desire to develop the educational and political program of fascism to its greatest potential. Mussolini wanted to deeply influence the nature of the Italian people, and to create "the physical and moral type of the new Italian." He also reiterated his commitment to marching with "Germany, in order to give Europe peace with justice, which is what all the people yearn for deeply."[51] The following day he inaugurated the FIAT automobile factory in Mirafiori designed by Vittorio Bonadé Bottino, a project he had seen beforehand. The quality of the services offered by the factory qualified it as a model for the "social progress of work," based on the directives of the regime. However, most of the fifty thousand workers there, standing on the clearing before the new factory for his visit, were not so convinced of that "social progress." The "inseparability" of the people and fascism that Mussolini glorified had already begun to show some cracks, and architectural exhibitionism did not seem to produce the desired effect on these workers with a more socialist tradition. Reports of the gathering made by the political police were radically different from the triumphant chronicles described in the press. Mussolini's words did not arouse an ovation, and the applause he did receive only came from the front rows. Many of the workers remained unperturbed, their arms folded. In order to get them involved, Mussolini tried to engage in a conversation, asking them if they remembered one

of the speeches he had made a few years earlier about the regime's social policies. But all the dictator managed to get out of them were a few
uncertain answers. Visibly angered, he cried out from the podium, "Well
if you can't remember, then read it again." Mussolini left Turin embittered by the cold welcome he had received, railing against "that damned
city."[52]

4 In the City Where Fascism Was Born

Milan, the city where fascism was born, and where Mussolini lived between 1912 and 1922, is tied to an important period in his political life. It
was the liveliest city in Italy from an economic standpoint, and a bench-
mark of fascism's capacity for modernizing the country. In Milan, more
than anywhere else, architecture could reveal the dynamic face of the
nation. In the late 1930s, Mussolini visited the city on many occasions.[53]

It was a late afternoon in May 1930 when Mussolini crossed Corso
Venezia to cut the ribbon for the planetarium and to congratulate its
architect, Piero Portaluppi. The following day, he was in Monza for the
Triennale, accompanied by Gio Ponti and Mario Sironi, where he lingered in the exhibition rooms of the Palazzo Reale. In the park he visited
the holiday home that had been designed by Ponti and Emilio Lancia,
as well as the Casa Elettrica created by some of the young members of
the Gruppo 7. As he took his leave, he praised Ponti and Sironi for the
"splendid" exhibition.[54] Once again in Milan, he presided over the ceremonies in Piazza Sant'Ambrogio, within the enclosure of the Monumento ai Caduti (War Memorial), whose plan he had examined a few
years earlier (figure 4). Ponti, Muzio, Alpago Novello, and Margherita
Sarfatti were there waiting for him.[55] The spotlight was not on the architects however; it was on the crowd of war wounded and veterans who
huddled around Mussolini. One reporter wrote that he was flanked by
people, that he could "read in the eyes and in the wounds of everyone."
Carlo Delcroix, a "hero wounded in war," painted an extraordinary, mes-
sianic portrait of the leader. According to Delcroix, this was a man who
had been summoned by God himself to "heal the wounds and fulfil the
vows of his people."[56] When he arrived in Piazza Duomo, Mussolini gave
a speech to celebrate the anniversary of Italy's entrance into World War
I. He transformed the war experience, which had been mythicized by
fascism, into an "epic of heroism and martyrdom," consecrated to the
deity of the fatherland.[57] He painted the war as the country's palingen-
esis, and as the foreshadowing of Mussolini's political movement. He
presented the date of the declaration of war as the birthdate of the "people's regime," which would then develop into fascism. Today, Mussolini

4. Alberto Alpago Novello, Tommaso Buzzi, Ottavio Calbiati, Giovanni Muzio, Gio Ponti, Monumento ai Caduti (War Memorial), Milan, 1926–9. While examining the preliminary drafts for the project, Mussolini remarked that the symbols of compassion prevailed over those that celebrated victory.

declared before a cheering crowd, that under the leadership of their Duce "the Italian people are the perfect masters of their fate."[58]

Mussolini visited Milan again in October 1932, on his way back from Turin. The first stop was Piacentini's Palazzo di Giustizia on Corso di Porta Vittoria, where work to demolish the old barracks was ending and digging was under way. The Roman architect was waiting for Mussolini so that he could take him to a room in the building site where the drawings were on display. He had also had a model made that showed a huge building with a tower for the archive that was about 60 metres tall. Having examined the project several months earlier, Mussolini was familiar with it, and showed great interest as he listened to the explanations. With journalists spread out before them, the two men put on a show of sorts. Mussolini asked how long it would take for the work to get done, and the architect replied that it would be finished in just four years. (It would actually take nine.) Mussolini then said that he wanted as many workers as possible there, to which Piacentini replied that the building would be able to accommodate up to 1,500 workers, seeing that it was "solidly made of bricks."

After leaving the building site, from Palazzo di Giustizia the dictator crossed the street to inaugurate the Casa dei Sindacati Fascisti dell'Industria (House of Fascist Industry Trade Unions), which was located on the other side. Mussolini praised the building made by Antonio Carminati's team for its "sober, modern, and powerful" look.[59] He then moved on to the building site of the Palazzo dell'Arte in Parco Sempione, where Muzio had arrived earlier to organize the dictator's welcome. Mussolini had followed this project with special attention. He had wanted to see and give the green light to the plan, and had personally supervised the progress of the works.[60] During the inspection, which lasted forty-five minutes, the script that had previously been acted out at the Palazzo di Giustizia was used again here. Mussolini asked questions whose answers he already knew, and Muzio gave the dictator the very answers he wanted to hear.

Besides Piacentini, Ponti also followed the dictator around the scaffolding at the Triennale. Ponti had prepared a project for the Torre Littoria (Fascist Party Tower), a metal structure to be built in the park. Mussolini, who was well informed about this project too, wanted the architect to show him the exact place where the foundations would be excavated. When, many months earlier, he had seen the first draft of the work, just 81 metres tall at the time, he had judged it too low, and had criticized the Milanese for being incapable of "coming up with something really daring." Mussolini felt that "in any case, it must be taller than the top of Milan Cathedral."[61] It was therefore decided that the building would be 110 metres tall, proof that fascist buildings were taller than those of the Church. Something similar had happened in Germany. While discussing the restoration of Augsburg, Hitler ordered that the Nazi Party Tower be built twenty metres taller than the spire of the city cathedral. The party's buildings should never be lower than the buildings of any other institution.[62] However, the policies of the two regimes vis-à-vis the Church differed greatly. A few months later, in fact, Mussolini changed his mind on the matter. Now that he was on good terms with the religious authorities – just that morning he had had a meeting with Cardinal Ildefonso Schuster, and they may even have talked about this particular topic – he declared that "what is human cannot surpass what is divine." Thus, Ponti was told to correct the plan once more so that the tower would be "at least one metre lower than the cathedral's 'Madonnina.'"

In early October 1934, Mussolini stayed in Milan for three days, his schedule filled with visits to numerous buildings. The Aeronautics

Exhibition at the Palazzo dell'Arte was an opportunity for an encounter with architectural culture, and Mussolini was welcomed there by Muzio, Ponti, Pagano, Maroni, and Luciano Baldessari.[63] As he had done two years earlier, Mussolini stopped at the Palazzo di Giustizia on Corso di Porta Vittoria; Piacentini was there to greet him. The architect had yet another model to show him, this time only of a façade, and then they were off to visit the courtyards and the unfinished rooms. The next stop was at the *Popolo d'Italia* headquarters, on Via Moscova, to admire the new offices designed by Pagano.

In the speech Mussolini gave in Piazza Duomo, before an "oceanic" crowd of half a million people, according to the regime's official press, he glorified the fascist corporate model, an alternative to capitalism and communism. He listed corporativism's future goals: at a social level, guaranteed work, a fair salary, and decent housing; in terms of foreign policy, the "complete and military preparation of the Italian people."[64] With some exceptions, including in Milan, fascism's commitment to social housing was little more than a demagogic promise, as proven by the disastrous housing conditions after the war. Between 1935 and 1939, 13,700 homes were built to accommodate up to 75,000 people, but in order to meet real housing needs, the Ministry of Public Works established that 320,000 rooms had to be built over a twenty-year period. This is easily explained if we consider the fact that the regime afforded more importance to the funding of monumental and celebratory architecture than to low-income housing.[65] This speaks volumes about the importance of the image of architecture for Mussolini. Moulding Italian identity by instilling in it the myth of ancient Rome through architecture had precedence over salubrious housing for all.

Mussolini visited Milan for the last time before the start of World War II on 30 October 1936. Welcomed by Pagano and Sironi at the Palazzo dell'Arte, he examined the rooms of the 6th Triennale and the new pavilion designed by Pagano. The following day he delivered the first sledgehammer blow at the Manica Lunga in Piazza Duomo to make room for the new Arengario. A decision had been made to build a monument of unquestionable political importance, dedicated to the "fascist faith" – in addition to being a pulpit for the dictator, it would also host the Shrine of the Fascist Martyrs – in a place that up until then had been dominated by the cathedral.[66] Later, Mussolini inaugurated Muzio's new headquarters of the Sindacato Giornalisti (Journalists Trade Union) on Via Monte Santo.[67]

On 1 November Mussolini was in Piazza San Sepolcro, on the site of the first Fascio di Combattimento, where the new Provincial Federation headquarters, designed by Piero Portaluppi, was to be built. While looking at the project, which was supposed to include a modern tower

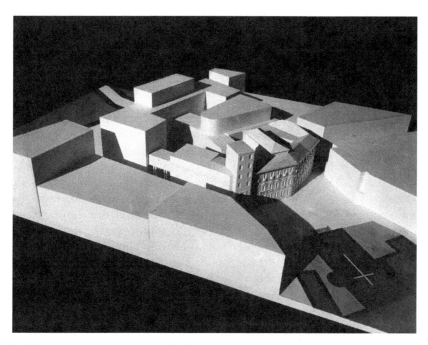

5. Piero Portaluppi, project for the headquarters of the Milanese Fascist Federation, model, 1936. The project was submitted to Mussolini on 1 November 1936.

adjacent to the historical palace, the architect presented a more extensive plan that would include the whole block. Although Mussolini agreed,
he also stressed the need to simplify the works: "All this is fine, but when
will it get started? Because this is what is most important" (figure 5).[68]
Mussolini was well aware of the procedures and the time it was going to
take, but here was an opportunity for him to express the people's intol-
erance for red tape, though he himself was ultimately responsible for it.
The works would not begin until one whole year after the first blow of the
sledgehammer.[69] Mussolini then stopped at the *Popolo d'Italia* to check
and give the green light to Tullio Nicoli's project for the Gruppo Rionale
Fascista "D'Annunzio." Surrounded by the scaffolding of the Casa del Fascio del Gruppo Rionale "Mussolini," he told the workers his usual story
about the time he worked on building sites himself.[70] When Mussolini
was shown the plans for Mario Bacciocchi's project, he asked that the
building be completed with a corner tower. Though just a few minutes
before he had been a worker among other workers, now he switched to
the role of architect. The handling of political consensus exploited the

principle of identification. It is hard to say whether this had been carefully prepared beforehand, or whether he improvised. One thing was for sure: the Casa del Fascio would get the extension he wanted.[71]

Standing before the people of Milan gathered in Piazza Duomo, Mussolini broached foreign and domestic politics. In the wake of the Ethiopian invasion, popular consensus had reached a peak, and Mussolini proved his great skill at leading the applauding crowd. There he was, claiming that if ever there were a "a country where democracy has been accomplished, then that country is fascist Italy." In Italy the regime had indeed initiated the process of integrating the masses in the body politic. This was presented as the "real" expression of democracy, certainly not the much-loathed parliamentary type of democracy; democracy of the absolute kind, based on a direct relationship between the leader and the masses. It was democracy built upon the figure of the Duce who embodied the "general will."[72] He now entrusted a pioneering role in the "promotion of the empire" to the "most fascist" of cities, the one that had witnessed the birth of the revolution. Later, we shall discuss how this ideological manifesto was translated into an urban image, and how Mussolini would personally intervene in shaping it.[73].

5 Architects in the Dictator's Entourage

Mussolini travelled by train, car, and ship. As a rule, his visits were short, the pace of his itinerary brisk and unrelenting. The image he wanted to present was that of an indefatigable leader who was endowed with exceptional intellectual and physical qualities. He exploited all available propaganda tools. Even the itineraries were designed to convince the people of his extraordinary qualities, since he was the living prototype of the "new man." For this reason, on a single day he might visit as many as six different towns, or drive as far as 300 kilometres.[74]

The dictator was inexorably attracted to crowded squares, to the thrill of being in contact with the people. His most important speeches were given before applauding masses, who quickly took to enthusiastic cheering. Much like an architect with his work before him, Mussolini felt he was an artist before his people. To his mind, politics was an art, the primary art, the "art of arts." He felt he could use politics to shape people, individually and collectively. He saw himself as an artist who had taken on the task of forging the Italian people, of modelling the populace. He was a sort of Michelangelo of politics, albeit working at a disadvantage, without the proper raw material, "the Italian race being a race of sheep."[75] The power of the word was of inestimable value to him, but another *instrumentum regni* was his polysemic physique: visible to all was the "rolling of the eyes, the contracting of the jaws with the lower one jutting out, the stance with legs apart and hands on his hips."[76] Mussolini also liked people to look at him: "While on a trip from Florence to Milan ... he even forgot to eat; he felt it was more important to stand next to the window so he could be admired by the endless crowds lining the railroad tracks, standing on the station platforms, and on the roofs of the farmhouses."[77] For those who had been waiting hours just to catch a glimpse of him, the encounter lasted a mere instant; however, that fleeting face would assume the enduring semblance of the legend.

In 1935, Mussolini began using planes to get around as well – fascism would create a whole epic based on these metaphors for modernity. On his three-engine plane he landed in Parma, Viterbo, Pantelleria, Bologna, La Spezia, Rimini, and Macerata. He used a seaplane to fly to Fiume, Naples, and Canal d'Arsia, where he visited the construction site for a new city designed by Gustavo Pulitzer Finali.[78] Sometimes his visits were a surprise, such as on the morning of 7 February 1939, when he unexpectedly landed at Perugia Airport. Quickly removing his coveralls, he changed into his fascist uniform, waiting for someone to whisk him off to the city, where he harangued the masses that had hastily gathered in Piazza Vittorio Emanuele. Something similar had happened the previous day in Naples, where he had gone to inspect the work that was under way for the Exhibition of Italian Overseas Territories, concerned that the works were not progressing fast enough. Once he had arrived at the building site, which was not ready for him, he stopped before the Palazzo dell'Arte designed by Filippo Mellia's team, and the Torre del Partito by Venturino Ventura.[79] Before going back to the airport, he made a quick stop in the city and had his driver park the car on Rione Carità, opposite the Palazzo della Provincia by Marcello Canino and the post office by Giuseppe Vaccaro (figure 6). The dictator had rejected Arturo Martini's initial maquette for the statues needed to adorn the building – a Saint Januarius receiving the blood of a soldier who died in war – warning that "blood can [only] be given to the fatherland."[80]

In Naples, due to the surprise nature of the visit, Mussolini met the project director but not the architects. When the visits were planned, as we said previously, the architect was almost always at Mussolini's side, even if only for a few minutes. At his sign, the architect would separate from the entourage, ready to illustrate the work, to show the drawings, to provide explanations. In Rome, Roberto Marino escorted Mussolini on his tour of the Ministry of Aeronautics; Gustavo Giovannoni was at the School of Architecture, Mosé Tufaroli Luciano at the Society of Authors and Publishers, Enrico Del Debbio at the building site for the Foro Mussolini. Piccinato and his team assisted him during the ceremony

6. Giuseppe Vaccaro, Palazzo delle Poste e dei Telegrafi in Naples, 1931–6.

for the founding of Sabaudia. Paolo Mezzanotte escorted him through the rooms of the new stock exchange and Augusto Magnaghi through the classrooms of the Scuola Arnaldo Mussolini in Milan. Emanuele Mongiovì showed him a model for the historical centre of Ravenna. Muzio was at his side at the opening ceremony of the headquarters of the Sindacato Giornalisti in Milan. Oriolo Frezzotti was with him at the inauguration of the Palazzo di Giustizia in Littoria, Fuzzi was there when he visited the Casa del Fascio in Predappio, Fagnoni was at the building site of the Scuola di Guerra Aerea in Florence, Vaccaro was standing in front of the School of Engineering in Bologna, Orfeo Rossato was at the Ossarium on Colle Laiten in Asiago, Pascoletti was there when he visited the Casa dell'Orfano di Guerra in Cividale. Provino Valle was also in attendance at the inauguration of the Tempio Ossario in Udine, and Bazzani was present when he visited the Palazzo del Governo in Forlì. Foschini was at Mussolini's side when he inspected the works for the opening of Corso del Rinascimento in Rome.[81] Foschini and Del Debbio obsequiously watched him as he wielded a sledgehammer at the Palazzo del Littorio (Fascist Party Headquarters), which they had designed for the Foro Mussolini in Rome. Concezio Petrucci was in the front row at

7. Alberto Ressa, project for the new Casa Littoria in Turin, model, 1938. The project was praised by Mussolini.

the inauguration of the newly founded city of Pomezia. Cesare Valle and Ignazio Guidi were in attendance at the inauguration of Carbonia. Inevitably, this is not a complete list. However, it will suffice to give some idea of the wide-ranging and ramified ties between Mussolini and the architectural world. We have deliberately omitted Piacentini's name from the list as we will thoroughly analyse his relationship with the head of state later on.

At times, Mussolini had words of praise for the architects. In Piazza della Vittoria in Brescia, he described Piacentini's buildings as "superb"; in Bologna, he applauded Santini's project for the Villaggio della Rivoluzione. In Guidonia, he praised his "camerata" (comrade) Alberto Calza Bini and his collaborators, while in Catania he congratulated Fichera for his plan for the Palazzo di Giustizia. In Redipuglia, while standing before the ossarium, he praised the work of Greppi and Castiglioni, adding that their monument would "defy the centuries and perhaps even the millennia."[82] In Turin, as he looked at the drawings and models for the new Casa Littoria, he praised Alberto Ressa (figure 7), while in Rome, he especially appreciated the work of the architects for the National Textiles and National Minerals exhibitions held at the Circus Maximus.[83].

Mussolini had his name put on the hundreds of buildings he visited, inaugurated, or initiated. Italy's modernization was personified by this commander-cum-builder. To make the the mythologization of Mussolini even more incisive and cohesive, the podium from which he made his speeches featured symbolic forms. In 1934 in Milan, before the "rural masses," the podium resembled a geometricized ploughshare; in Catania and Genoa the podium was a ship's prow; in Grottacalda, Sicily, the balcony was made from large blocks of sulphur, while in Pomezia it was covered with fruits and vegetables. In Trieste it was the "deck of a warship," while in Cuneo, close to the Alps, the podium resembled a rocky spur; lastly, at the Mirafiori FIAT factory in Turin the platform resembled an anvil. The setting was no less important than the speech itself; more than the words themselves, it was designed to capture the popular imagination. And just like the podium, Mussolini's face also changed, depending on the different masks he wore for each occasion. In September 1936, Giuseppe Bottai described one of these transformations. From the pulpit, built in Rome on Via dell'Impero, before the twenty thousand *avanguardisti* marching past, the governor noted with some dismay that Mussolini's face changed; it became "stony," "symbolic." "I could see his jaw tense up. It was a deliberate effort, one that confounds the person who would like to witness a man in all his candour."[84]

2 Mussolini's Rome

1 The Third Rome

In the fascist mythology built around Mussolini – as the primary engineer of a new Italy, of its modernization, and of its renewed architectural look – the dictator's process of identification with architectural and urban changes was most evident in Rome. Italy's capital, redesigned by way of the dictator's interventions, into which he would pour huge amounts of money, would also be the "Mussolinian city" *par excellence*.[1] The myth of Mussolini as the builder of cities was founded on his actual presence on the scene, which sometimes even affected the architectural choices made. A certain mistrust in the abilities of his collaborators, even his closest ones, and an inflated opinion of his own qualities convinced Mussolini to make many of the decisions himself, not just political but technical ones as well. As a result, his actions penetrated the domain of architecture.

It was between 1922 and 1923 that Mussolini, together with Margherita Sarfatti, conceived the idea of radically intervening in the city of Rome to change its appearance, to restore the glorious image of its past in order to relive its myth – one of whose essential elements was architecture itself – by building new monuments to rival those of antiquity; this idea informed the very first actions of the fascist government. "Malata di romanità" (fixation on the idea of ancient Rome), according to De Felice, Sarfatti, an art critic, provided the dictator crucial support in his elaboration of the myth of Rome, persuading him that under his guidance the imperial civilization could be reborn. At night, as they drove around the city, Mussolini and his lover Sarfatti pictured this new image.[2] The city offered outstanding raw material, which needed to be shaped to reinforce this myth. In March 1923, during the meeting of the Fascist Grand Council which led to the establishment of the Governorate, Mussolini declared that "the fascist government will introduce a new imperial Rome for a new Italy."[3]

Later, on two occasions Mussolini elaborated on his idea of establishing a new Rome, which he had only merely announced before. On 21 April 1924, having been awarded Roman citizenship, the dictator stated:

> I like to separate Rome's problems, the problems of twentieth-century Rome, into two categories: problems related to necessity and problems of greatness ...
> The problems related to greatness are of a different kind. We need to free all of ancient and medieval Rome of any mediocre distortions, we need to create a monumental Rome for the twentieth century. Rome cannot and must not be just a modern city, according to the ordinary meaning of the term: it must be a city worthy of its glory, and this glory must be renewed constantly to be passed down as the memory of the fascist era to the future generations.[4]

On 31 December 1925, when Filippo Cremonesi, the first governor, took office at the Campidoglio, Mussolini declared:

> My ideas are clear, my orders are exact ... In five years' time Rome must strike all nations of the world as a source of wonder: huge, well-organized, powerful, as it was at the time of the Augustan Empire. ... You will create spaces around the Mausoleum of Augustus, the Theatre of Marcellus, the Capitol, the Pantheon. Everything that has grown up around these buildings during centuries of decadence must be removed. Within five years' time, the great mass of the Pantheon must be visible from the Piazza Colonna through a large space. You will also free from parasitic and profane architectural accretions the majestic temples of Christian Rome. The age-old monuments of our history must loom larger in requisite isolation. Thus, the new Rome will spread over other hills, along the banks of the sacred river, and up the shores of the Tyrrhenian Sea ... A thoroughfare that will be the longest and the widest in the world will bring the breadth of this *mare nostrum* from a reborn Ostia to the heart of the city where the Unknown Soldier watches over it.[5]

These ideas were certainly not original. Demolition work to clear ancient monuments and open new roads had already been amply included in previous urban development plans. Already in 1913, Corrado Ricci, the general director of the Department of Antiquities and Fine Arts, had decided to clear the medieval houses built over the Fora.[6] Now, however, Mussolini's urban programs were more evidently ideological and educational. Surrounded by these gigantic buildings that told of ancient glories, the people would be captivated, they would feel proud of their illustrious past, they would be open to receiving the "inspiration" and emotional energy needed to bring about the fascist regime's ambitious projects.[7] To avoid any misunderstandings, this image of Rome was not the "authentic" one of the past, but rather one reinvented by the regime through the destruction and manipulation of the urban fabric: it was an architectural and urban invention deliberately created to breathe life into the fascist myth of the *Urbe*. Among those to whom Mussolini revealed his plans for the capital was Ojetti, one of his advisers in the artistic sector. Upon receiving him in Palazzo Chigi in the summer of 1926, Mussolini declared:

> You will see how we change Rome. In five years' time, the Pantheon, the Theatre of Marcellus, and the Mausoleum of Augustus will be cleared. In ten years' time, we will have built a majestic opera house ... In fifteen years' time, there will be a road twenty kilometres long and sixty metres wide crossing the Albani hills, all of it filled with villas and palaces.[8]

In this conversation with Ojetti, the project for the road towards the Albani hills was added to the one towards Ostia. Between the two axes of the city's development, the former was the most important to Mussolini. In this case as well, ideological reasons – giving Rome a seaport meant asserting its intention to rule the Mediterranean – prevailed over legitimate urban motivations.

It was the architect Armando Brasini who sought to realize Mussolini's idea of a neo-imperial Rome, anticipating by a few months the head of government's second speech on the subject, the one he delivered at the end of the year. Brasini was a close friend of Margherita Sarfatti, with whom he shared great enthusiasm for the world of the Roman Empire. It was Sarfatti who convinced Mussolini to commission Brasini to design the Italian Pavilion for the International Exposition of Decorative Arts in Paris, which was scheduled for that year, and it is likely that she played an important role in this urban initiative as well.[9] In April 1925, Brasini designed the new city centre, called Foro Mussolini, which required the demolition of whole neighbourhoods between the Corso, Piazza Borghese, and the Pantheon, isolating the ancient monuments – such as the obelisk and Palazzo Montecitorio, the Column of Marcus Aurelius, the Temple of Hadrian, and the Pantheon – and creating new and majestic squares closed off by gigantic colonnades (figure 8).[10] Thus conceived, Mussolini's Rome seemed capable of subsuming two opposite ideas: the Futurist anxiety that longed to take an iconoclastic sledgehammer to all old, "decadent," and "parasitical" buildings, and an ancient imperial vision of the new city.[11]

8. Armando Brasini, project for the centre of Rome, perspective drawing, 1925–6. According to Mussolini, by freeing up the space of the ancient monuments and demolishing whole blocks, the project perfectly fulfilled the directives on the future of Rome, announced in 1925.

With excellent timing, Piacentini responded to Brasini's project by designing what was known as the Grande Roma (Great Rome), discussed later on. The rivalry between the two architects was fierce, and during this phase Mussolini seemed to prefer Brasini, whose inspiring principles he would indeed claim as his own three years later. Indeed, in 1928, Mussolini explained to the new governor, Spada, that Brasini's project fell within his "preliminary guidelines expressed in late 1925 at the Capitol: isolate the great ancient monuments; open large roads and squares; build monuments whose architecture could serve as a sign of the fascist age. I therefore give my approval by way of principle to this urban development plan, and I want the necessary paperwork to be carried out quickly."[12] While Brasini diligently sent him three large perspective drawings for an overall vision of the Foro Mussolini, Spada worked on the "grandiose project for imperial Rome" according to the orders issued by Mussolini.[13] The next step was the proposal to set up a committee with special powers for the implementation of the plan devised by Brasini, who was charged with directing the works. But when the time came for the work to actually be done, faced with difficult financial and administrative challenges, the head of government pulled the brakes and decided to postpone the project for "better days."[14] Behind the initiative was a propagandistic motive, and the plan was never realized. However, this does not mean that Mussolini's urban policies aimed at clearing out the ancient monuments, outlined in the mid-1920s, never came to fruition. While Brasini's projects were never realized, spaces would be created around the Mausoleum of Augustus, the Theatre of Marcellus, and the Capitol in the following years.[15] The only area that remained untouched was that which surrounded the Pantheon. As we shall see, however, the projects were many, and the only thing that stopped the demolition work from continuing was the fall of the regime.

The subsequent stage of the urban development plan marked a new and important step in building of Mussolini's Rome, and once again featured his active presence. Appointed to draft the new plan, the governor, Francesco Boncompagni, nominated a multifarious committee to create a new urban centre. Mussolini himself directly installed the committee, which comprised, among others, Piacentini, Bazzani, Brasini, Giovannoni, Alberto Calza Bini, and Antonio Muñoz: three academics, the director of the School of Architecture in Rome, the national secretary of the Architects Trade Union, and the dictator's trusted archaeologist. Mussolini established the guidelines for the plan, and he underscored the need to free the space around the imperial monuments and restore a "clear view" of the seven hills. He asked that the members of the committee balance artistic needs with traffic requirements, and he invited them to "see things on a grand scale," to think not about the Rome of 1930, but about the Rome of 1950, with their eyes turned towards the Rome of 2000.[16]

On 28 October 1930, Boncompagni, together with Piacentini and the other members of the committee, presented Mussolini with their plan. Large maps, about thirty perspective drawings, and several models were displayed in the rooms of the Museum of Rome, in Piazza Bocca della Verità. As he unveiled the work, the governor emphasized the collegial approach of the architects, the authors of a city plan that was "worthy" of the "Rome that is in the Duce's mind." A plan – Boncompagni continued – that "should have borne your name alone." A plan that not only needed Mussolini's approval, but demanded his careful examination. The knowledge underlying the discipline knelt before the genius of the politician: "You will either approve it or modify it depending on your supreme judgment."[17] It was a plan that, in the final analysis, had to appear as though Mussolini himself had conceived it.

To what extent was Mussolini involved in the urban design? On 28 October the works had actually not been completed yet – there was a total of fifty of them – and so they continued. Mussolini also continued to closely follow the developments. On 24 January 1931, he visited the Museum of Rome, where the material illustrating the future city was still on display. There, he "led" a discussion among the architects on the redevelopment of the area surrounding the Pantheon, as well as on the opening of a road between the Parliament and Ponte Umberto.[18] Two days later he attended the committee's final meeting, where the members summed up all the points over which differences of opinions had emerged. Ultimately, Mussolini authorized the publication of the report that had been prepared by Piacentini.[19] The urban development plan allowed Mussolini plenty of latitude for his final decision. Indeed, at the end of the report Piacentini wrote: "This, Duce, is the plan that we deliver to you. Your genius and your great knowledge, which even in this field make you equal to the great figures of the past ... will allow you to distinguish between what is more or less good about it."[20]

The plan was approved with a decree in July 1931, and it was converted into law the following year. In August, with Mussolini once again in attendance, it was presented to the Italian and foreign press. When, in March 1932, the decree came to the Senate for its conversion into law, Mussolini intervened in the brief discussion. He claimed to be "without false modesty, the spiritual father of the urban development plan for Rome." A plan that he did not believe to be perfect, but that was "the best urban development plan that could be conceived and implemented." Then, alluding to the contradictions that had emerged during the planning sessions, he pointed out that "it had been created by a committee, and that Napoleon warned that a mediocre general can win a battle, but five sublime generals might risk losing it."[21] Although he did not exclude the contribution of any of the members of the committee, from now on Mussolini would call on one of these "sublime generals" in particular, and that "general" was Marcello Piacentini.

After the "Rome of Augustus, after the Rome of Pope Sixtus V, the Rome of Mussolini [would be built]."[22] Presented as the "Mussolini plan," a document of "fascist civilization," the 1931 urban development plan was only partially carried out. Its overall implementation was in fact abandoned after a series of "varianti" (variants) were required to meet the demands of building speculation, and the ever-changing needs of Mussolini's policies. Ten years later the plan was revised with another variant ("Variante del 1941"). At that point an attempt would truly be made to give an architectural shape to the city, one that would be consistent with the turnaround in totalitarian politics: specific unity of direction and "the strictest supervision" of building projects replaced the flexibility of the 1931 urban development plan.

2 Demolishing "with No Holds Barred"

Muñoz, the inspector general of the government's Department of Antiquities and Fine Arts, was, according to Antonio Cederna, the "director of the largest theatre of demolitions in modern history." The archaeologist, who was very close to Mussolini, wrote, "in the great works to transform Rome ... what Benito Mussolini wanted was its full potential; the leader oversaw, advised, gave orders." Mussolini, Muñoz continued, followed "day by day" the enactment of that vast plan "down to the smallest details."[23] The text that contained these words was first and foremost used as propaganda, and Muñoz's attitude was unquestionably adulatory (figure 9). However, there were some elements of truth to it, and one of these was Mussolini's unrelenting interest in the public construction works that were under way in the capital. The correspondence between Mussolini and the various governors confirms Muñoz's version, especially as concerns Mussolini's constant, spasmodic, almost maniacal supervision. His interest went well beyond urban design in general; it ranged from the opening of a new road to the maintenance of the road surface, from conservation work to the surroundings of a new building, from the installing of a monument in one of the piazzas to the dangerous state of a damaged wall. Mussolini was even involved in the administrative technicalities, which he menacingly annotated in blue or red pencil.

This custom of combining essential matters with trivial ones, which could easily have been managed by some clerk, can be found, for instance, in a letter that was sent to Boncompagni in December 1929, in which Mussolini laid down a calendar for the most urgent work. The demolition works to free the ancient monuments and open up new roads were at the top of the list, but they alternated with much smaller interventions, such as the tearing down of the walls on Via Salaria that "hid some makeshift lorry depots." This heterogeneous to-do list confirms the improvisational aspects of urban planning at this time, as well as the "paternalistic" mentality that informed the city's management.

The orders Mussolini gave Boncompagni involved the demolition work around the Theatre of Marcellus and between Piazza Bocca della Verità and the River Tiber, where the plan was to instal a large garden with a fountain. This included tearing down the block to the left of the Monument to Vittorio Emanuele in order to create a piazza near the Vittoriano that would be "as big as St. Peter's Square." "We need to

9. Mussolini and Antonio Muñoz on Via Dell'Impero in Rome at the
inauguration of the bas-relief maps hanging on the walls of the Basilica of
Maxentius, 21 April 1934. Two years earlier, the Velian Hill had been excavated
in order to open up Via Dell'Impero, the street where the regime organized its
parades, with the evocative Fora in the background.

think," Mussolini added, "about the Rome of tomorrow, which will have a
population that is twice the size of today's." The dictator interrupted the
building of the new Palazzo della Confederazione Fascista degli Industriali until the houses that were there were torn down so that he could
"form an opinion as to what would happen with or without the building." In terms of circulation, the dictator implemented a project that was
especially dear to him, the creation of a "new and vast avenue near the
water," thus connecting Rome with the seaside. Then, without including
them in the list of works to be built immediately, he mentioned the construction of three "big streets" to connect "Piazza Venezia – Via Cavour –
the railway station; Piazza Venezia — Via Botteghe Oscure – Largo
Argentina; Piazza Venezia – Tor degli Specchi – the Testaccio and
Ostiense neighbourhoods." The building in which he himself lived
would lie at the intersection of these streets, and, significantly, all three

proposals were included in the 1931 urban development plan. The last two directives concerned low-income housing. Mussolini sent the governor some drawings of houses – "which seem to me to be low-income" – that had been built in Treviso. "If it is worth the effort, we need to copy them, in a series, without luxuries or ornamentation."[24]

Clearly, demolition was a large part of Mussolini's urban policy. In 1931, Boncompagni planned to tear down the old Pierleoni houses, on the bank of the same name, but was met with Pietro Fedele's opposition. Fedele was the former minister of public education, a professor of medieval history as well as the president of the Italian Historical Institute. Mussolini intervened in the dispute, ordering the governor to keep on "demolishing." Mussolini was irritated by the way those houses gave that part of Rome a "more than African" appearance. He mocked the former minister, urging him not to insist on defending the medieval houses. Otherwise "we will end up demolishing Senator Fedele's sadness as well, that of a man who foolishly becomes emotional at the sight of a bunch of outhouses."[25]

In February 1932, Mussolini stepped in again in favour of demolition work that was under way. He urged workers to proceed "unhesitatingly" in tearing down a group of houses located close to the Colosseum, opposite the Oppian Hill. The reasons he gave were aesthetic and, more importantly, related to traffic: "A square would be perfect in that area of heavy traffic."[26] Documents such as these clash, at least in part, with the public image of a wise and moderate Mussolini, respectful of ancient Rome, an image he wanted his biographer, Yvon De Begnac, to underscore: "Need we demolish at all costs so that the centre of Rome can breathe, or should we curb the use of the sledgehammer in dozens of hectares in this ancient city? I, personally, am in favour of clean air. However, the Middle Ages and the Renaissance should also be guaranteed the right to survive. The word is that of a new sack of Rome ... But I am keeping my eyes open. I do not tolerate extremes."[27]

3 The Keen Eye

One day, as Mussolini was being driven through the city, he noticed that the perspectival continuity of the houses on Via Quattro Fontane, opposite Palazzo Barberini, was interrupted by an empty space, a "deplorable omission" he instantly denounced to the governor. Mussolini felt it would be a "mistake" to erect a "building that has no volume" in that site, and instead suggested leaving the area green – a solution that had already been put forward by a newspaper. "An unexpected strip of green," he told Boncompagni, "with the big trees that already exist there would no doubt have an aesthetic and healthy effect!"[28] When, a few months later, Mussolini noticed that the area had been fenced off by a wall, meaning that his 'suggestion' had not been taken seriously, he expressed vexation: "I notice a wall. Either you build or you leave empty. Better to leave empty because of the greenery. In any case, it cannot remain as it is any longer."[29]

The building of a new Auditorium was no doubt a more pressing issue. With a budget in hand, Mussolini was informed of the preliminary phases of the plan, and he visited Piazza di Porta Capena so that he could personally assess the choice of the area where the new building was to go up.[30] Mussolini was not entirely convinced by the idea, however, mostly because he thought the budget, equal to about 38 million lire, was excessive. He was looking for an alternative, possibly ingenious, solution. But his idea, "to see whether the Basilica of Maxentius might not be used instead," was not just naive, it was also alarming. It was the expression of a mentality that, on the one hand, extolled the city's ancient Roman roots, and, on the other, showed a total lack of sensitivity towards ancient monuments. For the dictator, they were objects to be manipulated, instruments of ruthless policies.[31]

Mussolini's scornful attitude towards antiquity, not just medieval but Roman as well, was extended to the ruins of the Meta Sudans, the ancient fountain that stood beside the Colosseum and opposite the Arch of Constantine. The conical fountain hindered the new "triumphal" road that ran from Via dell'Impero (currently Via dei Fori Imperiali) and continued along Via dei Trionfi (currently Via San Gregorio). Mussolini did not hesitate to order the governor to "tear down the Meta Sudans, which is nothing more than a heap of rubble." Did the governor need a better understanding of what he was talking about? Mussolini drew a circle on a piece of paper. "A circle such as this one is sufficient."[32] In a case like this, the idea of a ruin might even be dangerous for the regime if it conveyed an archaic image, one that clashed with the regime's rhetoric and its efforts to modernize.

The presence of slums and people living in precarious conditions was unquestionably a sign of political failure. Mussolini was vexed by the chaotic "amassing" of families who had been evicted and sent to live in the city's outskirts in a place called Tor Pignattara, and he ordered that they be removed. It is likely that among those living in the shacks were the former inhabitants of the houses he had had torn down to create his imperial Rome.[33] He also lamented the "deplorable" conditions of the street that led to Porta Portese; he advised against the use of barbed wire to fence in the gardens, as children could get hurt falling down on it.[34] Annoyed by the constant interruptions in the site where several houses were being built near Villa Torlonia, his place of residence in Rome, he declared: "If in one month's time the work does not begin again, or if the buildings are not torn down, I will deal with it myself *manu militari*."[35]

With a keen eye, Mussolini surveyed every single thing that happened in the city, using his time to resolve even the smallest matters. For instance, he noticed that something was just not right around the monument to Chateaubriand, and he informed Boncompagni about it: "A monument to Chateaubriand is being built in Trinità dei Monti. A public toilet located nearby looks horribly out of place."[36] He also complained about the conditions of the area near Trajan's Forum: "It is overgrown with grass. If something isn't done soon, the cats will be back." Nor were the zebra crossings to his liking. Their "stripes have almost faded, and that is a sign of slovenliness. Better to do away with them entirely then. *Redo them.*" And there was the new landscaping for the trees at the Forum of Caesar: "One of the trees has had wooden scaffolding around it for three years. What are we waiting for to remove it? Am I the only one who notices these things?"[37] One particular order addressed to the Governorate staff bears witness to just how far his invasive supervision could go: "Fascists. 1 April. Time to take off your coats."[38]

If the location of the Auditorium was controversial, so was that of the Ministry of Foreign Affairs. In 1935, Mussolini urged Bottai, who was governor at the time, to make Via Porta San Paolo larger, because "that's where the Ministry of Foreign Affairs needs to be built."[39] However, he then changed his mind and chose the park at Villa Borghese. In 1937, it was still all up in the air. In November, Galeazzo Ciano wrote the following in his diary: "Brief conversation with the Duce. More or less reached agreement on the building of the new Ministry of Foreign Affairs."[40] It would rise up in Piazza Barberini and "have to be worthy of the age of Mussolini and of its future role: the Imperial Ministry." However, a competition was then announced and the area that was selected was in a completely different part of the city, near the Baths of Caracalla. And that wasn't the last of the surprises. Despite the presentation of the projects and the jury selection – the three best projects were the ones by Canino, Moretti, and Ponti – the competition was called off and, at that point, in 1940, it was decided that the Foro Mussolini should be built instead (figures 10 and 11). Evidently, no plan was ever definitively established, and there was much room for improvisation. These uncertainties in the urban planning could mostly be attributed to Mussolini himself, to his unwillingness to delegate, to his boundless faith in his own political genius, and to the fact that he could not deal with many of the problems because he was busy doing other things.

10. Gio Ponti (in collaboration with Guglielmo Ulrich, Eugenio Soncini, R. Angeli, Carlo De Carli, and L. Olivieri), project for the Ministry of Foreign Affairs in Rome, model, 1940. The ministry was to have been built in the area between the Baths of Caracalla and the Aurelian Walls, close to Porta Ardeatina.

11. Luigi Moretti, project for the Ministry of Foreign Affairs in Rome, model, 1940. The building, over 175 metres long, was meant to be comparable in size with the nearby Baths of Caracalla.

Despite these contradictions, after the Ethiopian War there was a turning point and a concrete plan to transform the city was drafted. This emerged clearly in the list of works to be carried out between 1938 and 1941, presented to Mussolini by the governor, Piero Colonna, in December 1937. The plan involved the historical part of the city, but it was strictly connected to the opening of the Universal Exposition, initially scheduled for 1941, but postponed to 1942 so that it would coincide with the twenty-year anniversary of fascism, referred to as the E42. In addition to the works that were already under way – the tearing down of the Borghi and the opening of Via della Conciliazione, the opening of Corso del Rinascimento, the reorganization of the Mausoleum of Augustus, the expansion of Via delle Botteghe Oscure – Colonna had a list, filled with charts, of twenty-one other important works to be completed. These included the Termini Station, the opening of new roads between Piazza Barberini and Piazza Santi Apostoli, between Via Vittorio Veneto and Piazza San Silvestro, between Piazza Parlamento and Ponte Umberto I, between Piazza San Bernardo and Via Vittorio Veneto, to which was added the construction of a road parallel to Corso Umberto, the building of Ponte dei Fiorentini and Ponte d'Africa, and the completion of the freeing up of the space around the Capitol.[41] Although many of these works had already been included in the 1931 urban development plan, they now fit within a different point of view, one more in line with the policies of the regime, and clearly aimed at highlighting the city's "imperial" image. Similarly, the podestà of Milan also provided Mussolini with a list of works to be built over a three-year period. Architecture was filling an increasingly important place on the political scene.

4 Visits to Building Sites in Rome

In Rome, there was not a single important work of architecture that had not been influenced by Mussolini's personal intervention, be that the examination of a drawing, a visit to the building site, or some inaugural gesture. Rome was changing its appearance and this metamorphosis was happening under his constant, far-reaching, and direct control. Throughout 1930, Mussolini followed the development of the works in Piazza Bocca della Verità based on a project by Clemente Busiri Vici;[42] in Via Bari the dictator cut the ribbon for the new monumental headquarters of the Dopolavoro Ferroviario by Mazzoni;[43] he visited the building site of the Ministry of Aeronautics by Marino;[44] he pretended to make an "unscheduled" visit to the Parco Nemorense, by Raffaele de Vico, to the works on Via Barberini, and to the Ostia sea-front.[45] He inspected the architecture of the Central Institute for Statistics designed by Aschieri.[46]

He inspected the Palazzo delle Esposizioni on Via Nazionale, where the 1st Quadriennale was soon to open, and together with Aschieri and Del Debbio, he evaluated several possible solutions for the exhibition design.[47] On the anniversary of his rise to power, he inaugurated the Poligrafico dello Stato (State Printing House) by Garibaldi Burba, and the Sacrario delle Camicie Nere (Shrine to the Black Shirts) by Pietro Lombardo at the Palazzo del Viminale.[48]

The following year, he visited the gardens in Monte Testaccio designed by De Vico and the building site of the Foro Mussolini by Del Debbio. The building site would remain open for the entire duration of the regime, and it was one of the building sites that Mussolini visited most often. Originally meant to be the Foro dello Sport (Sports Arena) to host the Olympics, it instead became a place for mass gatherings, thus acquiring a more political and symbolic value. Anticipating the other totalitarian regimes, for fascism sports was a catalyst of national identity. It was a powerful propaganda tool, able to involve even those who were most impervious to politics. Some of the values inherent to competitive sports – such as courage, willpower, strength, and self-denial – were identified as being characteristic of the "Italian race" and an essential part of fascism's "new man." By symbolizing both ideological and physical supremacy, the place where sporting events were held became Mussolini's place as well, a symbol of the new imperial Rome: "The Foro Mussolini will be bigger than the Colosseum and it will have more marble than St. Peter's," he predicted in 1929.[49] Here, akin to the great Roman emperors, Mussolini built his own forum, bestowing a genuine architectural backdrop to the myth of the Duce as the "new Caesar." Inaugural activities continued with the Casa dei Ciechi di Guerra by Aschieri: the architect, who met with Mussolini three times in little more than a year, was experiencing a moment of professional glory.[50] At the end of the year, Mussolini visited the scaffolding at the Theatre of Marcellus with Alberto Calza Bini. As he stood before the area that had been cleared of all the less important buildings, he warned against "the useless pedantry of the archaeologists" who hindered the isolation of such ancient constructions. He raged against Fedele and the "know-alls of old stones," who stood together in defence of "fetid walls."[51] Mussolini then followed Giovannoni to the building site of the new School of Architecture, where the work progressed slowly and the inauguration, planned for October, had to be postponed.[52]

In April 1932, escorted by Piacentini, Mussolini made the first of many visits to the site of the Città Universitaria. This will be discussed later on. On that same day, he walked down Via Barberini, which was under construction, and along with Corrado Ricci he visited the excavations of Trajan's Forum. From the ancient Roman Fora, he headed over to the

12. Enrico Del Debbio, Stadio dei Marmi at the Foro Mussolini in Rome, 1928–32. Mussolini inspected the building site at the Foro Mussolini more often than any other in Rome.

Forum of modern Rome that bore his name, welcomed there by Renato Ricci and Enrico Del Debbio, who accompanied him to the building site of the Stadio dei Marmi (Marble Stadium) and the Accademia di Educazione Fisica (Academy of Physical Education) (figure 12).[53] Within the context of the activity there, most of which simply involved disastrous demolition work aimed at isolating the Capitol in order to radically change its image, reinventing a past that had never existed, Mussolini also visited the new Museo del Risorgimento, whose construction was under way. Waiting for him there was Brasini, who showed him a drawing of the building that would connect the Vittoriano to the square created by Michelangelo. Mussolini then headed over to the Forum of Caesar together with Gustavo Giovannoni and Corrado Ricci, where they talked about the construction of the new palace of the Accademia di San Luca. This will be discussed later.[54]

Preparations for the tenth anniversary of the March on Rome were in full swing and Mussolini was once again surrounded by architects and construction workers. From his windows in Palazzo Venezia, he could directly follow the work that was being done on the Fora. On 29 October, the sacralization of the rite required that he, wearing a uniform and a fez with a white crest, ride horseback down the new imperial road like a commander from ancient Rome. The building of this wide road, which connected Piazza Venezia with the Colosseum, involved drastic measures in the archaeological area, including the demolition of the Velian Hill. Thousands of cubic metres of material dating back to Roman times were ultimately destroyed.[55] The new layout, surrounded by the evocative scenery of the Fora, would be one of the regime's most emblematic sites, the symbiosis – and aporia – of fascism and ancient Rome, of revolution and tradition. To the crowd gathered in Palazzo Venezia, Mussolini pointed out the transfigured meaning of the parade, "so formidable, so impressive," even greater than those memorable ones that Rome had witnessed in its glorious history. Such rites produced a strong propulsive energy among the masses, as Mussolini was well aware.[56] The following day he opened the Exhibition of the Fascist Revolution, its façade designed by Libera and De Renzi, the O room by Terragni, and the Sacrario dei Martiri Fascisti by Libera and Antonio Valente. Mussolini had visited Via Nazionale on many occasions as it was being developed.[57] The young architects involved in the project had the unprecedented and exciting experience of working on something that was overseen directly by "their" Duce, and of seeing themselves as being part of history.

The modern, almost Futurist, image of the Exhibition of the Fascist Revolution offset the one at the Foro Mussolini, which instead evoked ancient Roman tradition. Conducive to the celebrations of fascism, they were emblematic of the eclectic policy fulfilled in those years with regard to architecture. The complex was inaugurated on 4 November and it included the Accademia dell'Educazione Fisica; the Stadio dei Marmi, entirely made of Carrara marble, crowned with 60 statues of athletes donated by the Italian provinces; and the Stadio dei Cipressi (currently the Olympic Stadium), which had been excavated into the side of the hill, featuring grass terraces that could accommodate up to 100,000 people. There was also an obelisk made from a monolith of Carrara marble, 18 metres tall and weighing 380 tonnes, dedicated to Mussolini himself. A symbol of "national renewal," the marble block was shipped from the quarry of Carbonera in the province of Carrara owned by Cirillo Figaia, the "pirate of marble," and father-in-law of Renato Ricci, president of the Opera Nazionale Balilla, which had commissioned the works; it also, and more prosaically, spoke volumes about a never dismantled system of patronage.[58] Ten days later, Mussolini was celebrating the splendour of the new Ministry of Corporations, another work by Piacentini.

In the spring of 1933, Mussolini visited the building site on Via Taranto along with Cipriani, surrounded by the new houses created by INA. He then took a look at the plan to make Via dei Trionfi longer. He visited the Eastmann Dental Clinic designed by Foschini. Accompanied by Alberto Calza Bini, he checked on the state of progress of the works for the new Istituto Artigiani San Michele. Insinuations had spread concerning Calza Bini's skill, which had perhaps even reached as far as Mussolini. Rumour had it that "the architect De Renzi was actually the one who was studying and drafting all the projects that bore his [Calza Bini's] signature," and that at the Istituto delle Case Popolari, of which he was president, "the director, Engineer [Innocenzo] Costantini was really the one who did everything."[59]

A few months later, Mussolini devoted a whole day to visiting all the construction work that was under way. The tour began at 8 a.m. at the building sites of the INCIS houses on Via Tronto and Via Taro. In Piazza Bologna, he chatted with Ridolfi, and examined the architect's drawings and model of the post office. Ridolfi, a young architect, had won – alongside Samonà, Armando Titta, Libera, and De Renzi – one of the four competitions for the capital's post offices. Although it had already been selected, Ridolfi's project needed to be approved on site by Mussolini himself, causing a series of problems for the young professional, who wanted to make some important changes while the work was being done.[60] The inspection continued and, having left Piacentini at the Città Universitaria, Mussolini headed over to Via Taranto, where he met Samonà, who showed him a sketch of his own post office. After returning to the centre of the city, Mussolini met Piacentini once more at the building site of the Banca Nazionale del Lavoro on Via Veneto. Then he showed up at the building site of the post office building by Titta on Viale Mazzini. From there, Mussolini climbed to the top of the Capitoline Hill so he could watch while several houses were being torn down. After that, accompanied by Muñoz, he walked down to the Forum of Caesar. Once he had arrived at the Colosseum, he and his archaeologist discussed the fate of the Meta Sudans, mentioned previously, and the remains of the Colossus of Nero. He crossed Via dei Trionfi, and stopped before the site where the fourth post office, this one by Libera e De Renzi, was being built on Via Marmorata. Having left the two architects, in a few months' time he would find himself with his loyal collaborator Alberto Calza Bini – who was not, however, his favourite – amid the scaffolding of the Istituto Artigiani San Michele.[61] By the end of the day, he had visited a dozen work sites, met half a dozen architects, and given the impression of meticulously overseeing the major building site on the Capitol.

Another parade was held on 28 October 1933, celebrating the opening of Via dei Trionfi, the restoration of the Temple of Venus Genetrix in the Forum of Caesar, and the freeing up of the space around the Capitol. Lastly, amid an array of airmen and trumpet blasts, Mussolini made an exuberant entrance to the new Casa dell'Aviatore, designed by Brasini, in Piazza IV Novembre. And yet, one year before he had not been so kind to the architect. "Nothing short of an accident, occurring to the Assicurazioni sugli Infortuni of all things," was how he had judged the building during a speech to the Senate, which had initially been designated as the headquarters of INFAIL.[62]

5 Architecture and the Legacy of Fascism

Before the Fascist Party's second five-year assembly, Mussolini declared that "after the Rome of the Caesars, after the Rome of the popes, it is fascist Rome, with its simultaneity of past and present, that is admired around the world."[63] The remodelling of the ancient and the figuration of the modern were the two fronts of his architectural policy for the city. In the spring of 1934, Mussolini was in Ostia to visit Guidi's "Rationalist" primary school. A few days later, he followed Attilio Spaccarelli around the ramparts and corridors of the Mole Adriana, which had been "cleared" of 50,000 cubic metres of houses. That same afternoon, he strolled along Viale Aventino, the continuation of Via dei Trionfi towards the seaside, to get a first-hand impression of a road that he himself had wanted to be 50 metres wide.[64] In July, he visited the new building of the Foresteria Sud designed by Enrico del Debbio for the Foro Mussolini, and the new Stadio del Tennis (Tennis Stadium) by Costantino Costantini. He examined the marble model of the Palazzo delle Terme and he climbed up the scaffoldings of the building that was under way.[65] It was there that Moretti would design the leader's private lodgings, known as the Palestra del Duce (the Duce's Gym).

Wielding a sledgehammer and wearing a coverall, early on 22 October Mussolini delivered the first blow to a house on Via Soderini, so that he could literally have a hand in clearing the Mausoleum of Augustus. One month later, he was laying the first stone for the Collegio IV Novembre by Giuseppe Boni at Lido di Ostia (figure 13). Surrounded by workers, he asked to be filmed as he pushed a wheelbarrow full of concrete, held a shovel, and listened, arms akimbo, to the architect's explanations. From there, he headed to the Palazzo delle Poste (Post Office) for a detailed examination of the building designed by Mazzoni.[66] More demolitions awaited him at the intersection between Via Cavour and Via dell'Impero. There, on the site of the houses he was planning to have torn down, he wanted to create the Palazzo del Littorio, an edifice that would be worthy of "handing down to posterity, with a lasting and universal value, the age of Mussolini."[67] For this event, he made sure he was surrounded by a multitude of architects. In addition to Bazzani, Brasini, Alberto Calza Bini, Piacentini, and Portaluppi, who were members of the competition commission, he invited Clemente Busiri Vici, Boni, Gino Cancellotti, and

13. Mussolini laying the first stone of the Collegio IV Novembre, Rome, 12 November 1934.

De Renzi as well because of their connections with the Fascist Party. "The Mole Littoria," he told them, "would have to be worthy of Rome, of the site, and of Italian architecture." He set 23 March 1939 as the date for the works to be completed. That deadline would not be met, however.[68]

On 2 October 1935, from his balcony in Palazzo Venezia, Mussolini announced the invasion of Ethiopia. The colonial conflict became a national war, and Mussolini set in motion an efficient propaganda machine, which earned him huge support even from the least enthusiastic sectors of public opinion.[69] His aim was to build an empire, to turn the war into a powerful educational undertaking, a tool that could be used to shape the character of the Italian people, and to see whether, after thirteen years under the regime, the new fascist man was becoming a reality.[70] During the Ethiopian War, Mussolini's activity in the field of architecture knew no bounds. On the anniversary of the March on Rome, he celebrated the opening of Viale delle Piramidi, between Porta San Paolo and Viale Aventino. But the main event of the day was the opening of the Palazzo Postale designed by Libera and De Renzi in the Aventino area (figure 14). Mussolini looked at the exterior, moved through its rooms, and

14. Mussolini inaugurating the Palazzo delle Poste in Porta San Paolo in
Rome. To his left are Adalberto Libera and Mario De Renzi, 28 October 1935.

complimented the architects.[71] The following day Mussolini was once
again wielding a sledgehammer to celebrate the start of the demolition
work on Via delle Botteghe Oscure.[72] Together with Cobolli Gigli, the minister of public works, the leader visited the exhibition where the projects
for the Ponte Duca d'Aosta on the River Tiber near the Foro Mussolini
were on display, including the winning project by Fasolo.[73] In January of
the following year, Mussolini took part in the initiation of the Città della
Cinematografia (Cinema City). He spread mortar on the first stone of the
new complex, not before examining the model and asking Gino Peressutti
some carefully scripted questions as the journalists crowded around them.
Truth be told, during the previous months, Mussolini had summoned the
architect to Palazzo Venezia on several occasions, and made sure he was
kept abreast of the development of the project, with "the same attention
with which he followed the activities of the troops in Abyssinia."[74]

In April, at the Foro Mussolini the leader inspected the Olympic Stadium, whose construction was under way. After the successes of the Italian athletes at the 1932 Los Angeles Olympics, Rome had become a candidate to host the games in 1940. Displayed on a table near the site was a model of the project by Moretti.[75] Piacentini wrote that Rome wanted to compete with the buildings that went up in Berlin, where the 1936 Summer Olympics were hosted, so that it could show itself to be "even worthier" than the German capital.[76] However, Germany was looking even further ahead in time, and Albert Speer was designing a huge Olympic Stadium in Nuremberg that could accommodate up to 400,000 people (figure 15). Before the massive structure, Hitler claimed that even the Pyramids would vanish: "I build for eternity, because ... we are the ultimate Germany." In Italy, on the other hand, having lost the bid to host the 1940 Olympics to Japan, the focus was on 1944.[77] Beyond the Alps, the completion of the Nuremberg Stadium was scheduled for the following year. From that moment on, Hitler warned, the Olympics would be hosted "here and here alone." Long before the declarations of war, this architecture spoke volumes about Hitler's desire to dominate the world.[78] Both regimes, albeit in different ways and with diverse methods, used architecture to attain their political goals. Both of them believed war and architecture to be the basic tools for political action from a totalitarian perspective. Renato Ricci, who was the creator of the Foro, wrote to Mussolini that "war and the arts are the only tools able to make a country great and powerful for centuries."[79]

On that same morning, Mussolini inaugurated the Accademia di Scherma (Fencing Academy) in the Forum, designed by Moretti. Completely clad in Carrara marble, its corners rounded off, and its slabs polished, the building resembled a huge, compact marble block.[80] Before entering it, Mussolini admired its sculptural impact: the young, talented architect, just like the politician, had achieved "emotional transfiguration" that drew on the classical tradition. Returning to Palazzo Venezia, ranks of Balilla and a festive crowd spread out like wings as he passed by, enthralled by this charismatic figure. With grand paternalistic gestures he patted children on the head and responded genially to the crowds. In their eyes, he was a dictator with a human face. Little did they know that just a few days earlier he had ordered the use of forbidden chemical weapons against Ethiopian soldiers. Mussolini had specified that "any kind of gas and in any quantity" be used: this included mustard gas, which causes skin to blister and results in a slow and painful death.[81]

A few days later, Mussolini made one of his usual visits to the most important building sites in the capital. He started out at the Mausoleum of Augustus, where he examined Morpurgo's design for the area's layout.

15.   Albert Speer, project for the Olympic Stadium in Nuremberg, model, 1937. The stadium could accommodate up to 400,000 people. According to Hitler, the future Olympic Games would be held "here, and here alone."

He continued on to Palazzo Madama, where the model of Foschini's plan for the opening of Corso del Rinascimento was on display. He made a last stop at Lido di Ostia, where he visited the building sites of the fire station and the Collegio. He examined the model of the new Palazzo degli Uffici del Governatorato by Ignazio Guidi and Cesare Valle on Via del Mare.[82] According to the chronicles of his visit to the Mausoleum of Augustus, the labourers interrupted their work to welcome Mussolini with "lively enthusiasm." A censored picture instead shows that many labourers chose not to greet him, some of them even turning their backs to him.[83]

Early one morning, accompanied by Bottai, Mussolini headed to Castel Sant'Angelo to examine Piacentini and Spaccarelli's plan for the opening of Via Conciliazione, and to check the progress of the work and its architectural and contextual features.[84] After the dictator approved the architects' project – the fact that Spaccarelli was a former collaborator of Piacentini's should not be overlooked – Bottai proceeded to show him some other drawings. However, by then Mussolini was distracted by a growing crowd of people standing in front of him. With the documents before him, he was no longer listening to the governor, nor was he looking at what he was being shown. His magnetic attraction to and for the masses had taken over, and an embittered Bottai had no choice but to gather his papers.[85] Two days later, Mussolini inaugurated the headquarters of the Commando Generale della Milizia (General Command of the Militia) on Via Romania and the Mussolini Militia Barracks, both designed by Vittorio Cafiero. Before returning to Palazzo Venezia, the dictator made a quick stop at the bridge over the River Tiber that led to the Foro Mussolini. A few months before, he had seen the drawings for the headquarters; he was now checking on its state of progress: he wanted the people of Rome to know that he was constantly overseeing everything that was going on.[86]

Bottai remembered spending all of 28 October 1936 with Mussolini, going "from one inauguration to another." He began with Cesare Valle's Liceo Giulio Cesare, and continued with Costantini's indoor swimming pool at the Palazzo delle Terme, and Moretti's stadium at the Foro Mussolini. When they finally arrived at the Accademia di Scherma, they took a break so that Mussolini could participate in a duel. After that, they were on the move again, this time to the Piazzale Prenestino, where they inaugurated low-income housing for streetcar drivers.[87] When Mussolini returned to Palazzo Venezia, cheered by the crowd, he came out on the balcony to remind the people that on that very day, not just in Rome, but "everywhere else" in Italy, other public works were being inaugurated. The simultaneity of such events was carefully orchestrated. These works, built at the same time in many parts of Italy, conveyed an astonishing sense of unity. This intense architectural activity belonged to a national mythology aimed at underscoring the country's collective strength. It was an immense undertaking meant to involve the Italian people, to turn them into a politically cohesive mass who identified with the works that had been built by the regime. By taking part in this secular cult, the people felt close to their leader and became, like him, protagonists of the regime. However, the buildings did not only serve a policy of consensus in the short term. As Mussolini told the people, they would serve as "indelible marks" for "our children's children," proof of the "creative potential of the Italian people in the fascist age."[88]

What did the Duce and the governor say to each other in the long hours they spent together? Did they discuss the "imperial" future of the city? It seems they did not. At the end of the day, in his diary Bottai lamented that they had "talked little about the works in Rome, about the 1941 exhibition." What they had talked about at length was "the regime's war preparations." Bottai's overall impression was that Mussolini wanted to keep his architectural and urban ideas to himself so that he would not have to share them with anyone else, not even with the governor, who was in part responsible for them. Mussolini feared that his personal prowess might somehow be undermined, and he made sure that the governors, as well as others, never lasted long in their posts for fear they might get too much power. Mussolini was probably already aware that Bottai was going to be replaced a few days later. Fascist Rome could not belong to others, it had to be "Mussolini's Rome," exclusively so.[89] Even with his closest and most loyal collaborators Mussolini was often cynical and ungrateful, his sole interest being the cultivation of his own personal myth.[90] Relentless in his fixation with building, the very next day, after climbing up to the terrace of an old house on Via Borghi, he inaugurated the opening of Via della Conciliazione. In the following months, he opened the Collegio IV Novembre at Lido di Ostia, and visited the remodelling of Piacentini's Casa Madre dei Mutilati.[91] During all of these events, which were part of a broader fascist strategy, the idea of the "Man" as an image of a nation in the making was perpetuated. Thanks to his miraculous interventions, the Eternal City, and Italy as a whole, was taking on a new look, one that was modern, fascist, and now also imperial. Even the role played by the architects themselves, always there beside him, tended to vanish, swallowed up in the cogwheels of Mussolini's myth.

6 Rome, "Kingdom of the Unexpected"

On the afternoon of 14 January 1937, Mussolini welcomed Hermann Göring, the German minister of aeronautics, to Palazzo Venezia to work out a shared strategy regarding the Spanish Civil War. The following morning, he and the Nazi Party official visited the Foro Mussolini.[92] These two moments in political life, rife with meaning, underscored the parallel action coordinated by the regimes of both fascist Italy and Nazi Germany. The large-scale construction activity was accompanied by military escalation. First, Mussolini had declared war in Ethiopia; now, just three months after the conquest of Addis Ababa, he had sent troops to Spain. Mussolini would press ahead with the invasion of Albania, and as he prepared for it he was engaged in a great military stand-off with other European nations. The totalitarian drive gathered momentum. The regime's architecture, like its military ventures, had to be a means of public persuasion; it had to convey new values and new myths. Mussolini wanted to instil in the people the pride of "feeling permanently mobilized for works of peace as well as for those of war."[93] He wanted to

16. Mussolini and Piacentini on the terrace of the new headquarters of the
Banca Nazionale del Lavoro on Via Veneto in Rome, 5 May 1937. Behind them
are the arcades of the Albergo Ambasciatori, designed by Piacentini as well.

anthropologically transform the nature of the Italians, to turn them into
a race of warriors capable of dominating the world once again.

In the following months, Mussolini laid the first stone at the Termini
Station designed by Mazzoni. He also visited the Città della Cinematografia, which opened on 28 April.[94] On that same day he headed to the Tre
Fontane area to see the start of work on the E42. Along with Pagano,
Mussolini climbed up the wooden tower overlooking Rome and the sea,
trying to imagine the future city's buildings and streets. Accompanied by
Piacentini and other architects, Mussolini spent time in the pavilion, where
the drawings and the model were on display.[95] In early May, he visited the
artists' Palazzo della Confederazione, where he stopped to chat with Carlo
Broggi. He then headed to Via Veneto, where Piacentini was waiting for
him to cut the ribbon at the headquarters for the Banca Nazionale del
Lavoro: on the balcony – party officials discreetly to one side – the Duce listened to the architect's words as he gazed over the city (figure 16).[96] It was
the third time in eight days that the two had met to discuss architecture.[97]

At the Foro Mussolini, the leader inaugurated Piazzale dell'Impero, designed by Moretti, and the Fontana della Sfera, designed by Mario Paniconi and Giulio Pediconi. He once again inspected Moretti's Olympic Stadium, Costantini's indoor swimming pool, and the sun therapy room.[98] Moretti's plans for the future development of the Foro were on display in a room at the Accademia di Scherma. These would entail a new entrance to the capital: it would be the first monumental piece of architecture on a thoroughfare that would cross the city from north to south, a grand and triumphal route featuring a series of ancient and modern monuments all the way to the Colosseum and the Circus Maximus. This was the vast segment of a larger road that would connect the north and south of Italy, from Milan to Brindisi. A large-scale model represented the area, which extended for over 4 million square metres, equal to the surface area of Rome in the sixteenth century; here was living proof of fascism's imperial will, as its creator would proclaim. Clearly visible at the centre was the Arengo delle Nazioni, whose stands embraced a huge square for gatherings. Capable of accommodating up to 400,000 people, it was five times larger than Piazza Venezia, and two and a half times larger than the Zeppelinfeld in Nuremberg, the stadium that had inspired it (figure 17).[99] In the German city, Speer's stadium – 390 metres long, almost twice the size of the Baths of Caracalla, the architect emphasized – was ready to host the gathering of the Nazi Party in the autumn of 1934.[100] The project for the Arengo delle Nazioni, initially conceived to accommodate just 300,000 people, was first proposed to Mussolini by Renato Ricci in May 1935.[101] The competition between the Duce and the Führer, in which they used architecture to flaunt their political power, had begun. From that moment onward, the historical mass gatherings would be held at the Arengo. This was where the rites of the new fascist religion would be celebrated. The massive gatherings held there would symbolize the nation's collective energy.

Exhibitions and expositions played a leading role in the construction of the fascist imaginary, in the self-celebration of the regime, and in the process of engaging with the masses and educating them politically.[102] Between June and September 1937, Mussolini inaugurated as many as three major exhibitions. The first was the Mostra delle Colonie Estive e dell'Assistenza al Circo Massimo (Exhibition of the Summer Colonies and Aid to the Circus Maximus). The other two opened on the same day: one was the Augustan Exhibition of Roman Civilization on Via Nazionale, celebrating the second millennial of Emperor Augustus, and the other was the Exhibition of the Fascist Revolution in the new wing of the Modern Art Gallery, designed by Bazzani. For the latter exhibition, Mussolini

17. Albert Speer, Zeppelinfeld in Nuremberg, 1934–6.

asked that the exhibition space devoted to the war be limited, so as to focus more on the creation of the empire and thus extol the permanent meaning of the revolution. The exhibition was a living monument whose purpose was to indoctrinate the masses.[103] The simultaneous timing of these events was meant to emphasize the synthesis between ancient and modern Italy, personified by Mussolini as a new Augustus, and the normalization of fascism within the Italian historical tradition.[104] Both the façade designed by Alfredo Scappelli and the one by Bazzani were a declaration of the change that was under way: instead of the prism with the metal fasces that had been designed by Libera and De Renzi for the Exhibition of the Fascist Revolution, the triumphal arch motif was chosen for both events.[105] The following day Mussolini travelled to Germany. In the Olympic Stadium in Berlin he talked about the "many shared elements," the "parallels" between Nazism and fascism. Even his affinity for classicism in architecture was interpreted as evidence of common ground between the two regimes.[106]

However, it would be a mistake to believe that Mussolini's visits represented little more than an opportunity for him to show himself to the crowds by way of meaningless rhetorical scripts. For instance, at the beginning of October, Mussolini was genuinely involved in the inspection of the building site of the Borghi factory. Piacentini and Spaccarelli occupied him in a series of difficult technical architectural issues regarding various developments having to do with the façades of the new Via della Conciliazione, historical aspects of the buildings, and a complex analysis of perspectival views (figure 18).[107] With the project in question, at first the regulatory control of the Consiglio Superiore delle Antichità e Belle Arti was excluded, triggering a strong reaction from Ojetti, who threatened to resign, but did not. Mussolini wanted to control the project directly; he discussed matters with the architects as if he were their client, one that was neither inexperienced nor unskilled.[108] Piacentini and Spaccarelli soon met with Pope Pius XI, who also showed an interest in the architectural undertakings. On his way back from Castelgandolfo, the pope asked to be taken to the entrance to Via della Conciliazione. Like Mussolini, he personally wanted to assess, along with the two architects, the effects of the demolition of the Spina, and the new view of the Vatican Basilica and Michelangelo's dome.[109]

By laying the first stone of Minucci's Palazzo degli Uffici in October, Mussolini ushered in the building of the E42.[110] In this case, the architect was directly tasked with the job. For the other buildings, however, competitions were organized and Italy's best architects took part. The results – which, as we shall see, were closely controlled by Mussolini and Piacentini – would play a key role in the subsequent architectural events. On the anniversary of the March on Rome, at the Farnesina, in keeping with an ancient Roman tradition, Mussolini designated the perimeter of the Palazzo del Littorio, on the area that had been chosen for Moretti's Arengo (figure 19). The volume of the new building was the same size as the Reggia di Caserta. With its 720,000 cubic metres, it would be able to compete with some of Speer's grandiose buildings in Berlin. Not only did it surpass Hitler's Chancellery, whose construction would begin three months later, but it also outshone Göring's Palace. And this was no exception: the competition for the headquarters of the Ministry of Foreign Affairs in the Baths of Caracalla area involved a construction measuring 530,000 cubic metres. Piacentini's Palazzo di Giustizia in Milan, which measured 580,000 cubic metres, was equal in size to Göring's Palace.[111] The *platea magna* opposite the Palazzo del Littorio could accommodate up to 600,000 people, and was twice the size of St. Peter's Square and Place de la Concorde in Paris. Even if the comparison with Berlin was not supposed to be about colossal dimensions, but rather "civilization," Mussolini was aware of the power that derived from the effect of the "oversized" on the masses. In this case, for a building that was meant to

18. Mussolini, Piacentini, and Attilio Spaccarelli visiting the building site for the redevelopment of the Borghi, 8 October 1937. Virgilio Testa, wearing eyeglasses, can be seen behind Spaccarelli. During the visit, the two architects involved Mussolini in a series of complex architectural issues.

symbolize the regime, Mussolini, not unlike Hitler, relied on gargantuan proportions to psychologically impress the masses.

After considering the area of the Via dei Fori Imperiali and that of Porta San Paolo, Mussolini decided to locate the Fascist Party headquarters near the Forum dedicated to him; this move revealed a "spiritual and material approach" uniting the political headquarters and the centre for youth education.[112] However, it also revealed the capriciousness of the dictator's urban development decisions: initially he had chosen an area at the centre of the city, then he chose one to the south, until finally settling on an area that lay in the exact opposite direction. Though the latter decision seemed to have to do with locating the building on a north-south axis, this is a conspicuous example of Mussolini's unpredictability, which he justified by saying that Rome was unique in that way as well, that it was the "kingdom of the unexpected."[113] In November, Mussolini visited Quadraro, on the city's outskirts, to preside over the opening of the works for the new headquarters of the LUCE Institute.

19.   Mussolini marks the perimeter of the new Palazzo del Littorio in the Foro Mussolini in Rome. To the left, in the second row, are Enrico Del Debbio and Arnaldo Foschini in uniform, 28 October 1937.

Before the ceremony, Clemente and Andrea Busiri Vici showed him the plans and model for the project.[114] That same month, Mussolini opened the Textile Exhibition and the headquarters of the National Research Council. The following year, he gave the go-ahead for the building of the Via Imperiale, the thoroughfare connecting the city with the E42. During one of Mussolini's frequent inspections of the Universal Exposition area, he, along with Piacentini, visited the pavilion where the permanent exhibition of the projects and the huge model of the new city were on display (figure 20).[115]

7 Rome and Berlin: Parallel Action

On the evening of 3 May, Mussolini welcomed Hitler to the Ostiense Station on a temporary platform that had been specially designed by Narducci for the occasion. The previous year, the German dictator had solemnly welcomed Mussolini to Germany. On that occasion, the traditional diplomatic ceremonies were dispensed with and a spectacular event was organized instead. In Berlin, Mussolini and Hitler "had

20. Mussolini, Piacentini, Oppo, and Cini standing in front of the model for the E42. Partially visible behind Piacentini is Gaetano Minnucci, 6 July 1938.

strolled along the great east-west axis that Benno von Arent had turned into a triumphant pathway with hundreds of white cardboard pillars." Hitler had been extremely pleased with the results and ordered that the pillars be reproduced in stone.[116] Mussolini had likewise been impressed by the *mise en scène*, and he now wanted to emulate the Führer. Some areas of the city were transformed so that they resembled the ancient Roman empire. The streets were adorned with columns and obelisks, pedestals and urns, made of plywood and gesso made to look like faux marble. In this surreal and haughty Rome, Mussolini escorted Hitler on a "triumphal itinerary" which had been carefully planned down to the smallest detail. Together they visited the Borghese Gallery, the Baths of Diocletian, and the Mostra Augustea della Romanità, where Hitler was struck by the huge 80-square-metre model of imperial Rome. "It is a very interesting thing. The Roman Empire has never been rivalled ... And no other empire was able to spread civilization as much as Rome had (figure 21)."[117] They visited the Foro Mussolini, which reminded the German dictator of the building – albeit of different dimensions – designed by Speer that was being built to host Nazi Party meetings in Nuremberg.

21. Hitler listening to Ranuccio Bianchi Bandinelli's explanations and
Mussolini's comments during a visit to the Galleria Borghese in Rome, 7 May
1938. The following day, Hitler visited the Pantheon for the second time; it
became the inspiration for the Volkshalle.

On the eve of 8 May, the Olympic Stadium hosted a public performance
in honour of the Duce's guest. On the lawn, choreographies drew swas-
tikas, and on the slope of Monte Mario, Wagner's *Lohengrin*, directed by
Pietro Mascagni, was performed on a huge stage.[118]
    In the morning, Hitler went to the Pantheon for the second time. He
asked to be accompanied by Ranuccio Bianchi Bandinelli, the archaeologist serving as his guide and interpreter, and by Bottai, who had taken
over from Mussolini, leaving the retinue outside. For a quarter of an
hour he stood there in silence below the coffered vault, confessing that
he had stayed up all night studying all of the monument's construction
details. As he gazed at the perfect cupola, no doubt his thoughts went to
the dome of the Auditorium in Berlin, which was at an advanced phase
of planning, and for which he had personally made a few sketches. The
Pantheon's famous coffered ceiling would be reproduced in the building in Berlin (figure 22).[119] On that same day, while standing before the

22. Albert Speer, project for the Volkshalle in Berlin, model, 1938. On the left, the model of the Brandenburg Gate underscores the colossal dimensions of the new building. The building, Hitler remarked, "is worth more than three victorious wars."

Colosseum, Hitler expressed the idea of replicating it: he was referring to the Congress Hall by Franz and Ludwig Ruff in Nuremberg. Once he returned to Germany, he had the plans changed, increasing the building's capacity to 60,000 spectators, so that it would exceed the ancient amphitheatre by 10,000 seats, and achieve a volume that was twice the size of the Great Pyramid of Giza.[120] In Rome, he talked at length on the subject of architecture with his interlocutors and expressed one of his main concerns: "the solidity, the eternal quality of the building." Only granite would do for his buildings. In those days spent amid imperial remains the Führer's mind often shifted to his plans for Berlin. He even discussed them with Mussolini. Hitler hoped to transform the capital of the small state of Prussia into the real capital of Grossdeutschland. However, Goebbels emphasized, "the Führer did not share any of his projects' details with Mussolini" (figure 23).[121] He did not want Mussolini to know that the capital of the Third Reich was going to be more

23. Albert Speer, project for the centre of Berlin, model, 1937–40. The most representative buildings of the Reich would be built on the axis joining the northern and the southern railway stations. These were gargantuan constructions. The Führer remarked, "breathtaking! Only thus can we eclipse our only rival in the world: Rome."

majestic than Rome. To his closest collaborators, on the other hand, he confided that the Greater German Reich "would start in Norway and end in northern Italy."[122]

During the visit to Italy the two states did not achieve political accords, and the immediate results were apparently modest. However, the Führer's direct acquaintance with the capital's monuments did appear to be of great use to him, confirming some of his ideas and inspiring new ones. Albeit his motive was not explicitly stated, the inspection was not a secondary reason for his trip. And indeed, the Führer was grateful to Mussolini for having allowed him "all the time that was required to see all the artworks that interested me."[123] He had managed to look at those magnificent Roman monuments from the perspective of an architect seeking inspiration and confirmation of his ideas.[124] In the days after he returned to Germany, Hitler was filled with ideas and projects, "completely absorbed in his building plan." He confided in Goebbels that he was "deeply impressed" by what he had seen in Italy, and that he had immediately "expanded all his own projects."[125] Clearly, at an architectural level the two dictators were challenging each other. For both, architecture was indissolubly bound with political action. Hitler, even more so than Mussolini, understood its potential; the latter, almost as a reaction to the plans laid down by the Führer, committed himself to even more projects. For both men, the future domination of Europe could only be accompanied by the primacy of their respective countries' national architecture, the most genuine expression of the new political order. This parallel action in architecture reinforced the plan for the political and military hegemony of the two totalitarian states. A surprising coincidence of dates accompanied the race. The two most impressive architectural undertakings of the fascist and Nazi regimes – respectively, the E42 and the rebuilding of Berlin – were launched almost at the same time. In the summer of 1936, Hitler began to discuss the plans for Berlin with Speer. The following autumn, Mussolini selected the area where the new satellite city would be built. In January 1937, within a period of just twenty days, Mussolini commissioned Piacentini, Pagano, and their fellow architects for the E42 project, and the Führer appointed his architect as general building inspector for the Reich capital. On 28 April, Pagano illustrated the general project for the E42. Two days later, on the Chancellor's birthday, Speer presented his plans for the redevelopment of Berlin and, in particular, the model for the huge Volkshalle. In October 1937, in the Tre Fontane area, the first stone was laid for the Palazzo degli Uffici. In Berlin a similar ceremony took place on 14 June 1938 for the Palace of Tourism. Almost in reply, on 30 June work began on the Palazzo della Civiltà Italiana on the banks of the River Tiber.

In Berlin, the Palace of Tourism was the first building to go up on the massive north-south axis, which was 7 kilometres long and over 100 metres wide; it completely transformed Germany's capital city. At the beginning and at the end of the road, the Führer, in perfect agreement with Speer, had arranged for the construction of a massive domed Auditorium, the Volkshalle, which stood 280 metres high and could accommodate up to 180,000 people, as well as a 120-metre-tall Arch of Triumph. A triumphal north-south road was also a part of Mussolini's plans. Bottai wrote in his diary that "Nazi Germany seems to have become the land of comparison for our beliefs."[126] In Rome and Berlin, Mussolini and Hitler brought both architecture and the city into their totalitarian ideologies. The two allies already foresaw that, after the war, which they were preparing to fight and win, they were going to have to engage with and challenge each other, and that challenge would include architecture. Because of the political repercussions of architecture, the stakes were high. For the German dictator, such works were worth much more than winning a war. Hence, it was best, right from the start, to act cautiously, to not show all his cards, and to be wary of his ally. In their conversations in Rome, Hitler had not told Mussolini "everything about his construction plans." On that day in mid-June, just a few hours before the new and colossal works for Berlin – "the most magnificent building project of all time" – were to begin, Goebbels made the final changes to the speech that the Führer was about to deliver. The dictator asked his minister to be prudent. It was best if he did not "insist too much on the monumentality of our projects. Otherwise, Mussolini will not hesitate to copy us. [127]

8 The North-South Imperial Axis

Upon returning from Florence, where Hitler had ended his tour, Mussolini headed to Via della Conciliazione to examine the model of the entrance to St. Peter's Square. Piacentini and Spaccarelli escorted him on this third inspection. The models and drawings helped Mussolini envision the finished work. Later, he went to Palazzo Serristori, where the two architects had organized an exhibition of projects, both ancient and modern, for the redevelopment of the area around St. Peter's Square.[128] In the summer of 1938, another event marked the building of Mussolini's city. At the end of August, the leader examined the drawings and laid the first stone of the Ministry of Italian Africa on Viale Aventino, currently the Food and Agriculture Organization headquarters, designed by the Ridolfi team (figure 24).[129] He was now demanding that architecture have greater unity of direction, that it be more in synergy with the leading principles of his policies.

In late September, thanks to Mussolini's decisive mediation, Germany, France, the United Kingdom, and Italy signed an agreement in Munich to avert the risk of war, which had seemed inevitable to all. However, the truce was short-lived owing to the fact that, in Germany, the survival of the Nazi regime was indissolubly linked to the rationale of war and territorial expansion.[130] For Mussolini, the journey back to Italy became a genuine – and clearly more spontaneous – popular triumph for the "preserver of peace." "The Duce was welcomed in a way that I had never seen before," wrote Galeazzo Ciano. In Rome, standing in the middle of Via Nazionale was a huge triumphal arch made of laurel leaves that Achille Starace had had installed. But this only caused Mussolini to lose his temper.[131] He did not approve of the enthusiasm for "Mussolini the peacemaker."

24. Vittorio Cafiero, Wolfgang Frankl, Alberto Legnani, Mario Ridolfi, Ettore Rossi, Armando Sabatini, project for the Ministry of Italian Africa in Rome, 1938.

He thought it represented the expression of a middle-class affection for peace, which was not in line with the bellicose values practised by "fascism's new man." The Duce was not the "angel of peace," as the Italians would have liked to believed, but an ideologist of permanent war, firmly convinced of its pedagogical function: "When the Spanish war is over, I will invent something else: in any event, the character of the Italian people must be forged in battle."[132] His disappointment in the people's reaction convinced him to speed up the process of the country's complete totalitarianization. This led to the harsh speech he gave in October in which he railed against the middle class, which he did not consider to be a social class, but a state of mind. He declared that there "[is] an enemy of our regime, and the enemy [has] a name: 'the middle class'."[133] This political outlook was linked to the dictator's decision in mid-January 1939 to abolish the Camera dei Deputati, and replace it with the Camera dei Fasci e delle Corporazioni. The abolition of all democratically elected positions – their existence albeit already reduced to a mere formality – marked a further step towards the state's totalitarian turnaround.[134]

In the meantime, the city's metamorphosis continued. In February 1939, Mussolini headed to the Ostiense Station to look at the drawings, model, and types of marble that might be used for the Termini Station along with Mazzoni. The fact that Cini was present at the meeting confirmed the close coordination between this architectural project and the E42.[135] First, Mussolini visited the building sites of the Ministry of Italian Africa, Ponte San Paolo, and the E42.[136] Then in mid-March, he visited the Palazzo del Littorio, the Foro Mussolini, the Africa and Magliana bridges, and once again the Ministry of Italian Africa. After that, he inaugurated the Ponte Duca d'Aosta and the first section of Via Imperiale.[137]

The regime's policy was increasingly based on imagery, and reality had to be adapted to fit in with it. In his diary Galeazzo Ciano wrote that Mussolini, to prepare for the parade of the militia, "would spend half hours standing at the window in his office, hidden beyond a light-blue curtain, peering at the movement of the units ... He has introduced the bandleader's use of a baton, personally teaches the movements that must be made, and dictates the proportions and shape of the baton itself. He increasingly believes that form, as concerns the armed forces, also determines substance." This was not just theatrics or childishness, but rather a firm belief that form could successfully be used to change the nature of an individual. The introduction of the *passo romano* (Roman step), the dictator declared, "is the expression of moral strength."[138] These rituals – parades in which the participants used the *passo romano* and wore a black shirt, patriotic and fascist anniversaries, the prohibition of the formal *lei* when speaking, and the introduction of the *sabato fascista*, or fascist Saturday – were all created to transform the daily lives of the Italian people, to profoundly influence the emergence of the "new man."[139] These elements were essential to the regime's pedagogy, as were the buildings that surrounded the squares where the men paraded by, and the buildings that hosted their institutions. These rituals, along with the myths and the symbols – that is, the buildings that were being erected by the regime – were the basis for the new secular religion. "As I intended, fascism ... has become the secular religion of all Italians," Mussolini said.[140] We cannot exclude the idea that during this phase of his political life, Mussolini, not unlike Hitler, was convinced of the power of rites and symbols to instil in the people greater faith in the regime. Mussolini believed that appearance – architectural setting and ceremony – more than content guaranteed the continuity of the political system into the future, even after his death [141].

On 6 May in Milan, Galeazzo Ciano and Ribbentrop agreed on a period of peace lasting four or five years, which was the amount of time it would take to militarily prepare the nation before the outbreak of war. Previously, Mussolini had declared to the German minister that Italy wanted to forge an alliance with Germany, aimed at "changing the map of the world." On 22 May, the Pact of Steel between the two countries was signed in Berlin.[142] On 1 September 1939, Hitler invaded Poland, starting a war that, despite its global escalation, was initially intended to represent a short step, as had been the case with Czechoslovakia, in the gradual and continual process of expansion.[143] Italy, which from a military perspective was not ready to support its ally, declared non-belligerence.

25. Giuseppe Vaccaro, project for the central headquarters of AGIP on Via Imperiale in Rome, perspective drawing, 1939. Approved by Mussolini, the main façade was over 100 metres in width.

The fear of a war and hostility against Germany was widespread across most of the country. Apparently, however, the conflict did nothing to slow the regime's building activity in the capital: during this period, the idea was to direct attention to the regime's peaceful intent in order to emphasize fascism's social engagement, and, at the same time, "raise ... the temperature" of the people in preparation for war.[144]

In early October, Mussolini launched a new series of building projects, all located along the Via Imperiale, today's Via Cristoforo Colombo. The new administrative headquarters of Rome, the imperial capital, were to be situated there.[145] This was a major section of the north-south axis, with the Foro Mussolini at one end, and the Universal Exposition at the other. As with the E42, all of these works – including the thirty-four INCIS apartment blocks by De Renzi, Libera, Montuori, and Vaccaro, the AGIP headquarters featuring a 100-metre-long façade by Vaccaro, the ONC headquarters designed by Adriano Cambellotti's team, the INFAIL, the Fascist Confederation of Merchants, the Casa Malattia degli Addetti al Commercio, the National Female Boarding School, and eight hotels by Pascoletti (figure 25) – needed a unified architectural character. Mussolini examined the projects, and using a sledgehammer made the first furrow in the soil for each.[146]

The celebrations taking place on 28 October that year showed a leader with a "weary air about him."[147] Looking "unhappy and troubled," Mussolini launched the demolition of some of the houses that obstructed the view of the Campidoglio. He inaugurated the Liceo Virgilio on the Lungotevere Tibaldi, two new sections of Via Imperiale, the National Fascist Insurance Institute for Work-Related Injuries headquarters in Piazza Cinque Province, and the Palazzo degli Uffici del Governatorato. There, on display in one of the rooms, were models of Rome displaying the urban transformation that had been made by the regime, in short, Mussolini's imperial Rome.[148] Amid the overall mood of consensus – skilfully orchestrated by the regime's propaganda machine – that accompanied the building frenzy in the capital, several critical voices could also be heard. Several of the newspapers wanted to publish them, but they were immediately stopped by the censors. On the subject of building and public works in Rome, the minister for popular culture, Alessandro Pavolini, pointed out, "one must always consider that it is a huge problem. It must be seen as a problem at the centre of the empire, and therefore as a universal problem. This is why one should aim very high."[149] In other words, criticizing that architecture would have meant directly criticizing the dictator and his plan for the imperial city to which he was fiercely committed.

In February 1940, Mussolini reassured the new minister of public works that the work for the E42, "which is developing quickly, will be intensified." In April, he launched the start of the demolition in Piazza San Claudio; he again visited the works insulating the Campidoglio, examined the model for the restoration of the Circus Maximus, and inaugurated the *case autarchiche* in the new rural area of Acilia.[150] Mussolini made sure he was in attendance for the testing of the huge aluminium arch that was to shape the skyline of the E42.[151] He feverishly followed news of the German attacks on the Western front. He could not emerge from the conflict empty-handed, and was ready to intervene, but only "when we are sure that this will be *a very short war*."[152]

On 3 June, Italy accepted the request to postpone the Universal, but Mussolini had no intention of halting the work. Against the insistence of the army that iron be exclusively used for military purposes, Mussolini authorized its use for the E42. This was another clear sign of the importance of the project in his plans overall.[153] However, given the imminence of war, the leader's decision to allow the work to continue could hardly signal a desire for peace in the public eye. Rather, work on the E42 continued, because it was one of the "major works from the perspective of our civilization."[154] A civilization that believed equally in the value of war and architecture. And "Mussolini's war" – which had been expected, even though it arrived a few years earlier than planned – was now just around the corner.

3 At Palazzo Venezia

1 The Success of the Exhibition of the Fascist Revolution

Because of Mussolini's keen interest in Rome's architectural image, many architects vied for his attention and tried to earn his favour. Arriving on his desk at Palazzo Venezia were dozens of projects sent by some of the most famous architects, as well as by relative unknowns. There was two-way communication between architects and the head of government: the former tended to bypass institutional channels, but often, wishing to affirm his role as the Duce, Mussolini preferred to forgo intermediaries and to exert direct control over matters himself by establishing a one-on-one relationship with an architect. In so doing, he could make his decisions directly, thus emphasizing his role as the sole leader and stoking his legendary status.

Mussolini received drawings from Spaccarelli for the restoration of Castel Sant'Angelo from Spaccarelli as well as drawings from Giulio Arata for a stadium in Rome capable of holding up to 150,000 spectators. He examined the photographs of the model for the Santa Maria Novella Station in Florence, he weighed up and praised Vaccaro's project for the School of Engineering in Bologna, as well as Palanti's in the shape of a ship for Palazzo del Littorio, and he also inspected Mazzoni's plan to expand the post office in Littoria. He unfolded, on his desk, Figini and Pollini's blueprints for Rationalist solutions for a neighbourhood in Ivrea. Mussolini also examined the plans drafted by Guido Carreras for the redevelopment of Via dei Trionfi in Rome, which included a double marble staircase – 466 metres long, hence, 50 metres longer than Speer's Zeppelinfeld in Nuremberg – and could welcome up to 60,000 people. He looked at Vincenzo Civico's plan to extend Corso del Rinascimento towards Via Giulia in Rome, at Leonardo Paternà's for Piazza Imperiale at the E42, at Domenico Filippone's for the Palazzo della Civiltà Italiana, also related to the E42, and the plan for the redevelopment of the Forum of the Fascist Empire. Lastly, Mussolini examined Filippo Maria Beltrami's project for work on Piazza Duomo in Milan.[1] Mussolini also weighed up the projects coordinated by Canino for the Mostra Triennale delle Terre Italiane d'Oltremare.[2] A young Quaroni managed to directly address Mussolini about his plan for the Auditorium, thanks to his brother, Pietro, who was a diplomat at the Farnesina. Previously, Quaroni had even managed to send Mussolini his senior thesis project for a Ministry of Foreign Affairs at Villa Borghese.[3]

This is only a partial list. Many architects wrote to Mussolini or sent him a drawing or a publication describing their works, but only a few were allowed to personally meet with him to show him their work. About fifty architects actually sat in the antechamber, and then crossed, folders stuck under their arms, the great Sala del Mappamondo (Map Room). They had to traverse a total of eighteen metres in total silence before finally reaching the leader's desk, and when they finally did get that far, he rarely lifted his eyes from what he was doing. For some, this was a one-off event, while for others it was almost routine. Along with Piacentini, Alberto Calza Bini, who visited Mussolini's office a total of seventeen times, was a regular, followed by Brasini, who had eight visits, and Muzio, with four. Bazzani, Del Debbio, and Terragni met Mussolini three times each.

Mussolini met with Brasini so he could examine the drawings for the Colonial Exhibition in Paris, and Bazzani for the ones related to the post office in Forlì and the abbey church in Pescara.[4] The dictator conferred with Guido Zevi about building a ring road around the centre of Rome, and in the architect's presence he read the entire report and examined the site plans on display, pleased to be simultaneously compared with Sixtus V, Napoleon, Trajan, and Augustus.[5] Mussolini also welcomed to his office Palanti, an old acquaintance from Milan who had just come back from Argentina. And on several occasions he summoned Alberto Calza Bini in order to be kept up to date about the building of the Istituto delle Case Popolari.[6]

He talked about architecture with renowned German journalist Emil Ludwig as well in one of the meetings they had on an almost daily basis between late March and early April 1932. In their conversations – to be published shortly afterwards as *Colloqui con Mussolini* – the dictator was "brutally sincere" and said things that "from a political point of view, would have been far better if he had kept them to himself." He outlined a crisis scenario in Western civilization, and claimed that fascism was the new historical reality of the twentieth century, a "lifeline" not just for Italy but for all of Europe. He did, however, complain about how hard it was for the people – cynically described as "a flock" – to follow him, to truly be fascists. The point of his harsh analysis was to empha-size the need to launch a new phase, now that he had achieved a role of authority and earned wide consensus. In the following decades, the main political aim would be to intervene and gradually transform the Italians, to change them both physically and morally in a fascist sense. The importance Mussolini ascribed to architecture is confirmed in an interview with Ludwig:[7]

> "To my mind," Mussolini said, "the most important of all the arts is architecture, because it includes everything else."
> -"The idea is worthy of an ancient Roman," I responded.
> "I too am Roman, in that sense," Mussolini retorted.

What emerges from these statements is that Mussolini understood architecture as a representation of his power, essential to the prospect of earning consensus and "enduring" politically. His words did not express the idea of turning architecture into an instrument to edu-cate the masses, determine their behaviour, influence their opinions. Up until then, Mussolini had moved cautiously, perhaps because he didn't trust the insidiousness of the architectural milieu. However, although this did not emerge in Ludwig's interview, he was already developing that particular idea. Two days after the completion of the last part of the interview, Mussolini, along with Piacentini, went to see the place where Rome's Città Universitaria would be built. This was to be a sort of architectural workshop, whose main objective would be the achievement of a cohesive stylistic direction, the first step towards a more organic and incisive presence within the totalitarian state as a whole.

During that same period, another event strengthened Mussolini's idea of giving architecture an educational function for political ends. In the spring of 1932, in fact, preparations for the Exhibition of the Fascist Revolution were already in full swing. In May, Libera informed Terragni that he had recommended him for the exhibition design. About ten days later, Mussolini asked that Terragni, along with Del Debbio, Valente, and other artists, come to Palazzo Venezia to set down the "historical and artistic directives" for the exhibition.[8] On 8 October, shortly before the opening and while preparations were still under way, Mussolini himself headed to the Palazzo delle Esposizioni to spend time with these men.[9] After the opening, he summoned them to Palazzo Venezia, where he lauded Libera and De Renzi's "typically fascist" façade – a black cube with two smaller red cubes next to it, preceded by four huge stylized fasces in a very modern design – and expressed his satisfaction with the exhibition design inside. In one of the spaces, the Sala O (O Room), Terragni had installed a dazzling Futurist montage. Mussolini had closely witnessed the effective collaboration among young, talented architects – all of whom were fascists – and party officials, and he was pondering the potential for art to provide a political channel for the emotional drives of the masses. On that occasion, he announced his intention to create the new Fascist Party headquarters and an exhibition on fascism on Via dell'Impero, which had just been inaugurated (figure 26).[10] The Exhibition of the Fascist Revolution was a huge success, with over 3,700,000 visitors; it stayed open for two years, closing on 28 October 1934. The public's response was judged "excessive," beyond what had been optimistically predicted, and it could not simply be seen as an expression of consensus. Millions of people from all over Italy now made the pilgrimage to Rome, no longer just to pray in its churches, but also to revere the mementoes of the fascist religion, to admire the great architectural works the regime had erected, and, lastly, to worship their leader. Almost as if to savour these impressive results and to capture the arcane mechanisms that had been triggered by the exhibition in the people themselves, Mussolini visited the show some eight times, and when it finally closed, he again mingled with the architects.[11]

The growing success of the Exhibition of the Fascist Revolution in the media was followed by another success resulting from the reclamation of the Pontine Marshes and the construction of newly founded cities. After the inauguration of Littoria – an event that was reported both in the Italian press and in the major newspapers abroad – Mussolini decided it would be a good idea for him to be directly involved in the plans for Sabaudia. After holding the competition and assigning the project to a team headed by Piccinato, Mussolini met with the architects and examined their drawings. He paid special attention to the drawing of the Palazzo Comunale, checking to make sure that the tower rising adjacent to it could also be seen from the Via Appia Antica, stressing "the importance of its visibility and proportions with respect to its surroundings, and the meaning of the building itself." He expected the focus to be on those elements that had the greatest visual and symbolic impact, ones that had to be immediately recognizable to the people, and ensured that the architects "correctly" perceived the meaning that the work should express. On 5 August 1933, Mussolini attended the laying of the first stone. He would go on to oversee the city's construction, visiting the site on several occasions, and carefully examining the models produced by the architects.[12]

26. Mario De Renzi and Adalberto Libera, Exhibition of the Fascist Revolution in Rome, 1932. Mussolini asked the architects to design something "contemporary, modern, and bold, with no melancholy references to the decorative styles of the past."

2 Restoring Augustus

In June 1934, Mussolini welcomed to his Roman palazzo the team of architects, led by Giovanni Michelucci and Piccinato, who had designed the Florence Railway Station and the city of Sabaudia.[13] As we saw before, Piccinato had met with the Duce just eight months earlier, when the first stone of the new city was laid. However, that meeting was not as important as the one that took place in 1934.[14] Shortly before, in Parliament, Francesco Giunta and Roberto Farinacci had made a scathing attack on modern architecture, to the applause of the majority of the other representatives: "Enough with Sabaudia ... Florence Railway Station! Remember it and feel ashamed!"[15] Stepping in to defend the new architecture were members of Parliament Alberto Calza Bini and Cipriano Efisio Oppo. The clash in Parliament between traditionalists and modernists created a picture of a quarrelsome assembly rather than an efficient fascist state whose purpose was to harmoniously organize and govern. By summoning the architects to Palazzo Venezia, Mussolini determined to solve this architecture problem on his own. By publicizing the importance of this meeting – the following day the Stefani Agency would publish a detailed report in all the newspapers – Mussolini wanted to make it known that he was in no way against the new architecture, thus distancing himself from the reactionary positions of many members of Parliament. More importantly, he wanted to ensure that everyone understood that he alone, certainly not Farinacci's Executive Board, was entitled to deciding what the architecture of the fascist era should look like. Here was an example of an extreme attempt to put all the power in the leader's hands, one of the most overt signs of the regime's totalitarian tendencies.

This widely publicized meeting was tied to another meeting, one that the Duce denied, and that was supposed to have taken place during those same days in June. Le Corbusier himself had asked to meet with Mussolini, "the true expression of Authority." Playing the part of a modern Diogenes – the Greek philosopher who went around with a lantern in search of an "honest man" – the Swiss architect was looking for "men able to rule cities," and was especially drawn to dictatorships. From this perspective, fascist Italy seemed to him to be more advanced than other countries. "In Italy, as in Russia – the architect wrote to Guido Fiorini – this problem [of Authority] has been solved."[16] But in 1933, Le Corbusier's first attempt to travel to Italy had been scuttled by the Duce, who had been against the French architect's idea of delivering "lectures on the new forms of modern architecture."[17] Not until the following year, thanks to Pier Maria Bardi and Fiorini, did Le Corbusier manage to get the visa required to make the trip. After arriving in Rome on 4 June, with Bottai's help, Le Corbusier tried – to no avail – to schedule a meeting with the dictator so that he could explain to him some of his ideas regarding urban planning, as well as to make his case for the Pontinia project. The dictator had been informed that Le Corbusier was in Rome by Alberto Calza Bini, but had neither the time nor the desire to meet with him. Even the secretary of the trade union, concerned that the "most important representative of Rationalist architecture" might be successful with the public, suggested that the leader not authorize large rooms for the lectures that had been scheduled or allow the press to talk too much about him.[18] Only when Le Corbusier's trip was over, perhaps because it was clearly too late, did Bardi inform him that "the Duce was willing to meet him." As soon as he was back in Paris, Le Corbusier sent Mussolini a copy of the second volume of his *Oeuvres Complètes*, convinced of the affinities between his studies on the *Ferme Radieuse* and the regime's agricultural policies. In the months that followed, the French architect kept a close watch over Italy, and sent Bottai, who was supposed to act as his go-between with Mussolini, his research on Pontinia and the suburban area of Rome.[19] In light of Mussolini's unwillingness to meet with Le Corbusier, the dictator's encounter with Piccinato and the other architects in June, and his protective attitude towards them on that occasion, were important for several reasons. First, he managed to keep his distance from Farinacci's more conservative and unshakeable positions. Second, he was able to clearly show his opposition to a modern architecture that could not immediately be linked to a nationalist political discourse.[20] Despite its international popularity, Mussolini was not supportive of modernist architecture per se. He was, however, more than willing to support modernist architecture that figuratively recalled the values of Italian identity, and that, as a result, supported his policies. Architecture was of use to him when it bestowed a national image on modernity and consolidated the identity of the Italian people.

For Mussolini, it wasn't a question of preferring the modern or the traditional style in architecture, it all had to do with the instrumental use of the genre. Hence, after praising modern architecture, he exploited it to strengthen and extend the myth of the ancient Roman spirit. In one of the rooms in Palazzo Venezia he made sure that Morpurgo's plan for the area of the Mausoleum of Augustus was put on display. Here, in March 1935, Mussolini, along with Bottai, listened to Morpurgo's explanation of his selections. A month later, because the works were taking too long, he wrote to the governor about them: "Demolition work at the Mausoleum of Augustus. Inquire about progress and hasten if necessary."[21] Informed by Bottai about the status of the excavations, he learned that the diameter of the monument had turned out to be wider than was expected. The dimensions of the square thus had to be modified so that new buildings would be of a suitably monumental scale. Furthermore, work was being done to connect the piazza to the Lungotevere.[22] In May, both the architect and the governor were asked to come to Palazzo Venezia to describe the new model incorporating the requested adjustments.[23] The model showed a stark, isolated ancient monument, and around it a square closed off on all four sides, with a perspectival clearing for those coming from Via del Corso. The monument could be entered from the south, up a staircase with two avant-corps to either side, at the centre of which was a statue of Augustus on a podium. The solution was not to Mussolini's liking, however; he had the two avant-corps eliminated and the façade overlooking the River Tiber – which had been built just a few years before to a design by Andrea Busiri Vici – knocked down. A new layout for the square was planned, one that was open and U-shaped, thus overturning Morpurgo's original plan. Mussolini's decision was mostly ideological, since he wanted the monument and the river to be connected, just as they had been in Augustus's time. The idea was for the monument to "tower over everything in necessary solitude."[24]

In April 1936, the dictator once again examined a new model during his visit to the building site (figure 27). By then, Morpurgo, following his orders, had opened the square and freed up the western front all the way to the Tiber. Mussolini was clearly devoting a lot of time to this project. After the Ethiopian War and the proclamation of the empire, he had become the "true alter ego of Augustus."[25] What he valued about the first Roman emperor – who had restored order and discipline after the civil wars, imposed the universal values of the Roman spirit all around the world, and ordered the restoration of buildings in the city – was his grandeur; Mussolini used his image to draw similarities with the present and to fuel his own legend. Later, he also consulted Ojetti about the project. The critic disapproved of some of the architectural choices, especially the design of the façades overlooking the new piazza – they were the "same old tall stilts or pillars or whatever you call them" – and suggested recreating the ancient Roman atmosphere by crowning the Mausoleum with a ring of marble statues.[26] Mussolini and Morpurgo must have at least partly heeded his words, as those "stilts" later disappeared, to be replaced by the classical columns that Ojetti had longed for.

The area of the Augusteum was also the preferred choice for the Ara Pacis of Augustus, which had resurfaced from the foundations of a palace on Via Lucina and been partially reconstructed. The choice of a location had been controversial, and once again Mussolini's intervention proved decisive. The first thing he did was to reject the governor's idea of situating the Ara Pacis on Via dell'Impero, in the same area as the first-level competition for the Palazzo del Littorio. He then accepted Morpurgo's idea to situate the monument between Via di Ripetta and the Lungotevere, in an area occupied by houses, but which, as we saw previously, he wanted torn down.[27]

Mussolini's *renovatio urbis* meant valorizing the imperial past, a past on which to graft the myths of the present in a process of active modernization. Fascist policies were often founded on actions that combined contradictory ideas. However, this was not a communicative barrier for a regime that demanded many acts of faith from its supporters, such

27. Vittorio Morpurgo, project for the redevelopment of the area of the Augusteum in Rome, model, 1936. Mussolini intervened to have the buildings on the Tiber River demolished, thus turning Morpurgo's original urban design on its head.

as belief in its myths, that is, in representations that were able to support apparent contradictions and turn them into something productive. Therefore, while reinventing one part of the city of Augustus, at a meeting with the participants of the International Conference of Architects held at Palazzo Venezia, the dictator defended modernity. During the conference, a letter by Frank Lloyd Wright was read by his son John. Referring to his studies for Broadacre City, Wright identified fascist Italy as a country where his radical model of urban decentralization could easily be implemented. The American architect invited the Italian government to renew the country's architecture, and abandon ancient academic paradigms. Especially in the eyes of foreigners, the leader of the Fascist Revolution did not want to appear backward-looking. And so, almost as a response to Wright's criticism, in his farewell speech Mussolini described himself as a true champion of the new architecture. Speaking in French, he addressed his foreign guests by saying that he loved architecture – "J'aime l'architecture" – and particularly functional architecture, which he believed offered the true framework of contemporary life.

The dictator added that he was well acquainted with the issues at hand, that he had worked with architects on many occasions and discussed matters with them at length. Before those in attendance he provided concrete proof of his modern vision; he talked about the question of ancient cities and expressed the need to tear down anything that was old and bereft of artistic value, in order to safeguard the people's health. Then, with rather shaky reasoning, he boasted of having had the base of the Colossus of Nero torn down and destroyed, because it stood right in the middle of the route of the Via dell'Impero.[28]

3 Doubts aboutTerragni

As we saw previously, Mussolini had already met with Terragni on the occasion of the Exhibition of the Fascist Revolution. Later, around 1935, he discussed with Margherita Sarfatti the architect's project for the grave of his son Roberto on Col D'Echele.[29] In December of that same year, the Como architect, along with Figini, Lingeri, and Pollini, again met with Mussolini to present him with the first version of a project to expand the Brera Art Academy. It was clear that the dictator was keeping a close watch on Terragni's activities. He did not fail to remind him, in fact, that his project for the Palazzo del Littorio in Rome had been selected for the second-level competition. The truth of the matter, as we shall see later, was that Mussolini had excluded the drawing from the list of the best nine works. Then, he spent over an hour talking to the architects, examining the panels with the drawings "plan by plan," going into some of the details and looking at the plaster model (figure 28).[30] At a certain point, Mussolini pointed to a a pillar and, with a puzzled look, asked Terragni, "What's this?" "A pillar, Your Excellency," the architect replied.[31] But Mussolini was not convinced about the idea that had been submitted to him, especially as concerned locating a modern building in the midst of what was already there, and in this case it would be adjacent to the seventeenth-century Pinacoteca. His words – "Brera must remain Brera" – sounded like a rejection. In the end, Mussolini did give his approval, motivated by contingent political calculation, as he did not wish to appear anti-modernist before the team of young, combative architects from Lombardy, or hostile to their proposal for modernity. However, Mussolini already knew that the project would never come to fruition.

One year earlier, Terragni's team had presented its Project A for Palazzo del Littorio: the idea was for Mussolini to be able to appear before the masses on the main façade, atop a large curved wall suspended above the ground. In the report that accompanied the plan, Terragni had described Mussolini as a deity: "he is like a god, up against the sky, and there

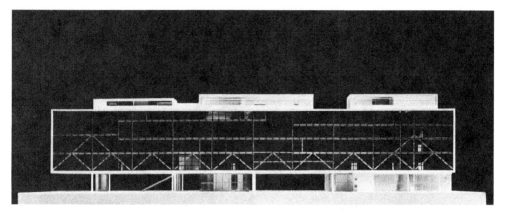

28. Luigi Figini, Pietro Lingeri, Gino Pollini, and Giuseppe Terragni, project for the extension of the Accademia di Brera in Milan, model, 1935. After carefully examining the project, Mussolini said that "Brera must remain Brera."

is no one else above him."[32] Terragni clearly understood the importance of using religious experience to connect the leader and the masses in an absolute, totalitarian democracy, and he had expressed this in the form of architecture. For the architect, the Duce was a living legend, the embodiment of the state itself, a figure whom one had to believe in adamantly. And precisely because he recognized these extraordinary talents in him, he found it inconceivable that, with regards to his Brera project, Mussolini could not understand the revolutionary value of Rationalist architecture, the only true fascist architecture. Through the harmony of abstract images, even Terragni's Rationalist architecture, albeit more cerebral than the kind based on arches, columns, and moulding, participated in the transformation of mundane time into the legendary and revolutionary time of Mussolini. Terragni continued to believe in Mussolini, he trusted him, "the architect of every real spiritual renewal," in his "fight for the architecture of the fascist age."[33] But his faith and that of his companions was unreciprocated. Mussolini did not back their work, and Bottai and the Superior Council of Antiquities and Fine Arts, which included both Piacentini and Giovannoni as members, ended up rejecting the project. Hinting at something that Mussolini was not insensitive to, the minister read back the opinion of the Council, which had found "the project to be inspired by 'rational' architecture of a foreign kind."[34]

Despite his failures, Terragni was still firmly convinced that his architecture offered the best possible interpretation of fascism. It was in this spirit, in October 1936, that Terragni gave Mussolini an issue of *Quadrante* – a

29. Giuseppe Terragni, Casa del Fascio in Como, photomontage with crowds, 1932–6. According to the architect, this building was the conversion into architecture of Mussolini's idea that "fascism is a glass house into which everyone can gaze freely."

magazine that was already familiar to Mussolini through writer and co-editor Massimo Bontempelli's essays. The issue was devoted to the Casa del Fascio in Como (figure 29). On this occasion, Dino Alfieri, whom Terragni had met at the Exhibition of the Fascist Revolution and was now minister for press and propaganda, acted as a go-between. According to Terragni, this building was the architectural translation of Mussolini's idea that "fascism is a glass house into which everyone can gaze freely." Mussolini must have seen that architecture, so cold and hard to understand, as unsuited to rousing the masses – regardless of the fact that photomontages showed it besieged by crowds – and representing the imperial climate. It is worth noting that the most famous fascist headquarters in all of Italy, which was popular with Italians themselves, was never visited by Mussolini, nor did it earn a single word of his praise.[35]

Already established in the Risorgimento era, the myth of Dante Alighieri was revisited by the regime in a nationalist and imperial context, and was transformed into a fascist myth. In March 1938, Rino Valdameri and the textile industrialist Alessandro Poss submitted to Mussolini their idea of building a "temple" dedicated to the great poet in Rome. In the following months, Mussolini took some time to reread Dante's Cantos. He saw Dante as a "master of Italian superiority," someone who had taught his readers to love Rome and the empire; he noted, though, that the poet had never directed his love to the Italians as a people, as men and women. The dictator especially appreciated Dante's separation of Italy as a place and set of institutions from Italians as a people. He shared the poet's thinking, and felt close to him. Mussolini, like Dante, believed that "although men die, although they pass on, the land, the works, the walls ... all those things remain!" It was the leader himself who chose the location for the monument to Dante, on Via dell'Impero, before the Basilica of Maxentius, the very same place that had been chosen for the first-level competition for the Palazzo del Littorio.[36] The dictator clearly felt that the area was strategic to the creation of a monumental itinerary of Mussolini's Rome, which from the north, at Moretti's Forum, ran south, to Piacentini's E42. Three years later, in November 1938, Lingeri and Terragni were once again in the Sala del Mappamondo, this time to illustrate their project for the Danteum.[37] Mussolini dictated that Dante be transformed into the protective deity of imperial Italy and an icon of popular devotion. In the report that accompanied the drawings, Terragni depicted Dante as a prophet who had envisaged the new empire. By using one of the most effective mythical transformations, that of Mussolini's salvific power, the architect identified the dictator as the very embodiment of the *Veltro* (Hound), that is, the figure that, according to the poet, would revive Italy's fate.[38] During the meeting, the dictator listened to the two artists' presentation while admiring the splendid watercolour illustrations. However, once again, their architectural choices did not convince him. Albeit rich in political metaphors, the architecture was still too conceptual. In an almost aggressive, angry tone, Mussolini attacked Lingeri, asking him, "How could the two of you mistreat Dante?"[39] All the same, he again approved the project, although he would later ask that some changes be made. Terragni, more than Lingeri, had made the most important decisions about the Danteum. He considered himself a "leader of men" in search of the absolute in art, the artist at the forefront of all Italian architects, one who had understood the importance of creating architecture that was equal in importance to that political experience, the unique and totalizing experience of fascism, and that it was he who was at Mussolini's side in the creation of the new man and the new art. But, in the late 1930s, Terragni entered a collision course with the architectural direction that Mussolini came to more and more openly support; his beloved dictator began to examine his work with more scepticism, and would often simply reject it.[40] Mussolini now felt that Terragni's abstract architecture lay outside the figurative tradition and even threatened the historical foundation of the idea of the nation based on the myth of ancient Rome. It was, in fact, difficult if not impossible to convince the people that those buldings characterized by rational and abstract forms could possibly express the continuity between fascism and ancient republican and imperial Rome.

Mussolini was involved with Terragni in another circumstance as well. The architect had opposed the demolition of the remains of Casa Vietti, a fifteenth-century dwelling in the historical quarter of Como. However, members of the public and many of the city's notables favoured demolition, as they believed the "ruins" were an obstacle to profitable property investments in the area. Terragni had prepared a project to restore the building, a plan that was perfectly in line with the artistic reform sought by Bottai, but which, as we shall see, clearly diverged from Mussolini's architectural choices in the late 1930s. Urged by, among others, his wife Rachele, who was a friend of the silk industrialist Ambrogio Pessina, the dictator personally followed the events, and "several times" involved Bottai in the matter.[41] When the building was set on fire and destroyed, Terragni sent him an article in which he appealed to his words over and over again, and denounced "the interests of businesses and financial groups." These were groups, with Pessina at the forefront, that Mussolini himself supported; the dictator had significantly put an end to the minister's reports in favour of Casa Vietti's preservation with a simple note: "Bottai is exaggerating."[42] Terragni's fascist faith, his blind trust in Mussolini, had once more been betrayed by a dictator who was obviously more responsive to the *vox populi*, and to the economic reasoning of the people of Como, than to the needs of ancient and contemporary art.

4 The Rejection of Brasini's Grandiose Architecture

Projects were ceaselessly presented in Palazzo Venezia even during the Ethiopian War. In March 1936, Mussolini approved the plan for Aprilia put forward by Concezio Petrucci's team, the winners of the competition, thus silencing those who had criticized the committee's choice. One such critic was Piacentini, who judged the project to be a step backward compared to Sabaudia (figure 30). Those who instead pushed for Mussolini's immediate approval of the project included Giovannoni, who

30. Concezio Petrucci, Mario Tufaroli, Filiberto Paolini, Riccardo Silenzi, view of the Piazza in Aprilia, 1936–7.

feared the intervention from above of his influential "friend Marcello." Giovannoni, who was his greatest supporter in the competition, believed Petrucci's vernacular language expressed a faithful interpretation of "the Duce's holy program, which is to make the urban population more rural, rather than to urbanize the rural population." And Mussolini, who in this case entirely shared the Roman engineer's point of view, had no difficulty giving the project the thumbs up.[43]

Once the Ethiopian War was over – at least officially – Mussolini was shown the plan for Addis Ababa by Cesare Valle and Ignazio Guidi.[44] Le Corbusier, on his part, once again failed in his attempt to persuade Mussolini to commission him to make a great public work. In September 1936, the Swiss architect sent his own drawings for Addis Ababa to Giuseppe Cantalupo, the ambassador, asking that he be allowed to discuss them directly with Mussolini. The letter that was enclosed with the project for the new African capital did arrive at Palazzo Venezia, but to no effect.[45] In October, Le Corbusier was again in Rome, invited by Piacentini to take part in the Convegno Volta, but again, the dictator was unwilling to meet with him. Mussolini did not want to commission a Swiss architect to design a "fascist" city, first, because he was a foreigner, and second, because the type of architecture that Le Corbusier imagined was rather distant from the objectives of "Roman building policy." "A fanatical Lutheran" was how Piacentini described Le Corbusier, "who is solely concerned with the technical elements ... We Italians are artists, and as such we are adept at shaping and adapting to the ancient."[46]

Hence, it was impossible for Le Corbusier to meet the dictator. In more general terms, after the Ethiopian War, Mussolini had become much harder to approach. The number of audiences considerably diminished as it became much more difficult for anyone to be admitted to Palazzo Venezia, even ambassadors and journalists who had been frequently and liberally welcomed there in the past. Significantly, however, this tendency did not include meetings with Italian architects.[47] Between 1928 and 1941, out of about seventy such meetings, six took place in 1934, nine in 1935, only five in 1936, with an increase to seven in 1937, and eight in each of the following two years.

Terragni's modernity in the second half of the 1930s did not earn Mussolini's favour, nor did Brasini's emphatic historicism. In February 1937, the architect had not yet given up on his gargantuan projects for Rome. Brasini still believed he was the interpreter, as he had been in 1925, of the idea of Mussolini's imperial Rome; and he was still convinced that he could appeal to the dictator's megalomaniacal side. Indeed, the creation of an empire and the ideological celebration that resulted from it seemed to favour him. Now more than ever, he was convinced that architecture had to express, as it had done in the past, the strength of a country and of the political regime that ruled it. In this spirit, and with the political support of the former undersecretary Giunta, Brasini unveiled to the dictator his model for the Mole Littoria. It was to be 200 metres tall, shaped like a truncated octagonal pyramid, with cannons jutting from its sides; it would "exceed the Church (St. Peter's), democracy (the Palazzo di Giustizia), and the Risorgimento (the Vittoriano)."[48] It would be set on a square platform 250 metres across and 10 metres tall, and on top of it would be a round terrace 135 metres in diameter. Adorned with Doric columns taller than those of Paestum, inside it would be a huge room measuring 65 metres in height and 65 in width. In that room the podium would be an arch similar to that of Emperor Constantine, and decorated with all the "Duce's great speeches." Surrounding it would be a tribune made of travertine that could hold up to 4,000 people. All around it the entrances would be marked by four propylaea topped by statues. One of these would represent the "Rome of the two empires" and feature the statues of its two founders, Emperor Augustus and Benito Mussolini. At the top of the pyramid, a huge beacon would cast a light from the Mediterranean up to Mount Soratte, about 40 kilometres from Rome, on whose rocky side the populace would be able to gaze at the Duce's profile.

During those same months in Germany – as was mentioned before – Speer was designing the Volkshalle, a huge domed building, for Hitler: 280 metres tall, it was intended to seat 150,000 people and was part of the great restoration plan for Berlin, destined to become the new capital of the Universal Empire. Hitler enthusiastically approved Speer's projects. The New Berlin would have to "surpass its only rival in the world, Rome" and "make St. Peter's and its square look like toys." According to Speer's calculations, St. Peter's would be able to fit in the Volkshalle seventeen times over.[49] The oculus of the dome would be 46 metres across, and it could contain the whole Pantheon, which had inspired it. From Hitler's point of view, the colossal structure would not be an end in itself, but rather a symbolic tool in his quest for domination. He explained to his architect, "Let a humble peasant set foot in our dome in Berlin: it will take his breath away, and he will soon understand to whom he owes his obedience."[50] The astounding dimensions alone would inspire a mystical feeling in the visitor's soul. The Volkshalle was conceived as a place in which to worship Nazism, imagined as a full-fledged religion, whose meaning for the Germans "would not be different from that of St. Peter's for the Catholic world."[51] Brasini's building sought the same meaning, but compared with the Volkshalle, it manifested a more marked expression of the cult of personality.

The architect proudly stressed that the final section of the Mole Littoria had the same diameter as the Pantheon. Curiously, as we just saw, the oculus of Speer's dome was the same size. This may simply have been a coincidence and not a deliberate challenge: at the time, Mussolini had not yet had the chance to familiarize himself with Hitler's Cyclopean architectural plans. The model for the stadium in Nuremberg would be exhibited in Paris in May 1937, whereas the plans for the Volkshalle would never be circulated. Nevertheless, Mussolini was well aware of the psychological effect that massive buildings had on the people, and he took that into account, although he never quite matched the excesses of the German dictator. About ten days after his meeting with Brasini, Mussolini gave the project the thumbs down. The estimate for the work was half a billion lire, and a note by his secretary stated, "Nothing can come of it. The Duce himself will inform the Executive Board." It was not just a matter of cost, however. Mussolini now required something different; he no longer held the same architectural vision he had ten years earlier, when he had supported Brasini's grandiose plan for Rome. The splendour, the magnificence, and the lavishness of Brasini's Mole Littoria were an expression of artistic individuality, one that no longer fulfilled the political needs in this phase of totalitarian turnaround. Brasini's plan seemed outdated, it belonged to a historical phase of fascism that had been superseded. During those very same days, the regime's administration had provided a plan for the E42 that was equally monumental and massive, but more complex, cohesive, and bound to the idea of architecture as the expression of Italian and fascist culture and as a tool for the education of the masses. As part of this plan Brasini was given an assignment nevertheless: designing the Istituto Forestale (Forestry Institute). But this did not entirely satisfy him. And so the scenographic architect, in search of better luck, offered his services to the Nazi government as well, perhaps to Göring. His proposal was to build a huge, phantasmagorical forum with a circular plan measuring one full kilometre in diameter, to be used for "performances for the masses," in the style of "imperial Roman architecture."[52]

5 Mussolini's Oversights

The list of major interventions in Mussolini's Rome included the opening of the Corso del Rinascimento. As early as August 1935, Foschini had gone to Palazzo Venezia with a plan for a new thoroughfare connecting Ponte Umberto I and Corso Vittorio Emanuele. In 1937 he met the dictator once again with some drawings for the same project but that had been in part modified.[53] The new road ran right into the church of Sant'Andrea della Valle; it involved demolition of a block of houses, the defacement of several buildings, including the church of San Giacomo degli Spagnoli, and the relocation of the Palazzetto delle Cinque Lune. There was a saying going around Rome at the time about Foschini, a professor of architecture at the University of Rome who taught planning to hundreds of future architects: "If each of his buildings is a rebirth, then every miscarriage is a blessed event." After the archaeological ruins of the Stadium of Domitian were discovered, the architect revised his initial ideas, leaving the part facing Piazza Navona unchanged, but rethinking the one facing Via Zanardelli so that the ruins would be visible. A model of the project was submitted to Mussolini for his approval, which he gave. In attendance at the meeting was Giuseppe Bevione, president of INA and the main financial sponsor of Corso del Rinascimento, as well as Bevione's right-hand man, Cipriani, who illustrated for the dictator another important construction plan: the new route connecting

Via Vittorio Veneto with Via San Bernardo, currently Via Bissolati, which would have the insurance company's financial support. During the fascist years, INA was a major financial backer for a series of radical and massive construction works in many Italian cities. Hailed by Mussolini as the expression of the "constructive will of fascism," this effort to modernize the city from an architectural standpoint, entrusted to the major insurance companies and banking groups, and with highly questionable results from an aesthetic standpoint, led to the expulsion of the most vulnerable people from city centres. The historical areas of cities were dramatically altered, and the remains of an ancient past were replaced by modern monuments of the regime.[54]

Mussolini examined plans for the modernization and fascistization of the city's historical centre, as well as plans for areas of urban expansion, areas that were the most affected by the city's demographic changes. For this reason, he welcomed De Renzi and Gaetano Maccaferri, who showed him the model for the new centre of the Magliana area. The architects emphasized the fact that it was the first of the "urban rural" settlements, the "closest to our agricultural mentality." Fascist ruralism, in fact, which opposed urbanization and supported a model of development based on agriculture and its "healthier" values, was cross-pollinated in this project with elements of urban architecture. Behind the ideological veil, consistently applied to the urban development plan flaunted by De Renzi before Mussolini, could be found a more ordinary speculative venture. The area, in fact, was on the main road to the E42 and was the target of voracious real estate developers. Moreover, this area, which had originally been excluded from the urban development plan, but was now rezoned to allow building, belonged to Maccaferri, the brother-in-law of Angelo Manaresi, a member of Parliament, former deputy minister of war, and podestà of Bologna.[55]

Mussolini's support for De Renzi's plan stood in contrast to his rejection at that time of another urban development plan, the one for Valle d'Aosta. Drafted by the BBPR team (Luigi Banfi, Ludovico Belgioioso, Enrico Peressutti, and Ernesto Nathan Rogers) together with Pietro Bottoni, Figini, and Pollini, the plan was financed by Adriano Olivetti, who gave Mussolini eighty-six photographic reproductions as a gift (figure 31). The young entrepreneur from Piedmont asked Mussolini to give his "high approval" to the plan, which was "the first attempt to solve ... all of the problems inherent to a region," and to establish the directives for its possible inclusion in the National Corporate Plan.[56] However, Mussolini failed to do so. The exhibition dedicated to the projects – which were actually limited to residential regeneration and the development of certain areas for tourism – opened in Rome on 5 July 1937. While Ministers

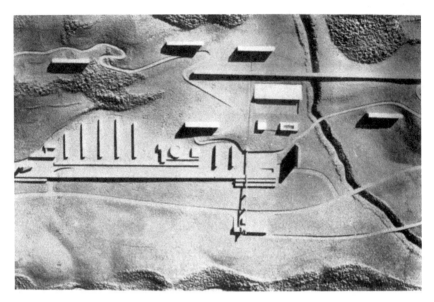

31. BBPR Group (Luigi Banfi, Ludovico Belgioioso, Enrico Peressutti, Ernesto
Nathan Rogers), Piero Bottoni, Luigi Figini, and Gino Pollini, Valle d'Aosta
urban development plan, model for Courmayeur, 1937. Mussolini did not
approve of these "Rationalist" projects.

Paolo Thaon di Revel, Bottai, and Cobolli Gigli went to see it, Mussolini, albeit much awaited, did not. Although some, like Bardi, praised the
choices included in the plan, identifying them with Mussolini's fascism –
the "Plan for Valle d'Aosta is Mussolini's fascism applied with the purest
devotion and also with the purest intelligence" – the dictator did not
want to give his approval to a project that contained such a radical formu-
lation of modern architecture, without throwbacks to figurative rurality.
Although he accepted the new modernity of De Renzi's "urban rural" settlements – where the rurality was clearly visible in the arc motif and the
stone cladding – he found it hard to get the bywords of ruralist ideology
to converse with architecture that was so abstract on a figurative level.

As a rule, Mussolini discussed the issue of residential settlements and
the serious housing crisis with Alberto Calza Bini, who visited Palazzo
Venezia on a regular basis. During one of those visits, with the minister of
public works, Cobolli Gigli, who was also in attendance, the architect and
member of Parliament presented a public housing plan to be carried out
over a five-year period.[57] A few months later, he reported the activities of
the National Association of Social Housing. On that occasion, Mussolini

stepped into the shoes of the town planner: he intervened in the selection of the type of lodgings, choosing intensive social housing in the big cities, and semi-urban and semi-rural constructions for the smaller towns. As concerned the latter, exercising his affinity for autocracy and ruralism, he ordered that they be provided "with pieces of land where the inhabitants can grow what they require for their domestic needs."[58]

However, Mussolini was more interested in the subject of the architectural projection of power rather than the social issue of housing. Bazzani was often at Palazzo Venezia in connection with a whole series of monumental projects, from the competition for the Auditorium in Rome to the Monumento alla Vittoria in Milan, from the Africa and San Paolo bridges in Rome to the Palazzo di Giustizia in Forlì.[59] The architect, who in 1937 had been commissioned by the Fascist Party to design the installation for the Second Exhibition of the Fascist Revolution, was seeking Mussolini's approval for a building venture in the historical centre of Forlì, where he was particularly active. He had convinced the Bank of Italy to purchase from the city's bishop a piece of land adjacent to the Palazzo del Governo (which he had designed) as a site for its new headquarters. Bazzani well knew, however, that in that city the most important urban issues were decided by Mussolini, which meant that he was going to have to directly address the dictator to get permission to design the building.[60]

In October 1938, the Milanese architect Vico Viganò visited the dictator's quarters. He had an outlandish idea to put forward, the design of a Gothic tower to be built in Piazza Duomo in Milan. Unexpectedly, the dictator approved it, scheduling its construction to be completed by 1942.[61] When the news was published in the papers it caused quite a stir. The podestà Gian Giacomo Gallarati Scotti was embarrassed and worried about having to tell Mussolini that he had approved the wrong project. The loyal Giulio Barella, former president of the Triennale and now manager of *Il Popolo d'Italia*, hastened to warn him that the construction of a bell tower so close to the Duomo was being "harshly criticized." Ojetti, while visiting Milan, remarked that "in Italy, the laws against the Jews were never discussed as much as this cotton candy bell tower, and a Gothic one to boot, has been in the past four days." Piacentini himself became involved, warning that "this bell tower ... would represent an element in opposition to any urban consideration and contrary to any historical, aesthetic, and stylistic objective."[62] Mussolini's decision puzzled his entourage. "None of us took this madman and his little project seriously," added Ojetti, "and then, out of the blue, without informing either the podestà or the prefect, Mussolini approved and signed it."[63] His personal secretary wondered, "who had allowed Viganò to meet with the Duce?" In an annotation in margin of the letter, Mussolini blamed Viganò himself, accusing him of having taken advantage of his good will. "You deceived me," he wrote. "You made me believe that it was part of the urban development plan." He then decided it was best to quickly hush up the matter, and have the *prefetto* summon the architect, "because he gets too nervous."[64] No doubt, for a leader who thought of himself as a connoisseur of all things architectural, the oversight was glaring. There is one thing that might have appealed to him, the demagogic potential of the project, and indeed the Gothic bell tower would be warmly welcomed by the Milanese people. Proving, in this case, that he had chosen the wrong "style," but "understood the soul of the people."[65]

6 Architecture for a Politics of Domination

Towards the end of the 1930s, architecture for Mussolini was increasingly becoming a crucial element in the government's strategic program. Right outside Rome, the E42 had been launched, while in the capital, in Milan, and in other major Italian cities important works were being built that would change the face of these places, leaving on them the mark of fascism, shaping the architectural scenarios necessary to educate the masses. Seven years after his conversations with Ludwig, while speaking to the journalist Nino D'Aroma, Mussolini once again emphasized his devotion to architecture. "To my mind, the two essential and most powerful arts, ones that are decisive and necessary for humanity are, and will always be, architecture followed by music. All the others are just games." This time, however, Mussolini made sure to underscore the aspects of architecture that signify "power" and "decisiveness." The projects that were under way and the major construction sites that had been opened throughout Italy were clear proof of this.[66] One of these was the new *Popolo d'Italia* headquarters in Milan. The building that housed the newspaper, founded by Mussolini in 1914 and whose history in part coincided with that of its founder and the birth of his political movement, was not meant to be a merely functional construction. Rather, the intent was for it to celebrate the cult of fascism in a central part of the city. Having become, after 1922, the government's unofficial organ, the newspaper was directly controlled by the dictator, who every evening from Rome gave the editor-in-chief directions over the phone. The plan for the new building in Piazza Cavour was commissioned from the loyal Muzio, who, in 1938, submitted a first proposal, which was later abandoned in favour of a second one. The most significant changes concerned the façade overlooking the square. Significantly, the geometrical partition in the initial plan was replaced by one that alluded to classicism (figure 32). A double row of pillars that protruded just slightly was attached to the

32. Giovanni Muzio, *Popolo d'Italia* building in Milan, 1938–42.

façade and, to close everything off, a cornice was added with a decorative motif that was reminiscent in an abstract way of Doric trabeation. "The outer appearance of the Palazzo," wrote the architect, "will be of austere simplicity and it will express a virile strength." In April 1939, Muzio was welcomed at Palazzo Venezia and was able to present his final project, which was approved by the dictator. On the façade overlooking the square, the architect had designed a balcony from which the dictator could make his public appearances. Connected to the balcony was the leader's office, a large room that measured 10 x 10 metres. Inside the building, Muzio also planned to faithfully rebuild some of the original rooms from the old headquarters, where Mussolini had founded and directed the newspaper, and where he had conceived the March on Rome. Hence, this was not just a simple office building with rooms for the presses, but also, in the words of editor-in-chief Giorgio Pini, a "house open to all Italians of faith." It was a sort of shrine to the fascist press, a temple for pilgrims to celebrate the religion of their leader.[67] Muzio's work was done for no charge and, according to Piacentini, who was always well-informed, Mussolini rewarded him by nominating him "accademico d'Italia" (Italy's academic-in-chief).[68]

The political success of the military conquest of Ethiopia now had to be consolidated with Italian and fascist efforts to "civilize" those territories, with the aid of architecture as one of the most persuasive tools of civilization.[69] Addis Ababa had to become, in a very short time, the "new Rome" on the African continent. As we saw before, Mussolini had been receiving urban development plans starting in the months right after the Italian occupation. After setting aside the project by Ponti and his partners, which will be discussed later, and leaving Le Corbusier's amid a random pile of papers, Mussolini turned to the plans drawn up by Cesare Valle and Guidi. In their final project, the political and administrative centre situated in the area between Viale dell'Impero, the main square, and ending with the Palazzo del Viceré recalled the ideas Piacentini had chosen for the E42. Detailed plans for the capital were then elaborated by Plinio Marconi, an associate of Piacentini, as well as by Guglielmo Ulrich and Cafiero. In November 1939, these designs were submitted to Mussolini by the podestà of the Ethiopian city, Carlo Boidi. Marconi was then commissioned to design the new city hall (figure 33), while Cafiero, Guidi, Ulrich, and Cesare Valle were tasked with building the gigantic Palazzo Imperiale. The latter building recalled the Reggia di Caserta and celebrated the magnificence and power of fascist Italy. Just as the ancient Romans had done, the regime wanted to use colossal dimensions to impress the local populations. By applying its own anti-egalitarian ideology, the regime promoted racial discrimination, drawing unfavourable comparisons between the "superb" architectural civilization of the Italian invaders, and the "wretched" of the *tukals*, made of straw and mud, of the native Ethiopians.[70]

The fascist politics exercised abroad needed to be accompanied by a coherent architectural strategy, one that could be adapted to other countries. This was the meaning of the visit to Palazzo Venezia by Piacentini and a team of recent graduates of the Scuola di Roma, the winners of the competition for the National Theatre in Belgrade (figure 34). For the architect and the dictator, who made sure that the press extensively covered the meeting, this honour was proof of the fact that "Roman architecture should be disseminated around the world," of the triumph abroad of the Italian "style."[71] Not far from this nationalistic and dominant display, was the presentation at Palazzo Venezia a few days later of the projects of Claudio Longo and Beltrando Savelli, two young architects who had also studied under Piacentini. The Case del Fascio they had designed for Salona d'Isonzo, Piedimonte del Calvario, and Canale d'Isonzo, small towns with significant Slavic communities, were part of an aggressive plan to Italianize and fascistize the populations on the eastern border.[72]

The regime's construction of monumental, sometimes Cyclopean, buildings stood in contrast with the dramatic housing shortages in the major cities, and with the disastrous sanitary conditions of rural housing.

33. Plinio Marconi, project for the City Hall in Addis Ababa, model, 1939.

34. Luigi Vagnetti, Luigi Orestano, Dante Tassotti, Pasquale Marabotto, project for the new opera house in Belgrade, model, 1939.

The regime, then, needed to demonstrate at least a surface commitment to this building sector as well. Hence, in January 1940, Mussolini summoned Alberto Calza Bini to Palazzo Venezia to learn about the need for affordable housing in the capital, as well as to examine the request for new low-cost housing in the area of the E42. Two months later, the architect and member of Parliament submitted to Mussolini the plans for the construction of new working-class neighbourhoods in Rome.[73] The issue of housing would prove to be even more dire in the wake of the destruction caused by the war. Moreover, successive military defeats would make it harder to justify the money spent to create audacious architecture celebrating imperial splendour, seeing that vast numbers of people did not even have a proper roof over their heads.

After Italy entered the war, there was a drastic reduction in the frequency of architects' visits to Palazzo Venezia. On one of these increasingly rare meetings, Libera, Muzio, Maroni, and Mario Cereghini went to see Mussolini in order to examine the design for the Museo degli Alpini on the Doss in Trento. Mussolini had supported the project since 1938. Then he had sent Ojetti to Trento, concerned that the museum would not blend in well with the Cesare Battisti Memorial by Fagiuoli. Later, while observing the military manoeuvres in Albania, Mussolini had a conversation with Cereghini. He had said he was "eager to see the project" and guaranteed the state's financial backing. Now, standing before the model and the sixteen panels illustrating the "new acropolis," he listened to the architects who, confident that they could interpret his idea, spoke to him about their desire to combine the symbols of Alpine architecture and those of Rome.[74]

7 Ponti's Suggestions

The relationship between Mussolini and Ponti was a unique one. Their first recorded meeting took place in December 1926, when the architect visited the dictator to outline his plan for the Monumento ai Caduti (War Memorial) in Milan.[75] Ponti's project for the Torre Littoria, to be built in Parco Sempione, was later presented by Barella to Mussolini for his approval.[76] The following March, Barella himself was welcomed by Mussolini to discuss the 5th Triennale. Ponti was on the board of directors and, with respect to the exhibitions of previous years, this one afforded fascism a much greater role in the field of the arts. During that meeting, Mussolini showed that he was particularly interested in the exhibition of architectural projects, many of which Ponti himself had inspired.[77] The Triennale focused on the relationship between "style and civilization," that is, the country's commitment to asserting its cultural and political supremacy. The houses that were to be built in the park, and that were commissioned from various architects, would have to represent a thorough "understanding of civilization today."[78] Through the arts, especially architecture, Ponti wanted to reaffirm Italy's spiritual and political prestige in the world. In *Il Popolo d'Italia* Ponti wrote that "today, only two arts, architecture and politics, try to understand, serve, and express" the "new orders that humanity, with passion and torment, seeks in depth."[79] The Milanese architect seemed to identify the confluence of architecture and politics, along a route where art's independence was not always defended, and when it was, it was done ambiguously. Mussolini wanted to be routinely informed about the developments of that particular Triennale, and Barella went to see him on two other occasions: the first was just a few days before the opening so that he could find out about the state of progress of the works, and the second was right after the opening, so that he could get an early account on its success.[80]

In 1934, during the competition for the Palazzo del Littorio on Via dell'Impero, Ponti thought of using that architectural complex to consolidate the "ideals of a new world".[81] His project, which differed from all the others, isolated Mussolini's office from all the other buildings, elevating it to a monument: Mussolini's glorification was embodied in the *domus lictoria*, one large room contained inside an isolated block on the parvis of the new acropolis. It was there that Ponti metaphorically brought together Mussolini and the Italian people. This *domus* that was so dear to Ponti, this Italian-style house that was the focus of plans to educate families from an architectural standpoint, was transformed into the *domus lictoria*, and transported to the top of the acropolis; at the same time, it was meant to convey that the Duce had left his palazzo to move closer to the people, settling in a home, that of fascism, the home of all Italians (figure 35).

The correspondence between Ponti and the dictator intensified in the second half of the 1930s, and grew even more frequent in the early 1940s. At this time, dissent against fascism and Mussolini was on the rise. Ponti was constantly reaching out to his political interlocutor, Mussolini, and because of the originality of his projects he stood out from his colleagues. In the second half of 1936, while preparations were under way for Italy's participation in the Paris Exposition – an event that, as we shall see later, was personally followed by Mussolini – Ponti sent the dictator the article he had written entitled "Battaglia di Parigi," which Mussolini read and praised.[82] For Ponti, who was also the director of *Domus*, the Paris Exposition, and indeed all future events – the E42 comes to mind – had to be thought of as "battles" aimed at valorizing Italy's artistic output and consecrating Italy as the "great global market of artistic production."

35. Gio Ponti, project for the first-level competition for the Palazzo del Littorio in Rome, 1934. In the foreground, the *domus lictoria,* Mussolini's office.

This cultural as well as economic strategy could only be implemented within the framework of the regime's policies.[83]

Mussolini himself sent the architect, along with Del Debbio and Vaccaro, on a mission to Addis Ababa. On his return, Ponti delivered a report to the dictator on the urban design of the Ethiopian capital, which Mussolini read on 18 December 1936. Through the report all three architects were in effect applying for the job of devising an urban development plan as an alternative to the one put forward by Valle and Guidi. The plan promoted by Ponti's team was based on superseding traditional colonial structures, offsetting them with a loftier idea of architecture, the "expression of our political, social, and artistic civilization." This was something that could transcend "everything that has been accomplished up to now in the urban design sector around the world," and therefore assert "a primacy that would go down in history." It was an "architectural plan," wrote Ponti, "the likes of which has never been seen before, unifying, bold, and extremely modern, the most responsible work that can be commissioned from an architect: the dream of modern city planning brought to fruition by Italy ... We can already envision it, and we already feel the extent to which Italians will love this visual object; outside of Italy we can feel all the Le Corbusiers with their eyes upon us." This ambitious plan represented an opportunity to show the world the supremacy achieved by new Italian architecture and by the fascist civilization. It would even be the envy of the likes of Le Corbusier, the Swiss architect who was spearheading the transnational innovative front and who had had the audacity to put forward his candidacy to design a city that Italy had conquered in spite of the hostility of the international community. However, as a modern architectural challenge to the world, this plan failed to persuade Mussolini, who gave it the thumbs down.[84]

Although his projects for the E42 had been rejected, Ponti actively collaborated on the exhibition, a "great national enterprise," the "brightest guiding light" for the future of the arts. He sent numerous articles to Mussolini through Osvaldo Sebastiani, the dictator's personal secretary, who at times informed the sender that Mussolini was pleased, and, occasionally, that he was struck by Ponti's inventiveness.[85] Ponti insisted on the theme of the "battle for art," on the meaning of the E42, a historical opportunity for "confrontation, which we ourselves have sought, with the whole world, in a field where Italy must by tradition excel."[86] Ponti suggested transforming the E42 into a great event that was not just dedicated to architecture, but that could also be used to drive the minor arts. He suggested that the exhibition could provide the stimulus required to improve the quality of national artistic production as a whole, in order to elevate it to the highest point in the history of Italian civilization, and to achieve dominance in the world market for quality goods. Ponti suggested establishing a national plan for the "mobilization of the production of art," funded by the state and lasting three years, entrusted to the Milan Triennale, whose board of directors included both him and Piacentini.

Ponti thus developed a national project for fascism aimed at relaunching artistic production, with major economic and financial repercussions for the assertion of Italian civilization. It is apparent here that there was a great deal of affinity between Ponti's cultural project and one aspect of the "confrontation" between civilizations that Mussolini sought. Ponti had identified an artistic inclination in the nature of the Italian people that led them to excel in the arts. According to the architect, these artistic skills had to be cultivated and bolstered because they could reward the Italian people with a leading role in the "new Europe." Mussolini, on his part, instead aimed to assign fascism and Italy a mission of "superior civilization," a "new order" to be imposed by the military as well as by construction activity – including architecture – on the other peoples of Europe.

8 "Rendering unto Caesar What Is Caesar's"

In the spring of 1940, Ponti sent Mussolini the article "Arte per il popolo." In it, the editor-in-chief of *Domus* pondered the meaning of Mussolini's slogan "moving towards the people," and how it could be applied
to the arts, in a broad sense and also with regard to architecture. Ponti
supported the independence of art – "art is art" – and seemed to be
against its demagogic use in politics.[87] He believed that art for the people was only that which bestowed beauty on the things that belonged
to everybody, hence, a street, a square, a public building. However, he
also believed that the creative process was absolutely independent from
the people, and was determined by art alone. He did not believe that
"moving towards the people" implied offering art that was dedicated to
the people, nor did he feel that it meant promoting art that could be
understood by the masses.

On this last point, at least as far as architecture is concerned, it is hard
to believe that Mussolini shared Ponti's opinion. In the second half of
the 1930s, the dictator used architecture to involve the people in the
fascist myths. Moreover, he thought that art had to be universally understandable. Was Ponti criticizing Mussolini? If so, it was veiled criticism
with a collaborative intent, certainly not strong enough to call into question the policies of fascism in the field of architecture. Or, based on a
second, more plausible, hypothesis, faced with the manifest interference
of politics, he was trying to indirectly uphold the thesis of a regime that
was sensitive to architecture's autonomy.

In November of the same year, Ponti sent Mussolini another short essay on the same theme, once again stressing the freedom of architecture
in the fascist regime. Shortly afterwards, the essay was fiercely criticized
by Pagano, who claimed it was an example of flattery, of superficial analysis, and the expression of a mentality that insisted on seeing everything
as "all beautiful, all splendid, and all easy."[88] In "Vocazione architettonica
degli italiani," Ponti underscored the "natural" passion that Italians felt
for architecture, a passion that, he believed, was "a state of mind." The
"court poet" – as Pagano, who was probably well aware of the relationship between his colleague and Mussolini, described Ponti – stressed that
the dictator's activity in the field of architecture was carried out with no
authoritarianism, nor with any intrusions. He praised Mussolini's ability
to valorize the qualities of each individual building, and at the same time
to reconstruct an Italian architectural identity:

> The Duce, this total Italian, was from the start a builder along the fate-
> ful line of the great and ancient Italians. He has expressed to the highest

degree, as with all his endeavours, the vocation of the architect. He has ushered in a revival of Italian-style architecture in Italy. He has given us architects an immense task; he has enriched us with the greatest possible experience, one that is excellent in every field ... He has engaged and valorized the thousand architectural personalities of this rich and diverse Italian race, from Piacentini to Muzio, from Pagano to Libera, from Ridolfi to Moretti, and from Terragni to Vaccaro.[89]

Ponti was well aware of the fact that art did not respond well to coercion; he also knew that such coercion did occur in Italy and thus chose to dissimulate. Had he perhaps forgotten the time that Mussolini had ordered him to raise and then lower the Torre Littoria in Parco Sempione, or when he had ordered him to stress heroism over compassion in the Monumento ai Caduti in Milan? However, Ponti was no doubt right when he emphasized the "endless amount of work" that the dictator had given the architects. In the letter that accompanied the article, Ponti explained that he had wanted to underscore just "how much we architects owe him: 'render unto Caesar what is Caesar's'"[90] On his part, Mussolini, after reading the article, jotted the following words in the margin: "The articles written by this architect are unquestionably original. In the one he just sent me ['Vocazione architettonica degli italiani'] he tries to demonstrate that Nature wanted Italians to be builders, and that the Duce has interpreted this vocation."[91]

The unique nature of the relationship between the architect and the dictator emerges in correspondence between them from a few months earlier. The Italian publishing house Bompiani had just released the Italian translation of Steinbeck's *The Grapes of Wrath*, and Ponti asked Sebastiani to make sure Mussolini knew about the book. "It describes," Ponti explained, "the expansion of landholdings in the United States, dispossessed farmers tragically forced to migrate in poverty. It is a striking allegation. It is the exact opposite of what fascism has done in the Pontine Marshes, in Sicily, and in Libya. The book should be read by every Italian, and every newspaper should recommend it." With the war at its peak, Ponti felt it was his intellectual duty to draw Mussolini's attention to the novel so that he could in turn recommend it to the Italian people; most importantly, however, to do so would be politically expedient, as the inequality and greed of American capitalism portrayed in the novel would reflect favourably on the regime's social policies. Nevertheless, Mussolini decided to keep the letter to himself.[92]

In March 1941, Ponti asked to be received by Mussolini to show him some "material illustrating an Italian component, so that it could then be compared with similar material coming from foreign countries." The architect's request was not granted, however.[93] In January of the following year, the publisher Aldo Garzanti met with Mussolini to discuss the idea of publishing Ponti's *La casa per tutti*. The topic of a "home for everyone," which had been introduced by Ponti in his magazine *Stile* in March 1941, was the focus of the 8th Triennale held in late October.[94] In an article he wrote for the *Corriere della Sera*, Ponti even referred to a speech Hitler had given on the same subject, thus expressing his own support for the political relevance of social housing.[95] Mussolini told Garzanti that he "sincerely approved of ... the ideas" of the architect.[96]

The following year Ponti advised Mussolini to read *L'industria d'arte in tempo di guerra*.[97] Here Ponti was offering Mussolini a socially oriented defence for the conflict that was under way. Ponti hoped to demonstrate that the war was justified "because it gave Italians work, vital space for work," which was required if they were to achieve the standard of life worthy of an "ancient civilization." Ponti envisioned Italy's artistic predominance over other countries in the postwar period. At the same time, he feared the dangers of maintaining the status quo, the loss of the efficiency of the skilled worker in the artistic sector, and therefore the risk that victory – which he had faith in – would turn to defeat.[98] Both Mussolini and Ponti were deeply worried about the difficult postwar period that awaited the country, and imagined a scenario in which Italy would be dominated by a victorious Germany.[99] Ponti believed that even though Italy could never compete with Germany in the heavy industries, it could assume a prominent position in artistic production, in craftmanship, and in related industries such as ceramics, textiles, glassware, and fashion.

In his search for points of convergence between his favourite themes and fascism, Ponti engaged in a series of risky balancing acts. A case in point was when – after reminding Mussolini that he had agreed with his "proclamation that this war is the supreme and resolute episode of a social policy that will result in vital spaces (justice among the people) and higher standards of life (justice within the people), and that these improved conditions would above all be realized through housing ("a home for everyone") – he suggested that he envision the theme of a "home for everyone" as an ideological reason, the highest and most heartfelt, for the fascist war: "a home for everyone can be a real resolution for this war, as clear as 'Trento and Trieste' was for the previous war. We are fighting for our homes." The idea of a "home for everyone" could thus take on the quality of an enterprise that would transform the virtues of war into the virtues of peace.[100] In essence, Ponti went so far as to suggest that Mussolini use the social issue of housing as an instrument of wartime propaganda.

9 Moretti Instead of Piacentini?

If ever there was an architect with whom Mussolini established a privileged relationship, it was Moretti. While Piacentini actually spent more time with the dictator, among younger architects it was Moretti, more so than Libera and Terragni, who received most of Mussolini's attention. Whereas Piacentini had achieved a position of renown in the "old" liberal governments, and was being recycled by the regime, Moretti had instead received his entire education during the "Fascist Revolution."[101] In 1934, at just 27 years of age, Renato Ricci appointed him director of the Technical Office of the ONB, with the important task of revising and approving projects at a national level.[102] Moretti was later invited, along with a few other colleagues, to take part in the competition for the ONB Museum, and for the positioning of the Colossus in the Foro Mussolini. The gigantic bronze statue designed by Aroldo Bellini was 86 metres tall and portrayed Hercules with Mussolini's features. It was also 26 metres taller than the statue Speer wanted to position on the grandstand at Märzfeld in Nuremberg, where the Nazi Party rallied each year. Ricci had initially wanted it to be even taller, so that it would be three times the height of New York's Statue of Liberty, whose structural details he had had sent to him.[103] Situated on the slopes of Monte Mario and dominating the city, the Colossus would have been one of the most spectacular and perhaps unsettling expressions of the cult of personality that fascism had built around the dictator.[104] Fascism counterbalanced the supranational myth of liberty that was typical of democracy, and that had become historically outdated, with the nationalist myth of Mussolini, the prophet of a new political religion. Interestingly, the Colossus was not simply one of the many visionary projects that were stored away inside a drawer and forgotten. The first parts of the Cyclopean statue, the head and one foot, had already been made. Only because of the sanctions levied against Italy by the League of Nations following the invasion of Ethiopia was work on the statue temporarily suspended (figure 36).

Moretti's first important work was the Accademia di Scherma, which was initially conceived as an experimental Casa del Balilla, but was later used as a reception area for the whole complex (figure 37). Without resorting to any of the traditional ornamental motifs, Moretti created a building that aimed at being both classical and modern, abstract and temporal; it was the ideal architectural setting for a politics based on the never-ending mythicization of the present. Encouraged by the success of the Accademia di Scherma, Moretti replaced Del Debbio as one of the architects on the Foro project, and in May 1937, he presented Mussolini with a new plan of the area, one that stretched all the way to the slopes of

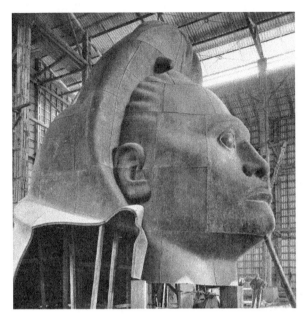

36. Aroldo Bellini, bronze head of the statue of Hercules with Mussolini's features, 1936. The 86-metre-tall statue of Hercules with Mussolini's face was to be located in the Foro Mussolini in Rome, behind the Arengo delle Nazioni.

37. Luigi Moretti, Fencing Academy at the Foro Mussolini in Rome, 1933–6.

38. Luigi Moretti, Arengo delle Nazioni at the Foro Mussolini in Rome, model, 1936. The huge area for gatherings could accommodate up to 400,000 people. The huge bronze statue was to be located behind the orator's podium. The Arengo delle Nazioni was reminiscent of the Zeppelinfeld in Nuremberg.

Monte Mario, and was filled with roads, gardens, open air theatres, and sports grounds. As part of the plan, the emerging and qualifying building was the Arengo delle Nazioni – discussed previously – which could house up to 400,000 people, and was towered over by Bellini's Colossus, now re-located to this site after the project for the ONB Museum was abandoned (figure 38).[105] When, in October 1937, Renato Ricci, Moretti's patron, was sacked, and the ONB, which had become the GIL, came under the direct management of the PNF, the architect was confirmed by Starace, proof of his ability to skilfully navigate the rough seas of politics. Unsur-prisingly, Quaroni, who was well aware of his fellow architect's rare skills, would always remember him for being "invincible in politics."[106]

Within the area of the Foro Mussolini, beside the Accademia di Scherma, Moretti designed two other highly significant buildings, which offer proof of favour afforded to him by the duce and the higher ranks of the regime. The first of these was Mussolini's own private quarters-cum-gym,

39. Luigi Moretti, the dictator's private lodgings and gym at the Foro Mussolini in Rome, 1940. Located in the Palazzo delle Terme, it was connected to the swimming pool via an elevator.

which was located on the first floor of the Palazzo delle Terme (figure 39). The architect divided the entire rectangular space with just two marble diaphragms: one marked the entrance, the other separated the rooms from the service area; opposite the entrance he placed a sculptural spiral staircase leading to the bedrooms on the upper floor. The walls were clad with black and white *paonazzetto* marble slabs, while the foyer was embellished with mosaics by Severini. A lift led directly from the living quarters to the Olympic-size swimming pool located on the floor below. Moretti's construction was fluid and the atmosphere rarefied, almost surreal. It was a space conceived for an exceptional man, a sort of demigod, and not some common mortal.

The second work the regime commissioned from Moretti was the Sacrario dei Martiri Fascisti (Shrine of the Fascist Martyrs), inaugurated by Mussolini on 28 October 1941. It was located in the building of the Foresteria Nord, which had been converted the previous year into the headquarters of the Casa Littoria (figure 40).[107] There Moretti created a cell

40. Luigi Moretti, Sacrario dei Martiri (Fascist Martyr Memorial) at the Foro Mussolini in Rome, 1940. Moretti was one of Mussolini's favourite architects. Yvon de Begnac, the dictator's biographer, portrayed them in their morning conversations amid the ruins of the Imperial Fora.

with an oval plan that was completely clad with marble, and whose curved wall was made from heavy blocks of rough-hewn white stone. At the centre, reminiscent of Christian liturgy, was placed an altar, a smooth white monolithic square, atop a red granite podium. There were no crosses (whereas there was a cross at the Shrine of the Exhibition of the Fascist Revolution), nor were there any of the fascist symbols or writings. In that room, whose atmosphere was esoteric and mystical, fascism was elevated to a political religion of the absolute, taking the place of the age-old traditional religions. In that cell, the divine absolute was replaced by a collective absolute, whose name was fascism. After he had finished Mussolini's apartment, Moretti was chosen to design the most sacred room in the entire complex. Neither the theme nor the task was new to him, however, if it is true that he had previously been assigned the project for the Sacrario (Shrine) for the old headquarters in Palazzo Vidoni.[108] Although no records have come down to us to prove that this was the case, it is hard to imagine Mussolini not having seen and given the thumbs up to both projects.

Around 1940, Moretti received yet another, even more prestigious, commission from the PNF, proof of his standing as Italian architecture's rising star. Though his work on the Foro Mussolini was confirmed, the area he was asked to deal with had grown much bigger – ten times the area that had originally been assigned to Del Debbio – and it included entire sections of northern Rome, such as the Flaminio neighbourhood. It is worth noting that this area was even greater than that of the E42, serving as its monumental counterpart to the north, the first tranche of the backbone leading from the city to the sea. The project, "Forma Ultima Fori," for which a model was made, shown to Mussolini, and then displayed in March 1942 in Florence, was introduced as the "most important construction work of the modern age."[109]

While Piacentini was commissioned to oversee the design of the E42, whose construction was by that time under way, Moretti was commissioned to direct the next colossal work by the regime. It was an assignment that was much like a passing on of the baton, almost an indication that Moretti had been chosen to replace Piacentini in the following decades. De Begnac, Mussolini's biographer, devoted much attention to the special relationship between the dictator and Moretti – who shared a unique understanding – describing their morning conversations, not in Palazzo Venezia, but amid the silence of the ruins of the Fori Imperiali.[110] In this case as well, the meetings were private, away from prying eyes, and appointments were made for odd times of the day. For the time being, not even the young fascist Moretti could be identified by anyone as Mussolini's architect.

4 In the Architect's Shoes

1 The Duce Approves

Mussolini's zeal for centralization was pervasive. Especially as concerned public works in Rome, his inclination to intervene, not only in political choices, but also in minor and at times insignificant administrative issues, was evident. The dictator felt he had to decide everything personally, an approach determined by his innate scepticism and his mistrust in other people, combined with an overblown belief in his own intellectual skills and political insight.[1] His exuberant individualism was also apparent in the many projects that required his personal approval. But what exactly did this approval entail? Was it merely a matter of image, a formality? Was putting his signature on everything a way of making sure that every single intervention related back to him, thus reinforcing the myth of his omnipotence? Or was it something more substantial?

Mussolini definitely wanted to exert direct control, for fiscal or other practical reasons, wherever possible on projects that were government-funded reasons. But he may also have wanted to express his aesthetic opinion. In some cases, he simply ratified decisions that others had made, but, often he expressed his own specific demands. He approved the project by Carminati's team of architects for the Casa dei Sindacati Fascisti dell'Industria in Milan: in this case, however, he gave the thumbs up for a perspective drawing featuring a giant order of half-columns, which, however, was not executed in the end.[2] He approved Foschini's project for the Istituto Odontoiatrico Eastmann in Rome.[3] Mussolini met with Brasini to view the drawings for the monumental Ponte XVIII Ottobre (currently known as Ponte Flaminio) over the River Tiber, which featured a huge arch at the centre, and asked him to remove the large colonnade. "His suggestion," the architect wrote, "was most valuable, and because of it the lines of the bridge gained originality and breadth."[4] Mussolini signed Brenno del Giudice's monumental traditional project for La Spezia Cathedral, solemnly declaring it "worthy ... of Italian art." A short time later, he also gave the green light to the modern Padiglione della Stampa (Press Pavilion) for the Milan Triennale; designed by Baldessari, it was characterized by large expanses of glass and brick.[5] He examined the drawings by Giovanni Magnaghi for the new Milan headquarters of the Gruppo Rionale Fascista Cantore.[6] He approved Fagnoni's drawings for the Sacrario dei Caduti Fascisti in the crypt of Santa Croce in Florence, as well as Spaccarelli's plan to clear out the Mole Adriana in Rome, and to repair the pentagonal city walls.[7]

While it seems Mussolini remained on the sidelines of the complicated affair concerning the Santa Maria Novella Station in Florence, requesting only that he be kept informed, he directly intervened in the Santa Lucia Station in Venice.[8] Umberto Puppini, the minister of communications, sent Mussolini the two plans drafted by Mazzoni for the passenger building. These represented two very different ideas as concerned the façade overlooking the Grand Canal: the first plan was rather traditional and was characterized by three large arches supported by pillars; by contrast, the second was modern, featuring a large curved glass wall and a row of round windows. Mussolini favoured the latter plan, discarding the former, which was, however, preferred by the Venetian authorities. And no sooner had the building site been opened than fierce local opposition arose, animated by disapproval of a building that many felt was unsuited to the lagoon environment, resulting in the work coming to a halt. The project Mussolini had chosen was not supported by the people, and for this reason he felt the right thing to do was to let it drop, and instead organize a public competition.[9] The dictator was not interested in exposing himself by taking on a fight in support of one architectural style or another. His sole objective was to garner support through architecture, not to fuel people's discontent.

Among other projects submitted for Mussolini's approval was Leo Stefano Balzano's design for the Caserma della Milizia (Militia Barracks) on Via Parini in Milan,[10] and Marino's plan for the Ministry of Aeronautics airmen's lodgings in Rome.[11] In December 1934, Mussolini met with Valentino Cencelli, president of the Opera Nazionale Combattenti, with the drawings for the new city of Pontinia: in approving the project, he praised the Ufficio Tecnico dell'Opera "for the rural environment that has inspired all the building plans."[12] Piccinato's "modern" Sabaudia was thus followed by "rural" Pontinia, designed by an anonymous draughtsman with Frezotti as consultant. The goal that Mussolini had expressed after Sabaudia's inauguration was now being put into practice. At the time, not satisfied with the architecture by Piccinato and his partners – the same architecture, lest we forget, whose praises he had sung in public – he had thought he could do without architects. His words to Cencelli reportedly were: "Enough with this rational, monotonous architecture. Next time, you and I will do the designing, with a draughtsman at our disposal following our orders."[13] Furthermore, he ordered the Opera Nazionale Combattenti not to initiate any competitions.[14]

Mussolini gave the green light to projects by Canino and Ferdinando Chiaromonte for the Questura (Central Police Headquarters) and the Palazzo della Provincia in Naples.[15] Following his visit to the "zona Dantesque" of Ravenna, the dictator ordered that the works be halted, disappointed by the modest results of the restoration; and yet, three years earlier he had authorized the regeneration of that same area.[16] Mussolini rejected the three projects that were awarded prizes by the jury for the competition for the town hall in Corridonia, and for a monument to Filippo Corridoni. Though the commission's decision had been described as "irrevocable" when the competition was first announced, after Mussolini actually saw the plans put forward he told the mother of the trade unionist who had lost his life on the Carso that her son was worthy of "something greater and more beautiful."[17] Mussolini was regularly updated on the situation of the RAS hotel in Forlì, and ordered that the building not be taller than the adjacent church of San Mercuriale. He also met with Fuzzi in regard to the idea of building the Casa del Fascio on the same site, and he personally tasked Giovannoni with the redevelopment of the adjacent area.[18] Mussolini favourably reviewed the plan for the isolation of the Arch of Augustus in Rimini, and for the regeneration of the square. He wanted the project to be completed by the end of the year, in time for the celebration of the second millennial. Having assumed the guise of a new Emperor Augustus, he wanted to instil in the people the idea of Rome's immortality and, by virtue of that, renew the values of discipline and obedience to orders.[19]

2 The Man with the Diktats

Mussolini's word was rarely questioned during the meetings. De Felice wrote that he grew "annoyed and impatient with those who criticized him, or did not share his judgment or his decisions and wanted to discuss them."[20] Generally speaking, Mussolini would listen to an architect's presentation, abruptly interrupt him with some questions, imply that he knew all about what was behind the plan, and encourage him when the work was to his liking.

In early 1937, Mussolini assessed the outcome of the competition for the Palazzo del Governo in Livorno and approved the winning project by Alberto Legnani and Armando Sabatini (figure 41). For

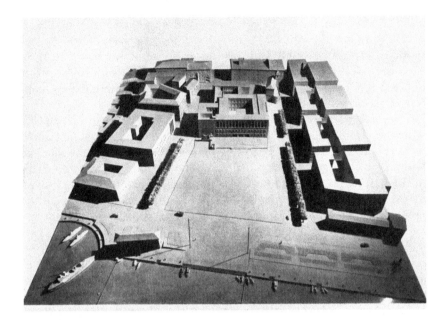

41. Alberto Legnani and Armando Sabatini, project for the Palazzo del Governo in Livorno, model, 1939. The drawings were submitted to Mussolini.

the same city, he also examined the project for the new square, which had been designed to be in harmony with the new building. To solve a problem with the area's urban layout, Piacentini's services were requested.[21] This led to Mussolini's approval of projects by "some young fascist architects" for the exhibition design of the Mostra Augustea della Romanità, through which he wanted to celebrate the unifying nature of the Roman world and the "infallible destiny" that led from Augustus to fascism.[22] A few months later, he met with Giulio Quirino Giglioli about Scalpelli's project for the Exhibition façade. A suggestion by Paniconi, who had given up on complete concealment and used fasces and trophies placed directly on the pre-existing façade, met with little success.[23]

Mussolini looked at Mazzoni's plan for the Termini Station in Rome, which will be analysed further on in this chapter.[24] He welcomed Ministers Alfieri and Cobolli Gigli to discuss the outcome of the competition for the tourism, customs, and legislative buildings on the Alpine ridges, which had seen entries by some fifty candidates.[25] The dictator ratified Minnucci's plan for the Palazzo degli Uffici for the Universal Exposition, which preceded the E42 buildings by a few months. Designed under

Piacentini's guidance, the palace represented a transitional phase – as yet unknown were the stylistic guidelines that would prevail during the exposition. All the same it conveyed a clear message. Indeed, it was modelled after the Città Universitaria, almost as if to give notice to the architects who needed to come to terms with the buildings of the E42 that this was to be their starting point.[26]

When Mussolini was asked to choose a site for the Ministry of Italian Africa – Villa Balestra at Valle Giulia and the Colosseum square were among the options – he decided on the entrance to what is currently Viale Aventino – a decision that was influenced more by a desire to get started as soon as possible than by solid urban planning standards.[27] Mussolini authorized Clemente Busiri Vici's project for the Casa degli Italiani all'Estero (Home for Italians Abroad), a building that served as a hotel capable of holding 500 guests in Piazzale Ostiense in Rome.[28] The dictator then met with Giacomo Paolucci di Calboli, president of the LUCE Institute, so that he could hear all the details concerning the project that had won the competition for the new headquarters, also designed by Clemente Busiri Vici.[29] That same day, Mussolini also met with Vincenzo Tecchio, commissioner for the Mostra delle Terre Italiane d'Oltremare (Exhibition of Italian Lands beyond the Sea), who showed him the general project for the exhibition in Naples.[30] Lastly, Mussolini looked at some drawings by Concezio Petrucci and his associates for Pomezia.[31]

In the spring of 1938, Rome prepared to welcome Hitler. Well in advance of his arrival, a committee chaired by Galeazzo Ciano started organizing the itinerary. They planned a triumphal route through the ruins of imperial Rome and the new streets built by the regime. They had the city adorned with banners, tripods, candelabra, pillars topped with eagles, and light fountains, and Nazi flags waving on flagpoles. They asked Narducci to temporarily set up the Ostiense Station and to embellish the Termini Station. De Renzi designed the decor for Campo di Centocelle, while Moretti designed that for the Olympic Stadium and the Foro Mussolini. The head of government afforded great importance to these designs. He examined them over and over again, choosing from various options and suggesting changes.[32] Quinto Navarra recalled, "Mussolini personally oversaw every detail and, for many days, did nothing but give orders and suggest that one ministry or another should speed up the preparations."[33] The previous year, the German dictator had gone to Munich to personally oversee the preparations for Mussolini's visit; the Duce was not to be outdone. As further proof of the Italian dictator's manic, often comic, attention to detail, for Hitler's train ride from Rome to Naples, cows had been put out to graze in the most beautiful meadows for the purpose of achieving a more picturesque result.[34] The spectacle implemented in the capital impressed Goebbels as well, who jotted in his diary, "A wonderful scene ... ancient Rome puts on a marvellous performance ... this city, this atmosphere! It's like living inside a fairy tale."[35] The ephemeral rearrangements bestowed a phantasmagorical appearance on the city, creating a "miraculous journey backwards through the ages," combining the images of the past with those of the present.[36] At the same time, they foreshadowed future spaces, ones that would be more uniform from an architectural standpoint, and would meet the needs of totalitarian politics. Mussolini's architectural policy for Rome would proceed in this direction.

In June 1938, the dictator gave the green light to Battigelli and Spangaro's design for the Casa del Fascio in Trieste.[37] A month later, he approved the "Roman" project by Fagnoni and Nordio for the new university in the same city, which, as we saw previously, would be the destination of his next trip.[38] Mussolini approved the drawings by Pascoletti and by Samonà for the Ponte d'Africa and the Ponte San Paolo, respectively. Shortly afterwards, he also gave the go-ahead for Cesare Valle and Ignazio Guidi's project for the Ponte della Magliana. The three projects had won their respective competitions and formed part of the plan for the network of roads that was redesigned in view of the Universal Exposition.[39] The dictator welcomed the project by the Ridolfi team for the Ministry of Italian Africa, and a few days later he approved the drawings by De Renzi, Guerrini, Paniconi, and Pediconi for the Mostra Autarchica del Minerale Italiano (Autarchic Exhibition of Italian Minerals) to be held at the Circus Maximus in Rome.[40]

In March, Mussolini travelled to Gardone for the funeral of D'Annunzio. On that sombre occasion, Mussolini approached Maroni, to whom he had directed gestures of affection that were more or less sincere, commissioning him to preserve the memory of the "commander," because of the "brotherhood that you shared, and the loyalty you have always shown me." A few months later, he pored over the architect's design for D'Annunzio's mausoleum.[41] Six years later, in February 1939, he reconsidered the matter of the Venice Railway Station, and examined the model by Angiolo Mazzoni and Virgilio Vallot.[42] He approved Valloni's project for the regeneration of Forlì's historical centre, and Mario Loreti and Cesare Valle's work on INFPS's general headquarters in Rome (figure 42).[43] Lastly, he gave the thumbs up for Pagano's drawings for the "Covo" headquarters on Via Paolo Cannobbio in Milan, which his nephew Vito, president of the School of Fascist Mysticism, had submitted to him in November 1939.[44]

42. Mario Loreti and Cesare Valle, project for the new INFPS headquarters in Rome, 1939.

3 With Pencil in Hand

Along with the myth of Mussolini the aviator, the miner, and the harvester – spread by the regime's propaganda machine – was that of Mussolini the architect. The attribution further enhanced the cult of his personality, imbuing him with superiority and versatility, and with intellectual faculties second to none. And yet, beyond the rhetoric, Mussolini at times did indeed play the part of the architect and did take part in decision-making. But did he have any genuine knowledge of the subject?

Despite his saying things like "I'm an expert on architecture" on more than one occasion, it is clear that he was unable to distinguish good architecture from bad. And yet he was not totally incompetent. His work as a bricklayer in his youth helped him to assess the quality of the construction of a building, and to understand whether a building had been built according to code. It also needs to be said that, over the years, precisely because of the many hours he spent among architects, his examination of countless blueprints, and his regular inspections of building sites, he did get to know many buildings, and thus also became more familiar with the subject of architecture. Moreover, it is likely that he developed his own aesthetic ideas. Paradoxically, Mussolini saw more works than any up-to-date and well-informed professional. Most importantly, however, during those years he came to fully understand that this particular genre could be used as a political tool, that it could play a role in the invention of the "new Italian." Mussolini directly intervened in specific architectural issues on countless occasions, asking for drawings that had been submitted to him to be modified, actually more than can be imagined, as can be seen in the following examples.

In 1924, Mussolini hosted an exhibition organized by Palanti in the library at Palazzo Chigi, which was still the seat of the head of the government. On display was a plan for a colossal Mole Littoria – shaped like a skyscraper, 250 metres across and 330 metres tall – to be built in the city of Rome. Two years later, when the same project was put forward once more with some changes, "based on Mussolini's personal suggestions," gone were the references that most clearly alluded to modernity. The building was now a large, chunky tower "just" 130 metres tall.[45] Despite Palanti's attempt to discuss funding, it is hard to believe that at that time Mussolini would ever have considered building such a colossal work, one capable of competing with Saint Peter's. Mussolini had other aims in mind. By identifying this gargantuan, multipurpose building with fascism – the first version was meant to host diplomatic offices, thermal baths, a Mussolinian Augusteum, and a church – he aimed to disseminate in the collective imaginary the idea of the founding of an extraordinary political regime, one that did not fear comparisons with the past. The larger the temple, the more it had to offer to the worshippers. In people's minds, the Mole Littoria became the visual representation of the coming of a new mythical age in Italian history.

In March 1926, Piacentini was hired to design the Arco della Vittoria in Bolzano. It seems that in this case Mussolini personally drew a sketch of the arch and arranged some of the monument's parts together with the architect.[46] According to Mario Lupano, Piacentini had to convince the dictator that it would not be a good idea to crown the arch with a cannon pointing towards Austria.[47] The architect made a quick sketch of Mussolini's aggressive proposal in his notebook. That same year, Muzio and Ponti were working on the Monumento ai Caduti in Milan, and Mussolini, who had contributed to choosing the monument's style, had a look at the plan.[48] Ponti wrote to Ojetti that the Duce had "said that the project moved him and that he appreciated the Italian consciousness of architecture." He also pointed out, however, that "there were too many symbols of the Pietà on what was supposed to be a building representing victory." The fascistization of the cult of fallen soldiers sought to extol heroism and sacrifice, and thus minimize traditional religious sentiment; the aim was to develop the myth of war and to stay silent as concerned human tragedy. Mussolini wanted the design to be modified so that images of victory prevailed over ones of compassion.[49] Once again in Milan, Mussolini became Mezzanotte's "unexpected collaborator" for the design of the Casa del Fascio. Only a small, narrow area was available for the several rooms and large conference hall that had been planned.

43. Alessandro Limongelli, project for the Memoriale ai Caduti (War Memorial) on Monte Grappa, model, 1927. Mussolini rejected the project because it was not to his liking.

Once again, Mussolini's "provident" suggestion came to the rescue: "If the reception hall is narrow, enlarge it with galleries along the sides."[50]

Alessandro Limongelli's plan for a Monumento ai Caduti in the Monte Grappa cemetery (figure 43) was not so fortunate. The underground ossuary, surmounted by a colossal lighthouse tower topped with a bronze dome and featuring a circular base measuring 60 metres in diameter, met with rejection simply because Mussolini did not like it, and for no other reason. The dictator's personal secretary wrote to the architect that he had "submitted the pictures of the project for the monumental cemetery on Monte Grappa to His Excellency and Head of Government, but, in confidence, I must inform you that the project was not to His Excellency's liking."[51] For the same site, Mussolini instead approved the alternative plan presented by Greppi and Castiglioni, which General Ugo Cei, the special commissioner for the reorganization of war cemeteries, submitted to him in September 1933.[52] Mussolini also had a say in the Colonia Marina (Children's Seaside Resort) in Cattolica, designed by Clemente Busiri Vici, reminiscent of a fleet of ships about to set sail (figure 44). After examining the drawings, the dictator told the architect to "double the access stairways." He even went beyond what he referred to as "observations" for the project, demanding that "the sea be more visible." He later changed his mind, however, and crossed out this last

44. Clemente Busiri Vici, "Le Navi" sun therapy colony in Cattolica, 1933–4. Mussolini asked the architect to "double the access stairways" to the "ships."

request in pencil.[53] In June 1934, Mussolini went to Cattolica to inaugurate the "flagship" and the four pavilions that resembled submarines. The choreography called for his taking a motorboat to get there and being welcomed ashore by the architect. After a scrupulous inspection inside, and after climbing to the roof of the "ships" in order to have a view of the whole, he judged this beautiful complex, whose design to some degree had been shaped by him, to be "stunning and perfect."[54]

Mussolini personally oversaw the various phases in the plan for the Exhibition of the Fascist Revolution. He met with the architects and visited the building site. It is likely he examined an early project by Del Debbio that had been presented to him by Alfieri.[55] In the end, Libera and De Renzi's project was chosen instead. Mussolini then intervened in Valente and Libera's final design of the Sacrario dei Martiri Fascisti (Shrine of the Fascist Martyrs). Mussolini decided that the original idea of placing a sculptural group in the middle of the crypt, with a naked figure holding the fasces and a fallen soldier at her feet, should be replaced by a "warrior cross" (figure 45). The image of the cross brought together the Catholic and fascist religions in an inspirational, Christological rhetoric of sacrifice intended for the masses, one that would tighten fascism's grip on the lower classes.[56]

Mussolini's visits to building sites were also meant to demonstrate his genius, as one capable of immediately solving an architect's most controversial and difficult problems. One such visit occurred at the post office on Via Taranto, designed by Samonà. Having been asked to choose

45. Adalberto Libera and Antonio Valente, Sacrario dei Martiri (Fascist Martyrs Memorial) at the Exhibition of the Fascist Revolution in Rome, 1932. Mussolini decided to replace the group of statues that were supposed to be located at the centre of the memorial with the "warrior cross."

between two options for the public entrance to the hall, Mussolini freed the architect from his dilemma, and chose the one referred to as the "podium," in which the flight of stairs was parallel to the façade.[57] The scene had very likely been carefully planned. However, another episode that took place during those same months failed to display Mussolini's alleged brilliance. The dictator had inspected and approved the project for Sabaudia designed by the Piccinato team. Later, while visiting the building site, Mussolini discovered that the height of the tower under construction for the Palazzo del Comune (Town Hall) was taller than the one in Littoria, a town that was destined to become the capital of the province. Out of respect for the administrative hierarchy, the only logical thing to do was to have the tower lowered from 42 to 32 metres in height. This decision puzzled the architects, because the height of the tower had already been discussed at length with the dictator during previous meetings. Piccinato and his colleagues sent Mussolini a note explaining their point of view. They felt that lowering the height was an "obvious mistake," and that the resulting structure would be "awkward and disproportionate." The dictator returned to the building site once more and, presumably aware that his idea was in fact unreasonable, decided to leave the original project unchanged.[58]

Not enough has been written about Mussolini's intervention in the competition for the Palazzo del Littorio on Via dell'Impero in Rome and its influence on Italian architecture. In this case, it is important to follow exactly what happened step by step. On 10 September 1934, the examining committee – chaired by Starace, but dominated by Piacentini due to his experience – rejected 28 projects. The public was able to view the remaining 79 from 23 September to 31 October. Meanwhile, the examining committee met again, on 16 and 18 October. During the discussions, Piacentini clashed with Bazzani, who was bent on rejecting not just the worst projects, but the ones that were judged to be "far too modern" as well. In the meeting that followed, Piacentini defended the efforts of Terragni, Ridolfi, and Moretti from Bazzani's attacks, claiming that their projects proved they knew how to reconcile stylistic needs with functional ones.[59]

In the first session, the committee selected 25 projects, then it divided them into three groups in the second session, indicating a range of preferences.[60] The first group included the Foschini, Vaccaro, and De Renzi team; the second included the Ridolfi, Terragni, del Giudice, Samonà, Rapisardi, Fasolo, Frezzotti, Libera, and Palanti teams; and the third one included Moretti and Torres. Giovanni Marinelli, the administrative secretary of the PNF, sent this classification to Mussolini, alongside a series of critical reviews.[61] On 12 November, Mussolini and Starace visited the Palazzo degli Esami to look at the projects on display.[62] On 29 December, the dictator directly summoned Piacentini's examining committee to Palazzo Venezia and chaired the final session. The solution to an architectural problem that was also "a historical landmark" – a building symbolizing fascism that was to be placed in the Imperial Forum – absolutely had to bear his seal, and could not simply be delegated to a jury. Marinelli made this quite clear: "the project will ultimately be chosen by the Duce."[63] When the meeting was about to end, a list was drawn up of the fourteen projects selected for the second-level competition.[64] Not only was the initial division into three groups, as suggested by the examining committee, partly subverted, but Mussolini chose only nine of the projects. He confirmed Vaccaro, De Renzi, and Foschini's team, but with one important detail: he clearly indicated his preference not just by putting the team at the top of the list, but also by drawing a line to separate it from the others (figure 46).

46.   Enrico Del Debbio, Arnaldo Foschini, and Vittorio Morpurgo, project
A from the first-level competition for the Palazzo del Littorio in Rome.
Solution A, model, 1934. Mussolini expressed a preference for this
design.

The dictator had chosen a project that was not modern. And yet,
a few months earlier, during an argument that arose in connection
with Palazzo del Littorio, he had expressed his support for modern
architecture. And it is worth remembering that, in the end, Foschini
would be the one to build the work. Mussolini then approved the
projects that had been entered by Torres, Rapisardi, Moretti, Palanti,
Ridolfi, and Frezzotti. He expressed his appreciation for Torres's ornamental composition over Moretti's clean-cut structure, just as he
preferred the symbolism of Palanti's building in the shape of a ship
over Ridolfi's huge curved wall perforated by rows of windows (figure
47). The other five projects were simply ones that were "added by
the committee to the ones chosen by the Duce." Among them were
works by Libera and Terragni, which Mussolini felt were unworthy of
construction but which Piacentini acknowledged to be of value (figure
48).[65] Piacentini asked that Margherita Sarfatti get involved, that she
"deal with the problem." But Mussolini's former lover, described by
Ojetti as the "arbiter" of Italian art, no longer held much sway over
the dictator.[66]
    Just six months before, Mussolini had announced to all of Italy that
he was a defender of the young generation of modern architects; now,
instead, he was showing his preference for Foschini's design, excluding
the two projects by Terragni and Libera, which were the most modern

47. Mario Palanti, project for the first-level competition for the Palazzo del Littorio in Rome, perspective drawing, 1934. Mussolini promoted Palanti's "ship" to the second-level competition.

48. Antonio Carminati, Pietro Lingeri, Ernesto Saliva, Giuseppe Terragni, Luigi Vietti with Marcello Nizzoli and Mario Sironi, project for the first-level competition for the Palazzo del Littorio in Rome. Solution A, model, 1934. Emerging from the opening in the curve wall was the podium where Mussolini appeared before the crowd. In the project report the dictator was described as a deity: "He is like a god, up against the sky, and there is no one above him."

designs as well as the best. Mussolini preferred the design of the older man, Foschini, an academic suspected of freemasonry, to that of a pair of brilliant young men who were unquestionably loyal fascists, and who had been raised in the myth of the Duce. Clearly, if there were still the need to underline it, architecture for the dictator was not a question of taste; whether or not the architects shared his own ideological creed was not important. Architecture was a political instrument that could be used to sway the masses, and it was for this reason that he was determined to exert his influence on architectural decisions.

4 Advising the Architects

In 1933, Mussolini surveyed Arata's drawings for the PNF Stadium. The dictator had personally tasked him with the project for a huge stadium in Rome with a seating capacity of 150,000. A first draft of the design had already been modified according to his "orders." He now approved the third version, specifically requesting that "travertine be used to clad all the external façades."[67] But nothing would come of this project either.

The Agro Pontino, where the land reclamation project had been most successful, was widely publicized by the regime. Littoria, the capital of the province, drew a particularly large number of tourists, including foreigners, who were attracted to the "amazing" change that fascism had brought to those marshlands. Mazzoni had built the post office there, one of his most successful works. The architect had added elegant, semi-cylindrical antimalarial nets to the windows, which were much appreciated by Filippo Tommaso Marinetti because of the Futuristic look they gave to the building. Mussolini did not like them at all, however, and they had to be destroyed. But that was not a question of aesthetics. More practically speaking, they openly contradicted the regime's message, which had triumphantly announced that "the bane of malaria" had been been defeated once and for all in the Agro Pontino.[68]

Mussolini also played a major role in the Redipuglia ossuary. He urged the abandonment of the old cemetery, which he had inaugurated in 1923; it was a distinctively sombre and evocative site marked by epitaphs and mementoes of war. Mussolini confided in Cei, the commissary, that he had never really liked the old cemetery because it reminded him of "a huge scrap metal deposit."[69] In no way did it meet the criteria of "greatness, monumentality, and perpetuity" that the regime required for places of worship. However, he needed a more practical, convincing reason to abandon the cemetery. Hence, in December 1935, Mussolini had Cei write up a public statement, drafted according to his orders, stating that the cemetery's hygienic conditions were very poor, and that the dictator had decided to build a new one in twelve months' time. In the meantime, Mussolini looked at photographs of the model for the new ossuary, designed by Greppi and Castiglioni, and gave it the thumbs up (figure 49).[70] The new work would be a resting place for over one hundred thousand fallen soldiers – more than in any other World War I cemetery. The fascist government wanted to be the leader in Europe even when it came to amassing the remains of fallen soldiers.[71] However, unlike the other ossuaries designed by the same two architects, who had a sort of monopoly on military necropolises, this one was different in that it accentuated the principle of architectural harmony, of unity in diversity. Gone, in fact, was the distinctive motif of the arched tomb, as used for the wide steps at Monte Grappa and Caporetto. In its place was a bronze fascia almost one hundred metres long that ran all along the vertical walls of the twenty-two wide steps that made up the ossuary. Inscribed on the fascia were the names of 400,00 fallen soldiers, the only names that were known. Still, the names vanished in the shadow of the much more visible word "Presente" (Here, Sir), which was obsessively repeated eight thousand times, the same word that could be found in fascist memorials, and that was pronounced in the ultimate fascist ritual, the *Appello* (Roll Call).[72] A word that could be found, for instance, in the most famous of the fascist memorials, the Sacrario dei Martiri Fascisti (Shrine of the Fascist Martyrs), designed by Libera and Valente, at the 1932 Exhibition of the Fascist Revolution in Rome. The same icon was now reproduced on the Carso, that is, in the sites where the country had fought a victorious war, whose "son" fascism declared itself to be. Redipuglia, previously the ossuary of the soldiers who had fallen in World War I, was transformed into a gigantic open-air fascist memorial. There, each of the fallen soldiers, with their own personal stories, and their own political beliefs – which couldn't possibly have had anything to do with fascism as the movement hadn't been founded yet – became unified. Now they were forced to repeat a single word, one that at the time was part of the fascist ritual, understood by all because of its pregnant political meaning. That "Presente" made everyone and everything the same. And anything that was not fascist became anti-homeland. Totalitarian integration, which in the second half of the 1930s involved civil society, even managed to swallow up the cult of those who had lost their lives in the Great War, regimenting it into its own prevaricating ideology. In this temple of the secular fascist religion, the regime could express the violence of its doctrine, against the dead as well as against the memory of the living. Here was a national monument capable, through its symbols, of reaching inside the conscience of the "new man" that the regime was forging. Mussolini would be struck by the symbolic and evocative

49. Giovanni Greppi and Giannino Castiglioni, Sacrario di Redipuglia (War Memorial), 1935–8. The large steps featuring bronze plates bore the names of 40,000 fallen soldiers. Carved into the head of each step, a total of 8,000 times, was the word "Presente!" It was the same word used in the fascist rite known as the *Appello* (Roll Call). When he inaugurated the War Memorial on 19 September 1938, Mussolini declared that the monument "will defy the centuries, and perhaps even the millennia."

strength of this monumental "temple of the faith" out in the open, and would visit it once more in July 1942.

Mussolini felt that the area overlooking the Basilica of Maxentius in Rome, an area that had been devastated by the demolition work resulting from the opening of Via dell'Impero, could only be salvaged by an architectural intervention. Upon the initiative of the publisher Valentino Bompiani, the Milan-based BBPR team drafted a plan for the Exhibition of Italian Civilization, an idea that foreshadowed one of the themes of the E42. The proposed building would occupy one floor and cover a surface area of 25,000 square metres, and would be located on the outskirts of the city, "on the Via Appia Nuova or the Via Appia Antica." On 9 April 1936, Mussolini, who from the beginning had known about the project, one in which both Bottai and Alfieri were involved as well, looked at the design, but did not approve of its location. Mussolini believed it would be "beneficial" for the building to rise over Via dell'Impero, in the area "that had been previously chosen for the Casa Littoria." Moreover, instead of the one-storey building proposed by the BBPR, Mussolini wanted a "building with several floors."[73]

Emilio Gentile wrote that the Case del Fascio were places of worship and indoctrination for the fascist religion, and that the party attributed symbolic value to some specific architectural elements, such as towers, objects borrowed from military architecture and which represented control. The national secretary of the Fascist Party ordered that there be one on each Casa del Fascio, "complete with bells ... that will toll for all our celebrations."[74] However, the guidelines in Starace's circular were not always applied, a case in point being the headquarters of the Gruppo Rionale Fascista Mussolini in Milan, designed by Bacciocchi. Mussolini himself, while visiting Milan, asked the architect to add a Torre Littoria to his plan. Once again, as for Piccinato's Palazzo del Comune in Sabaudia, and for Ponti's metal framework in the Triennale park, we see the importance Mussolini attached to the symbolism of this architectural element: the tower was a totemic object, an allegory of power. A process of identity-building grew around it in the community. By using symbols that spread myths capable of acting on the popular imagination, fascism implemented art in the service of government.[75]

The dictator's role in the competition for the Palazzo del Littorio was discussed previously. The decision to change the location – the Porta San Paolo district located near the Ostiense Station instead of Via dell'Impero, deemed too narrow for this type of building – meant that a second-level competition was necessary. Only the architects who had been selected at the end of the first phase were allowed to participate, and the deadline was set for July 1937. When the commission met in late August, the first thing it did was to reject the projects by Terragni, Fasolo, Libera, Palanti, and Samonà. In a later phase it eliminated another six, including the ones by Moretti and Ridolfi, ultimately choosing the project submitted by Foschini. Mussolini carefully supervised this second phase of the competition, just as he had the first. On 4 September, to Giorgio Pini's suggestion that the drawings for the various entries be published in *Il Popolo d'Italia*, Mussolini curtly replied, "No need, the winner has already been selected."[76] More than a month went by when a short article in the dictator's newspaper reported that the competition's results would be announced soon. It also mentioned the fact that the location might change again, and that the building could rise in the Foro Mussolini (figure 50). It wasn't until 23 November that Starace announced that Foschini's team had won. The news was accompanied by a drawing that was not of the winning project for the area of Porta San Paolo, but of a brand new one, for the Foro Mussolini. Meanwhile, Mussolini had had a chance to survey the drawings. In fact, Del Debbio – who had worked on them alongside

50. Enrico Del Debbio, Arnaldo Foschini, and Vittorio Morpurgo, project for the Palazzo del Littorio at the Foro Mussolini in Rome, perspective drawing, 1937. The size of the new building equalled that of the Reggia in Caserta. A total of 720,000 cubic metres in size, it rivalled some of the most grandiose buildings designed by Speer in Berlin.

Foschini and Morpurgo – requested an audience at Palazzo Venezia in order to illustrate "my new project."[77] He was welcomed there that very same day.

In January 1938, at the crucial moment when the winning projects for the competitions for the E42's Palazzo dei Ricevimenti e Congressi and Palazzo della Civiltà Italiana were to be chosen, Mussolini intervened once more. This crucial event will be described in detail later. Concurrently, the sessions of the examining committee for the renewal of Piazza Duomo as well as the creation of the Arengario took place in Milan. Once the competition was under way, the podestà Guido Pesenti presented Mussolini with a a folder containing the various entries and suggested holding a second-level competition limited to the four best projects. According to one report, "He leafed through the album, remarked on a few of the projects, but did not go into detail or make any suggestions. He did, however, approve of repeating the competition with the best applications."[78] Certain formal analogies – such as the orders of overlapping arches – tied Muzio's Arengario to the Palazzo della Civiltà Italiana by the La Padula team.[79] "As in many other Italian cities," wrote the novelist Corrado Alvaro, "this is a moment in time when the capital's architecture is closely monitored. The renewal of the centre of Milan recalls that of Rome."[80] How this unity of style was achieved is analysed later on.

For Mussolini, Forlì was a special city, tied to his place of birth. No sooner had he seized power than he elevated it to capital of the province, and the town was now getting organized for its new administrative role. For the Palazzo del Governo, Bazzani designed a large monumental hall. The architect defended his decision by saying that this particular idea fit with the "Italian tradition" vis-à-vis the palazzo. But Mussolini was not convinced, and he turned down the project with a peremptory "negative, too tall, waste of space."[81] The dictator also criticized the decorations chosen by the architect for the church of Saint Anthony in Predappio.[82] Also in Forlì, he intervened in the Palazzo di Giustizia designed by Leoni. The project that had won the competition had been examined and "personally approved by the Duce," who nonetheless called for some changes (figure 51).[83] The architect then presented the new project, completed "according to your wishes." Later, before moving on to the actual implementation phase, he wanted to again "submit the pictures of the project" to Mussolini's "enlightened judgment" in order to gain "his full approval."[84] Mussolini invited the architect to regularly update him on work on the projects: Leoni sent him pictures of the demolition and of the conditions of the site, as well as data on the number of workers. He showed him marble samples and got Mussolini involved in the choice of cladding.[85] On the morning of 2 September 1940, Leoni welcomed the dictator at the building site.

Even in the events surrounding this competition, issued in July 1937, Mussolini played a less than neutral role. In the commission phase, Domenico De Simone, an executive member of the Ministry of Public Works, allegedly favoured an architect who was a relative of his. In Italy, architectural competitions were far from transparent. Nonetheless, even when Mussolini had been a witness to instances of manifest irregularity in the past, he had never intervened. But here in Forlì he decided to step in. However, his reason for doing so was not redress in the case of a competition where cheating had taken place. He simply did not like the selection that had been made. And so he reconvened the examining committee and had them review the classification. Leoni himself recalled the episode: "Your intervention, Duce, altered the classification. Rumblings inside the ministry. A new meeting with the committee after it had been disbanded. A new resolution."[86]. And this time Leoni won.

51. Francesco Leoni, project for the Palazzo di Giustizia in Forlì, model, 1938. The dictator inspected and approved the project, with some changes.

Mussolini was at the centre of another event related to a competition. In early October 1939, he visited the area of the new headquarters of the Confederazione Fascista dei Commercianti in Rome. The projects that had been entered in the competition were on display at a temporary venue, awaiting the results. Mussolini looked at all the drawings, but paused to examine one in particular, which he praised. The plan was submitted by Vincenzo Monaco, a young Roman architect known to Mussolini because he, together with Amedeo Luccichenti, had designed the luxury home that Claretta Petacci, the dictator's mistress, had had built in Camilluccia that year. The day after the visit, Sebastiani, Mussolini's personal secretary, phoned Giorgio Molfino, president of the Confederazione dei Commercianti, "for an update." Molfino implied, even before the examining committee had had a chance to meet, that Monaco would be the winner. Which is indeed what happened.[87] In 1942, charged with abuse of public office, Molfino was expelled from the Fascist Party.[88]

While the podestà of Genoa may have been corrupt, in this specific case it was Mussolini himself who had asked him to break the law.

As we saw previously, Terragni and Lingeri visited Palazzo Venezia in November 1938 to illustrate the Danteum project that was slated to be built on Via dell'Impero, opposite the Basilica of Maxentius. This meeting was followed by another, without the architects this time, but with the two promoters of the project, Poss and Valdameri, as well as Cini. The fact that the commissary of the E42 was there had to do with the important decision to include the Danteum in the budget for the Universal Exposition. It is likely that on that occasion Mussolini intervened in order to make a few changes to the project. Valdameri referred to these requests, whose contents are unknown, in a letter to Terragni: "I need to ask you to work on the solution for the new façade according to the Duce's suggestions. The Duce is awaiting the project, which would be good for you to present in the meeting that we plan to have with him. Please let me know when you think you will have everything ready so that I can request a meeting. The matter is urgent, for as you know, everything must be ready for the E42."[89] It is common knowledge that Terragni, who was doing his military service, and was at loggerheads with Lingeri, would not collaborate.

5 Zigzagging Forward

Though Mussolini was a constant presence in architectural matters, not all his interventions were relevant. For instance, his meddling in the competition for the Palazzo del Littorio was much more significant than the changes he called for in the drawings for the Colonia Marina (Children's Seaside Resort) in Cattolica. Up to this point, it is difficult to perceive a clear preference in style on the part of the dictator. Though he personally monitored the matter of "style," he did not take a clear stand. Before the modernists and the traditionalists he assumed an instrumental attitude, mediated opposing positions, and backed whatever was politically convenient in that context. As soon as he settled in Palazzo Chigi, according to De Begnac, he was no longer in favour of monumentalism. The Galleria Colonna, inaugurated in 1922 and located on the square of the same name in Rome, "had not stirred his enthusiasm." "The marble, the faux marble, the capitals without a purpose, and the corbels with no objects on them to describe that encyclopaedia of bad taste rather inspired his harsh words as concerned contemporary architecture."[90] However, almost at the same time, Mussolini did give credit to the most monumental of traditionalist architects, naming Brasini "the architect of imperial Italy," and commissioning him to draft a plan for the Monumento Nazionale alla Vittoria (National Monument to Victory), to be built on the hill of Gorizia Castle.[91] Then, not only did Mussolini approve Brasini's project for the building of a huge classical forum in the heart of Rome, but he saw it as abiding by the guidelines for the Rome of the future as well.[92] Further, he supported the nominations of Brasini and Bazzani, also a traditionalist, to the Accademia d'Italia, praising the former's propensity for the monumental, and the latter's inclination towards "the scenic."[93] He also offered support to the Scuola Superiore di Architettura in Rome, an essential institution at the heart of the educational system, which, under Giovannoni's direction, educated its students to seek an Italian style that formally acknowledged the architecture of the past. Mussolini's other advisers included Ojetti, a traditionalist critic.

At the same time, Mussolini also intervened in favour of modern architecture. He did so in 1931, on the occasion of the 2nd Exhibition of Rational Architecture held on Via Veneto in Rome, in the art gallery that was run by Bardi and, not a minor detail, one that he personally funded with one hundred thousand lire to promote cultural events involving "modern Italian artists."[94] On the morning of 30 March, just a few hours before the opening, Mussolini visited the exhibition, poring over all the drawings. He lingered over a large photographic collage entitled *Il Tavolo degli Orrori* (The Chart of Eyesores) that had been mounted by Bardi. Among the "eyesores" that the critic described to him was Piacentini's INA Tower in Piazza della Vittoria in Brescia, which he would solemnly inaugurate soon afterwards, and the Italian Pavilion for the 1925 Paris Expo, designed by Brasini, whom Margherita Sarfatti had recommended to him for the project and whom he had personally chosen (figure 52). Before leaving the gallery, Bardi handed him the *Rapporto sull'architettura (per Mussolini)*, and Mussolini also spent time with a group of young architects, discussing "the problems of modern architecture andfascist expectations."[95]

Following that visit, which seemed to portend positive future developments, Libera and the other Rationalists who had been there deluded themselves into believing they had won: "As he was leaving, Mussolini clearly expressed his satisfaction, admiration, and enthusiasm for the MIAR [Italian Movement for Rational Architecture]."[96] However, the dictator was not unequivocally on their side, and those words of appreciation did not express an architectural belief but rather a political calculation, his support for a movement that attracted young architects. It was no accident that shortly afterwards Mussolini approved Bazzini's project for a post office in Forlì, and Muzio's for the Palazzo dell'Arte in Milan, both of which had little to do with the Rationalist creed. He also

52. Mussolini visiting the 2nd Exposition of Rationalist Architecture on Via Veneto in Rome, 30 March 1931. To his right, Gaetano Minnucci and Pier Maria Bardi. Seen from the back is Adalberto Libera.

turned down a meeting with the Roman Rationalist architects headed by Minnucci, who, through Margherita Sarfatti, sent him a memoradum denouncing the Architects Union for its retaliation against modern architects.[97] A few months later, however, Mussolini reiterated his support for the Rationalist group, authorizing the follow-up to the Exposition of Rationalist Architecture that was held in Florence in 1932.[98] And he took their side once more at the Exhibition of the Fascist Revolution in 1932, explicitly asking architects and artists to design an exhibition that would be "of today, hence, extremely modern, and bold, with no melancholy references to the decorative styles of the past."[99] Mussolini profoundly disliked overly ornamental architecture, and before an ornate work by Brasini, he exclaimed, "It is easier to be ancient than authentically modern. It's terrible! When you think that for over fifty years, a hundred, two hundred, three hundred artists have thrived on such a small and very old idea and that they even squabble over it!"[100]

The episode surrounding the completion of the Loggia del Capitanio in Vicenza offers further proof that Mussolini proceeded in a contradictory way in his architectural choices. In 1926, the city's podestà decided on the completion of the building designed by Palladio. Fagiuoli was commissioned to do the job, and he completed the design by adding two supporting arches to the three that already existed. The project was endorsed by Piacentini and Giovannoni. However, the application was blocked owing to some objections. Among them were those of Ojetti and Margherita Sarfatti, who both criticized the tampering with the monument. In June 1928, the podestà Antonio Franceschini turned to Mussolini for the final say on the matter. The dictator approved the addition of the two arches; the following day the headlines read, "Thanks to the Duce the Loggia del Capitanio will be completed." However, a few days later, D'Annunzio wrote to Mussolini to say that he was absolutely against the completion of the project. At that point, Mussolini, who did not want to argue with the poet, backed down and warned Franceschini that "D'Annunzio says the idea of completing the Loggia del Capitanio is a dreadful one"; in other words, the idea that Mussolini himself had approved was "dreadful." He excused himself with D'Annunzio by blaming Franceschini: "Whenever you hear what he has to say you assume he's right, and that's what I did."

In this story, Mussolini moved independently of his advisers. He did not listen to Margherita Sarfatti, whose influence on architectural matters was perhaps not as crucial as is often thought. In truth, their relationship grew more tense over the following year. Mussolini energetically disapproved of his former lover's "ruse" of using other people as an alibi, of trying to make people believe that the positions of "your 900" are those of fascism, of mixing "my name as a politician" with "your artistic or would-be artistic inventions."[101] Mussolini did not heed Ojetti, either, who, in the meantime, had also been demoted from his post as director of the *Corriere della Sera*. Instead, he accepted Giovannoni's and Piacentini's ideas. But perhaps it is safest to say that he overruled the opinions of the experts and trusted his own insights. Then, however, he ran into D'Annunzio, his former political rival, who had opposed his leadership and whom he still feared. Mussolini wanted at all costs to avoid a clash with the poet, which would no doubt generate a lot of publicity. In a bout of realpolitik, he preferred to risk coming across badly, but at least settling the whole affair, and then privately admitting his inferiority to the poet. He gave the "vate" (poet) the role of "supreme arbiter" of the Vicenza affair, adding that his opinion on artistic matters could "always be reversed."[102]

A minor incident that took place eight years later proves that Mussolini did not easily forget the *volte-face* D'Annunzio had forced him to make. In May 1936, a new plan for the building drafted by Rossato was introduced; it left the loggia as it was, and included a new building set back in relation to it (eventually completed). When Mussolini inspected the airfield in Vicenza in July 1937, he asked to be taken to Piazza dei Signori for an unexpected visit to view Rossato's intervention.[103] Now, the diatribe with the poet would have a different ending. Mussolini's prestige had grown even in the eyes of D'Annunzio, who no longer considered him a social climber, but a "Dear and Great companion, who is ever greater."[104]

Mussolini's erratic behaviour also confused his collaborators, as Alfredo Rocco privately expressed to Ojetti. The former Minister of Justice, and now Rector of the University of Rome, was very close to Mussolini, and also followed him as concerned the developments in the Città Universitaria. Rocco said that "Mussolini was changing his mind on Rationalist architecture." He believed that the change was also "the effect of Hitler's condemnation of this type of architecture: he does not want Italy to take in what Hitler doesn't want." Ojetti was sceptical about giving Mussolini's words too much importance, wondering whether he would change his mind once more; but Rocco replied that "Mussolini always moves forward, but not in a straight line. He zigzags forward, giving opposite sides the impression, alternately, that he is getting closer to them; but he is actually following his own path instead."[105] Come 1934, Mussolini's path as concerned architecture remained unclear.

6 "I'm an Expert on Architecture"

Mussolini's attitude towards the architects who were designing the Florence Railway Station and Sabaudia was a clear indication of the zigzagging that Rocco had aptly described (figures 53–4). On 26 May a debate was held in the Italian Parliament concerning the possible conversion into law of the decree declaring that the work to build Palazzo del Littorio on Via dell'Impero in Rome was in the public interest. The discussion took on harsh and polemical tones. Alberto Calza Bini stated that the palazzo had to be worthy of "the greatness and power" that fascism had impressed upon the country, and that it had to serve as a "continuation of the tradition of Rome." His reassurance that Italian architects were "mature enough" to "create a work worthy of our age" was not taken into consideration, however, and was actually interpreted as an opening to modern architecture. Most of the interlocutors were openly hostile to this tendency. There were some who voiced their opposition to the Florence Railway Station on Via dell'Impero, saying that

53. Giovanni Michelucci, Nello Baroni, Pier Niccolò Bernardi, Italo Gamberini, Sarre Guarnieri, and Leonardo Lusanna, Florence Station, 1932–5. When Mussolini encountered the architects who designed both Florence Station and Sabaudia, he declared that "Florence Station is beautiful, and the Italian people will like it."

the new building must not to be "one of the aberrations referred to as Novecento style."[106]

A transcript of Mussolini's speech to the architects during the meeting has survived. The dictator used very explicit terms. He informed them that he had summoned them there so they would have no doubts about his thinking, his position in favour of modern architecture after what had happened in Parliament: "I want it to be clear that I am in favour of modern architecture ... I would be immensely unhappy if you thought that I didn't appreciate your works." He referred to the discussion in Parliament in order to side with them: "You need not fear being stoned, or seeing your station torn down by a furious mob ... the Florence Station is stunning, and the Italians will be pleased with it!" Then, moving to the matter of the criticism of Sabaudia, he added: "If there are some who say they've had enough, then I'm telling you it is I who have had enough! Sabaudia suits me just fine!" Lastly, Mussolini dismissed them

54.   Gino Cancellotti, Eugenio Montuori, Luigi Piccinato, and Alfredo
Scalpelli, Sabaudia, 1933–4. Against those who were critical of Sabaudia,
Mussolini claimed that, "If there are some who say they've had enough, then
I'm telling you it is I who have had enough! Sabaudia suits me just fine!"

with a promise: "I will order all the institutions, all the ministries, of air,
of public works, of communications, of national education, and all the
offices, to erect buildings of our day and age."[107]

It is worth mentioning that the transcript of that meeting was not
published. Mussolini's sharp words were not to be made public. The
press release by the Agenzia Stefani, published the following day in the
newspapers, was much more neutral. In it the dictator did not appear to
openly embrace modern architecture, as is instead clear from the transcript. The public report simply informed its readers that Mussolini had
met with the architects, that he had lauded them for their work, and that
his praise for them was to be extended to "all the young people who seek,
in architecture and other fields, to produce a form of art that fulfils the
sensibility and needs of our fascist century." In this case as well, Mussolini's behaviour was that of a clever politician, and not of someone who

had sincere feelings about the arts. Furthermore, he deceived those who, like Pagano, envisioned him as the "saviour" of modern architecture.[108]

Several days after the meeting, Mussolini was in Venice, where he met Hitler for the first time. Both men, albeit at different times, visited the Venice Biennale. Hitler, Ojetti noted, had his own personal taste. He lingered before Mauro Vagaggini's *Barca*, which the president of the exhibition, Giuseppe Volpi di Misurata, immediately gave him as a gift. Mussolini, instead, appreciated "the large, expressive statue of a peasant woman" in the Russian Pavilion, and several paintings on the theme of sports and propaganda. He spent very little time in the German Pavilion, "grimacing" while there. He overlooked the British one entirely, and, lastly, he admired a work by Manet in the French Pavilion. In the Italian Pavilion, he expressed his liking for the Futurists, and he quickly moved through the rooms devoted to nineteenth-century self-portraits. He confessed to Antonio Maraini and Giuseppe Volpi di Misurata, who accompanied him, that he was not an expert on painting. "To be able to understand painting you need to make comparisons. I'm an expert on architecture. I like architecture."[109] Mussolini's preference for architecture was also confirmed in another event, a minor one, reported by Margherita Sarfatti. While visiting the Vatican Museums, Mussolini wore a "look of disgust" before the tapestries by Raphael and Pieter van Aelst, but was instead charmed by the grandeur of the palazzi themselves. "These rooms, how vast they are, how skilled they were at building!"[110]

Mussolini was more at ease with architecture than with other art forms. To his mind, architecture was an instrument of power that he knew how to use, as he had been doing over the years, taking care not to impose a specific style. But then other developments, foremost the Ethiopian War and Italy's imperialist expansionism, an impending and decisive confrontation between emerging nations, the little time that was left to forge fascism's "new man," and the totalitarian acceleration that accompanied the accomplishment of this aim, drove him, without waiving his prerogative to prevaricate, to more clearly express his preferences. When Ojetti travelled with him to Libya in March 1937, Mussolini was coming around to these new beliefs. He was thinking about making architecture more effective in its support of his policies. The art critic was a member of the dictator's entourage, and on their way back from a visit to the ruins of Leptis Magna, he asked him if "the sight of the basilica had converted him to a love of columns." To which Mussolini drily replied, "Who says I don't like columns? I love columns."[111] Soon afterwards, he repeated the same words to Starace. He probably wanted this particular point of view to be known to the secretary of the Fascist Party as well. Evidently, the thought had a much deeper meaning than that of a merely informal exchange with the art critic.

Mussolini had known Ojetti for a long time. He admired him and knew he was a "fervent fascist," and was grateful to him for his role as a go-between with D'Annunzio whenever there were misunderstandings between the political leader and the poet. Mussolini admired Ojetti's journalistic prose and personally asked that he be present at the Accademia d'Italia to act as a mediator between Piacentini, Bazzani, and Brasini.[112] Nonetheless, during the first half of the 1930s, Mussolini supported certain architectural positions that Ojetti did not. Now that the empire had been founded, in Mussolini's eyes the profile of the critic became more important; he even seemed to have taken the place of Margherita Sarfatti in providing ideological support to the cult of *romanità*. Ojetti's well-known stance in favour of Roman architecture was increasingly informing Mussolini's plans. This convergence of visions led the critic to change his strategy, to forgo the themes that were dearest to him, such as the safeguarding of historical and architectural heritage, as long as it meant that Mussolini backed him on the matter of the new architectural style. In the past, on many occasions Ojetti had disagreed with the Duce on the issue of monuments, and had clearly said so. This had happened, as mentioned earlier, with regard to the completion of the Loggia del Capitanio in Vicenza, and the demolition of the Spanish Bastions in Milan. Ojetti had also fiercely criticized the theory of making space around Rome's ancient monuments, which Mussolini had promoted in a famous speech he delivered in 1925: "I must confess that this urge to see all of Rome from a single point of view, to reduce Old Rome to a desert dotted with monuments ... seems to be a contagious folly."[113] But now, in 1937, things were changing, advancing along the path that he had predicted for some time. And so, after initially being against it, Ojetti now praised the work of Piacentini and his patron for Via della Conciliazione. Mussolini's support for his theory of arches and columns was well worth his silence on the destruction of the Borghi.

Between 1936 and 1937, Mussolini's zigzagging seemed to ebb, and he apparently embarked on a clearer direction. Further to his visit to the spectacle of the ruins of Leptis Magna, as plans got under way on the E42 in January 1937, another trip left a lasting mark on the dictator's views on architecture. As was previously mentioned, in September 1937 Mussolini travelled to Germany to see Hitler. He and and the Führer went to Munich to see the Brown House, the Haus der Kunst – "a wonder of the new architecture" according to Hitler – and the Memorial to the Fallen Nazis, all works by Paul Ludwig Troost, Hitler's favourite classicist architect. Troost, "the man who revolutionized the art of building," had died in 1934 and been replaced by Speer. Mussolini told his host that he was "enthusiastic about the new German architecture."[114] The following day in Berlin, while crossing the city and also in the evening at the Reich Chancellery, Hitler told Mussolini about his plans to radically transform the capital of the Third Reich.[115] While in Munich, Mussolini also had the chance to exchange a few words with Speer, whose work he must have been acquainted with, having seen the photographs of the German Pavilion in Paris, the Zeppelinfeld, and the model of the massive stadium in Nuremberg.[116]

Like Mussolini, Hitler believed that war and architecture served to "totally nationalize the masses."[117] Truth be told, Hitler assigned architecture a much greater political function than Mussolini had so far. Just a few days earlier, while in Nuremberg to lay the first stone of the gigantic stadium, among other things, he specifically mentioned the topic at the annual assembly of the Nazi Party. The German dictator declared that the great Nazi buildings, "gigantic and imposing signs," were built for eternity, designed "like the cathedrals of our past, for thousands of years into the future." These buildings would contribute "more than ever to politically unifying and supporting" the people, and would "instil in the minds of the citizens of our nation the enduring self-awareness that they are Germans."[118]

Hitler had been in power for only a few years, and yet he seemed more determined than Mussolini to exploit architecture to transform society. The political function of this art form was at the heart of their conversations in the Bavarian capital. It is likely that Hitler was the one to introduce the theme. A few days after his meeting with Mussolini in Munich, Hitler told Speer that he had taken on the role of the teacher and that he "had lectured [Mussolini] on modern building." He said he was sure he had "convinced" him, and he added that he had made him realize that the "drawings made by Piacentini, his state architect, made no sense."[119] Hitler was keeping a close eye on the development of architecture in Italy, and had figured out that Piacentini was Mussolini's architect. Germany somehow meddled in Italian politics through architecture, confirming the central role that this particular genre was assuming in the ruling strategies of the two regimes.

But which of Piacentini's recent projects had the Führer seen? There are several hypotheses. At that point in time, the most important example of "state architecture" realized by the regime and commissioned from Piacentini was undoubtedly the Città Universitaria in Rome, which had been completed in October 1935. In that case, the Führer may have criticized the Roman work because he thought it not classicist enough. He was also certainly aware of the Italian Pavilion in Paris, which had been inaugurated in May 1937. The building in question did not feature any classical elements despite having been inspired by the ancient

Roman model of the Septizodium, and it was more modern than the German Pavilion. A third hypothesis, perhaps the most plausible one, is that Hitler actually saw the plans for the E42, approved by Mussolini on 28 April 1937, and published that same month in the magazine *Architettura*, edited by Piacentini. In truth, only a few perspective drawings were published in the magazine, which illustrated a modern city made of stainless steel and glass buildings, an expression of the "Judaeo-Bolshevik" artistic culture that the German Chancellor so detested. Those projects, which, as we shall see, were also signed by Piacentini, had actually been inspired by Pagano. But Hitler could not have known this. He simply identified them with the most famous architect at the time, and judged them to be nonsensical.

This surprising account by Speer, however, contains some distortions. In spite of Hitler's "lecture," in spite of the "enthusiasm" he had allegedly expressed for the new German architecture, Mussolini moved independently. And Piacentini was anything but cast aside. Nevertheless, the meeting did make an impression on Mussolini, and strengthened his support of classical architecture, which he revealed to Ojetti, for instance, in July. But above all, during his visit to Germany, he was able to directly witness the importance that Hitler attributed to architecture in governing the masses, and this urged him to act in a more determined way, and to speed things up. He in no way wanted his German counterpart to get ahead of him. Now, however, he began to give his architects more precise directions. In February 1938, Cipriano Efisio Oppo warned Alberto Alpago Novello, a member of the committee for the Piazza Imperiale at the E42, that "Mussolini now demands from everyone 'romanità,' monumentality, Italianness, greatness, solidity."[120] *Romanità*, or ancient Roman style, increasingly became the aesthetic model for the totalitarian state. A huge shift, noted Ojetti in a passage taken from the final draft of his *Taccuini*, "compared with three or four years ago, when we were stuck on big, Novecento-style boxes, and Mussolini referred to them as fascist architecture because he believed they were the architecture of the future. So Hitler was of use for something."[121]

Another testimony, obviously a self-interested one, further confirms this German influence on Mussolini's turnaround: according to Speer, "what [Mussolini] had learned in Munich and Berlin would be demonstrated at the Universal Exposition in Rome in 1942."[122]

5 Piacentini and Mussolini

1 The Architect of the Littorian Order

Unlike Hitler, Mussolini did not have a personal architect. Alberto Calza Bini, the head of the architects' trade union between 1923 and 1936, was not his personal architect. In spite of their many meetings and Calza Bini's dynamism, Mussolini did not seem to have much confidence in him. He did, however, reward his untiring parliamentary activity by making him a senator for life in 1943. Nor was Del Debbio his personal architect. The architect who replaced Calza Bini, serving from 1936 to 1943, was much more of an architect than the former union leader, but his political presence was weaker than that of his predecessor. Perhaps Mussolini preferred some architects to others, such as Moretti, who was even younger and more artistically gifted than Speer, but the dictator did not want to commit himself to a single person. Impartiality allowed Mussolini to manage his relationships in the insidious world of architecture and to prevent another person, someone who might be identified as Mussolini's architect, from eclipsing his image as a builder. For this reason, he commissioned his works from a variety of professionals. Indeed, as we shall see later on, in the Città Universitaria as in the E42, the dictator made sure that the identity of the architect practically disappeared within the collective work. He also believed that the architecture that represented the regime should not be identified with the style of a single architect, but should rather appear to be the result of a shared outlook linked to a specific historical moment.

Although Mussolini did not have a personal architect, there was one architect with whom the dictator had a close relationship: Marcello Piacentini. From the early 1930s Mussolini turned to Piacentini, as needed, for political purposes that required a higher architectural profile, beyond the planning of a single building, however representative it might be. From the moment he came to power, Mussolini was in Piacentini's line of sight. From the very outset, the architect proved that he knew how to interpret in an original way some of the underlying principles of fascist ideology; for instance, in the Roman urban tradition he knew which elements to use to support the "strength of mystic suggestiveness" of the fascist state.[1] It was along these lines that, in December 1923, Marcello, together with his father Pio Piacentini, put forward the idea of relocating the seat of the government to the Campidoglio. By doing so, "the concepts of the city of Rome, the state of Rome, and universal Rome would thus be unified, and convey one single concept."[2]

Already during his first months in power, Mussolini identified Piacentini as an innovative artist on the Roman cultural scene. Moreover, in his conversations with De Begnac he mentioned that, at the time, alongside numerous buildings built with incredibly bad taste, there were "fortunately ... the early works by Marcello Piacentini."[3] With that frame of mind, in October 1924, in the months that followed the assassination of the socialist Giacomo Matteotti, Mussolini went to Bergamo to inaugurate the Torre dei Caduti, a tower dedicated to the war dead. There, he was praised for a work of urban renewal designed by Piacentini, whose activity had begun long before the March on Rome. It was the first of many buildings by the Roman architect that Mussolini inaugurated.

The following year, Piacentini presented his plan for the Grande Roma (Great Rome), which interpreted Mussolini's program for the urban transformation of the capital, in response to the recent project by Brasini (figure 55). Piacentini's plan went against the tendency to create a new centre within the ancient city. He suggested the building of a new monumental forum consisting of Viale della Vittoria, measuring 80 metres wide and 2 kilometres long, gained from pushing back the Termini Station, extended to an area beyond the Aurelian Walls. Piacentini claimed that Brasini had misunderstood the famous speech Mussolini had given on 31 December 1925, its meaning was "as transparent as diamonds." By contrast, his own plan provided a literal interpretation of Mussolini's claim in that speech that "Rome will expand over the hills."[4] But the truth of the matter is that the speech contained urban development directives that diverged from Piacentini's, in terms of both the amount of demolition work proposed for the ancient city, and the direction in which the new Rome should develop, that is, towards the sea.

In a subsequent version, which may have been presented precisely in response to the speech Mussolini gave in December, Piacentini more clearly leaned into the fascistization of his "Great Rome": he replaced the palazzo, initially located opposite the Baths of Diocletian at the end of Viale della Vittoria, with a Mole Littoria, which was not as massive

55. Marcello Piacentini, project for Grande Roma, perspective drawing, 1925–6. At the centre, in front of the Baths of Diocletian, the Mole Littoria. Grande Roma was the response to Brasini's project for the centre of Rome.

as the one designed by Palanti, but substantial nevertheless. Piacentini, who before the war was known to have spent time in the Masonic and radical-democratic circles of Ettore Ferrari and Ernesto Nathan – the latter of whom had been forced to drink a large dose of castor oil in 1923 – was already racing to immortalize fascism less than two years after Matteotti's assassination.[5] To get the attention of Mussolini, who seemed to favour Brasini, Piacentini did what was necessary to form a bond with Margherita Sarfatti, spending time in her Roman salon, and designing her home.[6]

In 1926, the commission for the Arco della Vittoria (Victory Arch) in Bolzano consolidated the relationship between Mussolini and Piacentini. In the dictator's plans this arch replaced the Monumento Nazionale (National Monument) – also in the shape of an arch – that according to Brasini's plan was to rise up on Gorizia Castle. The monument in Bolzano was not just any ordinary work, it wasn't simply a

memorial to fallen soldiers. It took on a much more ambitious meaning: it was meant to be the symbol of an entire victorious nation built in
a city that had recently been conquered. The cleverly organized campaign to raise funds and its great success were proof of that. It involved
the entire country, from north to south, and at the centre of the campaign was the government itself. A few years later, Hitler organized a
similar fundraising campaign for the Volkshalle in Berlin, even though
he did not really need the money. What both dictators wanted was to
involve the entire country and to make the people identify with the
architecture they had helped to build.[7] For the Victory Arch, Mussolini
contacted the architect personally.[8] Piacentini promptly expressed his
aspiration to "create the true fascist monument" and to become the
loyal interpreter of Mussolini's ideology. Indeed, Mussolini wanted to
identify Italy's victory with the *ante litteram* victory of the regime. Once
the work had been finished, he would say that the arch in Bolzano was
the "architectural seal of the fascist soul," his personal "spiritual" gift
to the Fascist Party, despite the fact that he was not yet a member.[9]
Here, architecture, in some of the details, had a voice, it became the
"personification of a fascist symbol," in Ponti's words (figure 56).[10] The
fourteen columns supporting the triumphal arch were interpreted as
bundles of smaller columns, without a capital, but topped by the Littorian axe.[11] This work openly declared the idea of creating a new Littorian architectural order, as well as the idea of identifying victory with
fascism. Piacentini's following works did not translate political ideology
into architecture as naïvely or explicitly. But Mussolini himself, who was
sensitive to the demagogic seduction of architecture, and its effect on
the masses, may have influenced the ideas put into effect in the monument in Bolzano.[12]

Significantly, Mussolini personally examined Piacentini's drawings for
a new architectural order some time between his circular letter dated
December 1925, in which he imposed fasces on all government buildings, and the decree dated 12 December 1926, in which he declared
that the fasces were the official emblem of the Italian state. However, in
Bolzano it was not just a question of putting a symbol on a monument. It
went much further: the monument was meant as a component of an architectural language. If Mussolini demonstrated arrogance in wanting to
impose a party emblem as a symbol for the whole country, the architect
went even further and added an ornamental element of political value,
in keeping with the ancient tradition of architectural orders. Piacentini
provided a detailed description of the problems he encountered in designing the new order. He gave considerable attention to the division
of the base of the column into lobes so that it would not resemble the

56. Marcello Piacentini, Arco della Vittoria (Victory Arch) in Bolzano, 1925–6.
The architect applied the Littorian order to the columns.

Egyptian type or the fluted shaft. He justified the elimination of the base
and the capital as a means to accentuate the fasces.[13] The fasces was not
simply a decorative motif; it represented the creation of a new order to
eternalize the new regime. Was this really what Piacentini thought of
fascism? Did he really believe that this political regime would influence
the history of civilization such that it would warrant a new architectural
order? Probably not, at least not during this phase. But he played along
with flattery, cynicism, and skill.

Piacentini put his professional abilities and his architectural qualities
at the service of the ideological and political needs of fascism, and Mussolini liked the results. From that moment onwards, the dictator and the
architect engaged in a series of contracts. Even before the monument
in Bolzano had been inaugurated, Piacentini was sending Mussolini
drawings for the new Ministry of Corporations, and he was beginning to
conduct research on the new Fascist Party stadium. The following year,
for the inauguration of the Casa Madre dei Mutilati in Rome, Mussolini
arrived with the architect at his side.

2 A Special Rapport

After being nominated a member of the Accademia d'Italia in September 1929, "moved and honoured by this new gesture of esteem," Piacentini expressed his gratitude and devotion to Mussolini.[14] That same year, he sent the dictator the new project for Rome, which he presented together with the Gruppo Urbanisti Romani. Although the architect wrote that the plan "seems to broadly fulfil the guidelines of what Your Excellency has so clearly and incisively laid down," and in spite of a hint at the idea that the dictator was very keen on extending development towards the sea, the truth of the matter is that the 1929 proposal harkened back to an idea that had already been illustrated in the 1925 plan for Great Rome, that of freeing a new monumental centre in the area by pushing back the Termini Station. Mussolini had never openly supported this idea. What was new about it, however, was the introduction of new satellite towns in a southeast direction, in the Castelli area. The proposal favoured both ruralization and decentralization, policies that Mussolini had previously expressed in his Ascension Day speech, and in the article "Sfollare le città" (Decongesting the Cities).

The 1929 proposal was accompanied by a letter written by Piacentini to the dictator in which the architect offered to collaborate on a solution to Rome's complex urban issues: "I would be extremely proud to in some way contribute to resolving this difficult problem, and would dedicate all my passion to it." Encouraged by the "repeated gesture of benevolence" he had been given, Piacentini asked whether he could meet Mussolini to explain the drawings: "The drawings are at the Palazzo delle Esposizioni, but I can bring them wherever Your Excellency orders me."[15] There is no evidence that Mussolini ever visited the Mostra dei Piani Regolatori (Exhibition of the Urban Development Plans) at the Palazzo delle Esposizioni, or that he saw those drawings somewhere else. What we do know, however, is that he was familiar with Piacentini's 1929 plan. He even referred to it in a conversation with Zevi several months later, expressing his negative opinion; similarly he extended his disapproval to both Giovannoni's La Burbera and Brasini's plans.[16] And yet the latter had received – as noted earlier – his explicit support. Clearly, Mussolini's political practice did not exclude, depending on the interlocutor and the circumstances, contradictory statements.

Mussolini accepted Piacentini's offer of collaboration, and the following year the dictator assigned him to Rome's Urban Development Committee, where he would play a leading role. In the early phases of the committee's work, Brasini tried to impose his grandiose and disruptive ideas: these were mostly a rehash of the proposal he had made in 1928, which Mussolini had approved. Actually, no sooner had he been assigned to the committee than he sent the leader a collection of drawings illustrating the future layout of the capital. But it was Piacentini who ultimately emerged as the dominant figure in the group.[17] That is how Muñoz described him: "His Eminence Brasini boldly brandished his yellow pencil, with a cut here and a slash there: if he had been allowed, he would have demolished half of Rome, but then, what's worse, rebuilt it to his own liking. His Eminence Bazzani, always the pleasant man, with his rapid-fire eloquence would occasionally foist some flowery lecture upon his colleagues. His Eminence Piacentini, an old sea dog if there ever was one, easily made his point."[18] Piacentini was the one drafting the new urban development plan, and when he presented the final report to Mussolini he said, "In following your path we have endeavoured to make it worthy of Rome, worthy of Italy, worthy of you."[19]

Meanwhile, Mussolini had other opportunities to become acquainted with Piacentini's work. In March 1930, Delacroix, chairman of the Associazione Nazionale Invalidi e Mutilati di Guerra (War Injured and Amputees Association), submitted the final project for the Monumento a Cadorna (Monument to Cadorna), to be installed in Pallanza on Lake Maggiore. Mussolini approved the work and set a date for its inauguration.[20] The relationship between Delacroix and the architect was excellent, and it led to new assignments and architectural collaborations on projects for the association's provincial headquarters.[21]

On 23 September 1930, Mussolini and Piacentini met in Piazza Barberini in Rome. They visited the works under construction in the area and walked along the street of the same name. The dictator especially appreciated the dimensions of the new street: "It is a wide avenue. It's a shame we can't also widen Via del Tritone between the Ministry of Corporations and Corso Umberto I." He also admired the architectural lines of the buildings and the new movie theatre.[22] Piacentini later approached Mussolini to offer him expert advice on the lighting in Piazza Venezia, showing him the favourable results he had achieved with the lighting in Piazza della Vittoria in Brescia.[23] As previously mentioned, Mussolini would inaugurate the piazza in November 1932. The buildings overlooking fascist Brecia's new forum included the INA Tower, one of the "eyesores" of contemporary Italian architecture presented by the Rationalists to Mussolini at the Via Veneto Exposition. While it cannot be proven that Mussolini intervened in the matter, on the day of the inauguration the tower looked different, more modern than the one in the drawing Bardi had submitted eighteen months earlier. The final work had a flat roof and the openings had an almost Rationalist cut. More importantly, there was no longer an arched motif on the side walls, though it was maintained on the façade.[24]

Among the most prestigious of Piacentini's commissions in that period was one with the Ministry of Corporations on Via Veneto. The history of the building is complex. In October 1927, a first project, signed by Piacentini and Vaccari, was submitted by the leader of the Fascist Union, Edmondo Rossoni, to the dictator; the project was given his approval.[25] The new building was originally meant to host the headquarters of the Fascist Unions. Although the building site opened the following year, the plans had in the meantime changed, and in 1929 the idea was to transform the Casa dei Sindacati (Trade Unions Building) into the new Ministry of Corporations headquarters. The initial budget, estimated at 40 million lire, caused Mussolini to react with indignation: "Spending 40 million lire is more than just absurd! ... The new Ministry of Corporations headquarters must not cost more than 8 to 10 million lire."[26] His stand against a building that was too costly was crystal clear. Years later, though, he had adopted a radically different approach. He assigned more importance to the representative nature of state buildings and to the functions of monumental architecture. Although never as profligate as Hitler in terms of spending on architecture – money was no object as long as his objectives were achieved – Mussolini allocated generous sums to lavish buildings, in particular to the E42, to the detriment of social housing for example. Besides, building "useless" arches and pillars and using expensive types of marble no longer seemed absurd when they could be employed to sway the people towards fascism and its mythology. But to go back to the Ministry on Via Veneto, having understood the "diktats," the two architects came up with a new project, built between 1930 and 1932, which took into account the new budget. In the meantime, Bottai kept Mussolini abreast of its progress, as well as of technical decisions, often going into great detail.[27] However, Piacentini also kept a close watch on things, and was ready to come to the aid of his important client. When the works were almost finished and the cabinet was called to discuss the matter of the new ministry headquarters, Piacentini, who was aware of the government's agenda, promptly sent the dictator a "report that I am sure will be of interest to you."[28]

3 Committed to the Party

That Piacentini was well aware of what was going on in Mussolini's cabinet is clear from the previous episode, but his level of awareness can also be gleaned from what Ojetti had to say in the *Taccuini*. During one of his visits to Florence, the architect gave the critic the heads up concerning the new posts that would be filled by some party officials who had recently stepped down. He also told him about a recent dinner that had taken place between Mussolini and the minister of communications, Costanzo Ciano, the dictator's son-in-law's father, shedding light on the dictator's odd, often reserved behaviour vis-à-vis certain topics that directly concerned the competency of Ciano. Piacentini's understanding of how Mussolini's mind worked served him well over the course of their many conversations.[29]

Further proof that Piacentini was favoured by the regime was the fact that he was commissioned to design the Palazzo di Giustizia in Milan. On 5 February 1932, the architect crossed the threshold of Palazzo Venezia to show Mussolini the drawings for the new building, and received the leader's praise for its "grandioso e razionale" appearance.[30] The building was one of fascism's greatest constructions, its surface area exceeding that of the Palazzo di Giustizia in Rome, featuring a façade that was 120 metres in length and 38 in height, and completely clad in marble. The following August, Mussolini was personally informed that the work was under way, and, as noted earlier, he visited the site whenever he went to Milan.

A few months after seeing the plans for the Palazzo di Giustizia, Mussolini asked Piacentini to design the Città Universitaria in Rome, another project that was a priority for the regime. In expressing his gratitude, the architect vowed to make it a symbol of Mussolini, fascism, and Rome.[31] This project turned into an extraordinary instrument of political propaganda. In a relatively short period of time, about three years, a massive complex for the purpose of educating young people, the most important university campus in the country, was built. It was a concrete example of the country's modernization, a model both for Italy and other countries. Piacentini worked on the project alongside Mussolini, who supervised it himself. The dictator wanted all the university buildings to be located in the same area; he monitored the work's progress, selected the architect, examined the drawings, visited the building site, discussed the choice of marble, flagged deficiencies, and, eventually, inaugurated the complex in October 1935, according to schedule. The project was exceptionally well received by the public. It is thought that over half a million people visited it in the first few days after its opening.[32] This mass pilgrimage in effect served to sanctify fascism, no longer the political ideology of the Exhibition of the Fascist Revolution: here was proof of its realization, an idea translated into marble, an architecture for the people.

That same year, Piacentini also submitted to the dictator a project for the Palazzo della Confederazione Fascista degli Industriali that was planned for Piazza Venezia, on the corner of Via del Corso. Mussolini, the architect recalled, "sang his praises (I have a letter with the marks he made in blue pencil): but because of the general economic situation the project never came to fruition."[33] Later, in early June 1933, Mussolini welcomed Arturo Osio, general manager of the Banca Nazionale del Lavoro, who showed him Piacentini's project for the bank's new headquarters.[34] In October, Mussolini went to see the construction site on Via Bissolati. Mussolini did not like the idea of completing the new layout by creating two superelevations over Via San Basilio and Via San Nicola da Tolentino, so he asked Piacentini to address the problem. Soon afterwards, the architect sent Mussolini a model that showed how the area could be regenerated, along with a detailed memorandum.[35]

Over the course of his career, Piacentini never designed a Casa del Fascio, but this does not mean he did not have a relationship with the PNF. In fact, he transformed the former Stadio Nazionale, which he himself had designed in 1911, into the new PNF Stadium. He also advanced a proposal, as discussed before, for a huge Mole Littoria to be built next to the Baths of Diocletian.[36] In 1928, he declared he had given the party his "spiritual labour" for some time, in spite of the fact that he was not a card-carrying member. The dispute between him and Marinelli over his fee for the stadium works provides a glimpse of Piacentini's relationship with the political apparatus, but also of his professional practice. The PNF's administrative secretary claimed that the architect's absence from the building site meant he should be paid less, but Piacentini demanded to be paid the full sum, only to hand it over entirely to the party.[37]

The PNF was also involved with the Exhibition of the Fascist Revolution on Via dell'Impero, for which Piacentini, in November 1933, sent Mussolini a brand-new drawing.[38] The meaning of Piacentini's desire to do so is illustrated in a few events. In December 1932, Mussolini had decided to have the Fascist Party headquarters and the Exhibition of the Fascist Revolution built on Via dell'Impero; consequently, a competition for the two projects was announced in December 1933.[39] Piacentini's proposal thus arrived shortly before the competition. Furthermore, the architect would help to set up the competition, designing the layout of the area, and he would also be a member of the jury. More than a full-fledged plan, his proposal seemed to suggest a hypothesis, perhaps requested by the dictator himself, who was eager to see how the façade could be resolved on Via dell'Impero based on the competition's terms and conditions. This episode offers further proof of the special relationship between the two men.

Another meeting took place in the same period, and this time the source is Piacentini himself, in a postwar report in which the architect was somewhat reticent about his relationship with the dictator. "I once spoke to him face to face, because I wanted to prevent the Palazzo delle Esposizioni on Via Nazionale, which my father had designed, from being knocked down." An idea was floating around to replace the building with the permanent grounds of the Exhibition of the Fascist Revolution. Piacentini continued: "I was brusquely greeted, but my reasons were many and sound, and I expressed them all clearly without holding back. In the end I won, and if the building on Via Nazionale is still standing there today, then it's thanks to me."[40] It's hard to know to what extent Piacentini's reasoning influenced Mussolini's decision. No doubt the dictator would have had no qualms about tearing down a building that he felt represented the much-loathed liberal Italy. It is instead more likely to imagine that he was already thinking about relocating the Exhibition of the Fascist Revolution to Via dell'Impero: amid the fora of ancient Rome, in that extraordinary place that so inspired the collective imaginary, he could use architecture to create a permanent display of fascism.

Nor was Piacentini excluded from the architectural ventures tied to the conquest of the empire. Shortly after Addis Ababa was occupied, perhaps solicited by Mussolini himself, the architect wrote to him about implementing a general urban development plan for Ethiopia, reminding him of how the Roman legionaries went about colonizing the places they conquered by bringing "their architecture in all the most solemn expressions," thus bestowing on the "entire Mediterranean empire an indelible character of unity, strength, and greatness." Acting as an interpreter of his ideas – "I think this is the path that Your Excellency wishes to impose, that is, bringing the Roman architecture to our new empire" – Piacentini suggested a new "building project" to give the new colony "a coherent and consistent architectural imprint."[41] Meanwhile, the project for the entrance to St. Peter's Square in Rome was launched as well, involving the opening of Via della Conciliazione and the demolition of the "spina dei Borghi" (thorny problem of the Borghi); the latter had not been included in the 1931 urban development plan (figure 57). Then, in January 1937, the dictator commissioned him to design the E42 and, lastly, in 1941, to review the urban development plan for Rome.

Piacentini understood better than anyone what Mussolini wanted from architects: a type of architecture that was stylistically adaptable to meet the needs of politics. Ojetti, described him thus in 1932; this was a time when, the critic and the architect had more divergent positions from each other than in the latter half of the decade: "Marcello Piacentini came by, triumphant and indefatigable: a man who knows his trade, but who has the habit, in these times of great uncertainty, of wanting to follow all the latest fads."[42] He nonchalantly subordinated the moral vision of architecture to the demands of politics. But in following Mussolini's constant wavering, it seems he had found a shared goal with the dictator, that of bestowing a unity of direction for the architecture of fascist Italy.

57. Marcello Piacentini and Attilio Spaccarelli, project for the opening of Via della Conciliazione in Rome, model, 1936.

4 Side by Side

Piacentini's numerous meetings with the dictator confirm the close ties between the two men. In the statement he produced for his post-fascism purge trial, Piacentini wrote that he had gone to Palazzo Venezia, "a few times … along with some other people to discuss issues of a technical nature."[43] Between 1931 and 1939, Mussolini welcomed him to Palazzo Venezia on at least twenty occasions. The first time they met was in February 1931 to discuss the urban development plan for Rome. They then met again to discuss the matter of the Palazzo delle Esposizioni on Via Nazionale and the Palazzo della Confederazione Fascista degli Industriali in Piazza Venezia. They met twice to discuss the Città Universitaria, in November 1932 and in October 1933. The second time Piacentini was accompanied by Rocco. In December that same year, Piacentini was in the Sala del Mappamondo (Map Room) on two other occasions: on 14 December, the architect was there to plan the 19th Venice Biennale along with Volpi and Maraini, and the following day to illustrate the project for the completion of the Casa Madre dei Mutilati in Rome.[44]

Piacentini embarked on a comprehensive study in Milan, in addition to the one he had undertaken in Rome, so that he could closely monitor the works under way and play a leading role in the city's urban transformation. That way he could monitor what was happening in the centrally located Piazza Diaz in Milan, where the financial interests of the SCIA were focused. This jointly owned Italian-American company commissioned the Scottish architect Alister MacDonald, son of the first Labour Party prime minister, Ramsay MacDonald, who had expressed support for Mussolini following Matteotti's assassination. However, such an important area of the city could not be entirely assigned to a foreign architect, and Piacentini was asked to collaborate with him. MacDonald seemed to be willing to share the project, and said he was flattered to be able to work with such an illustrious colleague. Mussolini, who was determined to impose his strict control on the transformation of the square, personally supervised the project. Both architects were summoned to Palazzo Venezia to receive "inspiration" from the dictator.[45]

With nonchalance and cunning, Piacentini mixed his professional activity with some speculative real estate investments. In early March that same year, Piacentini, along with Brasini and Giuseppe Belluzzo, formerly the minister of economy – and one of the major supporters of the public sector through state-controlled companies – presented Mussolini with a proposal for the creation of a huge public-private company to fund the implementation of the urban development plan in central areas of Rome. The works would be considered "urgent," and they would receive a sort of political-ideological shield, and be part of the backdrop of the grand celebrations planned for the two-thousand-year anniversary of the empire of Augustus in 1937.[46]

Mussolini believed that by extolling the millenary and imperial values of Latin civilization, and Roman and fascist universalism, the Mostra Augustea della Romanità would counter the Exposition Internationale des Arts et des Techniques organized in Paris by Léon Blum's Front Populaire government in 1937. The Italian Pavilion in the French capital had to be equally grand.[47] Once he had been assigned the project, Piacentini submitted the drawings twice to Mussolini. The plan was dominated by a great tower with overlapping loggias – which Ojetti believed was inspired by Septimius Severus's Septizonium – and preceded by a statue of an equestrian – the Genius of Fascism – about to ominously cross the waters of the River Seine (figure 58). In May, when the works had been finished, Piacentini returned to Palazzo Venezia to report on their completion

58. Marcello Piacentini, Giuseppe Pagano, and Cesare Valle, project for the Italian Pavilion at the International Exposition in Paris, perspective drawing, 1936–7. The project was submitted to the dictator on 11 July 1936.

and the outcome of the exposition.[48] Beyond the river, and clearly visible from the Italian Pavilion, was the German Pavilion designed by Speer, across from the Soviet Pavilion by Boris Jofan. Speer had submitted his drawings for the building months before to the Führer, who had previously rejected the projects chosen by the minister of economy. Speer's aim was to first and foremost create a monument that could tower over the Soviet building: ultimately, the German Pavilion was six metres taller than the Soviet one. The official catalogue clearly expressed Germany's desire to demonstrate its strength as a nation. Money was no object if it meant achieving that target, and indeed the German building cost from six to eight times more than the other buildings at the Paris Expo. Speer listed his pavilion, along with Troost's Haus der Kunst in Munich and the buidings in Nuremberg – models of which were on display in Paris – among the best examples of the new German architecture.[49] It is likely that during their second meeting, Piacentini and Mussolini exchanged a few words about the striking contrast between Speer's and Jofan's build-ings. It is likely that they also talked about the Third Reich's bold archi-tectural ambitions.

Between 1937 and 1938, Piacentini went to Palazzo Venezia three more times to discuss the projects for the E42: the importance of these meetings will be analysed further on. In June 1939, accompanied by Bot-tai and the podestà of Milan, he delivered to Mussolini a project for a 60-metre-tall building in the well-known Piazza Diaz area. Although Bacciocchi had been sent to assist Alister MacDonald, it was Piacentini alone who supervised the architectural decision-making.[50] In December of that same year, Piacentini, along with Ojetti, met with Mussolini to illustrate two new works: the new headquarters of the Accademia d'Italia, to be built on the Janiculum in Rome, and the memorial to Guglielmo Marconi, to be built in Pontecchio Marconi. To avoid "lengthy explana-tions," two models were installed on the first floor of Palazzo Venezia.[51]

While visiting the building sites and during the inaugurations, Piacen-tini was often at Mussolini's side. Many examples of their collaboration have already been described. Others include the presentation of the new urban development plan for Rome and the opening of the first part of Via del Mare;[52] the inspection of Via Barberini and the movie theatre of the same name, publicly praised by the Duce;[53] inspections of the building on Via della Conciliazione, during which Mussolini expressed "impressions and remarks" that the architect would take into account (figure 59).[54] However, among all of the projects visited, one in particu-lar was close to Mussolini's heart, and that was the E42. During his first visit, in April 1937, it is possible that Pagano spoke with Mussolini more than Piacentini. Once the first competitions had come to an end and the superintendent for architecture had been nominated, it was up to the architect and no one else to present the large model and the drawings on display along the walls of the pavilion that was meant to serve as a permanent exhibition of the projects. Piacentini was at the peak of his success, a true leader of Italian architecture, with only a few rivals. He had seduced and then destroyed the "Rationalist" front in Milan. He was praised by Ponti as "one of our greatest architects, a man who excels and represents us all."[55] Once again, then, Piacentini escorted the dictator during a detailed visit to the E42 in April 1939 (figure 60).[56] After exam-ining the updated model, and watching a short film about the progress of the works, they headed to the site of the Palazzo della Civiltà Italiana, which was already at an advanced stage, and they inspected the life-size wooden models of the colonnade in Piazza Imperiale. The architect ex-plained the projects for Via Imperiale – an overall site plan, perspective drawings of the squares and of the monumental buildings – drafted by a

59. Mussolini walking along the first part of Via del Mare. The second and third figures to his left are Marcello Piacentini and Armando Brasini, Rome, 28 October 1930.

group of ten of his recent graduates, formerly students of the School of Architecture in Rome (figure 61).

Lastly, in October 1941, Piacentini showed Mussolini the "Variante" for the urban development plan in the rooms of the Palazzo delle Esposizioni on Via Nazionale.[57] Between 1930 and 1940, then, Piacentini and Mussolini met some fifty times, and that does not include their secret meetings, documentation of which has not been found.[58] Mussolini met with the architect as frequently as with any one of his ministers. But unlike the ministers, who were constantly and deliberately being switched around and shuffled in and out so that none of them could gain too much power, Piacentini, albeit with ups and downs, was at Mussolini's side throughout the twenty years of the regime. This fact cannot be overlooked if we consider that the architect was not a new member of the regime, that he had ties to the old ruling class, and that he did not see his support for the regime as an act of blind faith.

60. Mussolini, Vittorio Cini, and Marcello Piacentini, with a folder tucked under his arm, at the E42. On the left, Gaetano Minnucci, Rome, 18 April 1939.

5 In Praise of Organizational Perseverance

Piacentini and Mussolini wrote to each other as frequently as they met. In 1929, as already noted, Piacentini wrote to Mussolini to invite him to see the Mostra dell'Abitazione e dei Piani Regolatori held at the Palazzo delle Esposizioni. On display in the section dedicated to the city of Rome were the plan for the GUR, to which he had contributed, and Giovannoni's La Burbera project (figure 62). The latter called for the opening of two large roads, a *cardo* and a *decumano*, which cut through the centre of the Renaissance city, gutting it, and forming a large square, a new "Foro Mussolini," at the intersection of Via Montecitorio and Piazza di Spagna. Piacentini adamantly opposed this vast and useless destruction, and he accused Giovannoni of having reneged on his original theories in defence of the historical area. Mussolini turned down the invitation, probably to avoid further heated debate, and he justified his absence with his "many engagements."[59] In April 1930, in the speech he gave on the

61. Marcello Piacentini with Augusto Baccin, Beniamino Barletti, Adriano Cambellotti, Nello Ena, Pasquale Marabotto, Otto Matelli, Luigi Orestano, Aldo Tomassini Barbarossa, and Luigi Vagnetti, project for Via Imperiale in Rome between the Aurelian Walls and the E42, perspective drawing, 1938–9. The drawings were shown to Mussolini on 18 April 1939, during a visit to the E42.

occasion of the instalment of an Urban Development Plan Committee for Rome, Mussolini digressed briefly about the Monumento al Milite Ignoto (Monument to the Unknown Soldier), noting that because Rome was a "fair city ... the white stain of the Vittoriano was out of place."[60] Piacentini seized the opportunity to suggest coating the Botticino marble that had been used to make the monument. The coating process, he recalled, had traditionally been used in the treatment of stone, and so it would therefore be a good idea to apply "a bit of Roman colour" to the Vittoriano: "If Your Excellency thinks this experiment is fitting, I would be more than happy to deal with it."[61] He later wrote to Mussolini to suggest a supply of tapestries for the new Palazzo delle Corporazioni.[62]

In June 1934, on the occasion of the well-publicized reception at Palazzo Venezia of the architects who designed Sabaudia and the Florence

62. La Burbera group (Pietro Aschieri, Enrico Del Debbio, Gustavo Giovannoni, Vincenzo Fasolo, Arnaldo Foschini, Alessandro Limongelli, Giuseppe Boni, Giacomo Giobbe, Felice Nori, and Ghino Venturi), project for the redevelopment of the centre of Rome, perspective drawing of the great piazza, 1929.

Station, Mussolini expressed his appreciation of the "lovely" church of Cristo Re in Rome designed by Piacentini, which he thought "perfectly fulfilled its spirit and its purpose." The architect wasted no time in sending him a letter of gratitude, for his words to the young architects and in regard to his work. "Allow me, please, to express my deepest gratitude for what Your Excellency said about the church of Cristo Re."[63] Mussolini had not yet actually seen the church. He would have a chance to see it later, however, as he himself recalled. "One spring morning, when Rome was still asleep, Marcello Piacentini accompanied me through the streets of the Vittoria neighbourhood, which he himself had designed ... The façade of the church of Cristo Re had just been completed. The bricks from the old sixteenth-century sites triumphed on that wall decorated simply with bronze statues made by Martini. A priest met us on the parvis ... The architect Piacentini listened to what I had to say."[64]

In July 1934 Piacentini – who must have had informers in Palazzo Venezia – became aware that Mussolini was planning a visit to Sabaudia, the newly founded city that the king had inaugurated the previous April. The city had been designed by the team led by Piccinato, formerly a pupil of Piacentini, a collaborator in his firm and now his assistant at the

Graduate School of Urban Studies. As he presented the dictator with the issue of *Architettura* dedicated to Sabaudia, Piacentini noted that "Sabaudia, albeit rigorously rational, is Italian, alive, warm, and sculptural." This was proof, the architect added, "that the development of Mussolini's architecture is in full swing."[65] As we saw before, Mussolini's opinion of Sabaudia was controversial. Its architecture was not "rural" enough, and it was hard for the people to grasp its Italian nature. Perhaps it wasn't exactly what he had expected. But he would have appreciated the words of Piacentini, who was so careful to place the work within a broader process of convergence between architectural language and political policy.

Slightly over a month after the inauguration of the Città Universitaria in Rome and its ensuing political success, Piacentini sent Mussolini a report on the project for the University Campus in Rio de Janeiro. The architect had gone to Rio in August 1935 to inspect the site, make arrangements with the local authorities, and work on the first studies, with the promise, which he did not keep, to return the following November.[66] Later, with cynicism and the usual ruthlessness, Piacentini sent Morpurgo abroad to "collect data, pass around lots of paper to make those fools believe that the project is moving forward, and then leave for Rome." But that is not exactly how things went: the Brazilians forced them to honour their commitment and deliver the working drawing. And while in Rio, Morpurgo asked his friend Foschini to "explain to M.[arcello] that he lives because I forge counterfeit money."[67]

Lastly, while the war raged, Piacentini sent Mussolini a publication about the new Palazzo di Giustizia in Milan (figure 63). He explained to him that he wanted to impress on "the biggest building made by the regime ... fascism's strong and universal nature." Mussolini could only agree that "Mussolinian architecture" was "at the height of its development." This was truly a modern temple that materialized all the myths of the fascist creed. The notion of strength, expressed by its huge dimensions, and that of universality, expressed by its classicism, were easy to understand and would appeal to the masses. The architect "ardently" yearned to personally give the dictator the book, but he did not dare distract him from "much more serious concerns at this time."[68]

Although Mussolini said that he perceived in Piacentini a "simplicity and love ... of unpretentious construction material," their affinity certainly went beyond matters of taste.[69] What Mussolini especially appreciated were Piacentini's superb organizational skills. The architect did not belong to the herd of feeble and insecure collaborators with whom the dictator had surrounded himself.[70] When Marinetti criticized the decision to bestow the title of "accademico d'Italia" to architects whom the Futurist Antonio Sant'Elia "would have spit at," the dictator replied by

63. Marcello Piacentini, Palazzo di Giustizia in Milan, 1931–41. This is one of the largest buildings created by the fascist regime. Mussolini inspected the project and visited the building site on many occasions.

asking him whether Sant'Elia had "Piacentini's organizational persever-
ance," if he would know how to deal with "the issues of great classical
architecture."[71] A few years later, even Claretta Petacci, Mussolini's mistress, asked for Piacentini's advice as concerned her villa in Camilluccia
in Rome. However, Mussolini's trust in Piacentini was not unconditional.
The mistrust he was famous for was also assigned to the dynamic architect. Piacentini's phone was tapped and the political police monitored
his activity. And there were many surprises in the reports Mussolini received. Apparently, Piacentini had accepted bribes in connection to several of the building sites in Rome and in Milan. But although Mussolini
knew about the corruption, he feigned ignorance. Mussolini knew that
he could use the information to blackmail the rich and powerful architect at the right time, if the need arose.[72]

6 Architecture towards a Style

1 In Rome's Città Universitaria

Mussolini and Piacentini played leading roles in many events, but two events are especially noteworthy. The first concerned the Città Universitaria in Rome.[1] On 16 February 1932 approval was given for the establishment of a consortium for the building redevelopment of the University of Rome; the consortium was officially founded on 4 April. On 18 February, Mussolini sent a letter to the minister of national education, Balbino Giuliano, that contained a series of "directives." In it he stated that the new university campus would have to be able to accommodate ten thousand students. He also asked that the "working drawings of all the buildings" be drafted. He imposed the simultaneous construction of the buildings; he set the date for the work to begin on 1 October 1932, and the inauguration ceremony to be held on 21 April 1935, the anniversary of the founding of Rome. He encouraged the minister not to waste any time: "Thirty months are enough to build a university campus destined to carry the legacy of fascism through the centuries to come." However, the letter also contained an important afterthought: "P.S. The monumental part should include buildings for the Schools of Letters, Law, and Political Science. A lecture hall that can accommodate up to 3,000 students should be located at the centre."[2] Though this was a general recommendation, it still appeared in the final plan. The architect commissioned to draw up the plan thus acknowledged Mussolini's "architectural" suggestion.

The agreement was signed on 4 April the estimated budget was a total of 70 million lire, with 54 million lire to be financed by the state. That same day Piacentini sent a telegram to Mussolini thanking him for commissioning him to design the Città Universitaria.[3] It can be hypothesized that that same day the dictator had sent Piacentini a telegram confirming the commission. Just a few days later, Mussolini went to inspect the site of the Città Universitaria, accompanied by Giuliano, the university rector Pietro De Francisci, and Piacentini.[4] The architect had already prepared a series of plans that illustrated where the buildings would be located, which he then showed Mussolini. This leads us to deduce that Piacentini had already been informed about the visit, or perhaps that he had been contacted by Giuliano after the latter had learned of it in a letter from Mussolini dated 18 February.

Twenty days later, on 26 April 1932, Mussolini wrote to Giuliano once more. This letter tells us he had received a project for the Città Universitaria, but that it was not the first, as it had been preceded by another. Furthermore, we learn that Mussolini had not liked the previous plan: "The current plan no longer resembles the first one, which was *excessively decorative and theatrical.*" This second plan met with Mussolini's approval, who urged Giuliano to "move quickly, without waiting a single day, towards the working plans."[5] Hence, not only had Mussolini suggested the general layout, but he had also rejected the first plan, justifying his decision with his opinion on the architecture. Here was a Mussolini who chose projects, whose interest spilled over from the political sector to the architectural one. In this circumstance, the Duce's role was more prominent than the one acknowledged to him by Piacentini when the architect wrote, "It was he who set the limits and the characteristics of the theme, to elevate the main university campus in the Mediterranean, expressing therein the best and most modern of Italy's construction techniques."[6]

Towards late April 1932, Piacentini had already sent Mussolini the urban layout of the complex. It likely also contained some perspective sketches that prompted the dictator to express the opinion mentioned previously. Other architects, in addition to the first twelve, were summoned to design each of the buildings. The decision to assign the project to a team coordinated by a leader rather than to just one architect dated back at least to 5 April.[7] Hence, it took place at the same time as Piacentini's official appointment. Which of the two men came up with the idea of a group project for the Città Universitaria? Was it Mussolini or was it Piacentini?

After the fall of the regime at the end of the war, in one of testimonials he presented during his trial, Piacentini claimed that "I alone had been assigned the project for the Città Universitaria. But then I suggested that the work be handed out to seven other architects, whose names I had myself indicated."[8] However, Piacentini's claim contrasts with something he himself had said in 1935, upon completion of the work: "Mussolini asked me to call to my side some of the best young architects from every region in Italy, sharing the vast project among them."[9] An article published in

Mussolini's newspaper, *Il Popolo d'Italia*, in early April 1932 also confirms this version of events. The author wrote that Piacentini, albeit assuming the role of director, would share the commission with "other architects," and added that the decision was "in accordance with the Duce's orders."[10] Minnucci, who, as we shall see, also played a role in this episode, stated that Piacentini, "abiding by the Duce's orders, summoned many architects to collaborate on the project."[11]

These records lead to the conclusion that it was Mussolini who forced Piacentini to share his assignment with other architects, and transform this major, demanding public work into a team project. The point was to demonstrate that architects in Italy were not divided by fierce quarrels between innovators and traditionalists, as in the 2nd Exposition of Rational Architecture on Via Veneto, but, rather, that they would be able to march as one in the direction determined by their leader. All the same, Piacentini played a pivotal role in drafting the list. At first, it included only six names: Foschini, Aschieri, Pagano, Michelucci, Ponti, and Gaetano Rapisardi. Later, the list also came to include Giuseppe Capponi.[12]

In the spring of 1932, as we saw before, Mussolini personally monitored the development of the Città Universitaria. He was Piacentini's number one client. His interest did not fade after the implementation of the first phases of the project, but rather continued throughout the course of its construction. In early May, Mussolini spoke to Piacentini about the type of marble to be used for the cladding. The dictator chose white Carrara marble, but, in this case, his decision did not seem to be based on architectural reasons; rather, it had to do with the economic advantage for the state in a purchase of this kind.[13] In mid-May, Mussolini asked Giuliano for an update on the work in progress.[14] At the end of the month, the area was completely cleared of the shacks where two hundred families had lived. In the meantime, Piacentini had handed out assignments to the other architects. They met several times to set "the financial boundaries, the architectural direction, the building procedures, and the choice of materials." By late May, all of the architects would be expected to present the preliminary projects for the buildings assigned to them, by late August the specifications would be ready, and by the end of September the work could finally begin in earnest[15]

Actually, some of the procedures went even more quickly than planned. Indeed, on 12 August, Piacentini was able to announce to a very satisfied Mussolini that the first contracts had been signed and that the work could begin earlier.[16] The dictator particularly valued the architect's organizational skills: "Must one nurture esteem for all those whom one employs? Rather, I would say appreciate them for what they can do. They are cogs in the wheel that, once they have been worn out, can be disposed of without giving it a second thought."[17] Though Piacentini was one of those "cogs," one who cleverly ensured that Mussolini would need him to the very end.

While the first excavations were under way, the architects were devising the preliminary plans. Foschini had already submitted some of his drawings and he was eager to hear what Piacentini had to say about them. Aschieri, Capponi, and Michelucci had some requests for him as well.[18] Records indicate the delivery in late August of an initial version of all the buildings.[19] Pagano was aware of the historic importance and novelty of the venture. In his magazine, in January 1933, he described what it meant: "to impress a unified character upon a group product, in harmony with our day and age, that is, the age of fascism."[20]

2 "Life Today" Requires a "Unity of Direction" in Architecture Too

In late November 1932, Mussolini was once again at centre stage, meeting with Piacentini for an update on the state of progress of the works. Informed by the architect about bureaucratic delays caused by the Public Works Committee dragging its feet in its examination of the drawings, Mussolini wrote to Minister Araldo di Crollalanza telling him to hurry things up: "If need be, have the committee meet on a permanent basis."[21] On 19 December, the first model and the drawings of the Città Universitaria were unveiled to the press. The perspective drawings prepared by Montuori, who was working for Piacentini at the time, enhanced the homogeneity of the intervention.[22]

Mussolini did not hide his concern about the number of workers employed at the building site. In January 1933, after another visit to the site, he realized that fewer people were working there than had been initially planned for.[23] The following day, when asked for an explanation, Piacentini sent the dictator a detailed schedule that included the number of workers who would need to be hired in the months to come. Only in October was the building site at full capacity, with two thousand workers on the payroll.[24]

In February, the drafting of the projects was still under way. Rocco wrote to Alessandro Chiavolini, Mussolini's personal secretary: "I would love for the head of government to examine the projects, which are now at an advanced stage, and the state of progress of the works for the university buildings. I would bring him the drawings and the photos myself; I think he should also be given a chance to see the plaster maquettes, which were recently finished, and the samples of the building materials." The letter ended with Rocco's invitation for Mussolini to visit the building site.[25] Indeed, on 11 March, Mussolini was there, meeting Piacentini and the other architects. Also present were Rocco and the philosopher and former minister Giovanni Gentile. Mussolini was shown the new drawings and the second model, as well as samples of building materials.[26] The principal changes concerned the connection between the Rettorato (Administration Building) and the Schools of Letters and Law, the dimensions of the latter, and the Institute of Physiology.

After that meeting, in May 1933, Ponti made some changes to the façade of the Institute of Mathematics, eliminating the portal with pillars.[27] Actually, many of the projects underwent changes. In addition to the projects by Aschieri and Michelucci, the building that was to house the Rettorato was deprived of its tower even though the foundations had already been laid.[28] In September, Mussolini inspected the building site once more, as usual accompanied by Piacentini. The dictator again looked at the drawings and the model. He then headed to the Institute of Hygiene, which had been designed by Foschini and was only missing its roof, as well as to the Institute of Physics designed by Pagano. These two buildings were the ones at the most advanced stage of construction; for some of the others, the foundations were still under construction.[29] Nevertheless, building activity was definitely in full swing. In 1934, Piacentini weighed the risks of improving the connection between the Città Universitaria and the Termini Station. In September he sent Mussolini a master plan, and the following month the dictator summoned him to Palazzo Venezia. The architect's proposal may also have included a design for the new railway terminal; however a memo from the dictator's secretary read, "In any case, the station will not be built."[30]

Mussolini probably carried out another inspection in September 1934. Piacentini wanted to know when exactly he planned to visit so he could be there as well.[31] This made for a total of five visits by the dictator to the building site: once in 1932, once in September 1934, and three times in 1933. His constant concern with the construction demonstrates that Mussolini attributed great political importance to this architectural enterprise. In March 1935, the inauguration, which was initially scheduled for 21 April, was postponed to 28 October, the anniversary of the March on Rome. Mussolini, who in some ways empathized with the architect, who was under great pressure from the imminent deadlines, made sure someone "inform Piacentini that he can take his time, as long as he's ready for 28 October" (figure 64).[32]

The critic Roberto Papini best articulated the meaning of Piacentini's operation: he "was up to his assignment not only as an architect, but as a coordinator of minds, that is to say, an orchestrator of fantasies." Papini added that not only was the project "an act of strict discipline, worthy of these times," but a "miracle accomplished" by a dozen architects "from

64. Città Universitaria in Rome, bird's-eye view, 1932–5. Mussolini rejected the first site plan Piacentini submitted to him, because he thought it was "excessively decorative and dramatic."

all over Italy, each from a different place and with a different personality, but who all agreed perfectly on a unity of style."[33]

How was this "unity of style" achieved among architects who were so different from each other? By outlining a symmetrical urban plan, one that harkened back to the classical style of the basilica. By using common architectural elements, such as matching windows, cornices with the same moulding, and the same materials for the cladding, namely travertine, ceramic stone bricks, and red or yellow stucco. Above all, by having each of the architects sacrifice something of their individuality.[34] The result of this was a single rationale, which was to a great extent artificial because it was imposed top-down; individual tendencies were acknowledged, only to be synthesized in a superior and harmonious whole.

"Unity of style" did not mean that everything had to be the same. Quite the contrary, each of the buildings in the Città Universitaria had its own distinguishing features. Furthermore, the "monumentality" that became apparent when one walked across the nave and transept of that open-air basilica gradually faded into the features of the façades at the rear and the secondary squares. The project's language embraced both past and present; it was modern but at the same time "solemn and enduring," and it recalled the "renewed spirit of the race."[35] Piacentini, with his meticulous management, showed that under the fascist government it was possible to build harmonious architecture, that this unity among architects, under Mussolini's patronage, bode well for more positive general developments in Italian architecture.

On 31 October, Mussolini attended the inauguration. Illness forced Piacentini to skip the ceremony. The head of state, in a short speech, recalled the medieval origins of the University of Rome, and then addressed the ongoing political situation, the Ethiopian War, and "our soldiers, bearers of civilization." He then attacked the League of Nations for the "shame" of the economic sanctions levied against the "Italy of the Blackshirts." Mussolini uttered only a few meaningful words about the buildings. He mentioned Piacentini by name, even though he did not usually acknowledge individual architects in his speeches. He emphasized the harmony between the regime's political program and architectural accomplishment: "I hired the architect Piacentini, who summoned architects from many provinces to his side ... and [they] turned our wishes into a reality made of marble and stone."[36] This convergence between the political ambitions of fascism and architecture served as a backdrop to Rector De Francisci's inaugural speech, in which he warned that "from a totalitarian conception, such as that of fascism, there can be no divide between thought and action," between culture and political decisions.[37]

Ten days later, after he had recovered from his illness, Piacentini echoed De Francisci's words. For the opening of the new academic year of the School of Architecture, where he had recently accepted the post of dean, Piacentini turned to the students to say that "today's life, a collective one designed for the masses, our fascist life, where every element of individuality is subordinated to the supreme, and even spiritual, interests of the state, requires a unity of direction to accomplish [... the] renewed national soul."[38] This unity of direction was architecture's response to fascism's political turnaround in the mid-1930s, characterized by a more marked tendency towards totalitarianism. Although the Città Universitaria was certainly not the first collaboration between Mussolini and Piacentini, it was the most important one up until then. It was the first project in which Mussolini tasked the architect with coordinating other architects to "impress a unified character" on the work of the regime. It turned out to be a successful experiment for both men, one they would attempt once more, on an even larger and more complex scale, with the E42.

3 The E42 and the Matter of Style

After the Città Universitaria, the E42 was the other important project that resulted from Mussolini and Piacentini's collaboration. In the history of architecture between the two world wars, the E42 was particularly important. It was the most significant example of the fascist regime's attempt to develop its own style. The E42 represented a turning point that profoundly influenced the relationship between the regime and architecture. The style of the city with which fascism most wanted to be identified had to be enduring; it had to identify architecture with that specific time in history. Mussolini decided to overcome his previous ambivalence, that is, the ambiguity of the style he had pursued up until then. Between 1937 and 1938, when summoned to choose whether to side with the modernists or the traditionalists, the leader gradually decided to identify the "Mussolinian city" with architecture that was reminiscent of Roman classical antiquity.

The "Mussolinian city" represented a milestone in the relationship between architecture and politics. In a visible way, it marked fascism's participation in architectural choices. It promoted a stylistic direction supported by Mussolini, who personally followed the whole evolution of the E42. Again, this was not a first. However, in this case, the dictator was more involved than he had been previously, and his interference had much broader repercussions. Unlike for the Città Universitaria, he now nominated a commissary, Vittorio Cini. At first, he had named another, most likely Alberto Pirelli, but then Bottai, who had perhaps been informed that the Milanese industrialist was unavailable, suggested Cini or Volpi for the post.[39] The appointment of a commissary did not mean that Mussolini would step back from decision-making. On the contrary, through Cini – whom he admired and for whom he felt "perhaps, some affinity" – he was even more persistent in his control and presence.[40]

Mussolini had chosen a commissary who, like the other candidates, had an impressive résumé and came from the world of industry and finance. The E42 was a major venture that was going to require a massive funding, and Mussolini needed to appoint someone with a prestigious name. Tullio Cianetti, then deputy minister of corporations, perhaps exaggerating but successfully conveying the pivotal nature of the event, said that in those years "all the productive activity in Italy was focused on the Universal Exposition."[41] The dictator himself, when presenting the progress report at the Campodoglio in the spring of 1939, asked that the entire country make a great unified effort, that it mobilize in a "civil and pacific" way for the E42. "From now on, each Italian has to consider himself personally engaged." It was a conciliatory Mussolini, one who spoke of manifestations "inspired by the criteria of peace and collaboration" among nations.[42]

But did Mussolini really want peace? Wasn't peace antithetical to the model of the Italian warrior that he was making every effort to forge?

Hadn't he repeated over and over again that peace was "depressing, that it deprived man of his fundamental virtues," that only war could reveal his greatness?[43] What exactly did Mussolini want? An important document that had been presented to the Fascist Grand Council two months earlier reveals the Duce's strategy. This document offered "guidelines" for foreign policy, and it attributed anything but a peaceful role to the E42. Indeed, the financial plans for the exposition determined that, after an initial construction phase, the money spent would be completely recuperated with the massive presence of foreign visitors, several million according to Piacentini's calculations. The event was expected to be a huge economic success. And with that valuable foreign currency, Mussolini would be able to reinforce the state's finances and be ready for the war, which was not expected to happen before 1943–4. It was clearly stated in that meeting of the Fascist Grand Council that Italy was ready to declare war as soon as the "1942 exposition is over, an exposition that must strengthen our monetary reserves."[44] "We have the E42 in sight, and it will earn a great deal of currency. We don't have enough ordnance and we need time to produce it," Mussolini confided to Pirelli.[45] In other words, architecture was going to pay for the war.

Mussolini took an active part in choosing the location. From the outset, the location for the E42 was meant to be a throroughfare connecting Rome to the sea, in accordance with the idea the dictator had expressed in 1925. On 21 October 1936, accompanied by Bottai, Alfieri, Cini, Oppo, and Bonomo, Mussolini inspected the site for the first time. The area was extensive, stretching from Ponte della Magliana to the Lido.[46] On 15 December, the group visited the Tre Fontane area, which became the site of the exposition.[47] Mussolini himself chose the five architects tasked with drafting a master urban development plan. Piacentini, Pagano, Piccinato, Vietti, and Ettore Rossi were selected from a shortlist drawn up by Cini, which also included Vaccaro, Libera, Del Debbio, Terragni, Michelucci, Montuori, Muratori, and Muzio. Next to Muzio's name Cini wrote the word "excellent," while on the draft he crossed out the names of Ponti and Peressutti. Significantly, Piacentini was number one on the list. Mussolini respected the order suggested by the commissary, except for Rossi – "architect of the Board of Tourism" – whom he chose over Vaccaro, Libera, and Del Debbio, even though they came before Rossi.[48]

Piacentini was the only definite name on Cini's list. It is worth remembering that already in the *Programma dell'esposizione* (Program of the Exposition), dated November 1935, the scenario that was now emerging had already been envisioned: "a group of the most intelligent, youngest architects in Italy, led by the most illustrious architect in the kingdom, will study an urban development plan and a technical project capable of constituting a whole new artistic complex, essentially in the fascist style."[49] Clearly, the "illustrious architect" was Piacentini, who was involved in the initiative from the earliest stages. Moreover, the coincidence in the date – the Città Universitaria was inaugurated that same month – and the hierarchical role he was given confirmed the intention to continue with the method that had been successfully tested with the Città Universitaria. Moreover, even before he was appointed, with the confidence of someone who already has a grip on the situation, the architect drew a picture of the transformations that Rome would undergo in view of the exposition. These included the idea of combining the event with the 1944 Olympics – both were planned to take place at the seaside – and thus coordinating the sports facilities for 1941 with those for 1944.[50]

In 1937, Piacentini was the most powerful architect in Italy, controlling both of its principal branches, the profession itself and the university.[51] He had building sites in Turin, Genoa, Milan, Bolzano, and Trieste, as well as in Rome. He signed the project for the pavilion that represented Italy at the Paris Expos. In that period of time alone, Piacentini was designing the central areas of half a dozen cities in Italy. Mussolini knew about Piacentini's activity. The architect himself had shown him some of those projects, whereas he had looked at others during his meetings with the podestà of the cities in question. It is worth mentioning some of the accompanying conversations.

In November 1934, Mussolini met with Paolo Thaon di Revel, podestà of Turin, who showed him the plans for the second half of Via Roma;[52] the podestà who succeeded him, Ugo Sartirana, would then keep the dictator abreast of the status of the works.[53] Piacentini tasked Pascoletti, who relocated to Turin for that very purpose, with managing the building site. The Roman architect would be at Starace's side on the day the new street was opened.[54] Also in November 1934, the podestà of Trieste, Salem, travelled to Palazzo Venezia where he updated Mussolini on the progress of works under way in that city, and particularly in the area of the Città Vecchia.[55] After that meeting, Salem asked that the project for the Palazzo delle Assicurazioni Generali be given to a "famous architect," in other words, to Piacentini.[56] Furthermore, he wanted the other buildings that were to be built in the same area and that would give the city a fascist identity to "harmonize" with Piacentini's project. He thus invited the managers of the Banco di Napoli to negotiate directly with Piacentini. In February 1937, the podestà met with Mussolini again to advise him as to the buildings' progress.[57]

Again in 1934, Mussolini welcomed Molfino, the podestà of Genoa, who presented him with a proposal for the works that had already started, and for those that had been planned for the city.[58] In December 1936, he met Cesare Colliva, the podestà of Bologna, who showed him the plan for the city's redevelopment, which hinged on Via Roma, and would involve Piacentini.[59] Mussolini also visited the new square in Bolzano; he was well-informed, as we saw before, about the architectural and urban situation in Milan. Mussolini thus had a clear picture in his mind concerning the projects that Piacentini was working on, and the architectural ideas behind them. The significance of the decision to involve him in the E42 project became even clearer: he had established himself as the architect tasked with transforming the major Italian cities, and more than ever the future of architecture lay in his hands.

In the first ten days of January, the team of five architects was already hard at work shaping the new Mussolinian city. In those same days in Germany, Hitler was discussing plans with Speer for the new Berlin.[60] Piacentini and his colleagues began studying and drafting the first projects in the temporary headquarters on Via Veneto in Rome.[61] Around mid-January, during a press conference, Cini pointed out that the main features of the exposition were universality, "definitiveness," and "style." Never had the matter of style been presented in such explicit terms. Now it was part of the program for the event. Cini remarked that "the style of the buildings must establish the ornamentation of the future city: it must reveal the tendencies of an age. The young people who for years have been awaiting a style worthy of our tradition, and at the same time in keeping with the originality of modern Italian civilization, have an opportunity, which may never again be as great and as varied, to view buildings that are synchronized, monumental, and all situated in the Italian capital."[62]

4 The Swing towards Classicism

What did Cini really mean when he talked about style? Piacentini seemed to have a clearer sense of this after meeting with the general commissary: "I left the conversation we had yesterday feeling immensely satisfied: I now see things more clearly and feel ready for the sprint ... I believe that the largest buildings of the exposition, which will become permanent, should constitute a huge forum. Imagine putting yourself at the centre of the ancient Roman forum surrounded by squares, colonnades, passages, arches, etc., and seeing the Colosseum down there on the left, and the Campidoglio down there on the right. It is a vision that is simultaneously classical but modern, in fact, very modern; and gathered together here will be all the exhibitions that extol our Latin and fascist civilization ... If you should have the opportunity to meet His Excellency our leader in the coming days, it might be a good idea to see whether he approves of such an idea: that way we can continue on safer ground."[63]

A first master plan, named "project A" by Pagano, was laid out in March. Piacentini, who was always in contact with Cini, wrote that he had prepared "a new study, based on the classical axial scheme, one that is better studied and proportionate, adding on the margins some of my associates' ideas that seem wonderful: the result of this is a whole that seemed more lively and closer to the ground, albeit still remaining classical."[64] This project led to "Project B," developed further and presented to Mussolini by the five architects on 8 April. The leader had just returned from his trip to Libya, where he had expressed his admiration for columns. After that meeting, the project was revised once more and presented to Mussolini on 28 April. That was the day chosen by the dictator to inspect the predetermined area. After climbing to the top of a platform from which he could survey the entire area, Pagano explained where the buildings were going to be located. Mussolini then headed to a dedicated pavilion where the drawings and the model of the exposition were on display.

The dictator gave the plan the thumbs up, even though he didn't fully agree with the project, according to which the E42 would be a modern city with buildings made of glass and steel (figure 65).[65] Piacentini had also signed the drawings. But Piacentini was crafty: he chose to take a back seat and wait for the right time to take control. Indeed, in this last phase Pagano seemed to be acting as the group's leader. A generation younger than Piacentini, Pagano had collaborated with him on the Città Universitaria, and when the project was finished their relationship seemed to have grown stronger: "The friendship and esteem born of this friendly collaboration will last forever," remarked Pagano, belying the animosity that eventually developed between the two architects.[66] Their collaboration continued with the Italian Pavilion for the Paris Expo, where Pagano's task was to deal with the interior. Whereas in 1932 he had recognized Piacentini as the "head" of Italy's modern architects, now that the E42 was under way it looked as though he wanted to work as his equal. And this time Mussolini had not appointed Piacentini director, as he had clearly done for the Città Universitaria. Unlike Piacentini, the forty-year-old Pagano had an undeniably fascist past. His belief in fascism was beyond question. Now it was he who presented the projects to the dictator. Piacentini indulged Pagano: he knew Mussolini far better than his younger colleague, and he sensed that the idea of the city as imagined by the architect was decidedly different from the one imagined by the dictator and by Cini.

After the plan had been approved, a plan that, as we shall see, was anything but final, they moved on to phase two. There were five competitions for the main buildings that would make up the exposition. In

65. Giuseppe Pagano, Marcello Piacentini, Luigi Piccinato, Ettore Rossi, and Luigi Vietti, project for the E42, perspective drawing of the monumental axis, 1937. These drawings were shown to Mussolini on 28 April 1937; he approved them, although he probably did not agree with the architectural choices, which he considered to be too modern.

May, Piacentini was drawing up the guidelines for the competitions with respect to the definition of the architectural expression. At that point, several signs of the shift towards classicism emerged. The guidelines stated that "the classical and monumental sentiment, in the pure sense of the attitude of the spirit ... must be the basis for inspiration, albeit with modern and functional forms."[67] The type of architecture described was supposed to combine – just as fascism did in politics – tradition and innovation. The former element would become increasingly dominant, not just in "spirit," but from an aesthetic standpoint as well.

On 25 June, Mussolini was handed the report on the urban development plan. That may also have been the day that the diverging opinions of Pagano and Piccinato on one side, and Mussolini on the other, first became evident: "Mussolini insisted on a straight line traversing the new city with one major thoroughfare (Via Imperiale) from Rome to the sea. We instead insisted on separating the traffic from the internal roads so that transit would be on the outside – but to no avail."[68] A few days later, on 28 June, Mussolini once again visited the Tre Fontane area.[69]

On 30 June, Cini delivered the second report on the exposition to Mussolini. This time it clearly stated that the new city had to "create the ultimate style of our age: that of the twentieth year of the fascist era: the E42 style."[70] The E42 style would "unveil the character of an era." This was a true model of the regime's architecture, much more than Sabaudia or the Florence Station, and even more than the Città Universitaria in Rome. The architects were tasked with designing buildings inspired by a "classical feeling," according to "the criteria of monumentality and the grandiose," shaping buildings "destined to last so that in fifty or one hundred years' time their style will not seem aged or, even worse, worthless."

In the following months, work on the urban plan continued. In September, Cini wrote to Minister Alfieri to say "that our urban development plan can still undergo several changes."[71] At the end of the month Mussolini visited Nazi Germany and the two dictators discussed architecture. Hitler's explicit hostility towards modern architectural language must have driven him to notice Mussolini's classicist turnaround, and to convince him that architecture inspired by the Roman tradition worked better in reinforcing, on the domestic front, a policy of domination over the masses and, beyond the national borders, one of imperial expansion. It was no accident that Piacentini visited Munich ten days before Mussolini had. He had seen the works by Troost, including the Haus Der Kunst, which had been inaugurated with great pomp and ceremony by Hitler in July 1937. For the German dictator it was an architectural model, a temple of "true and everlasting German art."[72] Piacentini took the opposite view. His low opinion was directed at Hitler's underlying classicist and anti-modernist architectural choices (whose artistic presumption Piacentini scorned), not how it had been put into practice: "I have been to Munich and other places in Germany. As concerns theory we could, to a certain degree, agree with the great artist that is Hitler: but when it comes to the actual realizations. God forbid! I say NO ... Munich: a mere calque of architecture or parody."[73] Germany's obsession with replicas was rather far-removed from what Piacentini had in mind for the E42: classical, even figurative, yes, but interpreted on the basis of a modern conception.

Meanwhile, Piacentini took over command of the planning for the E42, and in early December, he was nominated head of Architectural Services, which de facto meant ousting the other four architects that Mussolini had originally summoned to collaborate (figure 66).[74] Contact

66. Marcello Piacentini, urban project for the E42, model, 1937–8. After
the initial working group (Piacentini, Pagano, Piccinato, Rossi, and Vietti)
submitted their plan, the project was taken over by Piacentini alone. In
December 1937, Piacentini was appointed superintendent of urban planning.

between Piacentini, Cini, and Oppo intensified. Those who were members of this circle, such as Ojetti, said they had "heard the orders echoing
in their words, and had perceived Benito Mussolini's scrutiny in their
anxiety."[75] Now Piacentini was free to direct the entire stylistic operation
on his own and implement a whole series of measures to bring to fruition
the architectural direction the dictator demanded. This was an extremely
important role, but one he needed to minimize in his testimonies for the
purge trials: "He was an adviser for architecture (an honorary position)
on the Committee for the 1942 Exposition, without designing any of
the buildings."[76] This statement was false, and as concerned his salary to
impart "unity of direction" on the E42, he was actually paid 30,000 lire
per annum.[77]

5 At the E42 "History Is Built"

At the E42, Mussolini did not limit himself to inspections or overseeing
the construction; rather, he directly intervened in planning solutions. Initially, he was involved in the decisions made by the architects who were

tasked with drafting the urban renewal plan. As noted earlier, Mussolini wanted a large thoroughfare to cross the city, against Pagano's and Piccinato's wishes. Piacentini also took part in all architectural decisions. A review of the series of events that took place between December 1937 and February 1938 sheds light on the decision-making process.

In December 1937, the various phases of the two competitions were coming to an end: the one for Palazzo dei Ricevimenti e dei Congressi and the other for Palazzo della Civiltà Italiana. Furthermore, the drawings for the third competition, the one for Piazza Imperiale, had to be submitted by 20 December. Piacentini was a member of the jury for the latter two competitions. On 13 December, the architect was appointed supervisor. That same day he wrote to Cini.[78] His report on the Palazzo della Civiltà Italiana was ready. The winner had been decided even before the jury met for the last time: it was La Padula and his group. However, several changes needed to be made to their project. Piacentini planned to summon the architect so that he could "suggest the changes."[79] On 18 December, the fourth and final meeting of the examining committee for the Palazzo della Civiltà Italiana was held. The report with the name of the winner was held back. The decision was made to wait for the results of the first competition, that is, the one for the Palazzo dei Ricevimenti e dei Congressi, for which a second-level competition had been launched with a 31 December deadline. Piacentini asked Cini if he could look at the projects that had been entered for this competition as well – as he was not a member of the examining committee in this case – "to balance out the two judgments."[80] This gave the Roman architect control over all three competitions.

The jury examined the projects for the Palazzo dei Ricevimenti e dei Congressi competition in the first half of January. On 5 January, Terragni wrote to Piccinato, who was a jury member. He thanked him for the support he had given him during the first phase of the competition, and asked for his support in the second phase.[81] The commission was unable to reach a unanimous decision and it is likely there was a heated discussion.[82] Libera came out the winner, after making some radical changes to the project as originally submitted in the first phase. Terragni and his team were defeated. Although the results of the competition were not made public, they were somehow leaked among the competitors.[83] On 15 January, the critic Carlo Belli sent his friend Terragni a telegram: "Libera wins Congressi. Padula Civiltà."[84] Two days later Terragni wrote to the painter Achille Funi. He denounced the "strange postponement of the official announcement of the results," relayed the opinion Muzio had expressed to him that "something strange is happening in Rome," and said he suspected that "Libera was redrafting his project." Naïvely, he asked that Cini be warned "so that deceit and mistaken judgments of such gravity do not occur."[85] Terragni was right to suspect that Libera was now revising his project. He mistakenly believed that Libera was leaning towards "overt modernity."[86] Meanwhile Pagano wrote to Oppo, "The situation has greatly changed ... it is best not to insist, but to leave Piacentini and Minnucci to their responsibilities."[87]

On 7 January, Cini asked to meet with Mussolini so that he could submit to him the projects chosen for the first and second competitions.[88] This decision was not made on the spur of the moment; it had been carefully planned. The third report on the E42 that Cini sent to Mussolini stated that the two winning projects would be submitted to the dictator.[89] If we bear in mind Terragni's suspicions and the "amendments" urged by Piacentini, the projects by the La Padula team and by Libera might already have been modified. In the same letter, Cini asked whether he had to be accompanied by Piacentini and Oppo. The request leads us to consider Piacentini's pivotal yet not indispensable role. In that precise moment, when some fundamental architectural and political decisions were pending, the hierarchical relationship between the dictator and the architect was clear for all to see. In his lucid prose, Ojetti managed to express the exceptional meaning of the real issue at stake: "History is being made at the E42, not houses."[90]

The meeting was scheduled for 22 January. At 6 p.m. that Saturday, Mussolini met with Cini first, and then he had Piacentini and Oppo come in. He was shown the two projects, neither of which satisfied him. He then requested a series of "adjustments" and ordered that the publication of the winners' names be postponed.[91] About ten days later, Cini informed Mussolini that "those projects" would be ready by 5 February. He added that the projects had been "revised, based on Your Excellency's directives."[92] Mussolini then met with Cini, Piacentini, and Oppo not on 5 February, but on February 11. In the meantime, the third competition, this one for Piazza Imperiale, also came to a conclusion. Besides the projects by La Padula and Libera that had been "done over," Piacentini showed Mussolini the project by the Quaroni team and by Moretti, co-winners of the third competition. In that case, the jury's work went ahead without any hitches.

On 11 February, the projects for the E42's main nucleus were all on display on Mussolini's desk in Palazzo Venezia. While the 22 January meeting was kept secret, this one was highly publicized. A press release reported on it, announcing that "Mussolini has approved the winning projects." Libera and La Padula's team, according to this reconstruction, had revised their project twice while the competition was still under way. This corroborates Libera's statement that he "was forced to design as many as five projects for the Palazzo dei Ricevimenti [e dei Congressi]" (figures 67 and 68).[93]

Mussolini had therefore looked at the projects twice, and had asked for changes. As we have seen previously, this was not the first time that

67. Ernesto La Padula, Giovanni Guerrini, and Mario Romano, project for the competition for the Palazzo della Civiltà Italiana at the E42, 1937–8. As with Adalberto Libera's project for the Palazzo dei Ricevimenti e dei Congressi, Mussolini asked that the drawings be changed even though the competition was ongoing.

something like this had happened, but the decision here was even more important. It did not merely indicate the architectural direction in the years to come; these buildings were supposed to show "even as many as four hundred years from now ... what we are today."[94]

However, the linearity of this path is only superficial. Leaving aside the emphasis on propaganda, the advancement of the E42 was actually at least in part improvised and not without its contradictions. The March 1938 report in which Federico Pinna Berchet asked that Mussolini find someone to replace him as general manager of the exposition clearly illustrates the true state of affairs. Pinna Berchet denounced a long list of irregularities, including the abandonment of the initial project that had been "carefully developed" to instead proceed "by trial and error, the sole concern being to finish at the earliest possible date"; the "twenty-two changes" that the urban development plan had undergone so

68. Adalberto Libera, project for the second-level competition for the Palazzo dei Ricevimenti e dei Congressi at the E42, model, 1937–8. While the competition was still ongoing, Mussolini called for some changes to be made to the project.

far; competitions held without a clear statement of the purpose of the buildings; the expectation to "use classical and Roman style to inspire the pavilions"; "the nonsensical" idea of building the five streets connecting the exposition with Rome so that they all converged in Piazza di Porta Capena; and, lastly, the total underestimation of the issue of accommodation.[95]

After the central area had undergone Mussolini's scrutiny, the other buildings followed suit. In June 1938, the fourth competition for the Palazzi delle Forze Armate (Armed Forces Headquarters) was completed. Announced in October 1937, the competition had a first and a second level, and De Renzi and Figini with Pollini were the co-winners: the two projects that were chosen were significantly different from each other, especially in their first versions. In March 1938, Cini tasked the BBPR group to study the project for the Palazzo delle Poste e dei Telegrafi: the commission was awarded to the second-place winners in the competition for the Palazzo della Civiltà Italiana. In the early months of 1938, Foschini was designing the church of Santi Pietro e Paolo. In July, Cini kept the tender for all these buildings on ice – that is, the museums that made up the buildings for the armed forces, the post office, and Foschini's church – until the dictator approved them.[96]

The drawings were examined by another special viewer besides Mussolini: Hitler. The submissions for the E42, which Germany joined on 25 October 1938, arrived on the German dictator's desk as well.[97] One hypothesis is that as early as September 1937, in Munich, the Chancellor spoke negatively about the E42 to Mussolini. Then, according to Speer, he again viewed the projects for the Roman Exposition. At the time, in 1937, the drawings illustrated modern buildings, but now, after being approved by the Italian dictator in July 1938, they featured façades with arches and columns. The Führer's reaction was wholly negative again. Though he thought he had taught the Duce something with his "lesson" on architecture in Munich, now he discovered that Mussolini was venturing down his own path. "He hasn't understood us!" exclaimed the Führer: "this is an empty, lifeless copy. But perhaps it is for the best, because it means we will stay in first place."[98] Much like Piacentini in his rebuff of the German dictator's works, Hitler dismissed the rival nation's architecture, referring to it as an "an empty copy," a "calque."

The competition for architectural hegemony and for cultural supremacy more generally had begun. The idea was that Italy and Germany would compete in this field after the war. The supremacy of the German race had to be founded on solid cultural foundations. Hitler acknowledged that Mussolini had the advantage of being able to rely on classical civilization, to harken back to the marvellous Roman architectural tradition, and to draw on the huge potential that the beauty of those monuments and of that mythicized past exerted on the masses. Thus, he made a special effort to see that Germany's predominantly military and economic power be supported "by the establishment and expansion of a great culture." To achieve this goal, he was willing to go beyond his leading role as a warrior: "I want to be a builder. It is only in spite of myself that I am a leader of armies."[99]

6 Terragni's Challenge, Pagano's Silence, Bottai's Dissent

Very few architects opposed the new stylistic direction, but Terragni and Pagano were among the dissenters. However, there was a paradox underlying this apparent opposition. There was, in fact, a certain political opportunism in Piacentini's embrace of fascism, in this case vis-à-vis the E42, whereas those who opposed Mussolini's stylistic choices had a fideistic attitude towards fascism. This was even more true in the grand scheme of the regime's architectural program, which deployed

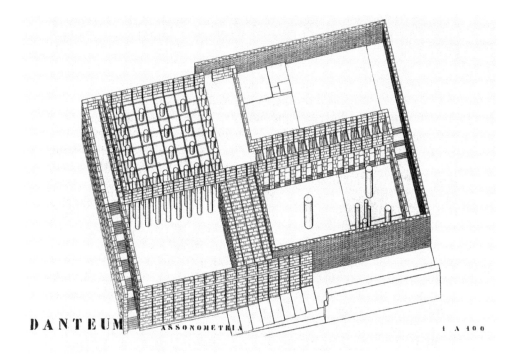

DANTEUM   ASSONOMETRIA   1 : A 100

69. Giuseppe Terragni and Pietro Lingeri, project for the Danteum in Rome, exploded diagram, 1938. It was to be built on Via Dell'Impero, opposite the Basilica of Maxentius. On 10 November 1938, Mussolini carefully examined the project and asked that some changes be made.

the pedagogical function of architecture on the front line of the enforcement of the Mussolinian project of forging "the new man"; the dissent jarred because it came from those who placed architecture at the service of the idea.

However, the regime found a solution for both factions. Terragni was allowed back into the game by being tasked with another prestigious commission: a project for the Danteum on Via dell'Impero (figure 69). In this case, the timing is of great importance. The first conversation between Mussolini, Valdameri, and Poss concerning the Danteum took place on 2 March 1938, and the following July, Terragni and Lingeri, who had been excluded from the E42 just a few months before, were already at work on the project. The decision clearly revealed the regime's unwillingness to exclude Terragni from the planning of Mussolini's Rome. According to those who assigned him the project, it was still possible to channel his dissidence within that "one single path" towards the achievement of a national architecture.

The choice of the site, Via dell'Impero, was significant. As we saw before, Mussolini had wanted the site of the BBPR's project for the Mostra della Civiltà Italica to be that urban void that had resulted from the new road that cut through the Fora. Now, a year later, the decision was made to place the Danteum in that area.[100] But Via dell'Impero was also at the centre of the monumental north-south axis connecting the Foro Mussolini and the E42, the model of fascist architecture. The area opposite the Basilica of Maxentius thus acquired even greater value. And to build up that area the regime did not choose an "accommodating" architect, but rather Italy's most intransigent defender of modern architecture. The challenge was significant, because overcoming Terragni's resistance meant overcoming the entire Rationalist front and therefore achieving a "unity of direction." Moreover, the architect planning the area, as seen in previous cases, had to directly come to terms with what the dictator wanted. If the rebellious Terragni did not want to follow Mussolini's directions, this time he would be opposing not the architect Piacentini, but the leader of fascism, towards whom he had up until then manifested an almost unlimited devotion. Proof of this was the aforementioned report for Palazzo del Littorio. Hence, any artistic dissent might lead to a political clash at the highest level.

Terragni seemed to sense all this: he was aware of the fact that he was facing the "terrible obstacle of a theme that is very close to rhetorical," and within a "hostile" historical context and environment. He wanted to demonstrate that it was possible produce modern architecture on that site, to make a building with the features of a monument – a "temple" – without resorting to stylistic formalism, something capable of arousing emotions with a "minimum amount of decorative or symbolist adjectivation."[101] Ultimately, the architect wanted to assert that modern architecture could convey those imperial myths that were accessible to the masses, and which lay at the foundations of fascist ideology. The first solution submitted to Mussolini did not oppose the unity of direction that characterized the new Rome, and it seemed to achieve an acceptable balance. The complex façade overlooking Via dell'Impero – on the city's monumental north-south axis – was mediated by building a neutral, stone-clad wall, while the columns on the inside were in abstract geometrical shapes, resembling cylinders rather than the architectural elements of classical tradition. Of course, we know that Mussolini would ask the architects to make changes – modifications "according to the Duce's suggestions" – and that Terragni eventually seemed to lose interest in the project.[102] Perhaps the myth of the Duce was beginning to show a few cracks, even for Terragni.

Things were different with Pagano. Whereas Mussolini considered the classicist architecture of the E42 to be instructional in so far as it conveyed the values of fascism through the celebration and renewal of the myth of ancient Rome, Pagano saw the architecture of the E42 as the exact opposite: it was anti-educational, false, and dishonest, so to his mind, it could not be truly fascist. Pagano felt that the real "cohesiveness" of a national architecture that could be understood by the people, architecture that "moved towards the people," should be based on simplicity, not arches and columns. Simplicity also meant morality as opposed to luxury, to the excesses of the classicist style, to useless ornaments.[103] Before this profound divergence in opinions – which, curiously enough, Pagano did not directly ascribe to Mussolini – the architect was offered a salary of 26,000 lire per annum to preserve his "silent consensus" for three years.[104] The agreement was signed on 26 March 1938 but, significantly, it was applied as of 1 January 1938 so that it also covered the period of time when Mussolini's interventions falsified the outcomes of the competitions. While in 1931 it had still been possible to discuss which architectural style best represented fascism, and to make public the heated debate between traditionalists and Rationalists, now, in 1938, when architecture's fate was actually being determined, this was no longer acceptable. The truth of the matter is that Pagano was only in part silent on the issue: he did make a few thinly veiled critical remarks on the architecture of the exposition. Then, when the three years of the agreement were up, he published fierce attacks against Piacentini and the E42 in *Costruzioni-Casabella*. In the February issue Pagano denounced the failure of the exposition, and noted how the competitions – though he was there, he did not sign the reports [105] – had been characterized by "acts of harm and deception." He went on to call those who had spent two and a half million lire to "monumentalize the void," … to make "senseless columns," as "squanderers of public money."[106] And just as quickly the magazine was seized from the newsagents and no longer sold. While some insinuated, perhaps rightly, that the articles had been "inspired" by Giulio Carlo Argan and Cesare Brandi, Piacentini urged Gherardo Casini, the general manager of the Italian Press Core, to intervene, and to carry out "what we said the other night."[107] He was considering replacing Pagano as director of *Costruzioni-Casabella* with people he trusted ("My men are ready"), and he did not want to wait any longer, urging Casini to immediately intervene with the publisher: "All you have to do is call Mazzocchi. I am at your disposal."[108]

Pagano, who certainly did not lack courage, openly challenged Piacentini, condemning his stylistic choices, denouncing the "false" nature of that architecture. But he did not see or did not want to see Mussolini's hand in this. Wasn't he perhaps the first among those "squanderers of the public money"? His closeness with some of the party officials, such as Bottai, his membership to the School of Fascist Mysticism, the time he spent in the milieu of the *Popolo d'Italia*, and the fact that he had experienced the events of the Città Universitaria and the E42 from within, had no doubt allowed him to gather clues that pointed at Mussolini's direct responsibility in the architectural decision-making. Pagano could not possibly have been naïve enough to think that the dictator was merely the victim of poor advisers, like Piacentini and Ojetti. It was his political faith that made him short-sighted, that kept him from bringing that name to the dock, and that led him to believe that the dictator would change his ways. His candidacy in 1943 for Minister of National Education, taking over for Bottai, must also be seen from this perspective.[109] A candidacy that, needless to say, did not get the thumbs up from the head of government.

Mussolini, in fact, could not lend support to the modernist front – likely a minority – in architectural culture; above all, he needed to isolate those sectors of the Ministry of National Education that supported it. The result of this was a wide rift between Mussolini and Bottai as far as architecture was concerned. Bottai had launched a reform that fiercely opposed the classicist architectural style the dictator sought for the E42, and for Rome. The minister had at first created an office for contemporary art and had promised his support so that "a clearly modern architecture could bestow the appearance of our day and age on our cities." More importantly, he ordered the creation of a new Restoration Charter – that is, the *Istruzione* drafted by Argan in 1939 and published by Marino Lazzari, general manager of the ministry, in 1942 – which even included the demand to make new constructions in the classicist style illegal. This meant rejecting all buildings featuring arches and columns whose construction was under way, and undermining Mussolini's entire plan, which hinged on architecture as a link to the myth of ancient Rome. The rift grew even larger when the minister decided to replace Piacentini, Giovannoni, and Gigli with Terragni, Roberto Longhi, and Bianchi Bandinelli on the National Committee for Education, Arts, and Science. The architectural and artistic policy pursued by the Direzione General delle Arti (General Direction of the Arts) – led by Argan – was clearly in contrast with that of Piacentini, which had Mussolini's support. These cunning moves by the former "postman" of anti-fascism in Turin, who had now penetrated the heart of the institutions, were rocking the foundations of the totalitarian regime.[110]

Nonetheless, Bottai's decision to make public a text that was so hostile to Mussolini's architectural policy vis-à-vis the E42 at that time seems to have been motivated by opportunism. In the fall of 1942, the minister could clearly perceive the impending crisis within the regime – Mussolini was no longer a leader who was always right, quite the contrary "to many, now he was always wrong" – and he did not rule out the possibility of a political collapse. In this context, which was probably also reinforced by Bottai's pro-modernist stance, the road to an Italy free from fascism was being paved. "He [Grandi], he and I, and Galeazzo [Ciano] are three men who could have earned a political position for ourselves even without fascism."[111]

For his policies, ones that so openly diverged from the dictator's decisions, that offered an image of fascism's artistic policy that was rather less totalitarian and much more "Italian," Bottai could have been removed from his office as minister. And at that point, for Mussolini, replacing him with Pagano would have meant going back on his word, and further demonstrating the significant tensions within the regime's policies. Mussolini chose Carlo Alberto Biggini to replace Bottai, and the first thing the new minister of national education did – Piacentini reassured him with a sense of relief – was to "declare he was against the defence of the avant-garde."[112]

7 The Totalitarian Acceleration and Architecture

1 Architecture for the Myths of the Totalitarian State

After the "resounding" success of the conquest of Ethiopia, Mussolini grew increasingly convinced that the relationship between the nations was about to change radically and that Italy had to be readied for "a new age." In the face of the crisis assailing the West, Mussolini wanted to lead the country to "its appointment with history," assigning it a special role, a mission for the "new civilization."[1] In the new global order, Italy's "civilizing role" would "naturally" stem from the fact that it was heir to the universal and classical spirit exerted by ancient Rome through its empire. Mussolini took charge of this plan to grant Italian civilization, which he believed superior to all others, the role of guiding and organizing a universal civilization. With this in mind, he decided to move quickly and hasten the process of the totalitarian transformation of society and the state so that they could meet the international challenge in the best possible conditions.

"The future belongs to the people who believe," said Mussolini, that is, to those who were energized by the animating myths. The myths – of ancient Roman roots, the empire, the nation, of Mussolini himself as the embodiment of the fascist principle – favoured the process of society's integration in the fascist state, and conveyed the notion of the "new man." Architecture thus became a powerful tool in fascism's hands, one that could be used to "shape" the character of the Italian people, to favour the political engagement of the masses in the development of political myths. It was becoming increasingly clear that the "arcane power" of architecture could be used by politics in the totalitarian plan to radically transform people's consciousness.[2] An example of this – the association is inevitable – came from Nazi Germany.

The E42 emerged within this turnaround in the historical process, marked by a race for the supremacy of civilization, a race in which architecture played a new role. It was no longer a matter of using architecture to show that Italy was one huge building site, and that fascism was moving towards the people; nor was it a matter of using architecture to glorify fascism, to build consensus, and to symbolize endurance. In that first phase, architecture could speak diverse languages, and Mussolini could uphold different trends with the same bold nonchalance. Nor was the aim of the E42 to fill state coffers, which had been depleted by the Ethiopian War and the Spanish Civil War, awaiting the war that would bring about the new world order.[3]

The E42 – whose theme, the "Olympic Games of Civilization," was no accident – marked the transition to a second phase, one that was characterized by the logic of "daring." Now architecture, in harmony with the "new times," was being asked to take a step further, to use a certain language, one that was more suited to the elaboration of the founding myths of fascism, *romanità*, and empire. "In Italy today," Mussolini would say, "it is no time for history …, rather, it is a time for myths ... Myths alone can shape and energize a people, one that is about to pave its own destiny."[4] By fuelling those myths, architecture was asked to influence the character of the Italian people, to intervene more incisively in the process of fascistization, so that the construction of the "new civilization" could move faster. The E42 would thus be used as a tool to educate the masses in a fascist sense, and thus bear witness to the mission of civilization. In Piacentini's words, it "has a specific mission to accomplish," and its realization would be "a conquest" on the part of "universal civilization."[5] Precisely because it was invested with this ideological weight, the E42 became a reference model for other important architectural interventions, both in Rome and in other cities.

To be able to fulfil the needs of a totalitarian policy, the architecture of the E42 above all had to be addressed to the masses, and the masses needed to be able to understand it. Hence, it could not be selective. It had to serve as a way of communicating with the people. Mussolini was very forthright on that point: "In art, just as in writing and talking, one must be understood, before all else understood."[6] This was why he could not accept modern architecture that featured glass palaces, such as the ones sketched out in Vietti's perspectives, initially submitted to the dictator by Pagano. That sort of architecture was far too abstract, it was hard to understand, and it lacked figurative references to the history of national architecture. It was detached from the values of popular culture; it drew inspiration from an architectural internationalism that jarred with fascism's policy of national expansion. Moreover, it seemed nearly incapable of producing those processes of identification that were demanded by fascist mythology. With the likely intention of eventually sharing his concern, in private Mussolini wondered, "When will these young people understand that this modern architecture cannot be the architecture of the empire?"[7] The fact that he now excluded modern architecture, which four years earlier he had publicly said he supported, was not because his taste had changed. It was because that architecture had become less appropriate to his political strategy.

The architecture of the empire had to symbolize a powerful myth – and the most powerful myth of all was that of ancient Rome – one that was capable of influencing the popular imagination as deeply and as broadly as possible in order to stir it to action. It had to become a tool of national identification and education for all. In that architecture it had to be easy to identify oneself, to find the essential, eternal, and universal features of Italian civilization. One had to be able to grasp the indissoluble link between the modernity of the present regime and ancient Roman tradition. That was why arches and columns had to be used: "a new, classical city" had to be built outside Rome, where visitors could be offered "a vision that will remind them of the Forum." It was a type of architecture that was conceived to foster the myth of the empire and the hegemonic policy of fascism. It was conceived to celebrate its creator, who was its embodiment. As Piacentini wrote, the architecture of the E42 was the *facies* of the Rome of Mussolini's day and age.[8]

The dictator's behaviour regarding the events of the E42 helps to reveal some of the mechanisms behind the myth of Mussolini. On the one hand, he seemed to act openly, carrying out inspections, approving the first urban plan in the presence of the press, elevating himself to the rank of guarantor of competition rules, almost theatrically exhibiting the transparency and immediacy of his decisions. The masses who identified with him saw themselves as being the true artificers of those decisions, the protagonists of a totalitarian democracy. But, on the other hand, Mussolini was scheming behind the scenes. Not satisfied with the first urban plan, he organized secret meetings, with the help of Cini and Piacentini, and he called for the projects by Libera and by La Padula's team to be modified. He deceived some of the fascists who trusted him, like Terragni, who believed the competitions to be fair. He was well aware of just how complex the architectural milieu was, and of the fierce differences of opinion that divided certain factions regardless of their belief in fascism. He knew that an architectural style could not be imposed by means of decrees or manifestos: so he subjugated architecture, determined its direction, without giving the impression of coercion, but rather by suggesting the idea of a voluntary flow. He offered the image of a natural process, as if between architects a shared sensitivity had emerged thanks to the fascist environment. He made sure that the projects hewed closely to his directives, and then he endorsed them by giving them the thumbs up, forcing architects to experience a preview of the totalitarian way.

For architecture to be relevant to this political program, it could not be the expression – as it actually was – of many different artistic personalities, ones that were distant from, if not incompatible with, each other. Rather, it had to display a unity of direction, it had to forgo individuality and become almost anonymous. In the ancient Roman world, Mussolini glimpsed the model of a relationship between the artist-individual and the community that had to be harnessed and framed within the totalitarian idea of the state. "Architecture," said Mussolini in May 1938, "is always anonymous: The Baths of Diocletian, the Baths of Caracalla, the Pantheon of Agrippa, the Forum of Caesar, the Forum of Augustus ... And today these architects expect to add their name tag."[9] The architect's individuality might have cast a shadow on the political meaning of the work. It was far better to replace the label with the name, carved in stone, of the person in charge.

One focus of the E42 project was the transformation of dozens of individual contributions into a single group work. Piacentini seemed to be the most suited to bringing this delicate and fundamental procedure to completion, and he personally revised numerous projects. The E42 Technical Office, headed by Minnucci, redesigned the buildings to iron out differences and accentuate similarities. Each individual building maintained a margin of recognizability, but its authorship was no longer that of a sole architect. Its authorship was now shared by so many that its origin became uncertain. The weakening of individual characteristics and the strengthening of a shared objective were necessary to activate the stylistic aim of the exposition, that is, to affirm that fascism, like the other great civilizations of the past, had its own architecture, its own style. It was not a style that was imposed, because that would have run counter to the essential nature of art itself; rather, it was a style that was spontaneously born in fascist times. That it had been skilfully planned beforehand had to be kept secret.

2 Piacentini's Architectural Unity

The global supremacy of fascist civilization had to correspond to architectural supremacy. The E42 had to demonstrate the power of the architecture of "the great Mussolinian age." Piacentini's intellectual contribution to fascism, the way he helped Mussolini to place architecture at the service of politics, emerged within this context. The architect was well aware of the instrumental value of architecture and its function as "handmaiden" to politics. In a newspaper interview, he explained that the greatness of a people must be measured in terms of the greatness of their monuments, accurately designating architecture's "circensian" task: "along with bread and games, we also need it to preserve the political order." He recalled the figures of Julius II and Napoleon, their names "consecrated throughout the centuries" precisely by virtue of their "powerful building policy." He alluded to the Duce, to the new Napoleon in the field of public works. Mussolini was impressed by the article, and saved it with his private documents.[10] But besides its circensian role, its help in maintaining a political consensus, Piacentini knew that architecture could have a much more active and pedagogical purpose for the masses. In introducing his magazine *Architettura*, Piacentini wanted to underscore the "most powerful functions" of architecture, the fact that it was "an immediate educational tool." He stressed each building's capacity to "represent" something.[11] To be able to deploy architecture's educational potential, a complex and engaging task, he forged an even closer alliance with fascism's leader.

The architect thus coherently welcomed the totalitarian turnaround urged by Mussolini, which resulted in greater discipline in the field of architecture. He clearly upheld this idea in November 1935, when he inaugurated the academic year. On that occasion, as seen in the previous chapter, he stated that "life today," in terms of both fascism and the mass population, "required a unity of direction." He claimed that in the greatest ages of the past "this principle was the foundation of architecture: the unifying spirit that elevated Greek temples and Roman amphitheatres, and that led to the rebirth of classical style in the Renaissance." He stated that unity was the distinguishing characteristic of the greatest past civilizations. However, he stressed that unity did not imply "the suppression of the imagination, or a uniformity of expression: it ought only to signify faith, rule, discipline" both in its study and in the work itself. In this "unity of direction" the personality of the artist expresses itself "in the balance of geometry, in the expressive quality of the details, and in that general sensibility ... that belongs to and distinguishes each individual."[12] With Mussolini's blessing, Piacentini applied the principle of the "unity of direction" to his work on the Città Universitaria. On that occasion, he praised the oneness between the "guiding spirit of the fascist constitution" and the "unity of direction" in the work of Italian architects.[13] The same principle was now present in the great venture of the E42. Its design was the result of a "shared ambition ... aimed at achieving a leading role," of "thinking big and in a unified way," and of an "assembly of the living forces of Italian art."[14]

In architecture, just as in politics, "unified" did not mean "uniform." In politics, fascism, in this phase of totalitarian evolution, sought to educate citizens, imposing upon them "a discipline, an awareness, and a will that are not uniform ... but rather unitarian and deeply centralized."[15] In architecture, Piacentini distinguished between "a unity of direction" and "uniformity." "Unity of direction" did not imply the disappearance of the artist's personality or, even worse, the imposition of a style. Piacentini avoided talking about a "fascist style" because it simplified a much more complex reality.[16] By contrast, "unity of direction" took into account both differences in trajectories of each artist and in the ongoing process. It clearly expressed the direction of an architecture characterized by shared figurative traits, and it implied the consensual participation of individual architects, who joined forces and participated in a common effort to build architecture that would be representative of an era.

The style of the E42 could not be the style of a single architect. Because it was the expression of the supremacy of the civilization of fascist Italy, it had to be the result of the collective work of the architects. "Unity of direction" entailed a desire for synthesis; it led towards an architecture consistent with a totalitarian vision of the state. Piacentini's specific contribution to the totalitarian transition of fascism could be measured through the elaboration of the concept and practice of architectural cohesiveness. There was a curious overlap between what Mussolini "felt" and some political statements made by Piacentini. He too spoke of the mutating relations between countries, the rise of totalitarian regimes, the crisis of cosmopolitan and international cultures, the peoples who had discovered renewed strength in their own history. The "new Renaissance" of Italian architecture proclaimed by the architect presented itself right on time for its appointment with history.[17] Piacentini had a unique rapport with the Duce, resulting from the large amount of time they had spent together, making him an exceptional interpreter of Mussolinian policies.

3 For Imperial Rome

Several times prior to the advent of the E42, Piacentini had supported the idea of a unitariness in architecture, stressing the need to direct various contributions within a wider vision of the whole. Already in the 1920s – when the fascists had not yet seized power – he had spoken about the "unity of composition" between the street and the house, about the need to let the community prevail over the individual, and of the need to limit the individual's artistic freedom.[18] Later, this time directed by Mussolini, he suggested the creation of a Rettore all'Edilizia (Head of

Construction) within the Governorate of Rome. Lastly, when the dictatorship was at its peak, he encouraged Mussolini to bring back the figure of the "building dictator": "I dream of a *Dittatore edile* in Rome, a person who, like the leaders of ancient times, has the skill and wants to take responsibility for imposing order."[19]

A laboratory for testing these ideas was the Città Universitaria in Rome, followed by the E42. However, in the capital, Piacentini had many other opportunities to practise directing and coordinating architectural projects. A series of such projects came about around 1935 with the launch of three important works right in the historical heart of the city, all characterized by an evident stylistic unity: the reorganization of Piazza Augusto Imperatore by Morpurgo, the opening of Corso del Rinascimento, which also included Foschini's new design for Piazza Navona, and the redevelopment of the Borghi to open access to St. Peter's Square, a project designed by Piacentini himself. As mentioned before, Mussolini kept an eye on all three projects. In the case of the Mausoleum of Augustus, the dictator intervened to "enhance the monumental nature of the architecture";[20] in Via della Conciliazione, he wanted to give the work a "sole conception," one "continually guided" by the Duce.[21]

Morpurgo and Foschini both had a close relationship with Piacentini. The former was one of his most trusted collaborators, whereas the latter was one of his closest associates. The strategy behind these interventions was not too different from the one implemented in the Città Universitaria. Piacentini was the director, and although his position was not official, he was still very active. His colleagues submitted their drawings to him, whereupon he made corrections and suggested alternative solutions. For instance, he suggested that Foschini knock down a pre-existing building because it was "picturesque in an old-fashioned way" but in a setting that was "broad, serious, noble." He then suggested "completely closing off" the curve in Piazza Navona so that it would be easier to imagine the ancient stadium, "reiterating the volume of the houses and completing the curve." The idea was accompanied by two rough sketches illustrating what he had in mind.[22] Instead of coordinating various buildings in a single site, as with the Città Universitaria, he was now overseeing three interventions in three distinct spots in the city's Renaissance district.

Piacentini introduced the three projects in a special issue of his magazine, *Urbanistica della Roma Mussoliniana* (Urban Planning in Mussolinian Rome). He wrote that the three interventions "shared a kinship," and that they assumed a "unified character." He stressed the link between this architectural vision and the totalitarian "political current": the one tended to support unified architectural initiatives, while the other aimed to achieve an "increasingly rigorous organization of social gatherings."[23] Those were three episodes, "three great and evocative pages of the monumental construction," to be viewed within the larger framework of the E42, and of the "Great Rome of the imperial plan."[24]

However, other works belonged to this unified design as well. One of these was the opening of a large "panoramic" avenue, 20 metres in diameter, running from Caffè Aragno on Via del Corso, through Piazza Parlamento, and all the way to the Ponte Umberto I, providing views of the dome of St. Peter's. Included in the 1931 urban development plan, the demolition work for this avenue involved, among other tasks, tearing down the church of San Nicolò ai Prefetti. The project was commissioned from Piacentini and Spaccarelli who, in July 1937, were busy with the working drawings: according to the two architects, the opening of that space in the heart of the Renaissance district would produce "a surprise similar to the one opened by Via dell'Impero." It would also constitute one of the two main axes crossing the historical city, specifically the one running from east to west (the other one ran from north to south).[25] When Muñoz asked whether these demolitions were endangering the oldest part of Rome, Piacentini replied that "in history there are strong eras and weak eras; a strong people must impose its will in every field ... In previous centuries, in Rome, the popes did just that; we are currently living in an age of power, one for which we want and need to leave a lasting sign."[26]

Two of the three works described above – the isolation of the Mausoleum of Augustus and the opening of Corso del Rinascimento – had already been included in the 1928 plan drafted by Brasini, who lamented the fact that his ideas for the city were often carried out by others. His plan followed the guidelines featured in the speech Mussolini gave in 1925 concerning the future development of the capital. We have already seen how the promises the dictator had made in the mid-1920s concerning the "liberation" of the area around the principal monuments of ancient Rome had come to fruition over the years. Among these the Pantheon was the sole exception. However, if the houses around this building, the most fascinating and best conserved from ancient times, were not destroyed, it was certainly not because Mussolini had any scruples about preserving the environmental context. Rather, it was because his demolition and reconstruction policies, the architectural "invention of tradition," was advancing by degrees. One thing is for sure: Mussolini had no intention of putting the work off for long. And indeed in 1938 he met with Brasini to examine one of his updated proposals on the reorganization of the area around the Pantheon. The solutions Brasini brought to the meeting must not have convinced him, however, because once again the architect's imaginative ideas remained solely on paper.[27] The dictator's renewed interest in creating a forum opposite the Pantheon is no doubt related to his plan to "liberate" the monument, prepared during those same months by Quaroni, who was very close to Piacentini at the time. We cannot overlook the fact that the young architect's plan was no less disruptive than the one put forward by Brasini, at least as concerned the tearing down of the areas adjacent to the Pantheon. Nonetheless, the reconstruction project he put forward resembled the buildings that Piacentini, Foschini, and Morpurgo were making, and it was more or less in line with the "unity of direction" of Mussolini's Rome.[28] That was enough to convince Mussolini to withhold support from Brasini, at least based on the plausible theory that he had examined both projects. A few years later, the area surrounding the Pantheon became one of the priorities of the 1941 Variante (Variant) of the urban development plan, and the object of a detailed intervention. The coordination of this project was again assigned to Piacentini.

Unquestionably, the Palazzo del Littorio, built in the Foro Mussolini after a second-level competition was announced for the area around Porta San Paolo, played an important role in this strategy of unified urban modelling. Because of its political meaning and huge size, but also because of the well-known controversies related to its building, the palazzo, which was designed by Foschini's team, marked a decisive step towards the establishment of a classicist style. The authors' choices were paradigmatic: they explained that they had designed an architecture that was "rooted in the everlasting and ever resurgent greatness of Rome," and that they had sought in this work "the only [result] that promised not to be ephemeral" because "this is a building that must remain standing for the centuries to come." This was why, they stated, they harkened back to the solid tradition of the Italian palazzo, and bestowed on the façades an "absolute unity," the same one that had ennobled the finest examples of civil architecture from the Renaissance.[29] Piacentini, who must have known about the plan as it was being developed, could only greet the work of his "dear friends Del Debbio, Foschini, and Morpurgo" with enthusiasm. He praised its "very Italian" character and the architectural layout that had "something military about it." He applauded the renewal of Italian architecture that now harkened back to the "sacred laws of the past," the same ones that he himself had recommended to the architects working on the E42.[30]

As a thoroughfare connecting the Universal Exposition to the city's historical district, the design of Via Imperiale required an architectural layout consistent with the exposition. In this case, a new law obliged the buildings lining the four squares that marked this route to "achieve a unified architectural character," and others to feature "the same architectural façade." The architectural solutions, as we saw before, were designed by ten young architects, coordinated by Piacentini and approved by Mussolini.[31]

Lastly, the Termini Station constituted yet another decisive step in the project to create a unified urban plan: its development was emblematic of the stylistic arc Mussolini imposed on architecture. On 16 February 1937, the dictator approved the first project by Mazzoni. The main façade – the crux of the matter – was characterized by a large portico topped by a room completely surrounded by glass, a metaphor for modernity, with a view on one side of both the city and the Alban hills. Mazzoni explained, "We did not want to create a monument"; Mussolini "personally" intervened in the project, "highlighting certain fundamental requirements."[32] These probably included separating the entrance, which would be adjacent on Via Principe di Piemonte, from the exit on Piazza dei Cinquecento. Piacentini recalled that "we owe this excellent idea to the Duce, who understood the effect of the large piazza on the incoming traveller."[33]

This first project, so modern in form and not unlike the first conception of the E42 that Pagano had presented around the same time, was almost immediately cast aside. Between August 1937 and January 1938, Mazzoni worked on a new draft, which was submitted to Mussolini on 15 January 1938. The architect removed one floor, eliminated the large glass hall, and drew a large projecting roof that was not taller than the pre-existing ones all along the façade. This second project also failed to convince the dictator, probably because it wasn't sufficiently monumental. It is worth remembering that, during the same period, the dictator was also examining designs for the E42 competition. In mid-February, Mussolini once again met with Mazzoni, who submitted the designs for the second project, as well as for a third one. Based on what the architect later recalled, the meeting lasted half an hour, during which the two men discussed the architecture of the travellers' building, which represented the main façade. Mazzoni defended the first idea for the project, the modern one, which Mussolini had approved the previous February. Mussolini did not express any preferences. However, the third project featured many significant differences compared with the first. In this version as well, the glass hall had been removed and in its place was a huge portico consisting of a series of cylindrical paired columns 18 metres in height – larger than the ones at the Pantheon – extending across a front of 230 metres.[34]

After meeting with Mazzoni, Mussolini met with Antonio Stefano Benni, the minister of communications, and approved the third project.

Between March and June, Mazzoni modified the pillars, adding capitals and tapering the shafts. In other words, he turned them into massive columns. As had happened with the E42, the design evolved from a modern image to something that was definitely more classical. The Termini Station was also subsumed into that unity of direction that resulted in the look of the E42, and Mussolini himself had supervised this metamorphosis. The model of the project thus modified – there were now 52 columns topped by capitals and arranged in a double row – was presented to the dictator on the platform at Ostiense Station in February 1939, where – for the third time – it was approved. It was later sent to the New York Exposition, after Ojetti gave it the thumbs up. In totalitarian countries, the potential for architecture to enthral the masses was clearly being played out on the theme of the column, its form and size: around the same time, Speer was designing a new station for the south of Berlin, with a façade featuring huge Doric columns, as tall as those in the Pantheon. The column symbolized endurance and universality for these regimes that wanted to impose their model on the entire world, and the fact that a column could be even larger than the kind that was used in ancient times spoke volumes about a new, insuperable power.

In 1940 in Rome, when the building site was in full swing, the sculptor Francesco Cocchia worked on a life-size plaster model of the capitals. Piacentini himself assisted Cocchia, designing some alternative solutions. In March 1941, accompanied by Mazzoni, Ojetti visited the building site of the Acque Albule, where life-size models had been prepared to show what the columns for the façade looked like (figure 70). He then reported back to the minister, saying that the cornice of the entablature had to be "more Roman, maybe with more dentils, as Piacentini has suggested."[35] As concerned the columns, he jotted down in his notebook: "Bigger than the ones at the Pantheon. Good tapering, no entasis ... the capitals have figures. To give them a more chiaroscuro effect Piacentini told Mazzoni and Cocchia to use only half-figures with a strong projection." The architect went from a capital shaped like the fasces in the Arco della Vittoria (Victory Monument) in Bolzano, to a figurative capital. Ojetti continued: "In short, His Excellency of the Arches and Columns is satisfied. And so is Piacentini."[36] Considering Ojetti wrote these words nine years after the dispute over arches and columns, one detects a note of vindication. Now, much more than before, the critic had Mussolini's ear. In the events surrounding the Città Universitaria Piacentini had prevailed, but now, Pagano bitterly observed, "Ojetti is always right and Piacentini is neither willing nor interested in contradicting him."[37] Rather than being unwilling, however, Piacentini clearly understood and supported Mussolini's turnaround.

70. Angiolo Mazzoni, project for the Termini Station in Rome, 1941, life-size model of the portico on the façade realized at the Acque Albule in Tivoli, 1941. The columns, which were bigger than the ones at the Pantheon, were designed based on suggestions made by Ojetti and Piacentini.

Ojetti observed that with the Termini Station and the E42, an Italian style, "the Roman and classical one," was reborn. This was not just the result of artistic sensitivity; it had come about for "political, and therefore historical reasons" as well, because "entire wars, bloody ones, are fought and held in the name and the august signs of Rome in its insignia."[38] This was yet another reference to Mussolini's parallel action, his effort to build and thus forge a new man, to impose on the rest of the world the supremacy of the fascist, Italian, and Latin civilization, which had now found a greater and more totalitarian expression in a classical, albeit modernized, architecture. This architecture renewed the splendour of the same vision of empire that was being fought for. By following those "political reasons" Mussolini promised to enable – once the war had been won – "as much as possible, and with total impetus" a policy that would allow "the genius of the Latin people, with Italy at its heart" to achieve a leading position. And the symbol of this policy, of this civilizing mission, "in disagreement with the world," was the E42; "On these initial foundations [the E42], conceived with the principles of a renewing art, we shall build the new age of intelligence of both Italy and its empire."[39]

4 The 1941 "Variante" of Rome's Urban Development Plan

The final episode in the totalitarian turnaround in architecture involved the review of Rome's urban development plan, which began with a directive from Mussolini in January 1941.[40] The decision to locate the E42 in the Tre Fontane area, and the resulting greater importance of the axis connecting the city to the coast, required a review of the previous urban plan of 1931. Piacentini, along with Giovannoni, Oppo, Paolo Salatino, and Virgilio Testa, headed the commission charged with drafting a plan for the 1941 Variante.[41] The first three men had been directly chosen by Mussolini. Piacentini and Oppo would provide continuity with the design of the E42. Moreover, the involvement of Giovannoni, known for his lack of enthusiasm when it came to modernist "trends," clearly pointed to Mussolini's new classicistic tendencies. As the elderly Roman engineer explained, "classical shapes are proof that the Italian language is still alive.[42]

Piacentini was well aware of the meaning of that urban revival, which he himself may have solicited, as well as of the possible extraordinary impact it might have within the gradual development of a fascist style. Referring to the city's future "physiognomy," he noted that it had entered a new and "highly important" stage after the founding of the empire and the construction of the E42. Consequently, he claimed that "nowadays, more than ever, one must dare, have a broader vision, and avoid falling back into the narrow-mindedness of the past."[43] Both architecture and politics were urgently needed to speed things up and had to be "daring." "To be daring" was what Mussolini now demanded, and Piacentini promptly echoed him. Architecture and politics proceeded in unison towards "supremacy in civilization."[44]

In reviewing the plan, Piacentini employed a large group of outside collaborators, to whom he assigned projects for the individual areas. Piccinato, Del Debbio, Marconi, Filippone, Fuselli, Concezio Petrucci, and Giorgio Calza Bini were among them, and all of them were beholden to Piacentini.[45] Some of them were asked to draft detailed plans for the central areas of the city, and for areas connecting the E42 with both the city and the sea. Piacentini commissioned the School of Architecture to work on three crucial sites: Piazza Venezia, the new piazza at the Termini Station, and the square opposite the Pantheon – in other words, he commissioned himself. A site plan of the area of the Pantheon has been preserved in the Piacentini archive: it called for the demolition of a portion of the surrounding buildings and the construction of a road – 30 metres wide at its narrowest point – connecting Piazza della Rotonda with Piazza Augusto Imperatore.[46] Piacentini was now applying this method of unified planning and design, first applied to single instances of urban architecture (the Città Universitaria and the E42), to the whole city. These projects, rendered in a holistic drawing, were at the basis of four huge models, which measured 300 square metres overall. All this, accompanied by a final report – more like a "book" as it was described by its author to his friend Ojetti – was presented to Mussolini on 29 October 1941 in the rooms of the Palazzo delle Esposizioni on Via Nazionale (figure 71).[47] Unlike the 1931 urban development plan, whose aim was to enlarge the city, this was a plan featuring a "superior and final order." But in 1931, the architect added, "the need for stately urban and architectural guidelines" had not yet "established its grip."[48]

During the same visit Mussolini was presented with, in addition to these two models, another massive model, that of the Foro Mussolini, which was being prepared by Moretti. It was the third and final version of the urban plan for the area, known as "Forma Ultima Fori" (figure 72).[49] In this most recent plan, the original core – which, between 1928 and 1932, Del Debbio had designed to cover a very small area – had been extended to cover over 10 square kilometres, almost competing in terms of size with the massive structure for Nazi Party assemblies Speer had designed for Nuremberg, spreading over an area of 16 square kilometres (figure 73).[50] In the Forma Ultima Fori plan, the Foro embraced the whole hillside valley of Monte Mario, developing eastwards beyond Tor di Quinto, all the way to the bight of the River Tiber. The eastern side would feature a horsetrack and a rowing pond. Near Villa Glori, the course of the Tiber would be changed, allowing for the creation of an artificial island. Farther to the south, beyond the river, the new plan also included changes to the Flaminio neighbourhood. A new axis crossing the Forum in a north-south direction would serve as a new northern entrance to the city. The area included in the new perimeter was redesigned and embellished to include gardens, sports grounds, arenas, terracing, and streets.

The Foro Mussolini and the E42 represented the two extremes of the monumental axis crossing the city. Starting from the Tor di Quinto plateau, the two roads, Cassia and Flaminia, formed one huge thoroughfare that stretched beyond the Ponte XXVIII Ottobre, whose construction was under way, to reach Piazzale Flaminio, which had been "enlarged and monumentally restored." Proceeding beyond Piazza del Popolo, along Via del Corso or the street parallel to it, one reached Piazza Venezia. From the "spiritual centre" of the city one continued along Via dell'Impero, went around the Colosseum and down Via dei Trionfi, and beyond the Baths of Caracalla, to finally reach the new Via Imperiale, which was "100

71. Mussolini examining the model of the Forma Ultima Fori, the urban development plan of the Foro Mussolini, in the rooms of the Palazzo delle Esposizioni on Via Nazionale in Rome. Holding the pointer, to his right, is Luigi Moretti. Cipriano Efisio Oppo and Gustavo Giovannoni are standing to his left, 29 October 1941.

metres wide," just twenty metres narrower than the street in Berlin. Once a person had reached the E42, the convergence of Via Ostiense, Via Marconi, and Via Imperiale itself would create a splendid composition, the southern counterpart to the trident of Piazza del Popolo.[51]

The idea of a north-south axis appeared in a rough map of Rome made by Moretti entitled *Il Foro Mussolini nel piano nazionale e nel grande piano imperiale di Roma* (The Foro Mussolini in the National Plan and in the Great Imperial Plan of Rome). Piacentini quickly outlined a similar plan.[52] Only a few letters between Piacentini, the architect to whom Mussolini handed over the direction of the country's architectural fate, and Moretti, one of his most likely successors, have been found, but it is likely that they were frequent correspondents.[53] The north-south road was important in light of Piacentini's proposal for an International City of Knowledge to complete the E42: "As imagined, north of the capital, a

72. Luigi Moretti, the Forma Ultima Fori urban development plan for the Foro Mussolini, model, 1941. The Foro, which covered over ten square kilometres, competed with the huge structure for party gatherings designed by Speer in Nuremberg.

huge area dedicated to the Education of Youth with the Foro Mussolini, the CONI and GIL headquarters, all the way to the great stadium; to the south towards the sea, after the monumental part of the city has been completed, this international city of knowledge should arise."[54] Overall, the 1941 Variante outlined an "imperial" plan, one of "global relevance," which sought to "make of the capital and its wonderful surroundings one great "unified work," one "so great it is daunting to the beholder."[55] Here again is evidence of the common psychological purpose assigned to architecture by Piacentini in Italy and Speer in Germany, that is, its splendour was used to impress, awe, and dominate the masses.

Unlike on previous occasions, this time the press did not draw much attention to Mussolini's visit to the Palazzo delle Esposizioni. The war was not producing the results he had hoped it would. The offensive in Greece had exposed the limits of the Italian army. In East Africa, the situation

73. Albert Speer, project for the area for Nazi Party gatherings in Nuremberg, model, 1937.

was disastrous. In May, Haile Sellassie had returned to Addis Ababa. Just five years after the Italian occupation, the "fateful hills" of Rome were deprived of its much-vaunted empire. In June 1941, Germany invaded the Soviet Union and Italy followed suit. In this critical situation, the dictator ordered that the news of his visit to the Palazzo delle Esposizioni not be made public and that the visit itself remain absolutely private.[56] He told the architects to "quietly continue along the path that was agreed upon."[57] The model was transported to the E42 and to a subcommittee, which included Piacentini, whose purpose was to hone the architects' studies. A new report, accompanied by some illustrations, was submitted to Mussolini later.[58]

The events surrounding the 1941 Variante in the urban development plan constituted another step towards the establishment of the regime's control over architecture. According to Piacentini, the Variante had to establish guidelines not just for areas of particular importance – such as Piazzale Termini, Porta Maggiore, Piazzale Flaminio, Piazza Barberini,

Piazza San Silvestro – but also for areas of residential expansion. Already one year before, when referring to the hilly exedras designed by Moretti north and west of the city, Piacentini demanded that "the location, the shape, and the colour (of the buildings) be strictly controlled, on a case-by-case basis, by the authorities."[59] Now Piacentini, addressing the head of the governor's cabinet, ordered that "in new residential areas, buildings shall no longer have individual features in the tastes of their owners or architects; rather, they must comply with a rigorous pre-established order, with the general harmony of the whole. The buildings shall no longer be detached, they shall be a subunit of a larger unit, which shall be the street and the piazza."[60] The new constructions of imperial Rome would fulfil a unity of direction. Individual citizens, deprived of their freedom to build, indirectly participated in the construction of the city's new fascist look, thus becoming protagonists in a vast collective process. Piacentini worked to make this plan come to fruition in the following months.[61]

Finally, Piacentini saw the opportunity to take on the role of "building dictator," a position he had already hoped to attain for himself in 1929, and that in 1943 he would complain of missing out on: "I should have been nominated *Edile* of Rome, but it all went up in smoke."[62] However, the fact that he had not officially been given this role did not mean that he had not carried out the job. At the same time, Mussolini did not want to give too much power to the architect who had been working at his side for over two decades. It was far better not to lavish him with titles, to avoid the risk that Mussolini's Rome might be identified as Piacentini's work.

5 Hitler's Plan for Imperial Berlin

The 1941 Variante for Rome seemed to be, even more so than the E42, Mussolini's response to the colossal plan for Gross-Berlin. In particular, the *via triumphalis* included in the 1941 Variante – which connected all the monuments of the ancient city, the Renaissance and fascist ones, and celebrated ancient as well as contemporary landmarks – competed with another *via triumphalis*, the north-south axis that Speer had designed for the German capital. Construction of Speer's axis – which was seven kilometres long, almost half the length of the Roman axis – with its gargantuan palaces, began in 1938, and was scheduled to be finished in time for the 1950 Universal Exposition to be held in Berlin; it would also be subject to further comparison with the E42. The two roads – the German one colossal, neatly structured, and rigid; the Italian one varied even in its effort to achieve uniformity, inviting constant comparisons with the past, and filled with noble interruptions – summed up the comparison between Hitler's and Mussolini's (and Speer's and Piacentini's) concepts of architecture.

In the summer of 1936, Hitler summoned Speer to discuss the redevelopment of Berlin; at the exact same time, Mussolini was doing what he needed to do to get work started on the E42. In January 1937, Speer was nominated general superintendent of urban planning for Berlin, with an office located inside the Academy of the Arts on Pariser Platz, not far from the Reich Chancellery.[63] Very often, towards evening, Hitler would visit Speer's office unannounced. They would examine drawings and discuss proposals, and the dictator would grasp a pencil and paper and make sketches, as an architect would. For many of the most representative areas, such as the staircases entering the buildings, the drawings bear corrections and suggestions in his handwriting.[64] According to Frederich Spotts, Hitler's involvement was even greater than what Speer recalled, and in any case nothing was ever done without his approval.[65] The office Speer supervised, the General-Bau-Inspektor, or GBI, which featured a team of eighty architects, only worked on the general plan, while the design of individual works was commissioned to architects such as Peter Beherens, Paul Bonatz, and Wilhelm Kreis, who were coordinated by the GBI. Speer kept the projects for the most representative buildings for himself, including, among others, the Volkshalle, the Arch of Triumph, the Reich Chancellery, the South Railway Station, and Göring's Palace.

Towards the end of 1936, he submitted a first plan for the Great Road, and on 20 April of the following year, on Hitler's birthday, he presented the dictator with the drawings – plans, cross-sections, elevations – of the Volkshalle. In January 1938, just one year after he had been assigned this task, Speer completed his plan for the new capital. In the first ten days of July, Goebbels examined the projects and wrote in his diary, "The map and the *maquette* of Berlin's entire redevelopment of Berlin ... [are] extraordinary. Speer has dealt with the task superbly. Berlin's new look exceeds everything that has been done up to now." Just a few days earlier, the first stone had been laid for the Palace of Tourism, the first building to go up on the axis; on that occasion the Führer recommended "greater architectural uniformity." In April 1939, again on Hitler's birthday, the architect completed the wooden model, which was three metres tall, of the Triumphbogen.[66] Meanwhile – almost at the same time as work on the E42 began – he ordered the demolition of the area required to build the Volkshalle. The granite was ordered, and a series of boats were built so that marble could be brought in from Scandinavia.[67] The Volkshalle was the most impressive building of all, the biggest hall in the world, and the new symbol of Hitler's Berlin. The dictator thought the building would exert a huge psychological influence on the masses. He was convinced that it could convey a sense of overwhelming strength to the people, even greater than the euphoria that usually followed a military victory. That building, he said, "was worth more than three wars won."[68] Elsewhere, he underscored the vital importance of architecture in Nazi ideology: "Listen to what I am telling you, dear Speer. These buildings are the most important things in existence."[69]

The great architecture of the Roman Empire, Hitler asserted, gave "Mussolini the opportunity ... to draw on the heroic nature of Rome."[70] The Duce, Goebbels continued, "claimed the entire history of the Roman age, from its most distant past, for himself. Compared to this, we are just nouveaux riches."[71] It was precisely the lack of a historical heritage as important as the one claimed by Mussolini that urged Hitler and Speer to seek superiority through colossal dimensions. Dimensions such as these were supposed to renew the German people's "awareness of identity," in other words, awareness that theirs was a superior race, whose destiny was to rule the world. In a secret report to the Wehrmacht chiefs, Hitler explained that his architecture fulfilled a "cold calculation." It aimed to convince the German people that they were second to none.[72] Hence, Gross-Berlin would have been filled with colossal buildings. The square opposite the Volkshalle, located in between the old Reichstag, Wehrmacht Palace, and the new Chancellery, would have been able to host a million people. The new Reichskanzlei, or Hitler's Palace, which included the Fuhrer's living quarters, would have been one hundred and fifty times larger than Bismarck's residence; the dining room alone would have measured three thousand square metres, and the theatre could have accommodated up to one thousand spectators. To reach Hitler's office, one would have had to walk down a five-hundred-metre corridor with columns. The message to the guest who walked such a long way to reach the office was clear: they had to "experience the feeling of paying a visit to the ruler of the world."[73] Many other colossal buildings, the most representative ones of the Third Reich, would have been built between the Volkshalle and the Arch of Triumph: ministry headquarters, the Soldiers' Pavilion, Göring's Palace, an opera house, theatres, and museums, as well as the headquarters of industrial companies, the AEG, some luxury hotels, and thermal baths. Beyond that, the North and the South Railway Stations would have been located at the farthest extremes of the axis: "Breathtaking! Only thus," Hitler claimed, "can we eclipse our only rival in the world: Rome."[74]

Speer visited Italy three times in the second half of the 1930s. He was undoubtedly fond of Greek architecture, and had recently travelled to Greece, but it was in Italy that he found the inspiration he needed for his future projects. Speer went to Rome for the first time in the fall of 1936 to study Michelangelo's cupola in St. Peter's, while in Berlin work on a gigantic dome for the Volkshalle was under way.[75] In October 1938, Speer visited Venice, Urbino, Rome, and Florence. Later, he claimed that Palazzo Pitti had inspired his project for the Reichskanzlei.[76] A few months later, in March 1939, he visited Puglia and Sicily with his wife and Magda Goebbels, and it was on that occasion that he met Piacentini.[77] On his way back, probably in early April, the Italian architect invited him to his Roman villa at the Camilluccia for an evening gathering held in his honour. During the event, Speer was introduced to "the most important Roman and Italian architects currently in Rome."[78] During this visit, Speer also attended an official luncheon organized by the management of the E42, and he likely visited the building site and saw the model of Mussolini's new city.[79] Upon returning to Germany, he said that "Hitler wanted me to describe to him my impressions from my journey in Italy."[80] A short time later, Speer drafted several studies for the German Pavilion for the E42.[81]

Speer and Piacentini kept in touch. The former provided material for the special issue of *Architettura* dedicated to the transformation of Berlin, Nuremberg, and other German cities. The issue did not include a model of the Volkshalle, however, even though it mentioned the building, nor did it include a model of the Arch of Triumph. As Speer recalled, the plans for the largest buildings were kept secret.[82] In his introduction to German architecture, Piacentini noted its "programmatic classicism," its emphasis on dimensions – "nowadays, in Germany, a metre is made of one thousand centimetres" – its uniform nature, its anti-individualism, and the fact that it was full-fledged state architecture. All the same, he carefully distanced himself from it. He did not distance himself from the architecture's political aims: after all, he stated, "we share the same ideals of heroism, including in the field of architecture." He claimed that the Italian "movement" naturally adhered to it, that it had a particular artistic "sensibility." He recognized its "solid" national "traditions," which were hardly present in Germany. He also acknowledged that in Italy, architecture was founded on "wholesome beliefs," whereas in Germany – he seemed to suggest – decisions were imposed from above.[83] In other words, he was claiming that, from this perspective, Mussolini's Italy was superior to Hitler's Germany. Piacentini also sent Hitler a copy of the issue: the architect wrote that the dictator "personally sent me his thanks."[84] The Führer had no doubt appreciated the classicist style of Piacentini's E42 as compared with the Città Universitaria; nevertheless, if we take into account his low esteem for Piacentini's work, which was reciprocated, his reply was nothing more than a gesture of common courtesy. Moreover, in the German translation Piacentini had carefully removed the most explicitly critical notes in the article written by Luigi Lenzi, which followed his own foreword. In it, the author stated in no uncertain terms that "dimensions, huge as they may be, are not enough to make a work of art."[85]

The following year, 1940, Piacentini wanted his magazine to feature the new piazza dedicated to Mussolini as well as part of the plan for Gross-Berlin on the secondary east-west axis, but Speer courteously turned him down. Because of the ongoing conflict, the architect did not want anything related to his plan for Berlin to be published, because he thought that those designs would be looked at in a completely different way in the victorious postwar atmosphere. He thus invited Piacentini to visit the building sites immediately after the war – within a few months, a year at most, or so he thought. The war, which was supposed to be short, was not expected to interfere with the plan. Indeed, in the fall of 1940, after Germany occupied France, the plans for the Great Road in Berlin "were more than ever on the Führer's mind."[86] For Hitler, the massive buildings of the Greater Berlin plan were on a par with wars in their importance: he had to undertake to assert German superiority and authority. The construction of Gross-Berlin was inextricably linked to the war of conquest. In May 1941, over three million forced labourers were employed in Germany, one million of whom were prisoners of war from conquered territories. Plans to build architecture on a pharaonic scale were predicated on the compulsory employment of three million Slavs for twenty years. The spoils of war were – both in terms of enslaved labourers and of materials – absolutely necessary to complete the city's massive buildings.[87]

In the summer of 1941, while Piacentini and his collaborators worked on the Variante for Rome, Mussolini kept an eye on Hitler's plans for Berlin. The Duce was curious, but he was probably worried as well. He discussed these matters with Ambassador Alfieri, who had had many opportunities to visit the Academy of the Arts, where Speer had his office.[88] There, in the large display rooms, were the models for the Greater Berlin plan: some, in 1:50 scale, were illuminated by spotlights in order to mimick the angles of the sunlight: "The model of the north-south axis extended from room to room for about thirty metres."[89] The official reason for the meetings between the ambassador and the architect was the construction of the new Italian embassy.[90] During their meeting on 20 August 1941, Alfieri reported that "the Duce is very interested in German architecture and has asked whether he, Alfieri, was in good standing with Speer." Speer himself, in his memoirs, recalled that "even Mussolini took an incredible interest in these plans" for Berlin.[91] The

Italian dictator wanted all the details so that he could take countermeasures. The Germans may have been clearly superior on the military front, but the competition on the architectural front was still open.

6 For Imperial Milan

Although Rome was unquestionably Mussolini's city, he also focused his attention on Milan. On many occasions he intervened in architectural issues there; on many occasions he asked for "detailed updates." The podestà often gave Mussolini the final word on some of the more controversial issues. As early as May 1930, Mussolini visited the city administration's technical office, where he examined the survey showing the width of the streets in the new urban development plan. Mussolini felt they were not wide enough to bear the volume of traffic in the years to come. He had also met with the podestà Marcello Visconti di Modrone at Palazzo Venezia concerning the demolition of the Spanish Bastions between Porta Nuova and Porta Venezia. There had been heated debate on the matter. Ojetti adamantly opposed the demolition, but Mussolini decided to approve the plan all the same.[92] Later on, the podestà visited the dictator to show him the working plan for the building of the Caserma della Milizia, the Museo dell'Aeronautica (Aviation Museum), and the underground transportation system.[93] However, it was not until 1936, when the Ethiopian War had ended and the foundation of the Italian empire was publicly announced, that a systematic plan for the works to be carried out was put in place. In a political climate of that kind, Milan aspired to be the most important city after Rome as concerned the revival of the ancient Roman myths, to which the regime assigned "the exquisitely political function ... of enhancing the spiritual values of the nation."[94]

Mussolini tasked the podestà Pesenti, a trusted figure from the early days of the fascist movement in Milan, with the renewal of the city.[95] Pesenti gave drafting an urban renewal plan top priority on his administrative agenda from 1936 to 1939, and, in July 1936, he submitted to Mussolini an architectural plan that was consistent with the new political climate. The most important project in this plan was the reorganization of Piazza Duomo. Mussolini approved the master plan drawn up by the city's Technical Office. It envisioned both the demolition of the Manica Lunga and the construction of a monumental "loggia-like" building to host the Arengario and the Sacrario dei Martiri Fascisti (Shrine of the Fascist Martyrs). The project also included knocking down the building opposite the Duomo in order to build a large Palazzo delle Corporazioni Fasciste in its place. According to this design, Piazza Duomo would no longer serve solely as the city's religious centre, but would assume an ever-growing political purpose. Other major projects were slated for Piazza San Babila, the Verziere and Bottonuto districts, and Piazza San Fedele.[96] Shortly afterwards, Mussolini gave the thumbs up for the City of Milan to issue a 250 million lire debenture to finance these works.[97]

Pesenti returned to the Urban Committee with news about his meeting with Mussolini, reporting all the dictator's comments about the various projects in great detail. It is worth mentioning a few of them. Mussolini had liked the drawing of the new Via dei Giardini, but he felt that the "straight road had to be given up," because it would come into contact with some of the new buildings. He thought opening a new street between Corso Venezia and Via San Damiano in order to isolate the northern side of the church of San Babila would incur "a considerable expense [that] would be hard to justify." He thought it would be worth "creating a small square on the northern side of the church." He asked that the southern face of Piazza San Babila, bordered by Via Durini and what is currently Corso Europa, be traced "on the alignment of the southern side of Via Borgogna." He judged the "aesthetic results" of the curved structure of the western façade of Piazza San Babila, located between Corso Europa and Corso Vittorio Emanuele, to be "highy questionable." He rejected the plan for a "building with a connecting colonnade" on the southern side of Piazza degli Affari, and he demanded that the façade overlooking the piazza be "straightened out" in order for it to be parallel to the stock exchange building. He felt the connection between Via Borgogna and Corso di Porta Vittoria was "superfluous." He judged the building of a square opposite the Palazzo di Giustizia, whose construction was under way, to be "indispensable" both in terms of circulation and "aesthetics." Lastly, he ordered that the parking area planned for the new junction between Piazza della Scala and Largo Cairoli be made "considerably" wider.[98] Mussolini looked closely at every single project, discussed them all one by one, and, when necessary, suggested alternative solutions. For all intents and purposes, he might be seen as one of the architects of the city's urban development plan. Surprisingly, he had nothing to say about the redevelopment of Piazza Duomo, but for that area, Pesenti recalled, the administration had appropriated "the studies and creative genius of His Excellency Piacentini." And that plan "was to the boss's liking."[99]

In March 1938, Mussolini urged the former podestà Giuseppe de Capitani to make every effort so that "the ancient Roman style of Milan would increasingly emerge in the works aimed at highlighting the remnants of the ancient imperial city."[100] On 9 December 1938, in Palazzo Venezia, two months after the "incident" of Viganò's Gothic tower, the Duce met with the new podestà, Gallarati Scotti, the party leader Rino Parenti, and many other Milanese party officials.[101] The meeting, which lasted over an hour, focused on the problem of implementing the urban development plan. Mussolini was handed an album that included the photographs of the current layout, and the plans that showed the future "imperial" design of the city.

Once again, Mussolini examined every single plan and made a list of priorities, which included the redevelopment of Piazza Duomo, Piazza Cavour, Piazza Diaz, Piazza San Babila, Piazza degli Affari, Piazza San Fedele, Piazza Bottonuto, Piazza del Verziere, Via dei Giardini, and the square opposite Stazione Milano Centrale. The ten interventions were to be completed within five years. The President of the Province showed Mussolini these documents as well as Muzio's design for the palazzo on Via del Vivaio.[102] In the interview he gave as he was leaving Palazzo Venezia, Parenti said that "the Duce has given the go-ahead to a complex design that will radically change the city, and bestow on it a new, imperial image." To achieve this "imperial" image, the podestà specified, a unified architectural model would be followed.[103]

In the December meeting, Mussolini was also shown a project that would not be included among the ten interventions. It concerned the new headquarters for the Questura (Police Headquarters), which was to be built opposite Piacentini's Palazzo di Giustizia. The Questura also fell within this unified model, and the architectural consulting was entrusted to the Roman architect.[104] Piacentini played another leading role on the Milanese scene as well. On 9 June 1939, as mentioned before, he met with Mussolini, the podestà, and Bottai to examine the overhaul of the southern side of Piazza Diaz and the project by Bacciocchi and Alister MacDonald. Mussolini approved the drawings and ordered the works to begin in the fall. The final reorganization of Piazza Diaz was scheduled to be carried out at the same time as that of Piazza Duomo.[105]

On 10 February 1940, Mussolini had another long meeting with the podestà in which they talked about the progress of the redevelopment plan. The dictator made it clear to the podestà that he was up to date on many of the details. The overall plan for ten simultaneous interventions was drastically reduced to just five. Priority was given to the work needed for Piazza Duomo with the Arengario by Muzio and his associates, Piazza Diaz with Bacciocchi and Piacentini's skyscraper, Piazza Cavour with Muzio's *Popolo d'Italia* building, Piazza San Babila with a work by Ponti, and, lastly, Via dei Giardini with a building by Enrico Agostino Griffini.[106] The budget for the realization of "imperial Milan" was cut due to the amount of money needed to prepare for war, a war that was supposed to bring glory to the empire. The parallel actions of combat and construction, on which the Mussolini based his pedagogy for forging "the citizen soldier," had to face economic reality.

7 A National "Unity of Direction"

Under Piacentini's leadership, the practice of architecture acquired a unity of direction that was not only limited to the capital. The architect's *longa manus*, of which we have seen much evidence, extended all the way to Milan. A case in point was the Arengario in Piazza Duomo. In January 1937, Piacentini, along with Giovannoni and Ojetti, was asked to describe the highlights of the new layout for the piazza and the proposed site for the Arengario project competition.[107] The two-level competition was announced in April 1937, and it ended in July 1938. Initially, Piacentini turned down an invitation to be on the jury and supported Ojetti's candidacy. In the transition between the first and second levels of the competition, the podestà, Pesenti, met with Mussolini, who approved the decision to advance to the second level of the competition with the four best projects. Muzio, who would end up winning, had two important conversations during that period: one with Ojetti, and the other with Piacentini.[108]

When the first level of the competition was over, Ojetti, who did not agree with the jury's decision, was replaced by Piacentini. With the architect now on the jury, work began on the second level. Project D, designed by Muzio's team, was selected by the jury. This project, which was to be built over the area of the demolished Manica Lunga, included two three-storey buildings, with arched openings on the ground floor and rectangular openings on the two upper floors. However, for Piacentini, this plan was not final, despite the fact that it had won the competition. He explained to Ojetti that, compared with the projects that had been rejected, this one had the advantage of being "calm, and for the time being it does not affect the rest of the piazza, which is the most important thing." The strategy Piacentini had in mind was the same as his strategy for the E42: "Yes, we'll award the prize, but then we'll start over again from scratch." Based on the jury's – that is, Piacentini's – suggestions, Muzio modified the project. And at that point, Ojetti was back in play. Ojetti paid his compliments to Muzio, who, in turn, confided to the critic that he had dedicated "a great deal" of his study to him. The architect was also eager "to hear his observations and suggestions. With your permission, I could come and talk to you personally."[109] The arch motif, which was appreciated by both Ojetti and Piacentini, prevailed, thus transforming the Arengario into "arched fretwork" (figure 74).

By 1938, Piacentini and Ojetti had become a winning team. Around the same time that he was choosing Muzio's project in Milan, the Roman architect asserted that "the affirmation of national values in totalitarian regimes," against internationalism and cosmopolitanism, was "destined

74. Enrico Agostino Griffini, Pier Giulio Magistretti, Giovanni Muzio, and Piero Portaluppi, project for the second-level competition for the redevelopment of Piazza Duomo in Milan and the creation of the Arengario, model, 1938. The project was made under Piacentini's supervision. Corrado Alvaro remarked that "renewal of the centre of Milan recalls that of Rome."

to have the broadest of repercussions." In parallel with the new political developments, architecture saw a rejection of Rationalism and the return to the national tradition, albeit with new terminology. What Italians were witnessing – Piacentini stated emphatically – was a "new rebirth," of "our own neo-Renaissance," a shift back to the essential style of classicism, and thus the use of arches and columns in "a rational and honest manner."[110] Ojetti endorsed him in one of the country's major newspapers, stressing that "Piacentini is right," reminding everyone that the E42 was a turning point, in which every single stone spoke "the same language as before," that of ancient and imperial Rome, "but with a new accent."[111] And the fact that this architectural tendency, besides being dominant and more or less official, was confirmed soon afterwards by a seminal text, the *Dizionario di Politica*. Published by the Fascist Party and presented to Mussolini, the work renounced architectural Rationalism, overtly abandoning it and identifying it as a product of enemy forces, like plutocracy and socialism, in their opposition to fascism.[112]

Piacentini's influence explains the "curious coincidence" between the figurative theme of the Arengario in Milan and the Palazzo della Civiltà Italiana at the E42.[113] Two surviving sketches demonstrate his clever, fruitful direction from behind the scenes. In the first, dated 1937, Piacentini drew the front of two structures framing the street that connected Piazza Duomo to Piazza Diaz, "suggesting" the overlapping arches motif present in the final version of the winning project. In the second, the loggias are rather similar to the ones that were actually built.[114] However, in Milan, Piacentini did not just intervene in the shape of the Arengario, the skyscraper in Piazza Diaz, and the Palazzo della Questura, as we saw before. He also modified the plan for the new Casa del Mutilato by Luigi Lorenzo Secchi, redesigning the layout of the façade, which he felt was too "uneven," so that it would be less "discontinuous" compared with the massive Palazzo di Giustizia nearby.[115]

Between 1937 and 1939, Piacentini oversaw projects for buildings in many other Italian cities. In early 1938, the podestà of Livorno Aleardo Campana tasked him with the reconstruction of the city centre. In June 1938, the architect had already submitted "precise directives" to the appropriate offices, and he had "looked over and led the studies."[116] First of all, he redesigned the piazza where the construction of Palazzo del Governo by Legnani and Sabatini was under way: open on the side of the old shipyard, it was seen as the city's new fascist forum, the location of the new Casa del Fascio and the Torre Littoria. He redesigned the area of Santa Giulia, reducing the extent of the demolition work and creating a new square. He asked Pascoletti, a loyal collaborator, to make perspective drawings illustrating Livorno's new fascist look. Later, he intervened in Via Vittorio Emanuele, suggesting the creation of a colonnade that ran all the way from the sea to Piazza della Repubblica, based on the model of one of his works for Via Roma in Turin.[117]

In Bolzano, where "he achieved a position of absolute power" – among other things, as the author of the urban development plan – he conceived the architectural layout of Piazza della Vittoria, a hub connecting the old Austro-Hungarian city with the new Italian city. Part of the original project – which included, on the area occupied by the narrowing of the riverbed of the Talvera torrent, the building of the Palazzo del Governo and the Municipio (City Hall), framed by two Roman columns – was inaugurated in 1938 (figure 75). Piacentini made sure that the projects for the INA and INFPS buildings located on the western side of the square were assigned to his associate Paolo Rossi

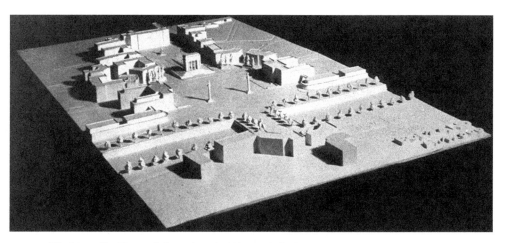

75. Marcello Piacentini, project for Piazza della Vittoria in Bolzano, model, 1933–9. After visiting the city, in November 1938 Galeazzo Ciano jotted down in his diary: "The appearance of the city is changing from Nordic to Mediterranean ... In ten years' time, or even less, it will be hard to recognize the Bozen of the past in Bolzano today."

de Paoli.[118] "The image of the city," observed Galeazzo Ciano during a visit, "is changing from Nordic to Mediterranean."[119]

In Bologna, Piacentini was asked to coordinate the work of eleven architects who were the co-winners of a competition for the redevelopment of Via Roma. In the early part of 1939, the architect presented the group project, designed on the basis of his guidelines, which configured the new architectural conception of the road. The project included the construction of a double curtain of buildings twenty metres tall in the southern part of Via Roma, and of four tower-shaped buildings in the northern part. For the latter, Piacentini included an idea by Bottoni, one of the winners. Albeit modified, the work's "Rationalist" inspiration was apparent. This work confirmed Piacentini's rare ability to remodel plans that at first sight seemed wildly inconsistent with each other, and to cooperate with architects whose cultural stances that differed greatly from his own. In May, Bologna's mayor showed the project to Mussolini.[120] In the nearby city of Parma as well, the mayor turned to Piacentini for advice on the redevelopment of the city centre and to make some changes to the urban development plan.[121]

In Genoa, Piacentini worked on a new look for both Piazza della Vittoria and Piazza Dante. In the former, as he was finishing drafting the plans for the INFPS building, he began work on Palazzo Garbarino e Sciaccaluga, which was meant to be a model for other similar buildings overlooking the piazza.[122] For the latter project, he was the consultant to the City Technical Office; his role was to advise on the overall plans and dimensions, and on which variations were to be adopted based on his recommendations. In Genoa he also designed the Invernizzi skyscraper, which was located on the other side of some other buildings in "Piacentini style," such as INA, designed by his friend Cipriani.[123] In Naples, he was tasked with designing the Banco di Napoli. Indeed, the fact that he was asked to design the headquarters of rival financial institutions further demonstrates Piacentini's power.[124] He was also asked to choose between several versions of Camillo Guerra's project for the Casa del Mutilato to be built on Piazza Duca D'Aosta, the most representative area of the fascist city. Guerra himself recalled studying the final version "under the esteemed guidance" of Piacentini, who made corrections to it.[125]

In Venice, plans were under way for the Santa Lucia Station. In February 1939, as we saw earlier, in a room in the Ostiense Station Mussolini examined the projects for both the Santa Lucia and Termini Stations, with designs that showed signs of an evolution towards classicism. The Venice Station was a one-storey building set on water and supported by ten pillars, with a façade interrupted by a row of arches.[126] Later, this first design underwent some changes: the pillars became columns with capitals, and more arches were added. The 1939–40 version was even more reminiscent of Rome, featuring a large portico without mooring. Considering his role as the artistic adviser for Venice, Piacentini must have been familiar with a wide range of projects.[127]

There were other cities in Italy where Piacentini was unofficially involved. In 1937 in Trieste, he was finishing the second block of the Palazzo delle Assicurazioni Generali. We have already mentioned that the podestà wanted the new buildings to fit in with the one designed by Piacentini. This city at the empire's border – and where Mussolini wanted to impose signs of *romanità* in order to highlight its Italian connotations: "Rome is here," he claimed during his visit – saw the construction of a university designed by Fagnoni and Nordio. Plans for this university were presented to the dictator in July 1938, at the same time that he was examining plans for the E42, the church of Santi Pietro e Paolo, and the Palazzi delle Forze Armate (figure 76).[128] When Trieste's podestà Enrico Salem was removed following the implementation of the racial laws, Piacentini lost some of his support in the city. However, considering the way this massive work echoes the classical style of the E42, it is likely that Piacentini had inspected the drawings. He was particularly close to one of the architects: Fagnoni had been his student in Rome, and Piacentini

76. Raffaello Fagnoni and Umberto Nordio, project for the University of Trieste, model, 1938. Mussolini saw the drawings in July 1938.

had headed the commission that had recently awarded Fagnoni a full professorship at the University of Florence. Moreover, Piacentini had asked the Florentine architect to design the Mostra dell'Artigianato (Arts and Crafts Exhibition) at the E42, and he would not forget to include Fagnoni in the establishment of a national architecture company, discussed further on.

In Udine, the plan for the area facing Piazza Duomo, which also included the Cassa di Risparmio by Foschini and Pascoletti, had been submitted to Piacentini, who had given it "his unconditional approval."[129] In Novara, when Cipriani asked him to share his expertise, Piacentini suggested a plan that would use a portico to connect the Credito Italiano building with the INA building on Via Cavour.[130] In Palermo, the construction of the Palazzo di Giustizia was under way, which was clearly a nod to its counterpart in Milan. Ernesto and Gaetano Rapisardi, the architects who designed it, often worked closely with Piacentini's firm. Indeed, Gaetano had been asked by his employer to design the School of Letters and Law for the Città Universitaria in Rome. Ernesto, on the other hand,

77. Gaetano Rapisardi, project for the Palazzo di Giustizia in Pisa, perspective drawing, 1936. Rapisardi was one of Piacentini's closest collaborators. He also designed, with his brother Ernesto, the Palazzo di Giustizia in Palermo. He worked with Piacentini on the Palazzo di Giustizia in Milan.

was Piacentini's right-hand man for the Palazzo di Giustizia in Milan. In 1938, Gaetano began work on the Palazzo di Giustizia in Pisa, winning a competition whose jury included Foschini, one of Piacentini's most loyal collaborators (figure 77). It is unlikely that the architects didn't show their work to Piacentini, that they didn't discuss the overall layout, or any of the more complex issues, with him. Piacentini "held the reins." Renato Bonelli described the climate of subordination, the almost military atmosphere that one breathed in those days, at least in Rome. Whenever an especially important project needed to be promoted, Foschini would always repeat, "Marcello, Marcello ... we have to call Marcello."[131]

Rome, Milan, Genoa, Livorno, Bologna, Venice, Palermo, Naples, Trieste, Bolzano, and Parma were the cities where Piacentini was more or less directly involved between 1937 and 1939. He was the brains behind the movement to coordinate the "unity of direction" in Italian architecture, with Mussolini's approval. It is important to bear in mind, however, that "unity of direction" did not imply the elimination of the pre-existing architectural features of these cities, whose histories and cultures were so different. This "unity of direction" corresponded to the creation of buildings that shared similar elements so as to bestow a unified character to a multiform whole; what had started in the workshop of the Città Universitaria had evolved into a great and complex national experiment.

Aware of the huge amount of power now in Piacentini's hands, Mussolini wanted to make sure the architect was under his control. The message he received from a city in northern Italy added nothing to what he already knew: "the interference of this very important figure is not limited, rumour has it, to Rome, where they say he is ruling at this point, but rather is extended to other cities as well, where his partisan and biased opinion prevails in every committee."[132] Still, the allusion to Piacentini's biases, which did in fact exist, could not overshadow the great design he aspired to, that is, to bestow a national stylistic uniformity upon architecture.

8 A Private Monopoly in a Totalitarian Regime

The "totalitarian" management of building competitions completes the picture of the power that Piacentini wielded over Italian architecture during the fascist years. Out of a total of 270 competitions, Piacentini was a member of 46 juries – practically speaking, all the important ones. Moreover, his most loyal collaborators, Alberto Calza Bini and Arnaldo Foschini, were involved in 37 and 28 juries, respectively.[133] And when they could not be present, they would send someone they trusted in their place, like Morpurgo, Marconi, Cancellotti, or Libera. This way, Piacentini could almost always determine the results of these competitions, or at least influence them. Also under Piacentini's – at times direct – control were the competitions for the E42, for Via Roma in Bologna, for the Teatro Regio in Turin, for the urban development plan in Rieti, for the Arengario in Milan and the Ministry of Italian Africa in Rome, for the Palazzo di Giustizia in Palermo, and, lastly, for Pomezia.

However, this minutious and widespread control over construction throughout Italy did not satisfy the architect's unbounded ambition. In the early 1940s, Piacentini orchestrated a series of manoeuvres to extend his hegemony to the architectural magazines as well. We discussed earlier how in April 1941, Piacentini, with Casini's help, sought to remove Pagano as editor of *Costruzioni-Casabella*. In July, *Architettura* absorbed *Rassegna di Architettura*, whose editor was Giovanni Rocco. Then, in October 1941, the publisher Gianni Mazzocchi, who already owned *Costruzioni-Casabella* and *Domus*, both edited by Pagano, attempted to purchase both *Architettura* and *Stile*, edited by Piacentini and Ponti, respectively. Piacentini keenly supported the enterprise, probably because he thought he could take advantage of the new concentration of ownership: one single magazine implied greater control over opinions, and it also allowed for the "styistic uniformity" he had already achieved in the public works sector. Even Ponti seemed to support these moves, lamenting that "Italy still lacks a great architecture magazine."[134] Later, when the plan failed, Piacentini tried to take over for Pagano at *Costruzioni-Casabella*.[135] When this attempt failed as well, he tried to create a new magazine under his direct control, albeit without his name ever appearing, assigning it to two of his most trusted associates, Piccinato and Aldo Della Rocca.[136]

The last piece in this complex mosaic of power was represented by the creation of a national architecture company. Between 1942 and early 1943, Piacentini tried to breathe life into the GAIU (Gruppo Architetti, Ingegneri, Urbanisti), a team of architects, engineers, and urban planners. Chaired by Piacentini himself, with twenty to thirty members – Fagnoni and Civico are the only names I have been able to confirm – the GAIU's mission was to create projects on a scale ranging from territorial to architectural, to be implemented both in Italy and abroad. With two main headquarters, one in Rome, the other in Milan, it would also have branches in other Italian cities where its members lived. The projects would always feature the signature of the president along with those of the actual architects. Furthermore, the fees would be divided among the members, with the exception of the president, who would receive a sum that was three times higher.[137]

The establishment of the GAIU was also related to the passing of a recent law that compelled Italy's major cities to draw up an urban development plan. It represented an attempt to establish a stable and organized form to a system of relationships between professional figures, which had already been subject to broad experimentation in previous years. Piacentini wanted the consulting he had already been doing behind the scenes to be officially acknowledged. He was no longer satisfied with being the anonymous director; he wanted his signature to visible on all the projects. The experience of the E42 left him with a sour aftertaste. He complained that his role as the person who oversaw everything had never been acknowledged, that although he had been the one to "pave the way for architecture" he had nonetheless been "left behind." Now he insisted that his position as leader be more obvious.[138] In Fagnoni's words, the GAIU would offer architectural "direction."[139] As an organization, this national architecture company was in step with the "unity of direction" that was suited to a totalitarian state; indeed, it appeared to be one of its offspring. However, one can only wonder whether Mussolini – who, at that time, was completely embroiled in his disastrous handling of the war – would ever have accepted Piacentini's elevation to such a lofty public pedestal.

Epilogue

Italy's entrance into World War II in June 1940 led to a near-total slow-down in the construction of architectural works in the public sector. During the first months of the conflict, however, there was selective mobilization in order to minimize production problems as much as possible.[1] Work continued on some important building sites, although progress was slow. In November 1940, the Palazzo della Civiltà Italiana was inaugurated at the E42. In July 1941, the rough structures of the Palazzo dei Ricevimenti e dei Congressi were tested.[2] That same year also saw the completion of the buildings that formed the perimeter around the Mausoleum of Augustus. In October 1941 in Milan, the roof of the Arengario was completed and work on the cladding began. Lastly, the building site of the Palazzo del Popolo d'Italia was still active in 1942.[3] In June 1942 in Trieste, the shell of the university campus was being completed.[4] In Rome, the collapse of the fascist regime caused the interruption of work on the Termini Station and the Ministry of Foreign Affairs.[5]

Clearly, Mussolini's commitment to architecture was significantly diminished. Already in April 1940, while war preparations were in full swing, Bottai had asked to see Mussolini along with Piacentini, but he had instead received a note from the administration saying it would be best "to avoid meeting in times such as these."[6] Nevertheless, as is evident from the efforts to keep the most high-profile building sites open, and from the events surrounding the Variante of the urban development plan for Rome, architecture was not entirely absent from the political agenda. Initially, Mussolini had thought the war would be short-lived, lasting no more than a few months. Even when the situation grew complicated, and in spite of both the disastrous invasion of Greece in October 1940 and defeats on the North African front – including the British Army's seizure of Tobruk in January 1941 – the dictator continued to believe the war would end soon. Especially at the beginning of the conflict, within the perspective of a short war, the program for the totalitarization of the country, and its architectural program, did not change. In view of the long timeline required for the creation of the "new man," the conflict, while forging the "warrior man," represented a short temporary delay in terms of all the regime aimed to achieve. After victory, everything would be easier and the dictator would emerge even stronger.[7] The architectural projects that he had approved would appear even more justified, and their construction would be accelerated. Architecture's "unity of direction" would finally be reached on a national scale. Those who had disagreed, such as Terragni, Pagano, Argan, and Bottai, would be silenced or pressured to conform to the dominant positions, for the sake of the absolute values of the totalitarian nation.

In late 1940 Cini submitted to Mussolini a change in the original plan for the E42, which was now called the EUR, Esposizione Universale Romana. The main features had not changed, but whereas before, for opportunistic reasons, the political side of the project had been kept largely hidden, now, within the context of the war, its objectives could be openly declared. The Olympics of Civilization, unlike any impartial competition between countries, was now envisioned as a one-sided demonstration of the power and the domination of fascist Italy. Its preliminary plan already contained an assertion of the fascist idea that the country would emerge victorious from the new world order that would follow the war – "the war we are fighting is a war of ideas" – and it would finally be able to impose its own idea of justice upon other peoples. To celebrate this "Novus Ordo" (new order), Cini proposed, once the war was over, the creation of a new great architectural work, "in the classical Roman style," aligned with Via dell'Impero, on the hill above the lake, framed by a huge metal arch, an "immense" Ara Pacis to celebrate Mussolini's peace and the triumph of fascist ideology (figure 78). It was to be a work that would celebrate fascist ideology, and would also serve as the venue for the Exhibition of the Fascist Party.[8]

The creator and designer of the fascist Ara Pacis would be Piacentini. At first, the architect rejected the project by Franco Petrucci and Mario Tedeschi for the Palazzo dell'Acqua e della Luce, whose original intended location was underneath the huge metal arch, and for which a competition had been organized. But then, in view of "recent international events that will culminate in the great victory of the Axis powers," he felt the need to create on the most important and conspicuous site of the exposition a colossal monument to "consecrate the peace between the peoples," and to celebrate the beginning of "a new chapter in human history, the advent of a new era," that is, a world ruled by Nazism and fascism.[9] In an unexpected twist, Piacentini, who up until then had

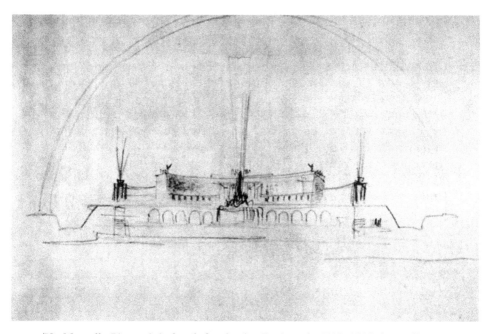

78. Marcello Piacentini, sketch for the Ara Pacis at the E42, 1940. According to its creator, the gargantuan monument to fascist peace celebrated "a new chapter in the history of humanity, the coming of a new era." The project was approved by Mussolini.

not directly taken credit for any of the buildings, despite intervening in most of them, assigned the E42 to himself; it was to be the most symbolic building of all, the very image of peace between peoples, imposed through an uncompromising policy of domination. Both the Ara Pacis and the metal arch clearly conveyed the idea of the competition between the two hegemonic empires: fascist Italy and Nazi Germany. The arch was the typological reinterpretation of the "gigantic Roman arch" that dominated the whole exposition; it was evoked by Mussolini in his speech at the Campidoglio, and it symbolized the ability of the new civilization to combine technology with the monumentality of antiquity.[10] The two constructions were an updated response to Speer's projects for Berlin, and they reflected the competition between the two countries in terms of size and message. Mussolini was presented with Piacentini's proposal for the Ara Pacis and gave it his approval on 4 January 1941.[11]

Nonetheless, the climate in some architectural circles was different from the triumphant one conveyed by Cini and Piacentini. It was precisely the appearance of the Palazzo della Civiltà Italiana in the Tre Fontane valley, the most iconic of the buildings with its fifty-four arches on each side, and the shapes, more or less covered with columns, of the other buildings that led to an even stronger rift within the world of Italian architecture. Pagano launched unprecedented attacks against Piacentini in *Costruzioni-Casabella*, identifying him as the person most responsible for architectural decisions. Piacentini fought back in an important article, published in July, entitled "Onore all'architettura italiana" (Praise to Italian Architecture), in which he presented a detailed summary of the architectural activity in Italy during the fascist regime, although the truth of the matter is that he focused on the 1930s.[12] The twenty-year anniversary of the magazine *Architettura*, which he had founded together with Giovannoni in 1921, offered him a suitable opportunity.

Piacentini wrote this article at a time when the war's outcome remained uncertain. In April, the British army had conquered Addis Ababa, but the German and Italian forces reconquered Benghazi. In that same month, Yugoslavia was attacked, and the Italian army invaded Slovenia, Dalmatia, and Montenegro. In June, Hitler ordered a blitz against Stalin's forces, and Mussolini was ready to intervene right beside him. Piacentini was well informed about these events. He frequented Bottai's circle – "rumour has it that he was, and still is, very close to Bottai"[13] – as well as that of Galeazzo Ciano, and his brother was a diplomat serving as a minister in Addis Ababa at the time. In June, ten days before the German attack against the Soviets, Piacentini learned from Bottai that Mussolini did not rule out the possibility of the war continuing until 1948.[14] However, despite the alarming rumours, Piacentini was still willing to believe in a "short war." He continued in his belief in the following months: "the great architect turns as yellow as a lemon if he only hears someone say 'that the war will be a long one.'"[15] It is likely he believed that the conflict would be resolved in a short period of time, and that the solution would be a diplomatic one discussed around a table. Once peace had been restored, Piacentini felt he could go back to drafting projects and managing building sites, giving new impetus to the quest for a more unified architectural direction. This, along with the facts, would silence the "heretic" Pagano.

It was in this architectural and historical context that Piacentini's article was published. He wrote that in the twenty years of the regime, architectural production had been "immense." The amount of building that had gone on in Italy could not be compared to "anything any other people in the same period had ever even imagined doing." Piacentini supported these claims with a long list of what he considered the 181 "best" and "most significant" works, including 32 urban development plans, 24 urban transformations, 11 railway stations, 6 universities, and 6 newly founded cities.[16] Piacentini's goal was to offer a complete and comprehensive picture of the various constructions reflecting the "development of Italian architecture." Furthermore, he wanted to emphasize the collective national value of the architectural output, and therefore did not mention the names of those who were behind it, just their works.[17] Piacentini also deliberately omitted some major works from the list, such as the Casa del Fascio and the Asilo Sant'Elia designed by Terragni for Como, and the Bocconi University in Milan by Pagano. Demonstrating his political acumen, he left out the E42, not so much because it was still unfinished, but because he absolutely wanted to discourage diatribes between architects and to focus instead on creating a sense of cohesion.

Piacentini did not set his program aside. Indeed, he reaffirmed the absolute importance, alongside the creation of "buildings for the people," of architecture that comprised "great art" for "great things," that could "express the race's eternal, immanent aspiration." This "great art" was not about "contingency; it did not have "an everyday function: it was something much nobler, something resembling religion." Mostly importantly, he wrote about the matter of style, acknowledging that in recent times this had been a preoccupation of architects in Italy: "these buildings have indicated, especially in the past few years, a rapid and progressive refinement, and a move towards a modern Italian conception, towards a *style*."[18] And what exactly was this move "towards a *style*" if not the promotion of the national unity of architectural direction discussed in the previous chapter? Was Piacentini not the director – at least broadly speaking, if not always successfully – behind this "fast-moving progressive refinement"? Was it not Piacentini who guided Italian architects, especially younger ones, many of them former pupils of his, from Piccinato to Luigi Valenti to Luigi Orestano, in this enterprise? Did he not prove wrong those critics, such as Pagano, who had frequently claimed that Italy lacked a leader?

This focus on style was possible – Piacentini continued – because at that time, as in the Renaissance, art had found an "order" on which to base itself. The "new order," that is, fascism, put Italy once more "in its great civilizing position." It "will give birth – the symptoms are all already visible – to our art, that of Italians."[19] Piacentini confirmed the modernity of the cultural impetus underlying the E42, albeit without ever naming it, a modernity that was also visible in other realms. The architect gave a new thrust to the leading role of architecture in the challenge for Italy's "supremacy of civilization." Once again, Piacentini tried to align himself with Mussolini's thinking. The reference the architect made to the "new order that we are preparing" recalled the values of Mussolini's "new civilization," one marked by "Roman knowledge and wisdom."[20]

In the event of a victorious postwar period, Italy would principally compete with Germany, whose hegemony it would contest. At that moment, architecture would be even more decisive in the rivalry for the leadership of civilization. This was because Hitler intended to extend the challenge precisely in that field. The Berlin that Speer had designed, with the active participation of the Nazi leader, was meant to be not only the capital of the Greater Germanic Reich, but also the "capital of the world." Standing before the huge model reproducing the avenue that crossed the city from north to south, Hitler, pointing to the great domed building, explained to Speer, "Here the eagle must no longer be represented above the swastika. The crowning of this largest building in the world must be an eagle atop the globe." In its powerful claws it would grip the sphere in a sign of merciless domination. Whereas Mussolini limited his aspirations to the construction of a Mediterranean empire overlooking the Indian Ocean and cultural leadership in the Western world, Hitler's goal, in no uncertain terms, was world domination.[21] The interests of the two powers clashed. Nazism, first and foremost, did not tolerate the idea of coexistence. The new Berlin was expected to be ready by 1950, at the end of the war.[22] The Führer was absolutely determined to continue with construction work during the conflict. In contrast to the situation in Italy, German military victories marked the height of the people's support for Hitler. In Russia – the dictator confided to his architect in the summer of 1941 – "we will find all the granite and marble we want."[23] Whereas the German project for the Aryan race's domination over the rest of the world roughly translated to the exaltation of architectural dimensions, the Italian project for the supremacy of the Latin civilization – which Mussolini, like Hitler, imposed with the use of force – was in no way limited to gargantuan proportions. Although the Germans were unsurpassed when it came to large-scale enterprises, the Italians, with their rich cultural and artistic tradition, both past and present, saw themselves as as the true masters.

In the summer of 1941, Mussolini and Piacentini were still on good terms. In August, near Pisa, Bruno Mussolini died during a military exercise, and the dictator commissioned Piacentini to design his son's tomb. He chose Piacentini, who had been harshly criticized by Pagano, for this private commission, and not one of the young "Mussolinian" architects, such as Moretti. The commission offers further proof of Mussolini's confidence in Piacentini. Only towards the end of 1941, when it became clear that combat in the Soviet Union would not be over before the start of winter, and that the Red Army could halt the advance of the Axis forces, did Mussolini gradually come to accept that the war would be neither quick nor easy. However, at that point, for the dictator the prospect was not entirely negative. A longer war would scale down his

German ally, introduce new opportunities, and allow Italy to participate in peace negotiations on more favourable terms.[24] On 29 October, with this in mind, Mussolini headed to the Palazzo delle Esposizioni on Via Nazionale to examine the Variante of the urban development plan, and the Forma Ultima Fori created by Moretti for the Foro Mussolini.

The 1941 Variante was the fruit of the highly didactic, hawkish atmosphere in which, years before, Mussolini had expressed the hope that the Italian people would go about their lives, engaged in "works of peace and works of war." The leadership's strict control over each work of architecture reflected the imposition of an increasingly militaristic – and therefore fascist – vision onto civil life. Mussolini now wanted these studies to continue, for, in the postwar period, Italy would have to challenge Germany in a sector – architecture and the arts in general – where it would hold the advantage. However, at the same time, he forbade the press from divulging any of the details on his massive architectural program, because he was convinced that the new situation on the Russian front would require the country's utmost military and economic effort.

On his part, Piacentini continued to support the architectural direction that he, more than anyone else, had contributed to defining. In December 1942, he illustrated the projects of the Italian winners of the three international competitions to demonstrate the leading role that Italian architecture had by that time achieved abroad, almost anticipating Italy's hoped-for future architectural supremacy over other countries (figure 79). The winning projects were by Attilio and Ernesto La Padula for the University Campus in Bratislava, the project by Vagnetti, Dante Tassotti, and Pasquale Marabotto for the Belgrade Opera House, and, lastly, Foschini's project for the Atatürk Memorial in Ankara, for which Muzio, Vaccaro, and Gino Franzi also received awards. The success of those architects, Piacentini claimed, was the result of the unparalleled activity of "totalitarian countries," especially Italy and Germany, in the field of architecture. The rebirth of the two peoples, who "now sense future domination and universal command in their hands and in their minds," was mirrored in their architecture, which was constituted by "genuine works of civilization." Almost all the architects who received awards in these competitions, Piacentini observed, were also working on the E42. The result of this was that that "architectural tendency" was proceeding "triumphantly at home and abroad." At the roots of architectural classicism, Piacentini believed, was not only the issue of "form," but something deeper that was tied to "unchangeable ethnic factors." Italians had always had a link to the "classicist spirit," which was "universal, anti-individual, and pro-state"[25]

But while extolling the victorious architecture of the age of Mussolini, which he saw as the "representation of a race," the mentality of a people,

79. Arnaldo Foschini, project for the Atatürk Memorial in Ankara, perspective drawing, 1942.

and an integral part of the "mission of civilization," the architect was beginning to break free of Mussolini as the war progressed in a catastrophic direction. November 1942 saw the first reports by the political police containing negative assessments of the dictator, who "has become a weakling, surrounded by too many totally incompetent people." In the following months, the "defeatist murmuring" grew, as did personal attacks against Claretta Petacci, the Duce's mistress, and reports on the adverse outcome of the war.[26]

When the regime fell, Piacentini refused to move to the north of Italy and join the Republic of Salò. He was imprisoned, but later released thanks to the help of the future pope, Giovanni Battista Montini, the replacement for the Vatican state secretary at the time. Piacentini was subjected to a purge trial and in his memoirs he denied ever having had "a personal friendship with Mussolini." His words were probably true, since the dictator had no friends and saw no one outside of work. Mussolini himself once confided, "I cannot have any friends, I do not have any."[27]

However, Piacentini did maintain, despite incontrovertible evidence, that his role in politics had been neutral, that he was a technician who was not part of the regime, merely an executor – an innocent one and indifferent to ideologies – of the orders he had received from Musssolini and the Fascist Party. He could not deny his visits to Palazzo Venezia, but he had only been there "a few times," he said, with other people and only "for reasons of technical expertise."[28] He thus alleged architecture's autonomy from politics on the grounds of false testimony, thereby inaugurating a successful defence, to be extended to the whole field of architectural culture.

The details of Mussolini's tragic and inglorious end are well known: how he was captured by the partisans while trying to reach the Swiss border disguised as a German soldier, how he was shot and hung upside down at a service station in Piazzale Loreto in Milan. But whereas the dictator fell, Piacentini survived, sailing, like many others, to other shores. Nevertheless, he would forever be known as the "regime's architect." He continued to work after the war, even on some of the projects he had begun during the regime, such as the Via della Conciliazione and the E42, which were eventually completed by the fledgling Italian Republic.

Mussolini willingly drew upon one of the primordial human needs: the need to shape one's identity. In these terms, the dictator used architecture to create his anthropological project to "remake Italians" and build the "new man." The more efficiently he could convey to the masses the values in which that "new man" was to be identified, the more successful his project would be. The monumental buildings, which were symbols of that political religion, were therefore built to last. Their forms were conceived not as part of a passing trend, but rather were intended to last over time. They were imagined as still being relevant not only in ten years' time, but in the centuries to come, "even in four hundred years," thus slowly fulfilling their pedagogical function, which was their explicit purpose. According to the entry in the *Dizionario del Fascismo*, the official text of the National Fascist Party (PNF), architecture "with its constant presence, slowly changes the character of the generations."[29] Architecture's goal was to revive, both in Mussolini's age and in hundreds of years, a sense of belonging to that Italian and fascist civilization, both ancient and superior.

During the fascist regime, architecture designed to transmit the memory of fascism to posterity was built all over Italy. Not only did the regime manipulate the memory of the dead, as in the Sacrario (War Memorial) of Redipuglia, but it also staked a claim on the memory of future generations. We might say that as soon as the dictator became aware of his imminent defeat and the end of his political journey, he also knew that he had managed to leave an almost indelible message through his architecture. He knew that the lack of a fitting architectural language would weaken the process of identification. Nonetheless, he was also convinced that the monuments would continue to convey meaning, and to convey the myth of a powerful and superior Italy whatever happened.

After the fall of fascism, these monumental works of architecture were not demolished, as was instead the case with other, less cumbersome, symbols of the regime. They could not be hidden or stolen like Mussolini's corpse.[30] There were, and are, hundreds of them, spread all across the country. For this reason, it was decided that the explanation for those forms, their meanings, should be forgotten. They were dismissed as false, rhetorical monuments, which somehow absolved them of their ignominious pasts. They remained as empty reliquaries in need of new meanings and purposes. In the landscape of early postwar Italy, they represented fragments of an interrupted project aimed at imposing a totalitarian vision on society, relics of the powerful alliance between the fascist dictator, his architects, and his people.

Paradoxically, it would be the task of the new republican Italy to complete some of the most significant works commissioned by the fascist dictatorship. The clearest example of this was, undoubtedly, the E42 (figure 80). In the early 1950s, Piacentini was nominated superintendent of urban planning, and Minnucci manager of technical services. After 1951, the Palazzo dei Congressi, the Museum of Italian Civilization, the church of Sts. Peter and Paul, and the Piazza delle Esedre were all completed. In Rome, work was finished on Via della Conciliazione, the Ministry of Foreign Affairs, and the Ministry of Italian Africa. The list continues with the Arengario in Milan, the University of Trieste, the Palazzi di Giustizia in Palermo, Forlì, and Pisa, and the offices of the Banca d'Italia in Naples.

Moreover, the Case del Fascio became police headquarters, Guardia di Finanza buildings, and tax offices. The headquarters of the Gruppi Rionali Fascisti became police headquarters, schools, or Radiotelevisione Italiana offices. The buildings of the Fascist Militia became barracks for the Carabinieri, and the GIL sun therapy colonies became charitable institutes. In Rome, the Accademia di Scherma became a court of law, the Palazzi delle Forze Armate at the EUR now hosted the Central State Archives, and the Ministry of Italian Africa became the Food and Agriculture Organization headquarters. In Nuremberg, Speer's Zeppelinfeld, the grandstand where the Nazi organizations marched before Hitler, was torn down, but in Rome the Foro Mussolini became the Foro Italico, thus restoring its original use as a sports arena.[31] Other works, ones that had not been built by the fascist regime, also resumed their original functions. Continuity between the new Italian Republic and the previous regime was perhaps most evident in architecture.

With the passing of time, those constructions gradually became part of the national cultural heritage. The identity of the Italian people is built on

80. Bird's-eye view of the EUR in the 1950s.

places of memory, and it includes these monuments, which recall the fascist myth created by Mussolini to educate the nation in the fascist creed. These monuments are part of the landscape and so they must be shared. While it is possible to choose which historical events should be celebrated, that is, to extrapolate the events that are considered the most important and the most instructive in history in order to build the shared memory of a nation, the same cannot be done for architecture. In this case, we find ourselves before a memory imposed by history, decided on by the regime, conveyed to and rooted in the people.[32] We see instruments of identity made to last, even, and above all, after Mussolini's death. Instruments that function slowly and, in most cases, escape the filter of critical assessment.

In the process of the homogenization of the past that characterized the end of the century, these buildings convey messages that are more hybrid, less menacing, less invasive than the original ones. But they re-emerge from the historical continuum precisely because they were built to last and to convey supremacy. The fact that they were built over a relatively short period of time and feature common figurative elements reinforces a dominant perception. Everyone, even those who are not particularly passionate about architecture, can identify them as "works of the regime." Moreover, their massive, solid, orderly, and sophisticated appearance immediately conveys what that grandeur must have looked like to the masses. They instil an idea of the apparent power that the country must have achieved during the twenty years of the regime. When taken out of their historical context, those buildings are projected onto a vision of past that is, to say the least, touched up, so that only their demagogical veneer is admired.

In Italy, the sense of belonging to a national community is relatively weak, and the country's architectural heritage represents an extraordinary resource on which the foundations of a national identity could be built.[33] However, as we have seen, that was precisely how architecture was used to great effect by the fascist regime, as no other modern country had done before. Hence, one wonders whether these examples of architecture – such as the Victory Arch in Bolzano, the Arengario in Milan, or the Palazzo della Civiltà Italiana at the E42 – could represent the country. Setting aside their different artistic qualities, do these monuments not convey a history dominated by dictatorship, by the oppression of democratic freedom, by wars of aggression against other peoples, by policies of racial segregation? Are they not the memory of values that absolutely cannot be supported in a civil country?

Italians have a primordial and perpetual propensity to tend to their individual interests, and to show a certain lack of interest in the common good: these are two of the reasons for the lack of democracy that weakens the country. The architecture of the past, with its symbolic function, could be the antidote to this process of the disintegration of identity. However, is it possible to reinforce a sense of collective identity, and therefore resist centrifugal forces, by exploiting a contaminated architectural heritage, which is anything but the expression of a superior civilization? In other words, is it possible to cure a country whose democracy is in crisis by figuratively identifying its historical memory through buildings that were the symbols of a dictatorship that preached and practised profound anti-democratic hatred? Are we perhaps grappling with yet another Italian paradox?

After a period of silence, that monumental architecture has once again started to fulfil its most intrinsic function: a demagogic appeal to the masses. Many Italians are now reconsidering the beauty of the cities and the palaces that were "built by the Duce," leading them to express a sort of absolution for a past that has been partly de-fascistized. The "arcane power" of that art is once again producing some powerful collective impressions. Ultimately, Mussolini's plan to use architecture to deliver fascism to posterity appears to have been a winning idea.

Notes

Abbreviations

AAF	Archivio Arnaldo Foschini, Università di Tor Vergata, Rome
ACS	Archivio Centrale dello Stato, Rome
AGG	Archivio Gustavo Giovannoni, Rome
AGT	Archivio Giuseppe Terragni, Como
AMP	Archivio Marcello Piacentini, Faculty of Architecture, Florence
BNF	Biblioteca Nazionale Firenze
CO	Carteggio Ordinario
CR	Carteggio Riservato
GIL	Gioventù Italiana del Littorio
GNAM	Galleria Nazionale d'Arte Moderna, Rome
MART	Museo di Arte Moderna e Contemporanea di Trento e Rovereto
MI	Ministero degli Interni (Ministry of the Interior)
PCM	Presidenza del Consiglio dei Ministri (Presidency of the Council of Ministers)
PNF	Partito Nazionale Fascista (National Fascist Party)
PS	Pubblica Sicurezza (Public Security)
SPD	Segreteria Particolare del Duce (Special Secretarial Service)

Introduction

1 Margherita Sarfatti, *Dux* (Milan: Mondadori, 1982 [1926]), 259. Unless otherwise noted, all translations are by Sylvia Notini.

2 Renzo De Felice, *Mussolini il fascista,* vol. 1, *La conquista del potere 1921– 1925* (Turin: Einaudi, 1966); Renzo De Felice, *Mussolini il fascista,* vol. 2, *L'organizzazione dello Stato fascista 1925–1929* (Turin: Einaudi, 1968); Renzo De Felice, *Mussolini il duce,* vol. 1, *Gli anni del consenso 1929–1936* (Turin: Einaudi, 1974); Renzo De Felice, *Mussolini il duce,* vol. 2, *Lo Stato totalitario*

1936–1940 (Turin: Einaudi, 1981); Renzo De Felice, *Mussolini l'alleato*, vol. 1, *L'Italia in guerra 1940–1943* (Turin: Einaudi, 1990).

3 Specifically, Emilio Gentile, *Il culto del littorio: La sacralizzazione della politica nell'Italia fascista* (Rome-Bari: Laterza, 2001 [1993]); George Mosse, *La nazionalizzazione delle masse: Simbolismo politico e movimenti di massa in Germania (1815–1933)* (Bologna: Il Mulino, 1975). A significant contribution on the theme of the sacredness of architectural spaces can be found in Sergio Bertelli, ed., *Il teatro del potere: Scenari e rappresentazione del politico fra Otto e Novecento* (Rome: Carocci, 2000).

4 Emilio Gentile, *Fascismo di pietra* (Rome-Bari: Laterza, 2007).

5 Following early analysis by Bruno Zevi, *Storia dell'architettura moderna* (Turin: Einaudi, 1950), and by Giulia Veronesi, *Difficoltà politiche dell'architettura in Italia 1920–1940* (Milan: Comunità, 1953). Authors directly involved in historical events (also due to their age) starting from the 1960s include Cesare De Seta, *La cultura architettonica in Italia tra le due guerre* (Bari: Laterza, 1972); Luciano Patetta, *L'architettura in Italia 1919–1943: Le polemiche* (Milan: Clup, 1972); Riccardo Mariani, *Fascismo e "città nuove"* (Milan: Feltrinelli, 1976); Henry A. Millon and Linda Nochlin, ed., *Art and architecture in the Service of Politics* (Cambridge, MA: MIT Press, 1978); Giorgio Ciucci, "Il dibattito sull'architettura e le città fasciste," *Storia dell'arte italiana: Parte 2: Dal Medioevo al Novecento*, ed. Federico Zeri, vol. 3, *Il Novecento* (Turin: Einaudi, 1982), revised edition: Giorgio Ciucci, *Gli architetti e il fascismo: Architettura e città, 1922–1944* (Turin: Einaudi, 1989); Dennis P. Doordan, "The Political Content in Italian Architecture during the Fascist Era," *Art Journal* 43 (Summer 1983), 121–31; Carlo Cresti, *Architettura e fascismo* (Florence: Vallecchi, 1986); Diane Ghirardo, *Building New Communities: New Deal America and Fascist Italy* (Princeton, NJ: Princeton University Press, 1989); Richard A. Etlin, *Modernism in Italian Architecture, 1890–1940* (Cambridge, MA: MIT Press, 1991); Dawn Ades et al., eds., *Art and Power: Europe under the Dictators, 1930–1945* (London: Thames and Hudson-Hayward Gallery, 1995); Giorgio Ciucci, ed., *Classicismo-Classicismi: Architettura Europa/America 1920–1940* (Milan: Electa, 1995); Marla Stone, *The Patron State: Culture and Politics in Fascist Italy* (Princeton, NJ: Princeton University Press, 1998); Leonardo Benevolo, *L'architettura nell'Italia contemporanea* (Rome-Bari: Laterza, 1998), 81–128; Paolo Nicoloso, *Gli architetti di Mussolini: Scuole e sindacato, architetti e massoni, professori e politici negli anni del regime* (Milan: Franco Angeli, 1999); Sandro Scarrocchia, *Albert Speer e Marcello Piacentini: L'architettura del totalitarismo negli anni trenta* (Milan: Skira, 1999); Francesco Dal Co and Marco Mulazzani, "Stato e regime," in *Storia dell'architettura italiana: Il primo Novecento*, ed. Giorgio Ciucci and Giorgio Muratore (Milan: Electa, 2004), 234–59; Borden W. Painter, *Mussolini's Rome: Rebuilding the Eternal City* (New York: Palgrave Macmillan, 2005).

6 Giorgio Ciucci, "L'urbanista negli anni '30: Un tecnico per l'organizzazione del consenso," in *Il razionalismo e l'architettura in Italia durante il fascismo*, ed. Silvia

Danesi and Luciano Patetta (Venice: La Biennale di Venezia-Electa, 1976), 28–31; Antonio Cederna, *Mussolini urbanista* (Rome-Bari: Laterza, 1979); Diane Ghirardo, "Italian Architects and Fascist Politics: An Evaluation of the Rationalist's Role in Regime Building," *Journal of the Society of Architectural Historians* 2 (May 1980), 109–27; Jeffrey T. Schnapp, *Anno X: La mostra della Rivoluzione fascista del 1932* (Pisa-Rome: Istituti editoriali e poligrafici internazionali, 2003).

7 De Felice, *Mussolini il duce*, 1:3–5, 54–5; De Felice, *Mussolini il duce*, 2:213–53.

8 Emilio Gentile, *Fascismo: Storia e interpretazione* (Rome-Bari: Laterza, 2002), 27–30.

9 De Felice, *Mussolini il duce*, 2:266–7, 286–7.

1 Travelling to See the Buildings

1 Renzo De Felice, *Mussolini il duce*, vol. 1, *Gli anni del consenso 1929–1936* (Turin: Einaudi, 1974), 244. On the myth of the Duce see Renzo De Felice and Luigi Goglia, *Mussolini: Il mito* (Rome-Bari: Laterza, 1983), 3–17; Luisa Passerini, *Mussolini immaginario: Storia di una biografia. 1915–1939* (Rome-Bari: Laterza, 1991).

2 Bruno Biancini, ed., *Dizionario mussoliniano* (Milan: Hoepli, 1939), 178.

3 Gustave Le Bon, *Psicologia delle folle* (Milan: Longanesi, 1980 [1895]), 96. The sentence has been attributed to Napoleon. In 1926, Mussolini considered Le Bon's book "an essential work which I often go back to these days." Simonetta Falasca Zamponi, *Lo spettacolo del fascismo* (Soveria Mannelli: Rubbettino, 2003), 42.

4 Sergio Bertelli, "Il teatro del potere nel mondo contemporaneo," in *Il teatro del potere: Scenari e rappresentazione del politico fra Otto e Novecento*, ed. Sergio Bertelli (Rome: Carocci, 2000), 17.

5 On journeys and the relationship with the crowd see Mario Isnenghi, *L'Italia in piazza: I luoghi della vita pubblica dal 1848 ai nostri giorni* (Milan: Mondadori, 1994), 310–24; Victoria De Grazia, "Andare al popolo," in *Dizionario del fascismo*, ed. Victoria De Grazia and Sergio Luzzatto, vol. 1, *A–K* (Turin: Einaudi, 2002), 52–4.

6 According to Mussolini, the Italian people were "a colloidal mass, and irresponsible by definition." Galeazzo Ciano, *Diario 1937–1943*, ed. Renzo De Felice (Milan: Rizzoli, 1990), 140 (22 May 1938).

7 Le Bon, *Psicologia delle folle*, 74.

8 Benito Mussolini, *Opera omnia*, ed. Edoardo Susmel and Duilio Susmel (Florence: La Fenice, 1951–80), 22:242.

9 Renzo De Felice, *Mussolini il fascista*, vol. 2, *L'organizzazione dello Stato fascista 1925–1929* (Turin: Einaudi, 1968), 362.

10 Barbara Spackman, "Discorsi del duce," *Dizionario del fascismo*, vol. 1, 429.

11 Mussolini, *Opera omnia*, 25:141–3.

12 Agostino Magnaghi, Mariolina Monge and Luciano Re, *Guida all'architettura moderna di Torino* (Turin: Lindau, 1995), 141.

13 Mussolini, *Opera omnia*, 25:146–7.

14 Ibid., 156.

15 George Mosse, *L'uomo e le masse nelle ideologie nazionaliste* (Rome-Bari: Laterza, 1988), 97–115. A chapter in the *Carta del Carnaro* is dedicated to "Edilità."

16 In 1926, D'Annunzio received 5,200,000 lire from Mussolini, which is equal to 3,300,000 euros. See Renzo De Felice, *D'Annunzio politico, 1918–1938* (Rome-Bari: Laterza, 1978), 199–200.

17 On the organization of the consensus, see Philip V. Cannistraro, *La fabbrica del consenso: Fascismo e mass media* (Rome-Bari: Laterza, 1975); Victoria De Grazia, *Consenso e cultura di massa nell'Italia fascista: L'organizzazione del Dopolavoro* (Rome-Bari: Laterza, 1981).

18 Mussolini, *Opera omnia*, 26:319.

19 "Il Duce entusiasticamente accolto a Lecce e a Taranto," *Il Popolo d'Italia*, 8 February 1934.

20 Bruno Tobia, "Dal Milite ignoto al nazionalismo monumentale fascista (1921–1940)," in *Storia d'Italia*, Annali 18, *Guerra e pace*, ed. Walter Barberis (Turin: Einaudi, 2002), 631.

21 "Il viaggio del Duce in Puglia," *Il Popolo d'Italia*, 9 September 1934.

22 "Il Duce accolto a Bolzano da oltre quarantamila persone," *Il Popolo d'Italia*, 27 August 1935.

23 Massimo Martignoni, "Il territorio e la memoria dei caduti," in *Monumenti della grande guerra: Progetti e realizzazioni in Trentino, 1916–1935* (Trent: Museo storico in Trento, 1998), 23–49; Tobia, "Dal Milite ignoto al nazionalismo monumentale fascista (1921–1940)," 613–19.

24 Mussolini, *Opera omnia*, 27:119.

25 Giorgio Rochat, "Le guerre del fascismo," in *Storia d'Italia*, Annali 18, 698–708.

26 De Felice, *Mussolini il duce*, 1:626–7; Augusta Molinari, "La giornata della fede," in *Dizionario del fascismo*, vol. 1, 507–8; Petra Terhoeven, *Oro alla patria: Donne, guerra e propaganda nella giornata della fede fascista* (Bologna: Il Mulino, 2006), 307–8.

27 "Il Duce comincia con il gesto del seminatore la vita nel nuovo Comune di Pontinia," *Il Popolo d'Italia*, 19 December 1935.

28 Yvon De Begnac, *Palazzo Venezia: Storia di un regime* (Rome: La Rocca, 1950), 554, 652.

29 "La seconda trionfale giornata del Duce nel bolognese," *Il Popolo d'Italia*, 26 October 1936.

30 Renzo De Felice, *Mussolini il duce*, vol. 2, *Lo Stato totalitario 1936–1940* (Turin: Einaudi, 1981), 394.

31 "Il Duce assiste nella parrocchiale di Premilcuore al rito nuziale," *Il Popolo d'Italia*, 25 April 1937. On Fuzzi, see the interview with Cesare Valle

in Ferruccio Canali, "Architetti romani nella 'città del Duce'," *Memoria e Ricerca* 6 (December 1995), 189. On the "provincia del Duce" see Patrizia Dogliani, *L'Italia fascista, 1922–1940* (Milan: Sansoni, 1999), 114–20.

32 Alfredo Forti, "La Stazione Centrale e Marittima di Messina," in *Angiolo Mazzoni (1884–1979): Architetto nell'Italia tra le due guerre* (Casalecchio di Reno: Grafis, 1984), 206.

33 Giuseppe Bottai, *Diario 1935–1944*, ed. Giordano Bruno Guerri (Milan: Rizzoli, 1994), 119 (4 September 1937); Passerini, *Mussolini immaginario*, 179.

34 Augusto Simonini, *Il linguaggio di Mussolini* (Milan: Bompiani, 1978), 191.

35 Carmelo Severino, *Enna: La città al centro* (Rome: Gangemi, 1996), 148–50.

36 Mussolini, *Opera omnia*, 28:240–1.

37 Ibid., 29:99.

38 Sergio Luzzatto, *L'immagine del duce* (Rome: Editori Riuniti, 2001), 179. The headquarters of the Gruppi Rionali Fascisti were the "Federico Florio," designed by Mario Angelini, and the "Nicola Buonservizi," designed by Luigi Daneri.

39 Fuselli collaborated with Piacentini on the extension to the Casa Madre dei Mutilati in Rome.

40 ACS, SPD, CR, 1922–43, b. 35, s. issue 9. See *Foglio d'Ordini* 181, 27 September 1937; ibid., 208, 27 August 1938; ibid., 238, 24 October 1939.

41 Emilio Gentile, *La via italiana al totalitarismo* (Rome: Carocci, 1995); Emilio Gentile, *Il mito dello Stato nuovo* (Rome-Bari: Laterza, 2000); Emilio Gentile, *Fascismo: Storia e interpretazione* (Rome-Bari: Laterza, 2002).

42 Mussolini, *Opera omnia*, 29:144–7; MacGregor Knox, *Destino comune: Dittatura, politica estera e guerra nell'Italia fascista e nella Germania nazista* (Turin: Einaudi, 2000), 166; Gianluca Gabrielli, "Razzismo," in *Dizionario del fascismo*, vol. 2, 474–5.

43 "Wiretapping," 24 November 1938, in ACS, SPD, CR, 1922–43, b. 38.

44 See *Le Tre Venezie* 10 (October 1938), 351–6. The end of August 1938 saw the removal of Edgardo Morpurgo and Arnaldo Frigessi from their charges as presidents of the Assicurazioni Generali and the RAS, respectively. Renzo De Felice, *Storia degli ebrei sotto il fascismo* (Turin: Einaudi, 1993), 283.

45 Bruno Tobia, "*Salve o popolo d'eroi...*": *La monumentalità fascista nelle fotografie dell'Istituto Luce* (Rome: Editori Riuniti, 2002), 140–5; Paolo Nicoloso, "Settembre 1938: Mussolini nella Venezia Giulia, Indirizzi totalitari e architettura per il fascismo," in *Torviscosa: esemplarità di un progetto*, ed. Enrico Biasin, Raffaella Canci and Stefano Perulli (Udine: Forum, 2003), 13–26. The Tempio Ossario was completed by Provino Valle after Limongelli's death in 1932.

46 Giovanni Giuriati, *La parabola di Mussolini nei ricordi di un gerarca*, ed. Emilio Gentile (Rome-Bari: Laterza, 1981), 56.

47 Mussolini, *Opera omnia*, 29:162–4; Joseph Goebbels, *Diario 1938*, ed. Marina Bistolfi (Milan: Mondadori 1996), 338 (27 September 1938).

48 On Carbonia, see Antonella Sanna, "Carbonia: progetto e costruzione dell'architettura e dello spazio pubblico nella città razionalista di fondazione," tesi di dottorato (PhD diss., XVII ciclo).

49 Bottai, *Diario 1935–1944*, 145 (13 April 1939).

50 Nino D'Aroma, *Mussolini segreto* (Bologna: Cappelli, 1958), 170.

51 Mussolini, *Opera omnia*, 29:273.

52 News on Mussolini's visit to the FIAT factory was found in Valerio Castronovo, *Fiat, 1899–1999: Un secolo di storia italiana* (Milan: Rizzoli, 1999), 560–4.

53 Mussolini visited in May 1930, December 1931, and October 1932, 1934, and 1936.

54 "Alla Mostra d'arte decorativa," *Il Popolo d'Italia*, 22 May 1930. Figini, Frette, Libera, and Pollini, who belonged to the Gruppo 7, and Bottoni designed the Casa Elettrica. Mussolini also visited the Casa del Dopolavorista, designed by Luisa Lovarini.

55 "L'aristocrazia della Guerra e della Vittoria dona al Duce il bastone del comando," *Il Popolo d'Italia*, 23 May 1930.

56 See Tobia, "Dal Milite ignoto al nazionalismo monumentale fascista (1921–1940)," 603–4.

57 Emilio Gentile, *Il culto del littorio: La sacralizzazione della politica nell'Italia fascista* (Rome-Bari: Laterza, 2001 [1993]).

58 Mussolini, *Opera omnia*, 24:246–7.

59 The designers were Antonio Carminati, Angelo Bordoni, and Luigi Caneva.

60 "Al Palazzo delle Arti sede della Triennale di Milano," *Il Popolo d'Italia*, 27 October 1932. The design for the Palazzo dell'Arte was approved by Mussolini on 9 July 1931.

61 Note by Dalmine, 29 September 1932, see Laura Falconi, *Gio Ponti: Interni, oggetti, disegni, 1920–1976* (Milan: Electa, 2004), 90.

62 Albert Speer, *Diari segreti di Spandau* (Milan: Mondadori, 1976), 113.

63 "All'Esposizione dell'Aeronautica," *Il Popolo d'Italia*, 6 October 1934.

64 Mussolini, *Opera omnia*, 26:351.

65 Note from Cobolli Gigli to Mussolini, 27 May 1939, in ACS, PCM, 1937–9, issue 3.2.10, n. 329. Note by Gorla for Mussolini, 26 November 1940, in ACS, PCM, 1940–41, issue 3.2.10, n. 2999. However, the prediction for of the Ministero delle Corporazioni included 600,000 rooms per year. See *Il Corriere dei Costruttori*, 15 December 1940. On the crisis of lodgings in the early postwar period, see Paolo Nicoloso, "Genealogie del Piano Fanfani, 1939–1950," in *Il piano Fanfani in Friuli*, ed. Ferruccio Luppi and Paolo Nicoloso (Pasian di Prato: Leonardo, 2001), 37, 56–7.

66 Mussolini, *Opera omnia*, 28:64–5.

67 "Alla nuova sede del Sindacato Giornalisti," *Il Popolo d'Italia*, 1 November 1936.

68 *Annali del fascismo* (November 1936).

69 "Starace approva il progetto e il finanziamento della nuova casa del fascio," *Il Popolo d'Italia*, 21 September 1937. For more on the event, see Ferruccio Luppi, "Sede della Federazione dei fasci milanesi," in *Piero Portaluppi: Linea errante nell'architettura del Novecento*, ed. Luca Molinari (Milan: Skira, 2003), 132–3.

70 Mussolini, *Opera omnia*, 28:72.

71 "La visita alla nuova sede del Gruppo Mussolini," *Il Popolo d'Italia*, 3 November 1936; "Gruppo Mussolini: Ecco la nuova sede che sarà completata con una torre alta 45 metri," *Il Popolo d'Italia*, 29 June 1937.

72 Alessandro Campi, *Mussolini* (Bologna: Mulino, 2001), 161–4.

73 Mussolini, *Opera omnia*, 29:70–1.

74 For more on the issue, see *Corriere della Sera*, 19 June 1939, about Mussolini's visits to Piacenza, Cremona, Parma, Modena, Bologna, and Rimini, and on 20 June 1938. In April 1932, Hitler travelled by plane to visit twenty different cities in the space of six days. Ian Kershaw, *Il "mito di Hitler": Immagine e realtà nel Terzo Reich* (Turin: Bollati Boringhieri, 1998), 52–3.

75 Emil Ludwig, *Colloqui con Mussolini* (Milan: Mondadori, 1970 [1932]), 127, 132, 182–3. "The Italian race is sheep-like. Eighteen years are not enough to transform it. One could need 180 years, or maybe 180 centuries ... I lack the material. Even Michelangelo needed marble to make his statues. If he had had only some clay, he would have been a simple potter." Ciano, *Diario 1937–1943*, 444–5 (20 June 1940).

76 Sergio Luzzatto, *Il corpo del duce* (Turin: Einaudi, 1998), 15–17.

77 Quinto Navarra, *Memorie del cameriere di Mussolini* (Naples: L'ancora del Mediterraneo, 2004 [1946]), 151. The memoirs are the result of rewriting by Leo Longanesi and Indro Montanelli.

78 The visit to Arsia took place on 7 August 1936. Francesco Krecic, *Arsia*, "La bianca città del carbone: La committenza, il progettista, l'architettura, la realizzazione. 1935–1937" tesi di laurea (MA diss., Facoltà di Architettura di Trieste, a.a. 2005–6).

79 The Palazzo dell'Arte was designed by Filippo Mellia, Nino Barillà, Vincenzo Gentile, and Giuseppe Sambito.

80 Flavio Fergonzi, "Dalla monumentomania alla scultura arte monumentale," in *La scultura monumentale negli anni del fascismo: Arturo Martini e il monumento al duca d'Aosta*, ed. Flavio Fergonzi and Maria Teresa Roberto (Turin: Allemandi, 1992), 195.

81 Leonardo Ciacci and Leonardo Tiberi, *La Roma di Mussolini* (Rome: Istituto Luce, 2003), DVD.

82 "Morti più vivi dei vivi," *Il Popolo del Friuli*, 20 September 1938.

83 The designers of the former were De Renzi, Guerrini, and Libera. The designers of the latter were De Renzi and Guerrini again, this time with

Paniconi and Pediconi. Mussolini held a dinner in Palazzo Venezia with the architects and the designers of the second exhibition.
84 Bottai, *Diario 1935–1944*, 111.

2 Mussolini's Rome

1 For more on funding, see Antonio Cederna, *Mussolini urbanista* (Rome-Bari: Laterza, 1979), 102–3. On the interventions by Mussolini, see Spiro Kostof, *The Third Rome. 1870–1950: Traffic and Glory* (Berkeley, CA: University Art Museum, 1973), and, more recently, Borden W. Painter, *Mussolini's Rome: Rebuilding the Eternal City* (New York: Palgrave MacMillan, 2005).
2 Philip V. Cannistraro and Brian R. Sullivan, *Margherita Sarfatti: L'altra donna del duce* (Milan: Mondadori, 1993), 240, 351; Giovanni Belardelli, *Il Ventennio degli intellettuali* (Rome-Bari: Laterza, 2005), 210–11. On the myth of Rome, see Emilio Gentile, *Fascismo di pietra* (Rome-Bari: Laterza, 2007).
3 Cederna, *Mussolini urbanista*, 48.
4 Benito Mussolini, *Opera omnia*, ed. Edoardo Susmel and Duilio Susmel (Florence: La Fenice, 1951–80), 20:234.
5 Ibid., 22:48.
6 On demolitions programmed in the urban development plans of 1873, 1883, and 1908, see Italo Insolera, *Roma Moderna: Un secolo di storia urbanistica, 1870–1970* (Turin: Einaudi, 2001), 27, 47–50, 92–3. On Ricci's hypothesis, see Giorgio Ciucci, "Roma capitale imperiale," in *Storia dell'architettura italiana: Il primo Novecento*, ed. Giorgio Ciucci and Giorgio Muratore (Milan: Electa, 2004), 398–9.
7 "By isolating the monuments, the relationship between ancient Romans and Italians is even more beautiful and suggestive." Benito Mussolini, *La mia vita* (Milan: Rizzoli, 1983 [1932]), 202.
8 Ugo Ojetti, *Taccuini, 1914–1943* (Florence: Sansoni, 1954), 233 (6 August 1926).
9 Cannistraro and Sullivan, *Margherita Sarfatti*, 351–4.
10 "Progetto di sistemazione del centro di Roma," *Capitolium* 1 (April 1925), 32.
11 "Grab the pickaxes and the hammers and mercilessly demolish the venerated cities." Filippo Tommaso Marinetti, "Manifesto del futurismo," in *Marinetti e il futurismo*, ed. Luciano De Maria (Milan: Mondadori, 1973), 8.
12 Letter from Mussolini to Ludovico Veralli Spada Potenziani, 14 April 1928, in ACS, PCM, 1931–3, issue 7.2, n. 2199.
13 Letter from Ludovico Veralli Spada Potenziani to Mussolini, 13 April 1928, in ACS, PCM, 1931–3, issue 7.2, n. 2199.
14 Letter from Mussolini to Ludovico Veralli Spada Potenziani, 2 August 1928, in ACS, PCM, 1931–3, issue 7.2, n. 2199; Note for H.E. the Prime Minister, 3 September 1928, in ACS, PCM, 1931–3, issue 7.2, n. 2199.
15 The idea of isolating the monuments predates Mussolini's rise to power.

16 "Il Capo del Governo insedia in Campidoglio la Commissione per il piano regolatore dell'Urbe," *Il Popolo d'Italia*, 15 April 1930.

17 "Il Capo del Governo inaugura i grandiosi lavori nella Capitale," *Il Popolo d'Italia*, 29 October 1930.

18 "Il piano regolatore dell'Urbe nei rilievi della stampa romana," *Il Popolo d'Italia*, 29 January 1931.

19 "Il Duce assiste alla chiusura dei lavori della Commissione per il piano regolatore di Roma," *Il Popolo d'Italia*, 27 January 1931. Bazzani was not present.

20 Governatorato di Roma, *Piano regolatore di Roma* (Milan-Rome: Treves-Treccani-Tuminelli, 1931); reprinted in *Storia dell'urbanistica* 5 (July–December 1983), 80–3.

21 Mussolini, *Opera omnia*, 25:85.

22 "Il piano regolatore dell'Urbe nei rilievi della stampa romana," *Il Popolo d'Italia*, 29 January 1931.

23 Antonio Muñoz, *La Roma di Mussolini* (Milan: Treves, 1935), x. On Muñoz, see Cederna, *Mussolini urbanista*, xix–xx.

24 Letter from Mussolini to Francesco Boncompagni Ludovisi, 12 December 1929, in ACS, SPD, CO, 1922–43, b. 839, issue 1927.

25 Letter from Pietro Fedele to Francesco Boncompagni Ludovisi, 18 September 1931, in ACS, SPD, CO, 1922–43, b. 839, issue 1932.

26 Letter from Mussolini to Francesco Boncompagni Ludovisi, 1 February 1932, in ACS, SPD, CO, 1922–43, b. 839, issue 1932.

27 Yvon De Begnac, *Taccuini mussoliniani*, ed. Francesco Perfetti (Bologna: Il Mulino, 1990), 346.

28 Letter from Mussolini to Francesco Boncompagni Ludovisi, 3 January 1934, in ACS, SPD, CO, 1922–43, b. 840, issue 1934.

29 Note by Mussolini for Francesco Boncompagni Ludovisi, 6 May 1934, in ACS, SPD, CO, 1922–43, b. 840, issue 1934.

30 "Il sopralluogo del capo del Governo nella zona della passeggiata archeologica," *Il Popolo d'Italia*, 12 December 1933.

31 Note by Mussolini, 19 February 1934, in ACS, SPD, CO, 1922–43, issue 509.428/3.

32 Note by Mussolini for Francesco Boncompagni Ludovisi, 19 June 1934, in ACS, SPD, CO, 1922–43, b. 840, issue 1934.

33 Note by Mussolini for Francesco Boncompagni Ludovisi, 6 August 1934, in ACS, SPD, CO, 1922–43, b. 840, issue 1934.

34 Notes by Mussolini for Francesco Boncompagni Ludovisi, 7 March and 18 June 1934, in ACS, SPD, CO, 1922–43, b. 840, issue 1934.

35 Note by Mussolini for Francesco Boncompagni Ludovisi, 6 July 1934, in ACS, SPD, CO, 1922–43, b. 840, issue 1934.

36 Note for Francesco Boncompagni Ludovisi, 24 September 1934, in ACS, SPD, CO, 1922–43, b. 840, issue 1934.

37 Notes by Mussolini for the Governatorato, 11 May 1936, 7 September 1935 and 19 January 1936, in ACS, SPD, CO, 1922–43, b. 841, fascc. 1935 and 1936.

38 Note by Mussolini for the Governatorato, 1 April 1936, in ACS, SPD, CO, 1922–43, b. 841, issue 1936.

39 Note by Mussolini for Bottai, 23 June 1935, in ACS, SPD, CO, 1922–43, b. 841, issue 1935.

40 Galeazzo Ciano, *Diario 1937–1943*, ed. Renzo De Felice (Milan: Rizzoli, 1990), 60, 121, 124 (22 November 1937; 4 and 11 April 1938).

41 "Opere di Piano regolatore da attuare nel quadriennio 1938–1941," typescript, 9 December 1937, in ACS, SPD, CO, 1922–43, b. 841, issue 1936. The other works included in the list were the Galleria del Gianicolo, the junction between Piazza dell'Augusteo, and the Lungotevere in Augusta, between the Ponte dei Fiorentini and Corso Vittorio Emanuele, between Ponte Mazzini and Piazza di Chiesa Nuova, the enlargement of Via della Vittoria, Via dei Due Macelli, Via San Giovanni in Laterano, Via di Porta Angelica, the connection road between Porta Cavalleggeri and the Statale Aurelia, the extension of Viale d'Africa, and the redevelopment of the block between Via Nazionale and Via Parma.

42 "Una visita del Duce ai lavori pubblici dell'Urbe e ad Ostia," *Il Popolo d'Italia*, 9 April 1930.

43 "Il Duce inaugura solennemente a Roma la nuova sede del dopolavoro ferroviario," *Il Popolo d'Italia*, 3 June 1930.

44 "Il Duce visita i lavori del palazzo del Ministero dell'Agricoltura," *Il Popolo d'Italia*, 3 August 1930.

45 "Un'improvvisa visita del Duce ai lavori in corso nell'Urbe," *Il Popolo d'Italia*, 23 September 1930.

46 "Il Duce visita la nuova sede dell'Istituto Centrale di Statistica," *Il Popolo d'Italia*, 2 November 1930.

47 "Una visita del Duce ai lavori del Palazzo delle Esposizioni," *Il Popolo d'Italia*, 5 October 1930.

48 "Il Capo del Governo inaugura i grandiosi lavori della Capitale," *Il Popolo d'Italia*, 29 October 1930.

49 Letter from Mussolini to the editor of the magazine *Capitolium*, August 1929, quoted in Valter Vannelli, *Economia dell'architettura di Roma fascista* (Rome: Kappa, 1981), 118.

50 "Il Duce alla Casa dei ciechi di guerra," *Il Popolo d'Italia*, 10 November 1931.

51 Nino D'Aroma, *Mussolini segreto* (Bologna: Cappelli, 1958), 35.

52 "La visita del Duce ai lavori del Governatorato di Roma," *Il Popolo d'Italia*, 6 December 1931; "Una visita del Duce alle opere pubbliche del Governatorato di Roma," *Il Popolo d'Italia*, 5 December 1931.

53 "Il Duce visita le maggiori opere pubbliche in corso di esecuzione alla Capitale," *Il Popolo d'Italia*, 7 April 1932.

54 "Il Duce visita i lavori del nuovo Museo del Risorgimento," *Il Popolo d'Italia*, 6 May 1932.

55 Andrea Giardina, "Archeologia," in *Dizionario del fascismo*, ed. Victoria De Grazia and Sergio Luzzatto, vol. 1, *A–K* (Turin: Einaudi, 2002), 88; Daniele Manacorda and Renato Tamassia, *Il piccone del regime* (Rome: Curcio, 1985), 181–94.

56 Mussolini, *Opera omnia*, 25:151.

57 Dino Alfieri and Luigi Freddi, eds., *Mostra della rivoluzione fascista* (Rome: Partito nazionale fascista, 1933), 30.

58 "Il Foro Mussolini inaugurato dal Duce," *Il Popolo d'Italia*, 5 November 1932; Mussolini, *Opera omnia*, 25:175. See Antonella Greco and Salvatore Santuccio, *Foro Italico* (Rome: Multigrafica, 1991), 49–52; Salvatore Lupo, *Il fascismo: La politica in un regime totalitario* (Rome: Donzelli, 2005), 380.

59 "Il Foro Mussolini inaugurato dal Duce," *Il Popolo d'Italia*, 5 November 1932; Mussolini, *Opera omnia*, 25:175. See Antonella Greco and Salvatore Santuccio, *Foro Italico* (Rome: Multigrafica, 1991), 49–52; Salvatore Lupo, *Il fascismo: La politica in un regime totalitario* (Rome: Donzelli, 2005), 380.

60 Sergio Poretti, *Progetti e costruzione dei palazzi delle poste a Roma, 1933–1935* (Rome: Edilstampa, 1990), 86.

61 "Il Duce passa in rassegna le grandiose opere in esecuzione alla Capitale," *Il Popolo d'Italia*, 15 September 1933.

62 "Mussolini consacra l'opera del regime," *Il Popolo d'Italia*, 29 October 1933; Cederna, *Mussolini urbanista*, 19. The INFAIL Palace was designed with Guido Zevi. Roberto Dulio, "Bruno Zevi: Le radici di un progetto storico. 1930–1950," tesi di dottorato (PhD diss., XV ciclo), 50. There was another discussion between Brasini and Mussolini concerning the competition for the Palace of the Soviets in Moscow. According to Brasini, the Duce "reacted quite violently" when he was informed that the architect had accepted the invitation to take part in the competition in Moscow in the fall of 1931. Luca Brasini, ed., *L'opera architettonica e urbanistica di Armando Brasini: Dall'Urbe Massima al ponte sullo stretto di Messina* (Rome: 1979), 17.

63 Mussolini, *Opera omnia*, 26:187. He gave this speech on 18 March 1934.

64 "Il Duce celebra il giorno del lavoro italiano inaugurando nuove grandiose opere nell'Urbe," *Il Popolo d'Italia*, 24 April 1934.

65 "Il Duce assiste al Foro Mussolini alla superba parata," *Il Popolo d'Italia*, 21 July 1934.

66 "Il Duce presenzia al Lido di Roma all'inizio dei lavori per il Collegio IV Novembre," *Il Popolo d'Italia*, 12 November 1934.

67 Announcement of the competition in *Architettura: Concorso per il Palazzo del Littorio*, special issue (December 1934), 4.

68 "Inviti demolizioni per costruzione Casa Littoria," in ACS, SPD, CO, 1922–43, b. 841, issue 1935.

69 Giorgio Rochat, *Le guerre italiane, 1935–1943: Dall'impero d'Etiopia alla disfatta* (Turin: Einaudi, 2005), 25–6.

70 Angelo Del Boca, *Italiani brava gente?* (Vicenza: Neri Pozza, 2005), 188.

71 "Le opere pubbliche dell'anno XIII," *Il Popolo d'Italia*, 29 October 1935. For more on Libera and the PNF see Paolo Melis, *Adalberto Libera 1903–1964: I luoghi e le date di una vita* (Villa Lagarina: Nicolodi, 2003), 141.

72 "Mussolini dà il primo colpo di piccone alla demolizione di via delle Botteghe Oscure," *Il Popolo d'Italia*, 30 October 1935.

73 "Il Duce esamina i progetti per il nuovo ponte sul Tevere," *Il Popolo d'Italia*, 13 December 1935.

74 "Il Duce approva il grandioso progetto per la costruzione della Città della Cinematografia," *Il Popolo d'Italia*, 27 December 1935; "Il Duce dà inizio ai lavori per la Città della Cinematografia," *Il Popolo d'Italia*, 30 January 1936; Natalia Marino and Emanuele Valerio Marino, *L'Ovra a Cinecittà* (Turin: Bollati Boringhieri, 2005), 193.

75 "Il Duce fra ardenti manifestazioni d'entusiasmo inaugura il monumento al Balilla e le nuove istituzioni del Foro Mussolini," *Il Popolo d'Italia*, 6 April 1936.

76 Marcello Piacentini, "L'Esposizione universale dell'anno ventesimo e la più grande Roma del piano imperiale," *Il Giornale d'Italia*, 14 October 1936.

77 Laura Iermano, "L'area della Farnesina: La trasformazione del Foro Mussolini nella Porta nord di Roma," in *Roma: Architettura e città negli anni della seconda guerra mondiale*, ed. Pietro Scoppola, Lucio V. Barbera, and Paolo Ostilio Rossi (Rome: Gangemi, 2004), 103–8; Ciucci, "Roma capitale imperiale," 403–7; Paolo Ostilio Rossi, "L'esposizione del 1942 e le Olimpiadi del 1944: L'E42 e il Foro Mussolini come porte urbane della Terza Roma," *MdiR* 1–2 (January–December 2004), 24–5.

78 Joachim Fest, *Speer: Una biografia* (Milan: Garzanti, 2000), 70–1; Albert Speer, *Memorie del Terzo Reich* (Milan: Mondadori, 1995 [1969]), 82–3; Alex Scobie, *Hitler's State Architecture: The Impact of Classical Antiquity* (University Park, PA: Pennsylvania State University Press, 1990), 80.

79 Note from Ricci to Mussolini, 22 June 1936, quoted in Niccolò Zapponi, "Il partito della Gioventù: Le organizzazioni giovanili del fascismo 1926–1943," *Storia contemporanea* 4–5 (October 1982), 604.

80 For more on the use of marble, see Marco Mulazzani, "Le opere nello spazio di Luigi Moretti," in *Luigi Moretti*, ed. Federico Bucci and Marco Mulazzani (Milan: Electa, 2000), 12; Rosalia Vittorini, "L'arte del costruire in marmo," *Casabella* 728–9 (December 2004–January 2005), 24.

81 Telegram from Mussolini to Badoglio, 29 June 1936 in Angelo Del Boca, *I gas di Mussolini* (Rome: Editori Riuniti, 1996), 152.

82 "La prima pietra degli Uffici del Governatorato," *Il Popolo d'Italia*, 22 April 1936.

83 "Il Duce visita le imponenti opere pubbliche in corso di esecuzione alla capitale," *Il Popolo d'Italia*, 8 April 1936. Image published in Sergio Luzzatto, "'Niente tubi di stufa sulla testa': L'autoritratto del fascismo," in *L'Italia del Novecento: Le fotografie e la storia*, ed. Giovanni De Luna, Gabriele D'Autilia, and Luca Crescenti, vol. 1/1, *Il potere da Giolitti a Mussolini (1900–1945)* (Turin: Einaudi, 2005), 158.

84 "Il nuovo volto della Roma mussoliniana," *Il Popolo d'Italia*, 21 June 1936.

85 Giuseppe Bottai, *Diario 1935–1944*, ed. Giordano Bruno Guerri (Milan: Rizzoli, 1994), 110 (1 September 1936).

86 "Il Duce inaugura la nuova sede del Comando generale della Milizia e la caserma 'Mussolini'," *Il Popolo d'Italia*, 23 June 1936.

87 "Le grandiose opere pubbliche inaugurate dal Duce," *Il Popolo d'Italia*, 29 October 1936.

88 Mussolini, *Opera omnia*, 28:63.

89 Bottai, *Diario 1935–1944*, 113 (31 October 1936).

90 Lupo, *Il fascismo*, 421.

91 "Il Duce inaugura al Lido di Roma il Collegio IV novembre," *Il Popolo d'Italia*, 5 November 1936.

92 "Il Duce e Göring acclamati da 25000 giovani al Foro Mussolini," *Il Popolo d'Italia*, 16 January 1937.

93 Mussolini, *Opera omnia*, 29:117. For more on the pedagogic meaning of the war, see Alessandro Campi, *Mussolini* (Bologna: Mulino, 2001), 180–4.

94 "Il Duce inaugura i lavori per la sistemazione ferroviaria di Roma," *Il Popolo d'Italia*, 17 February 1937.

95 "Il Duce inizia i lavori per l'Esposizione universale," *Il Popolo d'Italia*, 29 April 1937.

96 "Il Duce inaugura la nuova sede della Banca del Lavoro," *Il Popolo d'Italia*, 6 May 1937.

97 Previously, on 28 April and 1 May.

98 "Mussolini inaugura il piazzale dell'Impero," *Il Popolo d'Italia*, 17 May 1937; "La mostra dell'attività edilizia dell'ONB," *Il Popolo d'Italia*, 29 May 1937.

99 "Nuove opere grandiose al Foro Mussolini," *Il Popolo d'Italia*, 11 June 1937. See also Salvatore Santuccio, "Storia urbanistica," in Antonella Greco and Salvatore Santuccio, *Foro Italico* (Rome: Multigrafica, 1991), 18.

100 Speer, *Memorie del Terzo Reich*, 66–7.

101 Iermano, "L'area della Farnesina," 105.

102 For a complete picture on the exhibitions in the context of the relationship between the regime and culture, see Marla Stone, *The Patron State: Culture and Politics in Fascist Italy* (Princeton, NJ: Princeton University Press, 1998).

103 Ciano, *Diario 1937–1943*, 39 (23 September 1937).

104 Giardina, "Archeologia," 89.

105 On the comparison between the Exhibitions of the Fascist Revolution of 1937 and of 1932, see Stone, *The Patron State*, 245–53.
106 Mussolini, *Opera omnia*, 28:248–53.
107 On the document verbally described to Mussolini, signed by the two architects, and dated 7 October 1937, see ACS, SPD, CO, 1922–43, issue 7583.
108 Letter from Ugo Ojetti to Gustavo Giovannoni, 28 June 1936, in AGG, scatola varie R.
109 The meeting took place on 30 October 1937. Previously, Pope Pius XI had been able to examine the model of Via della Conciliazione, which Piacentini and Spaccarelli had presented to him on 28 June 1936. Carlo Confalonieri recalled that, in the Vatican gardens, the pope "often drew the borders of the new buildings with a rod." Carlo Confalonieri, *Pio XI visto da vicino* (Milan: Edizioni Paoline, 1993 [1957]), 216, 218–19.
110 "Il Duce pone la prima pietra del Palazzo degli Uffici," *Il Popolo d'Italia*, 21 October 1937.
111 The new Reichskanzlei measured 400,000 cubic metres, whereas Göring's Palace would measure 580,000 cubic metres. See Speer, *Memorie del Terzo Reich*, 166. For more on the dimensions of Palazzo del Littorio, see Vittorio Vidotto "Palazzi e sacrari: Il declino del culto del littorio," *Roma moderna e contemporanea* 3 (September–December 2003), 585. Göring's Palace (Reichsmarschallamt) was to have been built on the triumphal north-south axis, in front of the Wilhelm Kreis's Soldatenhalle.
112 "La casa Littoria di Foro Mussolini," *Il Popolo d'Italia*, 20 November 1937.
113 Mussolini's sentence was reported by Marcello Piacentini in "Per l'olimpiade della civiltà," *Il Giornale d'Italia*, 27 March 1940.
114 "Mussolini inizia al Quadraro i lavori per la costruzione della sede dell'Istituto Luce," *Il Popolo d'Italia*, 11 November 1937.
115 "Il Duce approva i progetti definitivi per l'Esposizione del 1942," *Il Popolo d'Italia*, 7 July 1938. The building projects on Via Imperiale were started on 21 April 1938.
116 Albert Speer, *Diari segreti di Spandau* (Milan: Mondadori, 1976), 144.
117 Adolf Hitler, *Conversazioni segrete* (Naples: Richter, 1954), 120 (2 November 1941).
118 Santuccio, "Storia urbanistica," 19.
119 "To a certain extent, we took inspiration from the Pantheon in Rome." Speer, *Memorie del Terzo Reich*, 185, 616. For more on references to the Pantheon and the Colosseum, see Scobie, *Hitler's State Architecture*, 32, 85, 112–14.
120 For more on the Colosseum, see Frederic Spotts, *Hitler and the Power of Aesthetics* (Woodstock-New York: The Overlook Press, 2004), 324–5. For more on Cheope's pyramid, see Luigi Lenzi, "Architettura del III Reich," *Architettura* 8 (August 1939), 478.

121 Joseph Goebbels, *Diario 1938*, ed. Marina Bistolfi (Milan: Mondadori 1996), 157 (12 May 1938).

122 Ranuccio Bianchi Bandinelli, *Hitler e Mussolini: 1938, il viaggio del Führer in Italia* (Rome: e/o, 1995), 32, 46–7. Fest, *Speer*, 118. For more on Hitler's visit to Rome, see Scobie, *Hitler's State Architecture*, 23–32.

123 Hitler, *Conversazioni segrete*, 419 (2 April 1942)

124 Renzo De Felice, *Mussolini il duce*, vol. 2, *Lo Stato totalitario 1936–1940* (Turin: Einaudi, 1981), 479–83; Spotts, *Hitler and the Power of Aesthetics*, 322–4.

125 Goebbels, *Diario 1938*, 157 and 181 (12 and 30 May 1938).

126 Bottai, *Diario 1935–1944*, 123–4 (12 July 1938). For more on Hitler's architecture, see Peter Adler and Guido Knopp, "L'architetto," in *Tutti gli uomini di Hitler*, ed. Guido Knopp (Milan: Corbaccio, 1999), 293; Fest, *Speer*, 83–5.

127 Goebbels, *Diario 1938*, 200 (14 June 1938).

128 "Il Duce esamina le prove di accesso a San Pietro," *Il Messaggero*, 12 May 1938.

129 "Mussolini pone la prima pietra della sede dell'Africa Italiana," *Il Popolo d'Italia*, 1 September 1938. The laying of the first stone took place on 31 August. The other architects were Vittorio Cafiero, Alberto Legnani, Giulio Rinaldi, Ettore Rossi, and Armando Sabatini.

130 Ian Kershaw, *Hitler: 1936–1945* (Milan: Bompiani, 2001), 181.

131 Ciano, *Diario 1937–1943*, 189 (29–30 September 1938); Paolo Monelli, *Mussolini piccolo borghese* (Milan: Garzanti, 1983 [1950]), 200.

132 Ciano, *Diario 1937–1943*, 56 (13 November 1937). Hitler was disappointed by the longing for peace the German people expressed after the diplomatic agreement with the Sudeten Germans. Ian Kershaw, *Il "mito di Hitler": Immagine e realtà nel Terzo Reich* (Turin: Bollati Boringhieri, 1998), 141.

133 Mussolini, *Opera omnia*, 29:187; De Felice, *Mussolini il duce*, 2:536–9.

134 Emilio Gentile, *Fascismo: Storia e interpretazione* (Rome-Bari: Laterza, 2002), 27–8.

135 "Il Duce esamina i plastici delle nuove stazioni di Roma e di Venezia," *Il Popolo d'Italia*, 4 February 1939.

136 "Mussolini visita le opere in corso a Roma," *Il Popolo d'Italia*, 1 March 1939.

137 The Ponte Duca d'Aosta was inaugurated on 26 March; Via Imperiale was inaugurated on 21 April.

138 Ciano, *Diario 1937–1943*, 245 (30 January 1939); Mussolini, *Opera omnia*, 29:189 (25 October 1938).

139 Simonetta Falasca Zamponi, *Lo spettacolo del fascismo* (Soveria Mannelli: Rubbettino, 2003), 143–82.

140 Mussolini, *Opera omnia*, 22:248.

141 George Mosse, *La nazionalizzazione delle masse: Simbolismo politico e movimenti di massa in Germania (1815–1933)* (Bologna: Il Mulino, 1975), 283.

142 De Felice, *Mussolini il duce*, 2:634; Carlo Gentile, Lutz Klinkhammer, and Steffen Prauser, *I nazisti: I rapporti tra Italia e Germania nelle fotografie dell'Istituto Luce* (Rome: Editori Riuniti, 2003), 62.

143 MacGregor Knox, *Destino comune: Dittatura, politica estera e guerra nell'Italia fascista e nella Germania nazista* (Turin: Einaudi, 2000), 119–20.

144 De Felice, *Mussolini il duce*, 2:711–13.

145 Ciucci, "Roma capitale imperiale," 411–14.

146 Il Duce inizia i lavori di grandiosi edifici lungo la via Imperiale," *Il Popolo d'Italia*, 5 October 1939. The Cambellotti Group was formed by Adriano Cambellotti, Nello Ena, and Otto Matelli.

147 Ciano, *Diario 1937–1943*, 362 (28 October 1939).

148 "Nuove grandi opere dell'Urbe inaugurate dal Duce," *Il Popolo d'Italia*, 29 October 1939); See Ciucci, "Roma capitale imperiale," 414.

149 Nicola Tranfaglia, ed., *Ministri e giornalisti: La guerra e il Minculpop (1939–1943)* (Turin: Einaudi, 2005), 11.

150 Giuseppe Gorla, *L'Italia nella seconda guerra mondiale: Diario di un milanese, ministro del re e del governo Mussolini* (Milan: Baldini Castoldi, 1959), 74 (9 February 1940). "Il Duce inaugura fra ardenti acclamazioni i lavori al Campidoglio e la borgata di Acilia," *Il Popolo d'Italia*, 21 April 1940.

151 "Il Duce alla Scuola di ingegneria e all'Istituto d'alta matematica," *Il Popolo d'Italia*, 11 April 1940. See also Bottai, *Diario 1935–1944*, 185 (10 April 1940).

152 Alberto Pirelli, *Taccuini 1922/1943*, ed. Donato Barbone (Bologna: Il Mulino, 1984), 259 (17 April 1940).

153 Dino Grandi, *Il mio paese: Ricordi autobiografici* (Bologna: Il Mulino, 1985), 558.

154 Tranfaglia, *Ministri e giornalisti*, 13.

3 At Palazzo Venezia

1 For more on Spaccarelli, see ACS, SPD, CO, 1922–43, issue 7.583; on Arata, ACS, PNF, serie II, b. 267, issue Ing. Arata; on the Florence Railway Station, "Una lettera del Ministro Ciano al Capo del Governo," *La Nazione*, 11 July 1932; on Vaccaro, "La scuola di Ingegneria di Bologna: Il progetto presentato al Capo del Governo," *Il Popolo d'Italia*, 6 August 1932; Simona Salustri, "Sapere e politica: Umberto Puppini e la Facoltà di Ingegneria," in *Giuseppe Vaccaro: Architetture per Bologna*, ed. Maristella Casciato and Giuliano Gresleri (Bologna: Editori Compositori, 2006), 114–17; on Palanti, ACS, SPD, CO, 1922–43, issue 509.519; on Mazzoni, ACS, SPD, CO, 1922–43, issue 132.862; on Figini and Pollini, MART, Fondo Belli, r. 40, c. 156; on Carreras: ACS, SPD, CO, 1922–43, issue 167.694. Speer boasted that the stands of the Zeppelinfeld he had designed were almost twice as big as the Baths of Caracalla. On Civico, see ACS, SPD, CO, 1922–43, issue 104.113/17. The project was designed with Dagoberto Ortensi and

Roberto Lavagnino. On Paternà Baldizzi, see ACS, PCM, 1937–39, issue 14.1, n. 200/8; on Filippone, ACS, SPD, CO, 1922–43, issue 509.327; on Beltrami, ACS, SPD, CO, 1922–43, issue 181.646.

2 "Direttive di Mussolini per la Triennale d'oltremare," *Il Popolo d'Italia*, 5 June 1938.

3 Note from the Foreign Ministry for the Duce's private secretary, in ACS, SPD, CO, 1922–43, issue 509.428/3. The project for the Auditorium was designed with Francesco Fariello and Saverio Muratori.

4 Brasini was received with Emilio de Bono and Pietro Lanza on 28 April 1930; in ACS, SPD, CO, 1922–43, issue 174.093/1. Ojetti recalled that he had met Brasini while he was waiting to meet Mussolini in the waiting room at Palazzo Chigi in June 1923. Ugo Ojetti, *Taccuini: 1914–1943* (Florence: Sansoni, 1954), 120. On Bazzani, see "I ricevimenti del Duce," *Il Popolo d'Italia*, 22 Octoer 1930; "L'accademico Bazzani ricevuto dal Duce," *Il Popolo d'Italia*, 5 June 1932.

5 Zevi was received on 3 January 1929. He recalled that Mussolini told him, "I like this project." Roberto Dulio, "Bruno Zevi: Le radici di un progetto storico, 1930–1950," tesi di dottorato (PhD diss., XV ciclo), 49. See also Valter Vannelli, *Economia dell'architettura di Roma fascista* (Rome: Kappa, 1981), 118.

6 Mussolini received Palanti on 12 June 1938, in ACS, SPD, CO, 1922–43, issue 509.519. On Calza Bini, see "I ricevimenti del Capo del Governo," *Il Popolo d'Italia*, 18 September 1929; "Calza Bini riferisce al Duce sulla ripresa edilizia dell'Urbe," *Il Popolo d'Italia*, 9 February 1930; "I ricevimenti del Capo del Governo," *Il Popolo d'Italia*, 21 February 1930.

7 Emil Ludwig, *Colloqui con Mussolini* (Milan: Mondadori, 1970 [1932]), 201. On the meeting see Renzo De Felice, *Mussolini il duce*, vol. 1, *Gli anni del consenso 1929–1936* (Turin: Einaudi, 1974), 45–7.

8 Emilia Terragni, "Sala O alla Mostra della rivoluzione fascista a Roma," in *Giuseppe Terragni*, ed. Giorgio Ciucci (Milan: Electa, 1996), 382. "Il Duce impartisce le direttive per la Mostra della Rivoluzione fascista," *Il Popolo d'Italia*, 10 June 1932. Libera and De Renzi, who had been involved in the exhibition project since the previous May, were not present at the meeting.

9 "Il Duce visita i lavori della Mostra della Rivoluzione fascista," *Il Popolo d'Italia*, 9 October 1932.

10 "L'alto elogio del Duce ai camerati che hanno collaborato alla organizzazione della Mostra della Rivoluzione," *Il Popolo d'Italia*, 1 December 1932.

11 "Il Duce visita per la settima volta la Mostra della Rivoluzione fascista," *Il Popolo d'Italia*, 24 October 1934; "Il Duce chiude la Mostra della Rivoluzione," *Il Popolo d'Italia*, 30 October 1934. For more on the exhibition, see Marla Stone, *The Patron State: Culture and Politics in Fascist Italy* (Princeton, NJ: Princeton University Press, 1998), 129–76. On the "excessive" response of the audience, see Jeffrey T. Schnapp, *Anno X: La mostra della Rivoluzione*

fascista del 1932 (Pisa-Rome: Istituti editoriali e poligrafici internazionali, 2003), 41–9.

12 See Riccardo Mariani, *Fascismo e "città nuove"* (Milan: Feltrinelli, 1976), 96–8. Mussolini received the architects on 27 July 1933. He visited the work site on 18 December 1933, 5 January, and 21 February 1934.

13 The architects were received by Mussolini on 10 June 1934. ACS, PCM, 1934–6, issue 5.2, n. 2776.

14 "I progettisti degli edifici di Sabaudia ricevuti dal Capo del Governo," *Il Popolo d'Italia*, 28 July 1933.

15 The minutes from the parliamentary meeting can be found in Luciano Patetta, *L'architettura in Italia 1919–1943: Le polemiche* (Milan: Clup, 1972), 363–4.

16 Letter from Le Corbusier to Guido Fiorini, 23 November 1934, quoted in Giorgio Ciucci, "A Roma con Bottai," *Rassegna* 3 (July 1980), 66–71.

17 The document is quoted in Marida Talamona, "Italia: Strategie per una seduzione, 1927–1940," in *Le Corbusier: Un'enciclopedia*, ed. Jacques Lucan (Milan: Electa, 1988), 251.

18 Note for the Prime Minister, 2 June 1934, in ACS, PCM, 1934–6, issue 14.3, n. 1475.

19 Ciucci, "A Roma con Bottai," 66–71; Talamona, "Italia," 247–51. See the statement by Carlo Belli reported in Diane Ghirardo, *Building New Communities: New Deal America and Fascist Italy* (Princeton, NJ: Princeton University Press, 1989), 62.

20 Le Corbusier was in Rome from 4 to 16 June 1934. Talamona, "Italia," 250.

21 Note from Mussolini, 1 April 1935. ACS, SPD, CO, 1922–43, b. 841, issue 1935.

22 Letter from Giuseppe Bottai to Mussolini, in ACS, SPD, CO, 1922–43, b. 841, issue 1935.

23 Morpurgo was received by Mussolini on 1 March and 6 May 1935.

24 For more on the issue of the Augusteum area, see the detailed reconstruction by Spiro Kostof, "The Emperor and the Duce: The Planning of Piazzale Augusto Imperatore in Roma," *Art and Architecture in the Service of Politics*, ed. Henry A. Millon and Linda Nochlin (Cambridge, MA: MIT Press, 1978), 270–325. See also Orietta Rossini, *Ara Pacis* (Milan: Electa, 2005), 108–13. He visited the work site on 7 April 1936. The two versions of the model, from 1935 and 1936, were introduced in *Architettura: Urbanistica della Roma Mussoliniana*, special issue (December 1936), 88–102.

25 Andrea Giardina and André Vauchez, *Il mito di Roma: Da Carlo Magno a Mussolini* (Rome-Bari: Laterza, 2000), 248–58.

26 Ojetti was received by Mussolini on 17 December 1936. His criticism appeared in the article "Sul sepolcro di Augusto," *Corriere della Sera*, 26 November 1936.

27 Monica Pignatti and Paola Refice, "Ara Pacis Augustae: Le fasi della ricomposizione nei documenti dell'Archivio centrale dello Stato," in *Roma:*

Archeologia nel centro, vol. 2, *La città murata*, ed. Anna Maria Bietti Sestieri et al. (Rome: De Luca editore, 1985), 408–10.

28 "Messaggio di Frank Lloyd Wright," in *Atti ufficiali: XIII Congresso internazionale architetti, Roma 22–28 settembre 1935*, ed. Plinio Marconi and Giuseppe Milandri (Rome: Sindacato Nazionale Fascista Architetti, 1936), 735–6. See Maristella Casciato, "Wright and Italy: The Promise of Organic Architecture," *Frank Lloyd Wright: Europe and Beyond*, ed. Anthony Alofsin (Berkeley, CA: University of California Press, 1999), 79; Dulio, "Bruno Zevi," 28. On Mussolini's intervention, see "Il discorso di Mussolini ai delegati del XIII Congresso internazionale degli architetti a Roma," *Casabella* 96 (December 1935), 4–5.

29 Giuseppe Bottai, *Diario 1935–1944*, ed. Giordano Bruno Guerri (Milan: Rizzoli, 1994), 134 (23 September 1938). See also Marina Sommella Grossi, "Monumento a Roberto Sarfatti sul Col D'Echele, 1934–1935," in *Il Cima: Giuseppe Terragni per Margherita Sarfatti: Architetture della memoria nel '900*, ed. Jeffrey T. Schnapp (Venice: Marsilio, 2004), 95–111.

30 "I problemi di Brera: Nostra intervista con il presidente dell'Accademia," *Il Popolo d'Italia*, 2 February 1937. The meeting took place on 17 December 1935.

31 Statement by Gino Pollini, 4 May 1958, reported in Antonio Acler and Luigi Travella, "Pietro Lingeri: L'uomo e l'architetto," tesi di laurea (MA diss., Politecnico di Milano, a.a. 1987–8), 1:87.

32 "Giuseppe Terragni," *Rassegna* 11 (September 1982), 62–3..

33 Telegram from Figini, Pollini, Lingeri, and Terragni to Mussolini, 16 December 1936, reported in Chiara Baglione, "Progetti per una nuova sede dell'Accademia di Brera," in *Giuseppe Terragni*, ed. Ciucci, 487.

34 Chiara Baglione, "Artigiani, artisti, industriali: Il mondo di Pietro Lingeri," in *Pietro Lingeri*, ed. Chiara Baglione and Elisabetta Susani (Milan: Electa, 2004), 15; Chiara Baglione, "Progetti per una nuova sede dell'Accademia di Brera," in *Pietro Lingeri*, 226.

35 Letter from Dino Alfieri to Pier Maria Bardi, 23 October 1936, quoted by Marina Sommella Grossi, "Sartoris e Terragni: la polemica sulla Casa del fascio," in *Giuseppe Terragni*, ed. Ciucci, 173–4. On the commentaries by Bontempelli, see Nino D'Aroma, *Mussolini segreto* (Bologna: Cappelli, 1958), 78. The building seemed to obtain a positive critical response from the PNF technical office at the end of 1941. Diane Ghirardo, "Italian Architects and Fascist Politics: An Evaluation of the Rationalist's Role in Regime Building," *Journal of the Society of Architectural Historians* 2 (May 1980), 110–11.

36 Letter from Rino Valdameri, 3 February 1939, reported in Baglione, "Artigiani, artisti, industriali," 27–8. On Mussolini's judgment of Dante, see D'Aroma, *Mussolini segreto*, 156–7.

37 Letter from Rino Valdameri to Osvaldo Sebastiani, 19 October 1938. ACS, SPD, CO, 1922–43, issue 509.374/3.

38 Thomas L. Schumacher, *Il Danteum di Terragni, 1938* (Rome: Officina, 1980), 44. For more on the fascist myth of Dante see Stefano Albertini, "Dante Alighieri," in *Dizionario del fascismo*, ed. Victoria De Grazia and Sergio Luzzatto, vol. 1, *A–K* (Turin: Einaudi, 2002), 388–91.

39 Statement from Carlo Cavallotti in Milan, 8 January 1988, reported in the dissertation by Acler and Travella, "Pietro Lingeri," 29.

40 For more on Terragni, "leader of men," see Paolo Fossati, "Il pittore: ufficiale e gentiluomo," in *Giuseppe Terragni*, ed. Ciucci, 105–11.

41 "The Duce involved me on many occasions in the issue of the Casa Vietti." Letter from Giuseppe Bottai to Osvaldo Sebastiani, 8 March 1940; letter from Ambrogio Pessina to Rachele Mussolini, 2 March 1939; both in ACS, SPD, CO, 1922–43, issue 178.018.

42 Bottai sent Mussolini the "Discorso ai comaschi," published in *Ambrosiano* on 1 March 1940. For more on the whole issue, see Paolo Nicoloso, "Progetto di concorso per il piano regolatore di Como e sua esecuzione a stralci," in *Giuseppe Terragni*, ed. Ciucci, 419–28.

43 Letter from Gustavo Giovannoni to Araldo di Crollalanza, 1 March 1936; letter from Araldo di Crollalanza to Gustavo Giovannoni, 12 March 1936; both in Mariani, *Fascismo e "città nuove,"* 118–20. See also Lucia Nuti and Roberta Martinelli, *Le città di strapaese: La politica di fondazione nel ventennio* (Milan: Franco Angeli, 1981), 126–8. Mussolini met with Petrucci, Tufaroli, and Silenzi on 9 April 1936. For more on Petrucci see Arturo Cucciolla, *Vecchie città-città nuove: Concezio Petrucci 1926–1946* (Bari: Dedalo, 2006).

44 Cesare Valle recalled "in 1936 we submitted to Mussolini the plan and that was the only time I met him." Ferruccio Canali, "Architetti romani nella 'città del Duce'," *Memoria e Ricerca* 6 (December 1995), 178.

45 Giuliano Gresleri, "La 'Nuova Roma dello Scioa' e l'improbabile architettura dell'impero," in *Architettura italiana d'oltremare, 1870–1940*, ed. Giuliano Gresleri, Pier Giorgio Massarenti, and Stefano Zagnoni (Venice: Marsilio, 1993), 170, 176.

46 Antonio Muñoz, "Marcello Piacentini parla di Roma e di architettura," *L'Urbe* 5 (May 1937), 25.

47 Renzo De Felice, *Mussolini il duce*, vol. 2, *Lo Stato totalitario 1936–1940* (Turin: Einaudi, 1981), 283.

48 Letter from Francesco Giunta to Mussolini, 15 February 1937, in ACS, SPD, CO, 1922–43, issue 174.093/3. Brasini was received on 11 February 1937. Giunta claimed that he had taken part in the creation of the building. See also Vannelli, *Economia dell'architettura di Roma fascista*, 383–5.

49 Albert Speer, *Memorie del Terzo Reich* (Milan: Mondadori, 1995 [1969]), 185. Speer was referring to the interior surface.

50 Joachim Fest, *Speer: Una biografia* (Milan: Garzanti, 2000), 89; Albert Speer, *Diari segreti di Spandau* (Milan: Mondadori, 1976), 23.

51 Speer, *Memorie del Terzo Reich*, 185.

52 A perspective drawing of the project, titled "Foro Imperiale Germanico," is kept at the Archivio Brasini. I thank Elena Bassi for having given me a copy of the document. See also Antonio Cederna, *Mussolini urbanista* (Rome-Bari: Laterza, 1979), xvii. Cederna dates the project to 1941; he found it in Berlin and indicated that Göring was the commissioner.

53 "Il Duce ordina l'esecuzione dei primi lavori per il Quartiere del Rinascimento a Roma," *Il Popolo d'Italia*, 22 August 1935. Foschini was accompanied by the president of the INA, Bevione, and by Testa.

54 "Il Duce approva il progetto del Corso del Rinascimento," *Il Popolo d'Italia*, 15 April 1937. He was presented the third lot. See Cederna, *Mussolini urbanista*, 219–21. For more on INA interventions in historical centres see Paolo Nicoloso, "Gli architetti: Il rilancio di una professione," in *La grande ricostruzione: Il piano Ina-Casa e l'Italia degli anni cinquanta*, ed. Paola Di Biagi (Rome: Donzelli, 2001), 85–6.

55 Mussolini met with De Renzi on 23 July 1937; ACS, SPD, CO, 1922–43, issue 175–757. See Mario De Renzi, *La Magliana nuova: Progetto di formazione del nuovo centro urbano rurale* (Rome: Tip. Poliglotta Cuore di Maria, 1937).

56 Letter from Adriano Olivetti to Mussolini, 22 May 1937, in ACS, PCM, 1937–39, issue 7.1.2, n. 1644. See Giorgio Ciucci, "Introduzione: Le premesse del Piano regolatore della Valle d'Aosta," in *Studi e proposte preliminari per il piano regolatore della Valle d'Aosta* (Turin: Comunità, 2001), xii, xiv.

57 "Duecento milioni all'anno per le case popolarissime," *Il Popolo d'Italia*, 6 January 1937. The meeting took place on 5 January 1937. "Rapporto al Capo del Governo sull'Istituto case popolari," *Il Popolo d'Italia*, 13 June 1937.

58 "Le direttive del Duce al Consorzio per le case popolari," *Il Popolo d'Italia*, 31 October 1937. Del Debbio was also present at the meeting.

59 ACS, SPD, CO, 1922–43, issue 155.146 and issue 553.474.

60 Bazzani, who was sure of interpreting the Duce's taste, ensured that it would be an architecture of a "certain dignity," with the façades "made of stone from Istria and the sides from local stones and bricks." Letter from Cesare Bazzani to Mussolini, 10 October 1938; letter from Cesare Bazzani to Osvaldo Sebastiani, 12 October 1938; both in ACS, SPD, CO, 1922–43, issue 509.429.

61 "Il campanile del Duomo sarà pronto nel 1942," *Il Popolo d'Italia*, 20 October 1938.

62 Piacentini's report to Bottai, "Memoria in difesa del prof. Marcello Piacentini," typescript, undated, in AMP, issue 112.2.

63 Ojetti, *Taccuini*, 499–501 (22 October 1938).

64 Note of the private secretary of the Duce, 21 October 1938; letter from Luigi Veratti to Mussolini, 9 December 1938, in ACS, SPD, CO, 1922–43, issue 509.267. Giorgio Pini, *Filo diretto con Palazzo Venezia* (Bologna: Cappelli, 1950), 183.

65 Ojetti, *Taccuini*, 500 (22 October 1938).
66 D'Aroma, *Mussolini segreto*, 188. The meeting took place in April 1939.
67 Letter from Giulio Barella to Osvaldo Sebastiani, 5 April 1939, in ACS, SPD, CO, 1922–43, issue 545.893. See also "La nuova sede del 'Popolo d'Italia' nelle sue grandi linee tecniche ed estetiche," *Il Popolo d'Italia*, 6 May 1939; Ettore Camesasca, ed., *Mario Sironi: Scritti editi e inediti* (Milan: Feltrinelli, 1980), 301–2; Emanuela Verger, "Palazzo de Il Popolo d'Italia," in *L'architettura di Giovanni Muzio*, ed. Franco Buzzi Ceriani (Milan: Segesta, 1994), 220–4; Fulvio Irace, *Giovanni Muzio. 1893–1982* (Milan: Electa, 1994), 148–61; Salvatore Lupo, "'Il Popolo d'Italia'," in *Dizionario del fascismo*, vol. 2, 408–10.
68 The nomination "is the salary for the Palazzo del *Popolo d'Italia*, which [Muzio] is building for free." Letter from Marcello Piacentini to Arnaldo Foschini, 12 June 1939, in AAF, various issues. Muzio was received in Palazzo Venezia together with the new academics on 5 July 1939.
69 Giorgio Rochat, *Le guerre italiane, 1935–1943: Dall'impero d'Etiopia alla disfatta* (Turin: Einaudi, 2005), 78.
70 Marida Talamona, "Addis Abeba capitale dell'impero," *Storia contemporanea* 5–6 (December 1985), 1114–19; Gresleri, "La 'Nuova Roma dello Scioa' e l'improbabile architettura dell'impero," 175.
71 "Udienze di Mussolini," *Il Popolo d'Italia*, 8 May 1940. The architects were Pasquale Marabotto, Luigi Orestano, Dante Tassotti, and Luigi Vagnetti.
72 Mussolini met Longo and Savelli on 31 May 1940; ACS, SPD, CO, 1922–43, issue 187.699; "Dono di case del fascio in provincia di Gorizia," *Il Messaggero*, 3 June 1940. See also Flavio Mangione, *Le case del fascio in Italia e nelle terre d'oltremare* (Rome: Ministero per i Beni e le Attività culturali, 2003), 271–2.
73 "Disposizioni del Duce per la costruzione a Roma di case popolari," *Il Popolo d'Italia*, 19 January 1940; "Rapporti al Duce," *Il Popolo d'Italia*, 8 March 1940.
74 Note from the private secretary of the Duce, 22 May 1941, in ACS, SPD, CO, 1922–43, issue 518.469/3. The architects were received by Mussolini on 31 May 1941. Cereghini, a lieutenant in the Alpine Corps, met Mussolini in Albania on 18 March 1941. For more on the whole issue, see Giovanni Marzari, "Acropoli alpina," in *L'architetto del lago: Giancarlo Maroni e il Garda*, ed. Fulvio Irace (Milan: Electa, 1993), 85–9.
75 Letter from Gio Ponti to Ugo Ojetti, 10 December 1926, in Irace, *Giovanni Muzio*, 133.
76 "L'altissima torre littoria che sorgerà al Palazzo della Triennale di Milano," *Il Popolo d'Italia*, 6 October 1932.
77 "L'interessamento di S.E. Mussolini per i problemi della Triennale," *Il Popolo d'Italia*, 15 March 1932.

78 Letter from Gio Ponti to Roberto Papini, 16 December 1931, reported by Fulvio Irace, *Gio Ponti* (Milan: Electa, 1988), 32.

79 Gio Ponti, "Perché interessa tanto l'architettura," *Il Popolo d'Italia*, 13 July 1932.

80 "Il dott. Barella ricevuto dal Duce," *Il Popolo d'Italia*, 25 April 1933; "Il compiacimento di Mussolini per l'andamento della Triennale," *Il Popolo d'Italia*, 18 May 1933. Barella met Mussolini to inform him on the evolution of the Triennale on 2 September 1933. Barella kept Mussolini updated via mail on the development of the program for the houses that were to be built in the park. See Massimilano Savorra, "'Perfetti modelli di dimore': la casa alle Triennali," in *Le case nella Triennale: Dal parco al QT8*, ed. Graziella Leyla Ciagà and Graziella Tonon (Milan: Electa, 2005), 116–17.

81 Gio Ponti, "'Domus Lictoria'," *Domus* 73 (January 1934), 1.

82 The article was published in October 1936 in *Domus*. Ponti wrote, "The Duce approved of these opinions when I wrote about the exhibition in Paris." Letter from Gio Ponti to Osvaldo Sebastiani, 25 February 1939, in ACS, SPD, CO, 1922–43, issue 511.102.

83 Letter from Gio Ponti to Mussolini, 5 June 1937, in ACS, SPD, CO, 1922–43, issue 511.102.

84 "Rapporto degli architetti Del Debbio, Ponti e Vaccaro sulla costruzione di Addis Abeba italiana," in Gresleri, "La 'Nuova Roma dello Scioa' e l'improbabile architettura dell'impero," 166, 171; letter from Ponti to Mussolini, 16 December 1936, in Maria Luisa Neri, *Enrico Del Debbio* (Milan: Idea Books, 2006), 285.

85 Ponti sent him "Mobilitiamo le nostre produzioni d'arte," and "Mobilitamo le nostre produzioni d'arte con un piano per potenziarle," which had been published in the *Corriere della Sera*, 17 and 23 February 1939. Paolo Masera, "L'ospitalità ai milioni di visitatori che verranno per l'E42," *Domus* 134 (February 1939), 73–80; Gio Ponti, "Mobilitiamo le produzioni d'arte per l'E42," *Domus* 135 (March 1939), 65–8.

86 Letter from Gio Ponti to Osvaldo Sebastiani, 11 April 1939, in ACS, SPD, CO, 1922–43, issue 511.102.

87 Gio Ponti, "Arte per il popolo," *Domus* 147 (March 1940), 69–70.

88 Giuseppe Pagano, "Potremo salvarci dalle false tradizioni e dalle ossessioni monumentali?," *Costruzioni-Casabella* 157 (January 1941); reprinted in Giuseppe Pagano, *Architettura e città durante il fascismo*, ed. Cesare De Seta (Rome-Bari: Laterza, 1976), 129–31.

89 Gio Ponti, *Vocazione architettonica degli italiani* (Milan: Tip. Sormani, 1940), special issue of the magazine *Il libro italiano nel mondo* (December 1940).

90 Letter from Gio Ponti to Osvaldo Sebastiani, 13 November 1941, in ACS, SPD, CO, 1922–43, issue 511.102.

91 Note by Mussolini, in ACS, SPD, CO, 1922–43, issue 511.102.

92 Letter from Gio Ponti to Osvaldo Sebastiani, 14 February 1940, in ACS, SPD, CO, 1922–43, issue 511.102.

93 Letter from Gio Ponti to Osvaldo Sebastiani, 5 March 1941, in ACS, SPD, CO, 1922–43, issue 511.102.

94 Massimo Martignoni, *Gio Ponti: Gli anni di Stile, 1941–1947* (Milan: Abitare Segesta, 2002), 106–7. For more on the program of the 8th Triennale, see Anty Pansera, *Storia e cronaca della Triennale* (Milan: Longanesi, 1978), 613; Giorgio Ciucci, "Gli architetti e la uerra," in *Storia dell'architettura italiana: Il primo Novecento*, ed. Giorgio Ciucci and Giorgio Muratore (Milan: Electa, 2004), 478–81. Ponti was a member of the executive board of the Triennale.

95 "This standard furniture from Germany belongs to the studies and the programs Hitler promoted for the 'house for everyone' in the speech he gave on 15 November 1941 in the middle of the war." Gio Ponti, "Umanità della casa," *Corriere della Sera*, 2 January 1943. Hitler's building program included the creation of "300,000 homes in the first post-war year." Fred Taylor, ed., *I diari di Goebbels*, (Milan: Sperling & Kupfer, 1984), 221 (19 November 1940).

96 Letter from Gio Ponti to Nicolò De Cesare, 2 February 1942, in ACS, SPD, CO, 1922–43, issue 511.102.

97 Gio Ponti, "Industrie d'arte in tempo di guerra," *Corriere della Sera*, 15 February 1942.

98 Ponti wrote to De Cesare on 21 February 1942, while he was waiting for a response from Mussolini: "Excellency, it would be a great comfort to me to know that the Duce has read this letter of mine. It contains an interpretation of the war and of the Italian work that I really hope will meet his ideas approval." ACS, SPD, CO, 1922–43, issue 511.102

99 Renzo De Felice, *Mussolini l'alleato*, vol. 1, *L'Italia in guerra 1940–1943*, tomo 1, *Dalla guerra "breve" alla guerra lunga* (Turin: Einaudi, 1996), 103–10, 283–90, 441–8.

100 Letter from Gio Ponti to Mussolini, 22 April 1943, in ACS, SPD, CO, 1922–43, issue 511.102. On that occasion Ponti asked to meet Mussolini.

101 One must consider that Moretti joined the PNF when he was 26 years old: he was a latecomer, for instance, when compared with Quaroni and Enrico Peressutti, who joined when they were 17 years old, with Fagnoni, who was 18, Belgioioso, who was 19, Astengo, who was 22, Libera and Albini, who were 23, and Terragni, who was 24.

102 Cecilia Rostagni, "Biografia," in *Luigi Moretti*, ed. Federico Bucci and Marco Mulazzani (Milan: Electa, 2000), 211.

103 ACS, Fondo Renato Ricci, b. 2, issue 4, s. issue 7. See Sandro Setta, *Renato Ricci: Dallo squadrismo alla Repubblica sociale italiana* (Bologna: Il Mulino, 1987), 509. The Statue of Liberty is 46 metres tall: Speer, *Memorie del Terzo*

Reich, 76. Moretti, Francesco Mansutti, Gino Miozzi, Paniconi, and Pediconi discussed the theme of the Museo ONB with Del Debbio. Marco Mulazzani, "Progetto di concorso per il monumento al fascismo e il museo della rivoluzione al Foro Mussolini," *Francesco Mansutti, Gino Miozzi: Architetture per la gioventù* (Milan: Skira, 2005), 70–2.

104 For more on the cult of the Duce see Emilio Gentile, *Fascismo: Storia e interpretazione* (Rome-Bari: Laterza, 2002), 219.

105 For more on the Arengo, see Laura Iermano, "L'area della Farnesina: La trasformazione del Foro Mussolini nella Porta nord di Roma," in *Roma: Architettura e città negli anni della seconda guerra mondiale*, ed. Pietro Scoppola, Lucio V. Barbera, and Paolo Ostilio Rossi (Rome: Gangemi, 2004), 105–7.

106 Antonella Greco, ed., "Gli obelischi, le piazze, gli artisti: Conversazione con Ludovico Quaroni," in *E42: Utopia e scenario del regime*, vol. 2, *Urbanistica, architettura, arte e decorazione*, ed. Maurizio Calvesi, Enrico Guidoni, and Simonetta Lux (Venice: Marsilio, 1987), 283–7.

107 Vittorio Vidotto, "Il mito di Mussolini e le memorie nazionali: Le trasformazioni del Foro Italico, in Roma," in *Roma*, ed. Scoppola, Barbera, and Rossi, 115.

108 Bucci and Mulazzani, *Luigi Moretti*, 214.

109 Salvatore Santuccio, "Storia urbanistica," in Antonella Greco and Salvatore Santuccio, *Foro Italico* (Rome: Multigrafica, 1991), 19.

110 Rostagni, "Biografia," 211.

4 In the Architect's Shoes

1 For more on Mussolini's unwillingness to delegate and his dispersive activity, see Renzo De Felice, *Mussolini il duce*, vol. 1, *Gli anni del consenso 1929–1936* (Turin: Einaudi, 1974), 20–4.

2 "La Casa dei Sindacati a Milano," *Il Popolo d'Italia*, 27 June 1930.

3 "I ricevimenti del Duce," *Il Popolo d'Italia*, 6 August 1930.

4 Letter from Brasini to Mussolini, 11 December 1930, in ACS, SPD, CO, 1922–43, issue 174.093.

5 The drawing signed by Mussolini was published in *Il Popolo d'Italia*, 7 December 1932; "Il Padiglione della stampa alla Triennale," *Il Popolo d'Italia*, 12 February 1933.

6 "La nuova sede del gruppo rionale Cantore," *Il Popolo d'Italia*, 8 March 1932. The project was designed by Stefano Balzano.

7 "L'approvazione del Duce al progetto della sistemazione in Santa Croce delle tombe dei caduti del fascismo fiorentino," *Il Popolo d'Italia*, 12 December 1933. The drawings by Fagnoni were submitted to Mussolini by Alessandro Pavolini; "Il Duce celebra il giorno del lavoro italiano inaugurando nuove grandiose opere nell'Urbe," *Il Popolo d'Italia*, 24 April 1934.

8 On 1 July 1932 Mussolini was updated by Costanzo Ciano on the pre-competition project by Mazzoni; then, a few days later, he was updated on the consensus obtained by that project in artistic and ministerial circles. See "Una lettera del Ministro Ciano al Capo del Governo," *La Nazione*, 11 July 1932; "Stazione di Santa Maria Novella: Firenze, 1932–1935," *Giovanni Michelucci. 1891–1990*, ed. Claudia Conforti, Roberto Dulio, and Marzia Marandola (Milan: Electa, 2007), 133–4.

9 Riccardo Domenichini, "I progetti di Mazzoni per la stazione ferroviaria di Venezia Santa Lucia," in *Angiolo Mazzoni: Architetto, ingegnere del Ministero delle Comunicazioni*, ed. Mauro Cozzi, Ezio Godoli, and Paola Pettenella (Milan: Skira, 2003), 189–96. See the statement by Mazzoni in "Appunti sulla mia formazione e sul mio lavoro di architetto e di ingegnere," in MART, Fondo Mazzoni, S21.

10 "Grandioso programma di opere comunali approvato dal Capo del Governo," *Il Popolo d'Italia*, 19 July 1934.

11 "Architettura aeronautica," *Il Popolo d'Italia*, 15 August 1934.

12 "L'approvazione di Mussolini ai progetti del nuovo comune di Pontinia," *Il Popolo d'Italia*, 16 December 1934.

13 Ugo Ojetti, *Taccuini: 1914–1943* (Florence: Sansoni, 1954), 435 (30 April 1934).

14 Riccardo Mariani, *Fascismo e "città nuove"* (Milan: Feltrinelli, 1976), 102.

15 "Mussolini approva i progetti per nuovi edifici pubblici a Napoli," *Il Popolo d'Italia*, 8 June 1935.

16 The visit took place on 15 April 1935. See Fabio Mangone, *Giulio Ulisse Arata: L'opera completa* (Naples: Electa, 1993), 178–80.

17 "Il Duce inaugurerà oggi il monumento a Corridoni," *Il Popolo d'Italia*, 24 October 1936.

18 Ferruccio Canali, "'Ambientamento' e 'restauro' a Forlì: Muzio, Giovannoni e l'Albergo della Ras (1937–1940)," *Parametro* 216 (November–December 1996), 76; Ferruccio Canali, "Architetti romani della 'Città del duce': Gustavo Giovannoni e la pratica dei diversi 'restauri architettonici' a Forlì," *Studi romagnoli* 47 (1996), 736–42.

19 "Elargizione del Duce per le case popolari e l'isolamento dell'arco di Augusto," *Il Popolo d'Italia*, 20 January 1937.

20 Renzo De Felice, *Mussolini il duce*, vol. 2, *Lo Stato totalitario 1936–1940* (Turin: Einaudi, 1981), 284.

21 "Il progetto dei palazzi del Governo e della Questura di Livorno approvato dal Duce," *Il Popolo d'Italia*, 7 January 1937; Elisabetta Pieri, "Il nuovo Palazzo del Governo di Livorno: La celebrazione del mito italico," *Quasar* 17 (January–June 1997), 149–54. For more on Piacentini's intervention, see Osanna Fantozzi Micali, "Livorno, "in Piero Roselli et al., *Fascismo e centri storici in Toscana* (Florence: Alinea, 1985), 71–2.

22 "La pianta definitiva della Mostra augustea della romanità presentata a Mussolini," *Il Popolo d'Italia*, 25 February 1937. The set-up was designed by Bruno Maria Apollonj, Claudio Ballerio, Pasquale Carbonara, Venerio Colasanti, Francesco Fariello, Vincenzo Monaco, Mario Paniconi, Giulio Pediconi, Franco Petrucci, and Ludovico Quaroni. For more on the exhibition, see Tim Benton, "Rome Reclaims Its Empire," in *Art and Power: Europe Under the Dictators, 1930–1945*, ed. Dawn Ades et al. (London: Thames and Hudson-Hayward Gallery, 1995), 121–2.

23 "Il compiacimento di Mussolini per i lavori preparatori," *Il Popolo d'Italia*, 24 June 1937; letter from Marcello Piacentini to Gustavo Giovannoni, 3 August 1937, in AGG, Carteggio 1930–47.

24 "La nuova stazione di Roma secondo le direttive del Duce," *Il Popolo d'Italia*, 28 February 1937; Paolo Mariani, "La stazione principale di Roma: dal nudo realismo alla folle vestizione," in *Angiolo Mazzoni (1884–1979): Architetto nell'Italia tra le due guerre* (Casalecchio di Reno: Grafis, 1984), 85.

25 "Disposizioni del Duce per gli edifici doganali turistici sui valichi alpini," *Il Popolo d'Italia*, 16 July 1937. Among the winners of the prize were Eugenio Montuori, Leonardo Bucci, Alberto Legnani, Armando Sabatini, Vincenzo Monaco, Amedeo Luccichenti, and Ludovico Quaroni.

26 "Il Duce approva il progetto per il Palazzo degli uffici," *Il Popolo d'Italia*, 9 September 1937; Antonella La Torre, "Il Palazzo degli Uffici," in *E42: Utopia e scenario del regime*, vol. 2, *Urbanistica, architettura, arte e decorazione*, ed. Maurizio Calvesi, Enrico Guidoni, and Simonetta Lux (Venice: Marsilio, 1987), 300.

27 Note from Cobolli Gigli to Mussolini, 5 August 1937, in ACS, PCM, 1937–9, issue 1.1.3, n. 2366.

28 "La Casa degli italiani all'estero: Il progetto approvato da Mussolini," *Il Popolo d'Italia*, 9 June 1937.

29 "Mussolini approva il progetto per la nuova sede del 'Luce'," *Il Popolo d'Italia*, 23 October 1937. Andrea Busiri Vici and Rodolfo Rustichelli also worked on the design of the project.

30 "Direttive di Mussolini per la Mostra coloniale di Napoli," *Il Popolo d'Italia*, 23 October 1937.

31 "Pomezia sarà fondata il 22 aprile," *Il Popolo d'Italia*, 17 February 1938. See also Daniela De Angelis, *Note su Concezio Petrucci: L'architetto delle "Città Nuove"* (Rome: Gangemi, 2005), 99.

32 "The Duce had seen the plans for the embellishment of Rome for the Führer's visit. He thought they were fine." Galeazzo Ciano, *Diario 1937–1943*, ed. Renzo De Felice (Milan: Rizzoli, 1990), 93 (4 February 1938). "Addobbi e illuminazioni dell'Urbe," *Il Popolo d'Italia*, 22 March 1938. For more on the approval of the project by Narducci, see "La nuova stazione ferroviaria di Roma-Ostiense," in *Rassegna dello sviluppo dell'Italia imperiale*

nelle opere e nelle industrie 11–12 (November–December 1940), 147–56. For more on the temporary pavilion of the Ostiense Railway Station, see Alessandro Morgera, "Roberto Narducci e la monumentalizzazione delle stazioni ferroviarie," tesi di laurea (MA diss., Facoltà di Architettura di Trieste, a.a. 2005–6).

33 Quinto Navarra, *Memorie del cameriere di Mussolini* (Naples: L'ancora del Mediterraneo, 2004 [1946]), 93.

34 ACS, PCM, 1937–9, issue 4.11, n. 3711/2.

35 Joseph Goebbels, *Diario 1938*, ed. Marina Bistolfi (Milan: Mondadori 1996), 142–3.

36 Federico Mastrigli, "Roma pavesata," *Capitolium* 5 (May 1938), 119–234.

37 Irene Sardei, "Due monumenti per il nuovo volto fascista di Trieste: Il teatro Romano e la casa del fascio," tesi di laurea (MA diss., Facoltà di Architettura di Trieste, a.a. 2004–5), 73.

38 "Il Duce approva il progetto della nuova Università elaborato dagli architetti Fagnoni e Nordio," *Il Piccolo*, 23 July 1938

39 "Il Duce approva i progetti di due nuovi ponti sul Tevere," *Il Popolo d'Italia*, 26 June 1938; "Il terzo ponte sul Tevere," *Il Popolo d'Italia*, 8 August 1938.

40 "Mussolini pone la prima pietra della sede del Ministero dell'A.I.," *Il Popolo d'Italia*, 1 September 1938; "La Mostra autarchica del minerale italiano," *Il Popolo d'Italia*, 3 September 1938.

41 "Il progetto approvato dal Duce per la tomba di Gabriele D'Annunzio," *Il Popolo d'Italia*, 20 November 1938; Yvon De Begnac, *Taccuini mussoliniani*, ed. Francesco Perfetti (Bologna: Il Mulino, 1990), 508–81. De Begnac's version, according to which Mussolini was much moved by D'Annunzio's death, contrasted with what Ciano reported: "I cannot say that the Duce was very moved." Ciano, *Diario 1937–1943*, 106–7 (2 March 1938).

42 "Il Duce esamina i plastici delle nuove stazioni di Roma e Venezia," *Il Popolo d'Italia*, 4 February 1939.

43 Canali, "'Ambientamento' e 'restauro' a Forlì," 80; "La nuova sede dell'Istituto di Previdenza sociale," *Il Popolo d'Italia*, 18 June 1939.

44 ACS, PNF, serie II, b. 261, issue Scuola di Mistica fascista. See Benito Mussolini, *Opera omnia*, ed. Edoardo Susmel and Duilio Susmel (Florence: La Fenice, 1951–80), 29:331. The "Covo," which had been the first headquarters of the "popolo d'Italia," became the headquarters of the Scuola di Mistica Fascista in 1939.

45 ACS, SPD, CO, 1922–43, issue 509.519. Mario Palanti, *L'Eternale: Mole Littoria* (Milan: Rizzoli, 1926). See also Emilio Gentile, *Il culto del littorio: La sacralizzazione della politica nell'Italia fascista* (Rome-Bari: Laterza, 2001 [1993]), 213–15.

46 Flavio Fergonzi, "Dalla monumentomania alla scultura arte monumentale," in *La scultura monumentale negli anni del fascismo: Arturo Martini e il*

monumento al duca d'Aosta, ed. Flavio Fergonzi and Maria Teresa Roberto (Turin: Allemandi, 1992), 177.

47 Mario Lupano, *Marcello Piacentini* (Rome-Bari: Laterza, 1991), 184. See also Ugo Soragni, *Il monumento alla vittoria di Bolzano: Architettura e scultura per la città italiana (1926–1938)* (Vicenza: Neri Pozza, 1993), 50.

48 Fergonzi, "Dalla monumentomania alla scultura arte monumentale," 145.

49 Letter from Gio Ponti to Ugo Ojetti, 10 December 1926, in Fulvio Irace, *Giovanni Muzio. 1893–1982* (Milan: Electa, 1994), 133.

50 See Raffaello Giolli, "La casa dei fasci milanesi," *1927: Problemi d'arte attuale* 3 (November 1927), 29–30; reprinted in Raffaello Giolli, *L'architettura razionale*, ed. Cesare De Seta (Rome-Bari: Laterza, 1972), 24–6.

51 Letter from Alessandro Chiavolini to Niccolò Gavatti, January 1928, in ACS, SPD, CO, 1922–43, issue 509.602/4. Gavatti was the president of the Roman committee for the War Memorial of Monte Grappa. For more on the controversy over the monument between the Catholic and the Fascist committees, see Livio Vanzetto, "Monte Grappa," in Mario Isnenghi, ed., *I luoghi della memoria: Simboli e miti dell'Italia unita*, (Rome-Bari: Laterza, 1996), 367–72.

52 "Mussolini approva il progetto per la sistemazione del Cimitero di guerra sul Monte Grappa," *Il Popolo d'Italia*, 13 September 1933.

53 Note in pencil on the letter from Piero Parini, 3 December 1932, in ACS, SPD, CO, 1922–43, issue 138.673/1.

54 "Il Duce inaugura a Cattolica la nuova Colonia Marina dei Fasci all'estero," *Il Popolo d'Italia*, 29 June 1934; Claudia Baldoli, "Le Navi: Fascismo e vacanze in una colonia estiva per i figli degli italiani all'estero," *Memoria e Ricerca* 6 (July–December 2000), 163–73.

55 Note for the prime minister 2 December 1931, in ACS, PCM, 1931–3, issue 14/1, n. 1628.

56 Gentile, *Il culto del littorio*, 200.

57 Sergio Poretti, *Progetti e costruzione dei palazzi delle poste a Roma, 1933–1935* (Rome: Edilstampa, 1990), 128. The visit took place on 14 September 1933.

58 Mariani, *Fascismo e "città nuove,"* 96–8.

59 Memorandum on the meeting of 10 September 1934; the meeting of 16 September 1934; see AMP, issue 81. For more on the competition, see Maria Grazia Messina, "L'orma fermata nella pietra: Il concorso per il palazzo del Littorio del 1934," in *Il teatro del potere: Scenari e rappresentazione del politico fra Otto e Novecento*, ed. Sergio Bertelli (Rome: Carocci, 2000), 117–47.

60 Carol Rushe, Progetto di concorso di primo grado per il Palazzo del Littorio a Roma: Progetti A e B," in *Giuseppe Terragni*, ed. Giorgio Ciucci (Milan: Electa, 1996), 439.

61 Marina Sommella Grossi, "Progetti di concorso per il Palazzo del littorio," in *Pietro Lingeri*, ed. Chiara Baglione and Elisabetta Susani (Milan: Electa, 2004), 210.

62 "Direttive di Mussolini per la costruenda Casa Littoria," *Il Popolo d'Italia*, 13 November 1934.

63 Letter from Giovanni Marinelli to Tito Vespasiani, 23 October 1934, quoted in Massimo Zammerini, in *Concorso per il Palazzo Littorio* (Turin: Testo e immagine, 2002), 12.

64 "Il concorso per il Palazzo del Littorio," *Il Popolo d'Italia*, 30 December 1934.

65 Sommella Grossi, "Progetti di concorso per il Palazzo del littorio," 210–12.

66 Letter from Giuseppe Terragni to Antono Carminati, 14 August 1934, in Sommella Grossi, "Progetti di concorso per il Palazzo del littorio," 210. Ojetti wrote about Sarfatti that "Mussolini allows her to decide everything concerning art." Ojetti, *Taccuini*, 204 (4 November 1925).

67 Letter from Giulio Arata to the chairperson of CONI, 11 September 1933, in ACS, PNF, serie II, b. 267, issue Ing. Arata. The assignment dated back to 1932.

68 Alfredo Forti, "Ricevitoria postelegrafonica in Littoria," in *Angiolo Mazzoni (1884–1979): Architetto nell'Italia tra le due guerre*, 148.

69 Anna Maria Fiore, "La monumentalizzazione dei luoghi teatro della Grande Guerra: Il sacrario di Redipuglia di Giovanni Greppi e Giannino Castiglioni," *Annali di architettura* 15 (2003), 239. For more on Redipuglia see Massimo Bortolotti, "Progetti e realizzazioni in Friuli Venezia Giulia, 1931–1938," *Parametro* 213 (March–April 1996), 33–40.

70 Letter from Ugo Cei to Osvaldo Sebastiani, 6 December 1935, in ACS, SPD, CO, 1922–43, issue 509.602/4.

71 Patrizia Dogliani, "Redipuglia," in Isnenghi, *I luoghi della memoria*, 382.

72 Gentile, *Il culto del littorio*, 48.

73 Letter from the general inspector to Giuseppe Bottai, 5 June 1936, in ACS, E42, b. 1023, issue 9770, s. issue 18, ins. 5. See also Riccardo Mariani, *E42: Un progetto per l' "Ordine Nuovo"* (Milan: Comunità, 1987), 16–17; Enrico Guidoni, "L'E42 città della rappresentazione," in *E42*, ed. Calvesi, Guidoni, and Lux, 2:20–2. Pictures of the designs are also published in Serena Maffioletti, ed., *BBPR* (Bologna: Zanichelli, 1994), 52–3.

74 Gentile, *Il culto del littorio*, 217–19; *Foglio d'Ordini*, 20 November 1932.

75 Hitler was also concerned about similar issues, such as whether the bell tower in Linz should exceed that of Saint Stephen's cathedral in Vienna, but not that of the Ulm cathedral. Albert Speer, *Diari segreti di Spandau* (Milan: Mondadori, 1976), 196.

76 Giorgio Pini, *Filo diretto con Palazzo Venezia* (Bologna: Cappelli, 1950), 125.

77 Sommella Grossi, "Progetti di concorso per il Palazzo del littorio," 210–16; letter from Enrico Del Debbio to Osvaldo Sebastiani, undated, in ACS, SPD, CO, 1922–43, issue 531.835; "La Mole Littoria a Roma," *Il Popolo d'Italia*, 13 October 1937; "Il grandioso progetto della Casa Littoria," *Il Popolo d'Italia*, 23 October 1937.

78 Letter from Marcello Piacentini to Ugo Ojetti, 13 January 1938, in GNAM, Fondo Ojetti, Cass. 58, I. For more on Ojetti's role in the competition, see Marta Petrin, "Ugo Ojetti e l'architettura italiana, 1936–1942," tesi di laurea (MA diss., Facoltà di Lettere e Filosofia di Udine, a.a. 2005–6), 28–40. See also Massimiliano Savorra, *Enrico Agostino Griffini* (Naples: Electa Napoli, 2000), 121.

79 Irace, *Giovanni Muzio*, 132. The group included Ernesto La Padula, Giovanni Guerrini, and Mario Romano.

80 Corrado Alvaro, "Case e uomini di Milano," *La Stampa*, 24 May 1939.

81 Letter from Cesare Bazzani to Mussolini, 24 August 1938, in ACS, SPD, CO, 1922–43, issue 155.146. See also Ferruccio Canali, "Il Palazzo del Governo," in *La città progettata: Forlì, Predappio, Castrocaro. Urbanistica e architettura fra le due guerre*, ed. Luciana Prati and Ulisse Tramonti (Forlì: Comune di Forlì, 2000), 182–5.

82 Ferruccio Canali, "Chiesa di Sant'Agostino a Predappio," in *La città progettata*, ed. Prati and Tramonti, 279. Mussolini also examined the projects for the new town of Predappio in 1925. Diane Ghirardo, *Building New Communities: New Deal America and Fascist Italy* (Princeton, NJ: Princeton University Press, 1989), 35.

83 Letter from [illegible signature] to Nicolò De Cesare, 19 August 1941, in ACS, SPD, CO, 1922–43, issue 553.474.

84 Letter from Francesco Leoni to Osvaldo Sebastiani, 11 November 1938, in ACS, SPD, CO, 1922–43, issue 553.474.

85 Letter from Francesco Leoni to Mussolini, 13 September 1941; letter from Francesco Leoni to Mussolini, October 1941; both in ACS, SPD, CO, 1922–43, issue 553.474.

86 Letter from Francesco Leoni to Mussolini, 13 September 1941, in ACS, SPD, CO, 1922–43, issue 553.474.

87 "Arch. Monaco. Rang Molfino to be updated. He thinks he will win the competition. Yesterday, during his visit, the Duce praised his project. The commission will make its decision in a few days." Note from personal secretary of the Duce, 5 October 1939; letter from Giorgio Molfino to Osvaldo Sebastiani, 18 October 1939; both in ACS, SPD, CO, 1922–43, issue 197.242. A description of the villa and of its inhabitants appeared in the report of an official from the Military Information Service. See Renzo De Felice, *Mussolini l'alleato*, vol. 1, *L'Italia in guerra 1940–1943*, tomo 2, *Crisi e agonia del regime* (Turin: Einaudi, 1990), 1536–40. See also Paolo Monelli, *Mussolini piccolo borghese* (Milan: Garzanti, 1983 [1950]), 186–7.

88 Giuseppe Bottai, *Diario 1935–1944*, ed. Giordano Bruno Guerri (Milan: Rizzoli, 1994), 577.

89 Letter from Rino Valdameri to Giuseppe Terragni, 13 April 1940, in AGT, Accademia Brera.

90 Yvon De Begnac, *Palazzo Venezia: Storia di un regime* (Rome: La Rocca, 1950), 337.

91 Mussolini personally wrote on a picture he presented to Brasini: ACS, SPD, CO, 1922–43, issue 174.093/1. On the project for Gorizia, see U.O. [Ugo Ojetti], "Il colle del Castello di Gorizia e il monumento alla Vittoria," *Dedalo* 5 (1923–24), 327–30. The project was approved by Mussolini.

92 In ACS, SPD, CO, 1922–43, b. 838, issue 1928. Antonio Cederna, *Mussolini urbanista* (Rome-Bari: Laterza, 1979), 56–7.

93 De Begnac, *Taccuini mussoliniani*, 326.

94 Francesco Tentori, *P.M. Bardi* (Milan: Mazzotta, 1990), 49–51. According to Angelo D'Orsi, Bardi "has most probably been hired by the Ovra, at least for some time." Angelo D'Orsi, "Bardi Pier Maria," in *Dizionario del fascismo*, ed. Victoria De Grazia and Sergio Luzzatto, vol. 1, *A–K* (Turin: Einaudi, 2002), 146.

95 "Il Duce inaugura una mostra di architettura razionalista," *Il Popolo d'Italia*, 31 March 1931.

96 Adalberto Libera, "La mia esperienza di architetto," *La Casa* 6 [1960], 173.

97 Michele Cennamo, ed., *Materiali per l'analisi cell'architettura moderna: Il Miar* (Naples: Società editrice napoletana, 1976), 448–50.

98 Sileno Salvagnini, *Il sistema delle arti in Italia* (Bologna: Minerva, 2000), 303.

99 Dino Alfieri and Luigi Freddi, eds., *Mostra della rivoluzione fascista* (Rome: Partito nazionale fascista, 1933), 8; J.T. Schnapp, *Anno X: La mostra della Rivoluzione fascista del 1932* (Pisa-Rome: Istituti editoriali e poligrafici internazionali, 2003).

100 Nino D'Aroma, *Mussolini segreto* (Bologna: Cappelli, 1958), 65. The episode took place in April 1933.

101 Letter from Mussolini to Margherita Sarfatti, 9 July 1929, in Salvagnini, *Il sistema delle arti in Italia*, 54–5.

102 Letter from Mussolini to Gabriele D'Annunzio, 20 June 1928, in Renzo De Felice and Emilio Mariano, eds., *Carteggio D'Annunzio-Mussolini (1919–1938)* (Milan: Mondadori, 1971), 250.

103 "Mussolini in volo a Vicenza, Padova e Ferrara," *Il Popolo d'Italia*, 28 July 1937.

104 See Renzo De Felice, *D'Annunzio politico, 1918–1938* (Rome-Bari: Laterza, 1978), 141–223.

105 Ojetti, *Taccuini*, 436 (1 May 1934). For more on Ojetti flattering the Duce, see De Felice, *Mussolini il duce*, 2:569.

106 "Il progetto per la Casa Littoria approvato per acclamazione alla Camera," *Il Popolo d'Italia*, 27 May 1934.

107 The document can be found in Federico Malusardi, *Luigi Piccinato e l'urbanistica moderna* (Rome: Officina, 1993), 364.

108 Giuseppe Pagano, "Mussolini salva l'architettura italiana," *Casabella* 78 (June 1934); reprinted in Giuseppe Pagano, *Architettura e città durante il fascismo*, ed. Cesare De Seta (Rome-Bari: Laterza, 1976), 19–27.

109 Ojetti, *Taccuini*, 437 (19 June 1934). The Russian statue that Mussolini noticed was "The Peasant" by Vera Moukina.

110 Margherita Sarfatti, *Dux* (Milan: Mondadori, 1982 [1926]), 257–8.

111 Ojetti, *Taccuini*, 475 (20 March 1937).

112 De Begnac, *Taccuini mussoliniani*, 43, 307, 326, 345, 579. Mussolini, who confided to Ludwig that he did not have any friends, said that he "has been friends for a long time" with Ojetti.

113 Cederna, *Mussolini urbanista*, 135.

114 Adolf Hitler, *Conversazioni segrete* (Naples: Richter, 1954), 223 (13 January 1942).

115 Nicola Timmermann, *Repräsentative "Staatsbaukunst" im faschistischen Italien und im nationalsozialistischen Deutschland – der Einfluß der Berlin-Planung auf die Eur* (Stuttgart: Ibidem, 2001), 245–6.

116 Speer, *Diari segreti di Spandau*, 145.

117 MacGregor Knox, *Destino comune: Dittatura, politica estera e guerra nell'Italia fascista e nella Germania nazista* (Turin: Einaudi, 2000), 121.

118 Adolf Hitler, "Gli edifici del Terzo Reich," in Anna Teut, *L'architettura del Terzo Reich* (Milan: Mazzotta, 1976), 81–2.

119 Speer, *Diari segreti di Spandau*, 144–5. For more on Hitler's influence on Mussolini concerning architecture, see Stephen Helmer, *Hitler's Berlin: The Speer Plans for Reshaping the Central City* (Ann Arbor, MI: UMI Research Press, 1985), 89–93.

120 Ojetti, *Taccuini*, 491 (2 February 1938). When Mussolini inaugurated Guidonia in October 1937, he declared that fascist architecture was "modern"; however, it was a unique city, the "City of the Aeronautics," a symbol of modernity and a project dating from 1936.

121 BNF, Fondo Ojetti, mss da ord., Manoscritti 5, 1 III, cc. 5–7.

122 "By then, the Duce was convinced that projects by his state architect, Piacentini, were meaningless: he would demonstrate what he had learned in Munich and Berlin at the Universal Exposition in Rome." Speer, *Diari segreti di Spandau*, 144–6. Mussolini's visit to Munich took place on 25 September 1937.

5 Piacentini and Mussolini

1 Emilio Gentile, *Il mito dello Stato nuovo* (Rome-Bari: Laterza, 2000), 248.

2 Marcello Piacentini and Pio Piacentini, "Idea per la residenza del Governo e per quella del municipio di Roma: Residenza del Governo al Campidoglio," December 1923, in ACS, PCM, 1928–30, issue 5.1, n. 5499.

3 Yvon De Begnac, *Palazzo Venezia: Storia di un regime* (Rome: La Rocca, 1950), 337.

4 "La grande Roma: Intervista con Marcello Piacentini," typescript, undated (after 26 January 1926), in AMP, issue 56.2.

5 Marcello Piacentini, "La Grande Roma," *Capitolium* 7 (October 1925), 413–20; Antonio Nezi, "Le sistemazioni metropolitane moderne: La 'Grande Roma' di Marcello Piacentini," *Emporium* 376 (April 1926), 254–63; Antonio Nezi, "Artisti contemporanei accademici d'Italia: Marcello Piacentini," *Emporium* 422 (February 1930), 94–8.

6 Philip V. Cannistraro and Brian R. Sullivan, *Margherita Sarfatti: L'altra donna del duce* (Milan: Mondadori, 1993), 357–8; AMP, issue 50.6.

7 George Mosse, *La nazionalizzazione delle masse: Simbolismo politico e movimenti di massa in Germania (1815–1933)* (Bologna: Il Mulino, 1975), 68.

8 Flavio Fergonzi, "Dalla monumentomania alla scultura arte monumentale," in *La scultura monumentale negli anni del fascismo: Arturo Martini e il monumento al duca d'Aosta*, ed. Flavio Fergonzi and Maria Teresa Roberto (Turin: Allemandi, 1992), 177.

9 Piacentini wrote about his support of the PNF, "to which I have been giving, for some time, my spiritual work, creating the War Memorial in Bolzano, which is the architectural seal of the fascist soul." Letter from Marcello Piacentini to Giovanni Marinelli, 17 October 1928, in ACS, PNF, serie II, b. 267, issue Corrispondenza arch. Piacentini.

10 Gio Ponti, "Architettura," *L'Illustrazione italiana* 44 (October 1933).

11 Ugo Soragni, *Il monumento alla vittoria di Bolzano: Architettura e scultura per la città italiana (1926–1938)* (Vicenza: Neri Pozza, 1993), 1–81.

12 See, for instance, Mussolini's support for the ship-shaped project by Palanti in the competition for the Palazzo del Littorio in Rome.

13 Marcello Piacentini, "Di alcune particolarità del Monumento alla Vittoria in Bolzano," *Architettura e Arti Decorative* 6 (February 1929), 255–8.

14 Telegram from Marcello Piacentini to Mussolini, 28 September 1929, in ACS, SPD, CR, 1922–43, b. 103.

15 Letter from Marcello Piacentini to Mussolini, 4 October 1929, ACS, SPD, CO, 1922–43, issue 104.113. A handwritten note on the letter says, "Telling that H.E. has been invited many times to visit this exhibition, but he has always been forced to decline."

16 Valter Vannelli, *Economia dell'architettura di Roma fascista* (Rome: Kappa, 1981), 118.

17 Letter from Brasini to Mussolini, 31 March 1930, in ACS, SPD, CO, 1922–43, issue 174–093. See also Giampaolo Consoli, "Armando Brasini (1879–1963)," tesi di laurea (MA diss., Facoltà di Architettura di Roma "La Sapienza," a.a. 1983–4).

18 Antonio Muñoz, *La Roma di Mussolini* (Milan: Treves, 1935), 76–7.

19 Ibid., 102.

20 "L'approvazione del progetto del Mausoleo a Cadorna," *Il Popolo d'Italia*, 18 March 1930.

21 Piacentini intervened, as we shall see, in the architectural decisions concerning the headquarters in Naples, Milan, and most likely also in Genoa.

22 "Il Duce conclude l'ispezione delle opere pubbliche alla Capitale," *Il Popolo d'Italia*, 24 September 1930.

23 Letter from Marcello Piacentini to Francesco Boncompagni Ludovisi, 18 August 1932, in ACS, SPD, CO, 1922–43, b. 839, issue 1932

24 See also Francesco Tentori, *P.M. Bardi* (Milan: Mazzotta, 1990), 54.

25 Gabriele Morolli, "Il palazzo e la sua architettura," in Franco Borsi, Gabriele Morolli, and Daniela Fonti, *Il Palazzo dell'Industria* (Rome: Editalia, 1986), 46.

26 Letter from Mussolini to Antonio Mosconi, 14 July 1929, in Morolli, "Il palazzo e la sua architettura," 59.

27 Report by Bottai to Mussolini, 5 January 1932, in ACS, PCM, 1931–3, 7.2 n. 3916.

28 Letter from Marcello Piacentini to Guido Beer 11 August 1932, in ACS, PCM, 1931–3, 7.2 n. 3916.

29 Ugo Ojetti, *Taccuini, 1914–1943* (Florence: Sansoni, 1954), 396–7 (28 July 1932).

30 "Il Capo del Governo approva il progetto per il nuovo Palazzo di Giustizia," *Il Popolo d'Italia*, 6 February 1932.

31 "I express to Your Excellency my gratefulness for the important assignment concerning the great work, to which I will enthusiastically commit myself to make it worthy of you and of Roman Fascism." Telegram from Marcello Piacentini to Mussolini, 4 April 1932, in ACS, SPD, CR, 1922–43, b. 103.

32 "La città universitaria è stata visitata da 500.000 visitatori," *Il Popolo d'Italia*, 10 November 1935.

33 Letter from Marcello Piacentini to Giuseppe Volpi, 18 November 1934, in AMP, issue 82.

34 "Il progetto per la nuova sede della Banca Nazionale del Lavoro sottoposto al capo del Governo," *Il Popolo d'Italia*, 4 June 1933.

35 Note for the prime minister (undated but confirmed1934); letter from Arturo Osio to Mussolini, 29 June 1934, in ACS, SPD, CO, 1922–43, b. 840, issue 1934.

36 Nezi, "Le sistemazioni metropolitane moderne," 254–63.

37 Letter from Marcello Piacentini to Giovanni Marinelli, 17 October 1928, in ACS, PNF, Servizi vari, serie II, b. 267, issue Corrispondenza arch. Piacentini. Marinelli rejected Piacentini's cheque for 20,000 lire.

38 ACS, SPD, CO, 1922–43, issue 104.113/21. For more on the event, see Giada Scussolino, "Un disegno inedito di Marcello Piacentini per la Mostra

della Rivoluzione fascista in via dell'Impero," tesi di laurea (MA diss., Facoltà di Lettere e Filosofia di Udine, a.a. 2004–5).

39 "La decisione del Duce per la costruzione sulla via dell'Impero della sede del Partito e della Mostra fascista," *Il Popolo d'Italia*, 2 December 1932. For more on the choice of Via dell'Impero, see Maria Grazia Messina, "L'orma fermata nella pietra: Il concorso per il palazzo del Littorio del 1934," *Il teatro del potere: Scenari e rappresentazione del politico fra Otto e Novecento*, ed. Sergio Bertelli (Rome: Carocci, 2000), 122; Vittorio Vidotto, "Palazzi e sacrari: Il declino del culto del littorio," *Roma moderna e contemporanea* 3 (September–December 2003), 584–5

40 "Memoria del prof. Marcello Piacentini al Presidente della Commissione di epurazione del personale universitario," typescript, undated (confirmed later than 3 February 1945), in AMP, issue 112.2.

41 Letters by Marcello Piacentini to Mussolini, 16 and 25 May 1936, in Giuliano Gresleri, "La 'Nuova Roma dello Scioa' e l'improbabile architettura dell'impero," in *Architettura italiana d'oltremare. 1870–1940*, ed. Giuliano Gresleri, Pier Giorgio Massarenti, and Stefano Zagnoni (Venice: Marsilio, 1993), 165–6.

42 "If you collect the pictures of all of his architectural works in a book, you will find not one, but rather twenty different architects." Ojetti, *Taccuini*, 396–7 (28 July 1932).

43 "Memoria del prof. Marcello Piacentini."

44 "Il programma della XIX iennale sottoposto al Capo del Governo," *Il Popolo d'Italia*, 15 December 1933; "Il Duce approva i progetti definitivi per la Casa dei Mutilati in Roma," *Il Popolo d'Italia*, 16 December 1933.

45 "I am happy to work according to the inspiration of Y.E." Letter from Alister MacDonald to Mussolini, 8 February 1934, in ACS, SPD, CO, 1922–43, issue 510.505. XXX Renzo De Felice, *Mussolini il duce*, vol. 1, *Gli anni del consenso 1929–1936* (Turin: Einaudi, 1974), 328.

46 Note presented by Belluzzo, Brasini, and Piacentini on 27 February 1934, in ACS, SPD, CO, 1922–43, issue 104.113/1. On Belluzzo, see Franklin H. Adler, "Belluzzo Giuseppe," in *Dizionario del fascismo*, ed. Victoria De Grazia and Sergio Luzzatto, vol. 1, *A–K* (Turin: Einaudi, 2002), 154.

47 ACS, SPD, CO, 1922–43, issue 135.015.

48 The project had been submitted to Mussolini for the first time in March 1936 and then again on 11 July 1937. Marida Talamona, "Italie," in *Paris 1937: Cinquantenaire de L'Exposition Internationale des arts et des techniques dans la vie moderne* (Paris: Institut Française d'Architecture/Paris-Musées, 1987), 166–71. See also "Direttive di Mussolini circa la partecipazione all'Esposizione internazionale di Parigi," *Il Popolo d'Italia*, 12 July 1936; "Il Padiglione italiano pronto all'Esposizione di Parigi," *Il Popolo d'Italia*, 2 May 1937. The riding statue was created by Giorgio Gori.

49 Karen A. Fiss, "The German Pavillon," in *Art and Power: Europe under the Dictators, 1930–1945*, ed. Dawn Ades et al. (London: Thames and Hudson-Hayward Gallery, 1995), 108–9; Karen A. Fiss, "In Hitler's Salon: The German Pavilion at the 1937 Paris Exposition Internationale," in *Art, Culture, and Media under the Third Reich*, ed. Richard A. Etlin (Chicago-London: University of Chicago Press, 2002), 316–42; Albert Speer, *Memorie del Terzo Reich* (Milan: Mondadori, 1995 [1969]), 98. The tower of Speer's pavilion was to have been reconstructed in Nuremberg.

50 "Il Duce approva e dispone la rapida esecuzione dei lavori," *Il Popolo d'Italia*, 10 June 1939.

51 Letter from Luigi Federzoni to Mussolini, 28 November 1939, in ACS, SPD, CO, 1922–43, issue 104.113/25.

52 On 14 and 28 April 1930. Only the meetings which took place after 1929 have been taken into consideration.

53 "Il Duce conclude l'ispezione delle opere pubbliche alla capitale," *Il Popolo d'Italia*, 24 September 1930.

54 "Spaccarelli and I have examined the project following the impressions and the suggestions of Y.E., which H.E. the Governor had communicated to us." Letter from Marcello Piacentini to Mussolini, 1 April 1937, in ACS, SPD, CO, 1922–43, issue 7583. Visits to the Borghi took place on 20 June 1936, 8 October 1937, and 11 May 1938.

55 Gio Ponti, "Idee di Gio Ponti sulla politica dell'architettura," *Il Giornale d'Italia*, 19 July 1938.

56 Visits to the E42 took place on 28 April 1937, 6 July 1938, and 18 April 1939.

57 The presentation of the model took place on 29 October. Mussolini was accompanied by Giovannoni and Oppo. See Vieri Quilici, ed., *E42-Eur: Un centro per la metropoli* (Rome: Olmo, 1996), 34.

58 It is difficult to believe that there was no contact between Piacentini and Mussolini concerning the design for the tomb of the Duce's son, Bruno.

59 ACS, SPD, CO, 1922–43, issue 104.113/10.

60 Benito Mussolini, *Opera omnia*, ed. Edoardo Susmel and Duilio Susmel (Florence: La Fenice, 1951–80), 24:269.

61 Letter from Marcello Piacentini to Mussolini, 16 June 1930, in ACS, SPD, CR, 1922–43, b. 103. "Discussioni sul Vittoriano," *Il Popolo d'Italia*, 26 September 1931.

62 The document is quoted in the letter from Alessandro Chiavolini to Mariano Pierro, in ACS, SPD, CO, 1922–43, issue 500.505/1.

63 Letter from Marcello Piacentini to Mussolini, 13 June 1934, in ACS, SPD, CO, 1922–43, issue 132.862.

64 Yvon De Begnac, *Taccuini mussoliniani*, ed. Francesco Perfetti (Bologna: Il Mulino, 1990), 328.

65 Letter from Marcello Piacentini to Mussolini, 7 July 1934, in ACS, SPD, CO, 1922–43, issue 132.862.
66 Letter from Marcello Piacentini to Mussolini, 2 December 1935. ACS, PCM, 1934–6, issue 5.1, n. 5568. Only the protocol recording of the letter survived. For more on Piacentini in Rio de Janeiro, see Mario Lupano, *Marcello Piacentini* (Rome-Bari: Laterza, 1991), 186.
67 The Brazilian minister of education forced Morpurgo to submit the project by October. Letter from Vittorio Morpurgo to Arnaldo Foschini, 2 October1937, in AAF, issue Varie.
68 Letter from Marcello Piacentini to Nicolò De Cesare, 23 April 1942, in ACS, SPD, CO, 1922–43, issue 536.663/4.
69 De Begnac, *Taccuini mussoliniani*, 326. Mussolini's statement on Piacentini has to be dated around the first half of the 1930s.
70 Renzo De Felice, *Mussolini il duce*, vol. 2, *Lo Stato totalitario 1936–1940* (Turin: Einaudi, 1981), 275.
71 De Begnac, *Taccuini mussoliniani*, 357.
72 Paolo Nicoloso, *Gli architetti di Mussolini: Scuole e sindacato, architetti e massoni, professori e politici negli anni del regime* (Milan: Franco Angeli, 1999), 157–8.

6 Architecture towards Stylistic Uniformity

1 This paragraph and the following one recall an article published under the title "Piacentini e Mussolini nella Città universitaria di Roma" in *L'Università e la città: Il ruolo di Padova e degli altri atenei italiani nello sviluppo urbano*, ed. Giuliana Mazzi (Bologna: Clueb, 2006), 231–45.
2 Letter from Mussolini to Balbino Giuliano, 18 February 1932, in ACS, PCM, 1934–6, issue 5.1, n. 2866/1.
3 Telegram by Piacentini to Mussolini, 4 April 1932, in ACS, SPD, CR, 1922–43, b. 103.
4 "Il Duce visita le maggiori opere pubbliche in corso di esecuzione alla Capitale," *Il Popolo d'Italia*, 7 April 1932.
5 Letter from Mussolini to Balbino Giuliano, 26 April 1932, in ACS, SPD, CO, 1922–43, issue 509.826/2.
6 Marcello Piacentini, "Metodi e caratteristiche," *Architettura: La città universitaria di Roma*, special issue (December 1935), 2.
7 "Il Duce visita le maggiori opere pubbliche in corso di esecuzione alla Capitale," *Il Popolo d'Italia*, 7 April 1932.
8 "Memoria del prof. Marcello Piacentini al Presidente della Commissione di epurazione del personale universitario," typescript, undated (confirmed after 3 February 1945), in AMP, issue 112.2
9 Piacentini, "Metodi e caratteristiche," 2.

10 "Il Duce visita le maggiori opere pubbliche in corso di esecuzione alla Capitale," *Il Popolo d'Italia,* 7 April 1932.

11 Gaetano Minnucci, "La Città Universitaria di Roma," conference paper given at the Institute of Roman Studies, 26 April 1937, typescript, in ACS, Fondo Minnucci, b. 10, issue 67.

12 Giuliano wrote that Piacentini distributed the assignments "among the six chosen architects." Letter from Balbino Giuliano to Mussolini, 14 May 1932, in ACS, PCM, 1934–6, issue 5.1, n. 2866/2. See also Gianfranco Caniggia, "Il clima architettonico romano e la città universitaria," *La Casa* 6 [1960], 285.

13 Letter from Marcello Piacentini to Mussolini, 2 May 1932, in ACS, SPD, CR, 1922–43, b. 103. The stone which was most used at the Città Universitaria would not be Carrara marble but travertine.

14 Letter from Mussolini to Balbino Giuliano, 13 May 1932, in ACS, PCM, 1934–6, issue 5.1, n. 2866/2.

15 Letter from Balbino Giuliano to Mussolini, 14 May 1932, in ACS, PCM, 1934–6, issue 5.1, n. 2866/2.

16 Telegram from Piacentini to Mussolini, 12 August 1932; telegram from Edoardo Rossoni to Piacentini, both in ACS, PCM, 1934–6, issue 5.1, n. 2866/2.

17 Yvon De Begnac, *Palazzo Venezia: Storia di un regime* (Rome: La Rocca, 1950), 567.

18 Letter from Arnaldo Foschini to Marcello Piacentini, 17 August 1932, in AAP, issue Università di Roma.

19 Claudia Conforti, "Istituto di Mineralogia, Geologia, Paleontologia e Istituto di Fisiologia generale, Psicologia e Antropologia della Città universitaria di Roma," in *Giovanni Michelucci,* ed. Amedeo Belluzzi and Claudia Conforti (Milan: Electa, 1986), 94.

20 G.P.P. [Giuseppe Pagano], "Registro (Dell'Università di Roma)," *Casabella* 61 (January 1933), 41.

21 Letter from Mussolini to Araldo di Crollalanza, 27 November 1932, in ACS, PCM, 1934–6, issue 5.1, n. 2866/2. Piacentini and Mussolini met on 26 November 1932.

22 "Il piano generale per la costruzione della Città Universitaria di Roma," *Il Popolo d'Italia,* 20 December 1932.

23 Telegram from Mussolini to Rocco, 23 January 1933, in ACS, PCM, 1934–6, issue 5.1, n. 2866/2.

24 "Programma di lavoro di Marcello Piacentini ...," typescript, 24 January 1933, in ACS, PCM, 1934–6, issue 5.1, n. 2866/2.

25 Letter from Alfredo Rocco to Alessandro Chiavolini, 18 February 1933, in ACS, PCM, 1934–6, issue 5.1, n. 2866/2.

26 "Dalla Città Universitaria al Porto di Fiumicino," *Il Popolo d'Italia,* 12 March 1933. Renato Pacini, "Il grandioso progetto della città universitaria,"

Emporium 475 (March 1933), 180. The first and the second model correspond to the scale models indicated by Lupano as "A" and "B". Mario Lupano, *Marcello Piacentini* (Rome-Bari: Laterza, 1991), figs. 121 and 123.

27 Stefania Mornati, "La Scuola di Matematica di Gio Ponti a Roma (1932–35)," in Pier Giovanni Bardelli et al., *La costruzione moderna in Italia: Indagine sui caratteri originari e sul degrado di alcuni edifici* (Rome: Edilstampa, 2001), 278–93.

28 Caniggia, "Il clima architettonico romano e la città universitaria," 294.

29 "Il Duce passa in rassegna le grandiose opere in esecuzione," *Il Popolo d'Italia*, 15 September 1933.

30 Note, 29 September 1933, in ACS, SPD, CO, 1922–43 issue 509.826/2.

31 Letter from Marcello Piacentini to Mussolini, 30 August 1934, in ACS, CR, 1922–43, b. 103.

32 Note from Mussolini, 17 March 1935, in ACS, SPD, CO, 1922–43 issue 509.826/2.

33 Roberto Papini, "Architetture se Dio vuole italiane," *L'Illustrazione Italiana* 44 (November 1935), 862–4; reprinted in Rosario De Simone, ed., *Cronache di architettura, 1914–1957* (Florence: Edifir, 1998), 287–90.

34 Giorgio Ciucci, *Gli architetti e il fascismo: Architettura e città, 1922–1944* (Turin: Einaudi, 1989), 132–3.

35 Piacentini, "Metodi e caratteristiche," 6.

36 Benito Mussolini, *Opera omnia*, ed. Edoardo Susmel and Duilio Susmel (Florence: La Fenice, 1951–80), 27:178.

37 Pietro De Francisci, "Università del tempo fascista," *Architettura: La città universitaria di Roma*, special issue (December 1935), 1.

38 "S.E. l'arch. Marcello Piacentini preside della Facoltà di architettura dell'Università di Roma," *Architettura: Supplemento sindacale* 2, 15 February 1936, 13–14.

39 Riccardo Mariani, *E42: Un progetto per l'"Ordine Nuovo"* (Milan: Comunità, 1987), 18

40 In the postwar period Cini defined Mussolini as "a most clever man, not always balanced; he has incredible abilities but he was notably superficial and volatile; he was impulsive and susceptible to flattery." For more on the complex relationship between Cini and Mussolini, see Renzo De Felice, *Mussolini l'alleato*, vol. 1, *L'Italia in guerra 1940–1943*, tomo 2, *Crisi e agonia del regime* (Turin: Einaudi, 1990), 1062.

41 Tullio Cianetti, *Memorie dal carcere di Verona* (Milan: Rizzoli, 1983), 293.

42 Mussolini, *Opera omnia*, 29:265–6.

43 Ibid., 26:259.

44 See the report given by Mussolini at the Gran Consiglio on 4 and 5 February 1939, in Renzo De Felice, *Mussolini il duce*, vol. 2, *Lo Stato totalitario 1936–1940* (Turin: Einaudi, 1981); 319–25. See also Dino Grandi, *Il mio paese: Ricordi autobiografici* (Bologna: Il Mulino, 1985), 524.

45 Alberto Pirelli, *Taccuini 1922/1943*, ed. Donato Barbone (Bologna: Il Mulino, 1984), 217 (4 May 1939).
46 "Un sopralluogo di Mussolini alla zona nella quale sorgerà l'Esposizione Universale del 1941," *Il Popolo d'Italia*, 22 October 1936.
47 Luigi Di Majo and Italo Insolera, *L'EUR e Roma dagli anni Trenta al Duemila* (Rome-Bari: Laterza, 1986), 24–6; Mariani, *E42*, 18.
48 ACS, Fondo Cini, b. 1, issue 42.
49 "Programma dell'Esposizione Universale e Mondiale di Roma, XX Annuale," November 1935, in ACS, Fondo Cini, b. 3, issue 61. See Patrizia Ferrara, "L'Eur: Un'ente per l'E42," in *E42: Utopia e scenario del regime*, ed. Tullio Gregory and Achille Tartaro, vol. 1, *Ideologia e programma dell'Olimpiade delle Civiltà* (Venice: Marsilio, 1987), 74–5.
50 Marcello Piacentini, "L'Esposizione universale dell'anno ventesimo e la più grande Roma del piano imperiale," *Il Giornale d'Italia*, 14 October 1936.
51 For more on Piacentini's power in the academia, see Paolo Nicoloso, *Gli architetti di Mussolini: Scuole e sindacato, architetti e massoni, professori e politici negli anni del regime* (Milan: Franco Angeli, 1999).
52 "Il Duce elogia l'attività del podestà di Torino," *Il Popolo d'Italia*, 2 November 1934.
53 "Il rapporto al Duce del podestà di Torino," *Il Popolo d'Italia*, 13 October 1935.
54 See the picture published in *Il Popolo d'Italia*, 1 November 1937.
55 "L'alto elogio del Duce ai Gerarchi delle Province di Trieste e di Gorizia," *Il Popolo d'Italia*, 21 November 1934.
56 Diana Barillari, "Architettura e committenza a Trieste: Piacentini e le Assicurazioni Generali," *Archeografo Triestino* 63 (2003), 607; Paolo Nicoloso, "Architetture per la città fascista, 1933–1939," in *Trieste 1918–1954*, ed. Paolo Nicoloso and Federica Rovello (Trieste: Mgs Press, 2005), 48–52.
57 "Il Duce riceve le gerarchie di Trieste," *Il Piccolo di Trieste*, 13 February 1937.
58 "Il Prefetto e il Podestà di Genova ricevuti dal Capo del Governo," *Il Popolo d'Italia*, 23 May 1934.
59 "Rapporto al Capo del Governo sul risanamento di Bologna," *Il Popolo d'Italia*, 20 December 1936.
60 "5 January. The Führer discusses his plans for the reconstruction with Speer ... the Führer shows me his plans for the renovation of Berlin ... they are truly majestic." From Goebbels's diary, 5 January 1937 Frederic Spotts, *Hitler and the Power of Aesthetics* (Woodstock-New York: Overlook Press, 2004), 356.
61 "L'Esposizione del ventennale fascista secondo le precise direttive del Duce ampiamente illustrate dal sen. Cini," *Il Popolo d'Italia*, 13 January 1937.

62 Enrico Guidoni, "L'E42 città della rappresentazione," in *E42: Utopia e scenario del regime*, vol. 2, *Urbanistica, architettura, arte e decorazione*, ed. Maurizio Calvesi, Enrico Guidoni, and Simonetta Lux (Venice: Marsilio, 1987), 36.

63 Letter from Marcello Piacentini to Vittorio Cini, 23 January 1937, in ACS, Fondo Cini, b. 1, issue 7.

64 Letter from Marcello Piacentini to Cipriano Efisio Oppo, 4 March 1937, in Guidoni, "L'E42 città della rappresentazione," 37.

65 The projects have already been discussed previously, and they are the same ones that would lead to Hitler's negative judgment in September in Munich.

66 The sentence by Pagano is quoted in Lupano, *Marcello Piacentini*, 176.

67 Mariani, *E42*, 66.

68 Guidoni, "L'E42 città della rappresentazione," 49.

69 Mariani, *E42*, 67

70 Di Majo and Insolera, *L'EUR e Roma dagli anni Trenta al Duemila*, 47–8.

71 Letter from Vittorio Cini to Dino Alfieri, 8 September 1937, in Guidoni, "L'E42 città della rappresentazione," 50.

72 Ian Kershaw, *Hitler, 1936–1945* (Milan: Bompiani, 2001), 48.

73 Letter from Marcello Piacentini to Ugo Ojetti, 18 September 1937, in GNAM, Fondo Ojetti, Cass. 58, I. Piacentini was in Munich on 4 September 1937.

74 Guidoni, "L'E42 città della rappresentazione," 51.

75 Ugo Ojetti, "Piacentini ha ragione," in Luciano Patetta, *L'architettura in Italia 1919–1943: Le polemiche* (Milan: Clup, 1972), 382.

76 "Memoria riguardante l'arch. Marcello Piacentini," typescript, undated, in AMP, issue 112.2.

77 Guidoni, "L'E42 città della rappresentazione," 51.

78 Letter from Marcello Piacentini to Vittorio Cini, 13 December 1937, in ACS, Fondo Cini, b. 1, issue 7.

79 Ibid.

80 Ibid. For more on the Palazzo della Civiltà Italiana, see Maristella Casciato, "Palazzo della Civiltà Italiana: Cronaca del concorso," in *Il Palazzo della Civiltà Italiana*, ed. Maristella Casciato and Sergio Poretti (Milan: Motta editore, 2002), 39–65.

81 Letter from Giuseppe Terragni to Luigi Piccinato, 5 January 1938, in Enrico Mantero, *Giuseppe Terragni e la città del razionalismo italiano* (Bari: Dedalo, 1983), 147.

82 According to Terragni, who was involved in the issue, however, the meetings were "highly argumentative." Letter from Giuseppe Terragni to Achille Funi, 17 January 1938, in Mariani, *E42*, 125.

83 See the letter from Davide Pacanowski to Domenico Filippone, 8 January 1938: "I was already informed in Milan that Padula would win the first

prize." Vieri Quilici, ed., *E42-Eur: Un centro per la metropoli* (Rome: Olmo, 1996), 74.

84 See Alessandra Muntoni, "Progetto di Concorso di primo e secondo grado per il Palazzo dei ricevimenti e congressi all'E42," in *Giuseppe Terragni*, ed. Giorgio Ciucci (Milan: Electa, 1996), 540.

85 Mariani, *E42*, 125.

86 Letter from Giuseppe Terragni to Achille Funi, 17 January 1938, in Mariani, *E42*, 125.

87 Letter from Giuseppe Pagano to Cipriano Efisio Oppo, 14 January 1938, in Mariani, *E42*, 181.

88 Letter from Vittorio Cini to Osvaldo Sebastiani, 7 January 1938, in ACS, SPD, CO, 1922–43, issue 509.832.

89 "III° rapporto sull'attività svolta al 31 dicembre 1937," typescript, in ACS, SPD, CO, 1922–43, issue 509.832.

90 Ojetti, "Piacentini ha ragione," 382.

91 Mariani, *E42*, 71.

92 Note by the private secretary for Mussolini, 2 February 1938, in ACS, SPD, CO, 1922–43, issue 509.832

93 Adalberto Libera, "La mia esperienza di architetto," *La Casa* 6 [1960], 174. The first two were drawn for the first- and second-level competition, the third and the fourth projects for this phase. The fifth likely resulted because of further changes required by Piacentini later on.

94 Ojetti, "Piacentini ha ragione," 382.

95 Report from Pinna Berchet to Mussolini, 15 March 1938, in ACS, SPD, CO, 1922–43, issue 509.832. Pinna Berchet verbally expressed her criticism during the meeting on 8 March 1938. Mussolini required a written report on it.

96 Note from the private secretary for Mussolini, 5 July 1938, in ACS, SPD, CO, 1922–43, issue 509.832.

97 Sandro Scarrocchia, *Albert Speer e Marcello Piacentini: L'architettura del totalitarismo negli anni trenta* (Milan: Skira, 1999), 109.

98 Albert Speer, *Diari segreti di Spandau* (Milan: Mondadori, 1976), 146.

99 Adolf Hitler, *Conversazioni segrete* (Naples: Richter, 1954), 89 (21 October 1941).

100 Letter from Rino Valdameri to Giuseppe Bottai, 3 February 1939, in Chiara Baglione, "Progetto per il Danteum," in *Pietro Lingeri*, ed. Chiara Baglione and Elisabetta Susani (Milan: Electa, 2004), 262.

101 Pietro Lingeri and Giuseppe Terragni, "Danteum in Roma: Note illustrative," *Casabella* 522 (March 1986), 40–1. See also Giorgio Ciucci, "La ragione teorica del Danteum," ibid.

102 Letter from Rino Valdameri to Giuseppe Terragni, 13 April 1940, quoted by Paolo Nicoloso, "Lingeri e Terragni," in *Pietro Lingeri*, ed. Baglione and Susani, 68.

103 Giuseppe Pagano, "Architettura nazionale," *Casabella* 85 (January 1935); reprinted in Giuseppe Pagano, *Architettura e città durante il fascismo*, ed. Cesare De Seta (Rome-Bari: Laterza, 1976), 47–8.

104 Guidoni, "L'E42 città della rappresentazione," 51. 26,000 lire equal to 20,000 euros.

105 On Pagano's missing signature, see Mariani, *E42*, 183. Pagano was nevertheless on the jury for the competition for the Palazzo dell Civiltà Italiana.

106 Giuseppe Pagano, "Potremo salvarci dalle false tradizioni e dalle ossessioni monumentali?" *Costruzioni-Casabella* 157 (January 1941); Giuseppe Pagano, "Occasioni perdute," *Costruzioni-Casabella* 158 (February 1941); both in Pagano, *Architettura e città durante il fascismo*, 129–41 and 142–5.

107 Letter from Marino Lazzari to Vittorio Cini, undated (confirmed after February 1941), in ACS, Fondo Cini, b. 1, issue 30.

108 Letter from Marcello Piacentini to Gherardo Casini, 28 April 1941, quoted in Guidoni, "L'E42 città della rappresentazione," 81.

109 ACS, SPD, CR, 1922–43, b. 36, issue 242.

110 Paolo Nicoloso, "La 'Carta del restauro' di Giulio Carlo Argan," *Annali di architettura* 6 (1994), 101–5. For more on Argan, see Mirella Serri, *I redenti* (Milan: Corbaccio, 2005), 135–9.

111 Giuseppe Bottai, *Diario 1935–1944*, ed. Giordano Bruno Guerri (Milan: Rizzoli, 1994), 323 and 328 (10 September and 7 October 1942).

112 Letter from Marcello Piacentini to Ugo Ojetti, 25 March 1943, in GNAM, Fondo Ojetti, Cass. 58, III.

7 Architecture and the Totalitarian Turnaround

1 Renzo De Felice, *Mussolini il duce*, vol. 2, *Lo Stato totalitario 1936–1940* (Turin: Einaudi, 1981), 254–330.

2 Piacentini wrote about the "arcane power" of the E42 in his letter to Cini, 11 March 1943, ACS, Fondo Cini, b. 3, issue 7.

3 According to De Felice, *Mussolini il duce*, 2:320.

4 Angelo Gatti, "Abbozzo per un ritratto di B. Mussolini," *Il Popolo d'Italia*, 27 March 1938.

5 Marcello Piacentini, "Classicità dell'E42," *Civiltà* 1 (April 1940), 23, 28.

6 Ugo Ojetti, *Taccuini: 1914–1943* (Florence: Sansoni, 1954), 538 (1 October 1939).

7 The sentence by Mussolini has been reported in Quaroni, "Giorgio Ciucci intervista Ludovico Quaroni," *Casabella* 515 (July 1985), 32.

8 Piacentini, "Classicità dell'E42," 23.

9 For more on Mussolini's sentence, see Ranuccio Bianchi Bandinelli, *Hitler e Mussolini: 1938, il viaggio del Führer in Italia* (Rome: e/o, 1995), 30–1.

10 "L'architettura del tempo fascista e l'edilizia moderna: Intervista a Marcello Piacentini di Alberto Simeoni," *L'Impero*, 31 March 1929.

11 Marcello Piacentini, "Il nostro programma," *Architettura* 1 (January 1932).

12 "S.E. l'arch: Marcello Piacentini preside della Facoltà di architettura dell'Università di Roma," *Architettura: Supplemento sindacale* 2 (15 February 1936), 13–14.

13 Marcello Piacentini, "Metodi e caratteristiche," *Architettura: La città universitaria di Roma*, special issue (December 1935), 2.

14 Marcello Piacentini, "L'urbanistica e l'architettura," *Architettura: L'Esposizione Universale di Roma 1942*, special issue (December 1938), 725–6; Marcello Piacentini, "Architettura del tempo di Mussolini," *L'Illustrazione italiana* 53 (December 1938), 1034.

15 Partito Nazionale Fascista, *Il cittadino soldato* (Rome: La libreria dello Stato, 1936), quoted in Emilio Gentile, *Fascismo: Storia e interpretazione* (Rome-Bari: Laterza, 2002), 251.

16 Piacentini rarely used the expression "fascist style." He had used it in the past, for instance in 1929, when he argued with Giovannoni on the future of Rome. At that time, he had proposed not only to protect the ancient city, but also to build a new one. At the time he wrote that the new city, which should be dedicated to "the beloved name of Benito Mussolini," would be the expression of "our own style, that is truly fascist and Italian." Marcello Piacentini, "Roma e l'arte edilizia," *Pegaso* 9 (September 1929), 319.

17 Marcello Piacentini, "Per l'autarchia: Politica dell'architettura 2, Nuova rinascita," *Il Giornale d'Italia*, 15 July 1938; reprinted in Mario Pisani, ed., *Marcello Piacentini: Architettura moderna* (Venice: Marsilio, 1996), 220.

18 Marcello Piacentini, "Nuovi orizzonti dell'edilizia cittadina," *Nuova Antologia* 1199 (1 March 1922), 60–72.

19 Around 1925, "thanks to the suggestion of the president of the Senate House T. Tittoni to B. Mussolini, [Piacentini] proposed the creation of the new charge of Rettore per l'Edilizia to the Governatorato of Rome, for which he proposed his candidacy." Mario Lupano, *Marcello Piacentini* (Rome-Bari: Laterza, 1991), 183; "L'architettura del tempo fascista e l'edilizia moderna. Intervista a Marcello Piacentini di Alberto Simeoni," *L'Impero*, 31 March 1929.

20 Letter from Vittorio Morpurgo to Osvaldo Sebastiani, 5 September 1938, in ACS, SPD, CO, 1922–43, issue 509.428/2.

21 Letter from Marcello Piacentini and Attilio Spaccarelli to Mussolini, 24 February 1940, in ACS, SPD, CO, 1922–43, issue 7583.

22 Letter from Marcello Piacentini to Arnaldo Foschini, 30 April 1936, in AAF, issue Varie.

23 "Premessa e criteri generali," *Architettura: Urbanistica della Roma Mussoliniana*, special issue (December 1936), 5–6.

24 Marcello Piacentini, "L'esposizione universale dell'anno ventesimo e la più grande Roma del piano imperiale," *Il Giornale d'Italia*, 14 October 1936.

25 Marcello Piacentini and Attilio Spaccarelli, "Dal ponte Elio a San Pietro," *Capitolium* 1 (January 1937), 19; "Una nuova grande via a Roma," *Il Popolo d'Italia*, 10 July 1936; Marcello Piacentini, "L'esposizione universale dell'anno ventesimo e la più grande Roma del piano imperiale," *Il Giornale d'Italia*, 14 October 1936; Antonio Cederna, *Mussolini urbanista* (Rome-Bari: Laterza, 1979), 82.

26 Antonio Muñoz, "Marcello Piacentini parla di Roma e di architettura," *L'Urbe* 5 (May 1937), 25.

27 Letter from Brasini to Bruno Biagi, 12 September 1938, in Archivio Brasini, Porano. The plan by Brasini involved the area between Corso Umberto, Via delle Botteghe Oscure, Via della Scrofa, and Via Tomacelli. The meeting with Mussolini took place on 12 June.

28 Quaroni's project was included in a broader plan for the arrangement of the area between Piazza Barberini and Corso del Rinascimento. See Pippo Ciorra, *Ludovico Quaroni, 1911–1987* (Milan: Electa, 1989), 81 and 164.

29 "Il concorso di secondo grado per la casa Littoria in Roma, Progetto vincitore: Arch. Enrico Del Debbio, Arnaldo Foschini, Vittorio Morpurgo," *Architettura* 12 (December 1937), 707–13.

30 Marcello Piacentini, "Il progetto definitivo della Casa Littoria a Roma," *Architettura* 12 (December 1937), 699.

31 Giorgio Ciucci, "Roma capitale imperiale," in *Storia dell'architettura italiana: Il primo Novecento*, ed. Giorgio Ciucci and Giorgio Muratore (Milan: Electa, 2004), 411–14.

32 "La nuova stazione di Roma secondo le direttive del Duce," *Il Popolo d'Italia*, 28 February 1937; Giorgio Pini, *Filo diretto con Palazzo Venezia* (Bologna: Cappelli, 1950), 86. For more on Termini Railway Station, see Paolo Mariani, "La stazione principale di Roma: Dal nudo realismo alla folle vestizione," in *Angiolo Mazzoni (1884–1979): Architetto nell'Italia tra le due guerre* (Casalecchio di Reno: Grafis, 1984), 81–94; Ezio Godoli, "Roma Termini: dai progetti di Mazzoni al concorso del 1947," in *Architettura ferroviaria in Italia: Novecento*, vol. 1, *Il Novecento*, ed. Ezio Godoli and Antonietta Iolanda Lima (Palermo: Flaccovio, 2004), 283–316.

33 Marcello Piacentini, "La nuova stazione di Roma imperiale," *Architettura: L'E.42 in Roma: Stato dei lovori e nuovi progetti – Le sistemazioni urbanistiche connesse: via Imperiale e nuova stazione di Roma Termini*, special issue (December 1939), 76.

34 "Come sarà la nuova Stazione di Roma," *Il Popolo d'Italia*, 27 February 1938.

35 Letter from Ugo Ojetti to Giovanni Host Venturi, 13 March 1941, in BNF, Fondo Ojetti, mss da ord. 250, Manoscritti 5, 8, c. 32. See Marta Petrin, "Ugo Ojetti e l'architettura italiana, 1936–1942," tesi di laurea (MA diss., Facoltà di Lettere e Filosofia di Udine, a.a. 2005–6), 105–12.

36 Ojetti, *Taccuini*, 556–7 (15 March 1941). Ojetti had examined the columns on the previous Tuesday.

37 Giuseppe Pagano, "Una solenne paternale," *Costruzioni-Casabella* 149 (May 1940); reprinted in Giuseppe Pagano, *Architettura e città durante il fascismo*, ed. Cesare De Seta (Rome-Bari: Laterza, 1976), 114.

38 Ugo Ojetti, "L'ultima internazionale," *Corriere della Sera*, 22 May 1941.

39 Nino D'Aroma, *Mussolini segreto* (Bologna: Cappelli, 1958), 230.

40 Italo Insolera, *Roma Moderna: Un secolo di storia urbanistica, 1870–1970* (Turin: Einaudi, 2001), 170–4.

41 Vieri Quilici, ed., *E42-Eur: Un centro per la metropoli* (Rome: Olmo, 1996), 20.

42 Gustavo Giovannoni, "Restauro dei monumenti e urbanistica," *Palladio* 2–3 (1943), 38.

43 Marcello Piacentini, "Per l'Olimpiade della civiltà," *Il Giornale d'Italia*, 27 March 1940.

44 De Felice, *Mussolini il duce*, 2:286–7.

45 Andrea Bruschi, "La Variante Generale del 1942 al Piano Regolatore di Roma," in *Roma: Architettura e città negli anni della seconda guerra mondiale*, ed. Pietro Scoppola, Lucio V. Barbera, and Paolo Ostilio Rossi (Rome: Gangemi, 2004), 55.

46 AMP, b. 193.1. The undated drawing, presenting the "Variante" on the title block, should refer to the Variante of 1941.

47 Letter from Marcello Piacentini to Ugo Ojetti, 22 October 1941, in AMP, issue 98.

48 Report from the Committee to the Duce, undated, in AMP, issue 195.1.

49 Salvatore Santuccio, "Storia urbanistica," in Antonella Greco and Salvatore Santuccio, *Foro Italico* (Rome: Multigrafica, 1991), 19.

50 Joachim Fest, *Speer: Una biografia* (Milan: Garzanti, 2000), 69.

51 For more on the two monumental poles of the north-south axis, see Paolo Ostilio Rossi, "L'esposizione del 1942 e le Olimpiadi del 1944: L'E42 e il Foro Mussolini come porte urbane della Terza Roma," *MdiR* 1–2 (January–December 2004), 13–28.

52 The sketch appeared on the back of the letter from Marcello Piacentini to Virgilio Testa, 18 September 1942, in AMP, issue 200.

53 For example, the letter from Luigi Moretti to Marcello Piacentini, 27 March 1941, in a meeting on the Variante to the city plan, in AMP, issue 197.3.

54 Letter from Marcello Piacentini to Vittorio Cini, 18 August 1942, in ACS, Fondo Cini, b. 1, issue 7.

55 Report by Borghese to Mussolini, typescript, undated, in AMP, issue 195.2. Published in *Urbanistica* 62 (April 1974), 69.

56 Bruschi, "La Variante Generale del 1942 al Piano Regolatore di Roma," 59.

57 Insolera, *Roma Moderna*, 171.

58 The report, presented by Italo Insolera and Alberto Mancini in *Urbanistica* 62 (April 1974), was written after 17 August 1942. This date had been determined based on a draft, preserved in the Piacentini Archive, that is slightly different from the published version, which contained a reference to the "recently promulgated" urban law. "Relazione della commissione al duce," typescript, undated, in AMP, issue 195.1. Piacentini was the author of chapters 2, 4, 5, 7, Giovannoni of chapters 1, 6, 12.

59 Marcello Piacentini, "Per l'olimpiade della civiltà," *Il Giornale d'Italia*, 27 March 1940.

60 Letter from Marcello Piacentini to Melis, 29 October 1941, in Bruschi, "La Variante Generale del 1942 al Piano Regolatore di Roma," 60.

61 "I have been thinking for some time about the coordination of the Rome city plan, which, as you know, I am passionate about." Letter from Marcello Piacentini to Vittorio Cini, 18 August 1942, in ACS, Fondo Cini, b. 1, issue 7. In this letter, Piacentini claimed he was opposed to the construction of "houses" that were not in keeping with the "solemn and unified tone" of the E42.

62 Letter from Marcello Piacentini to Vittorio Cini, 11 February 1943, in ACS, Fondo Cini, b. 1, issue 7.

63 Albert Speer, *Memorie del Terzo Reich* (Milan: Mondadori, 1995 [1969]), 92; Fest, *Speer*, 74.

64 George Mosse, *La nazionalizzazione delle masse: Simbolismo politico e movimenti di massa in Germania (1815–1933)* (Bologna: Il Mulino, 1975), 213.

65 Frederic Spotts, *Hitler and the Power of Aesthetics* (Woodstock-New York: The Overlook Press, 2004), 311–13.

66 Lars Olof Larsson, *Albert Speer: Le plan de Berlin, 1937–1943* (Bruxelles: Archives d'architecture moderne, 1983), 59; Joseph Goebbels, *Diario 1938*, ed. Marina Bistolfi (Milan: Mondadori 1996), 225 (8 July 1938) and 200 (15 June 1938); Speer, *Memorie del Terzo Reich*, 180, 184; Ian Kershaw, *Hitler: 1936–1945* (Milan: Bompiani, 2001), 291–3.

67 Albert Speer, *Diari segreti di Spandau* (Milan: Mondadori, 1976), 175; Work on the projects began in 1938; see Wolfgang Schäche, "From Berlin to 'Germania'," *Art and Power: Europe under the Dictators, 1930–1945*, ed. Dawn Ades et al. (London: Thames and Hudson-Hayward Gallery, 1995), 329.

68 Fest, *Speer*, 89.

69 Speer, *Diari segreti di Spandau*, 175.

70 Speer, *Memorie del Terzo Reich*, 67.

71 Goebbels, *Diario 1938*, 190 (5 June 1938).

72 Spotts, *Hitler and the Power of Aesthetics*, 321.

73 Fest, *Speer*, 23.

74 Adolf Hitler, *Conversazioni segrete* (Naples: Richter, 1954), 89 (21 October 1941).

75 "While I was designing the *Volkshalle* I went to study St. Peter's Basilica
    in Rome in great detail." Speer, *Memorie del Terzo Reich*, 187, For more on
    Speer's use of the ancient Roman models, see Alex Scobie, *Hitler's State
    Architecture: The impact of Classical Antiquity* (University Park, PA: Pennsylva-
    nia State University Press, 1990). For more on Speer's journeys in Italy, see
    Sandro Scarrocchia, *Albert Speer e Marcello Piacentini: L'architettura del totalita-
    rismo negli anni trenta* (Milan: Skira, 1999), 163–9.
76 Speer, *Diari segreti di Spandau*, 412.
77 When he got back from Sicily, Speer suggested to Hitler that he move the
    sarcophagus of Frederick II, which was kept in Palermo Cathedral, to Ber-
    lin. Speer, *Diari segreti di Spandau*, 460.
78 Letter from Marcello Piacentini to Alessandro Pavolini, 12 July 1940,
    quoted in Scarrocchia, *Albert Speer e Marcello Piacentini*, 351. For more on
    the visit to Rome, see Speer, *Diari segreti di Spandau*, 142.
79 Enrico Guidoni, "L'E42 città della rappresentazione," in *E42: Utopia e sce-
    nario del regime*, vol. 2, *Urbanistica, architettura, arte e decorazione*, ed. Maurizio
    Calvesi, Enrico Guidoni, and Simonetta Lux (Venice: Marsilio, 1987), 35.
    For more on Speer's visit to the building site, see Riccardo Mariani, *E42:
    Un progetto per l' "Ordine Nuovo"* (Milan: Comunità, 1987), 148. Speer was
    also invited to the opera by Alfieri. See Speer, *Memorie del Terzo Reich*, 179.
80 Ibid., 179. In his *Memorie del Terzo Reich*, Speer willingly played down the
    significance of his journey, claiming that he had been mostly impressed by
    the propaganda graffiti.
81 Scarrocchia, *Albert Speer e Marcello Piacentini*, 108–9. The drawings are dated
    May 1939.
82 Speer, *Memorie del Terzo Reich*, 161, 204.
83 Marcello Piacentini, "Premesse e caratteri dell'architettura attuale te-
    desca," *Architettura* 8 (August 1939), 467–8.
84 Scarrocchia, *Albert Speer e Marcello Piacentini*, 351.
85 Luigi Lenzi, "Architettura del III Reich," *Architettura* 8 (August 1939), 479.
86 Letter from Albert Speer to Marcello Piacentini, 10 September 1940, in
    Scarrocchia, *Albert Speer e Marcello Piacentini*, 352; Speer, *Diari segreti di Span-
    dau*, 56.
87 Schäche, "From Berlin to 'Germania'," 326–9. For more on the use of the
    prisoners and on the marble supply, see Scobie, *Hitler's State Architecture*,
    129–31; Paul B. Jaskot, *The Architecture of Oppression: The SS, Forced Labor and
    the Nazi Monumental Building Economy* (London-New York: Routledge, 2000),
    94–100. Jaskot demonstrated that the SS used prisoners to produce bricks
    and extract marble from the quarries, and that the prisoners were the main
    producers of materials for Speer's buildings in Berlin and Nuremberg.
88 Alfieri went to visit Speer's study in June 1940 and, on that occasion, he
    underlined the Roman character of the most representative buildings

planned for Berlin. Nicola Timmermann, *Repräsentative "Staatsbaukunst" im faschistischen Italien und im nationalsozialistischen Deutschland – der Einfluß der Berlin-Planung auf die Eur* (Stuttgart: Ibidem, 2001), 243.

89 Speer, *Memorie del Terzo Reich*, 160.

90 Dino Alfieri, *Due dittatori di fronte* (Milan: Rizzoli, 1948), 275. The old embassy was abandoned because it was within the area of Speer's new plan.

91 Scarrocchia, *Albert Speer e Marcello Piacentini*, 136. Alfieri visited Speer's study in June 1940. The ambassador was one of the main organizers of the Exhibition of the Fascist Revolution in 1932. Speer, *Memorie del Terzo Reich*, 160–72.

92 "I lavori pubblici e quelli in progetto approvati dal Duce: Il ritorno del Podestà dalla capitale," *Il Popolo d'Italia*, 29 January 1931; Andrea Bona, "Il Club degli urbanisti: Una battaglia per Milano," *Città immaginata e città costruita*, ed. Cristina Bianchetti (Milan: Angeli, 1992), 91–111.

93 "Grandioso programma di opere comunali approvato dal Capo del Governo," *Il Popolo d'Italia*, 19 July 1934.

94 Luigi Venturini, "La pianta di Milano romana ed i piani regolatori," *Il Popolo d'Italia*, 8 February 1935.

95 Daniele Bardelli and Pietro Zuretti, "L'Amministrazione comunale nel periodo podestarile," *Storia di Milano*, vol. 18, *Il Novecento*, tomo 1 (Rome: Istituto dell'Enciclopedia Italiana, 1995), 660.

96 "Il Duce per Milano: La sistemazione di Piazza Duomo ed altre importanti opere di piano regolatore," *Il Popolo d'Italia*, 31 July 1936. Mussolini approved a Victory Arch in Piazzale Fiume (now Piazza Repubblica) and for a Fontana dell'Impero in Piazza Duca D'Aosta.

97 Bardelli and Zuretti, "L'Amministrazione comunale nel periodo podestarile," 659.

98 Fondo Luigi Lorenzo Secchi, Politecnico di Milano, A. 18, issue 1. Register of the memoranda of the meetings of the advisory committee for the City Plan 1935–36–37, memorandum of the meeting of 3 August 1936. See also Cristina Bianchetti, "Portaluppi e Milano," in *Piero Portaluppi: Linea errante nell'architettura del Novecento*, ed. Luca Molinari (Milan: Skira, 2003), 262–6. I thank Cristina Bianchetti for allowing me to see this document.

99 "When on 20 July 1936 I was received by the prime minister, I submitted a project, one which he appreciated and which was mostly the result of the study and the creative talent of H.E. Piacentini." Letter from Guido Pesenti to Giuseppe Bottai, 4 December 1937, in GNAM, Fondo Ojetti, Cass. 86, Roma.

100 Note for the Duce, 18 March 1938, in ACS, PCM, 1937–9, issue 7.1.2, n. 4264.

101 Pesenti resigned on 24 May 1928 and was substituted by Gallarati Scotti. Bardelli and Zuretti, "L'Amministrazione comunale nel periodo podestarile," 660.

102 "Il Duce approva la sistemazione di dieci principali località cittadine," *Il Popolo d'Italia*, 11 December 1938.

103 "L'esultanza di Milano espressa dal federale," *Il Popolo d'Italia*, 11 December 1938.

104 "La sede della Questura," *Il Popolo d'Italia*, 7 December 1938; "La nuova sede della Questura," *Il Popolo d'Italia*, 5 March 1940.

105 "Il Duce approva e dispone per la rapida esecuzione dei lavori," *Il Popolo d'Italia*, 10 June 1939. Piacentini was by then an adviser to the Società Immobiliare Diaz, which had replaced the SCIA.

106 "Il Duce riceve le gerarchie milanesi," *Il Popolo d'Italia*, 11 February 1940; "Il Duce per Milano," *Il Popolo d'Italia*, 10 February 1940.

107 For more on the history of the competition, see Fulvio Irace, *Giovanni Muzio, 1893–1982* (Milan: Electa, 1994), 124–32; Massimiliano Savorra, *Enrico Agostino Griffini* (Naples: Electa Napoli, 2000), 118–32; Massimiliano Savorra, "Piazza Duomo," in *Piero Portaluppi*, ed. Molinari, 134–7.

108 Letter from Marcello Piacentini to Ugo Ojetti, 13 January 1938, in GNAM, Fondo Ojetti, Cass. 58, I, Roma. In the group, there were Muzio, Griffini, Magistretti, and Portaluppi.

109 Letter from Marcello Piacentini to Ugo Ojetti, 25 July 1938; letter from Giovanni Muzio to Ugo Ojetti, 26 July 1938; both in GNAM, Fondo Ojetti, Cass. 58, I and Cass. 51, 20. See Marta Petrin, "Ugo Ojetti e l'architettura italiana, 1936–1942," tesi di laurea (MA diss., Facoltà di Lettere e Filosofia di Udine, a.a. 2005–6). Ojetti considered the second-level project of Muzio's group much better than the first-level one, and he praised the role played by Piacentini. Ugo Ojetti, "Piacentini ha ragione," in *In Italia l'arte ha da essere italiana* (Milan: Mondadori, 1942), 271–8.

110 Piacentini, "Per l'autarchia. Politica dell'architettura," 2.

111 Ugo Ojetti, "Piacentini ha ragione," *Corriere della Sera*, 24 August 1938.

112 "Architettura," in *Dizionario di Politica*, ed. PNF (Rome: Istituto dell'Enciclopedia Italiana, 1940), 1:159. The dictionary was presented to Mussolini on 26 April 1940. See Alessia Pedio, *La cultura del totalitarismo imperfetto: Il Dizionario di politica del Partito nazionale fascista (1940)* (Milan: Unicopli, 2000).

113 Irace, *Giovanni Muzio*, 131–2.

114 The first sketch is reported in Lupano, *Marcello Piacentini*, 141; the second sketch is reported in "Marcello Piacentini e Roma," *Bollettino della Biblioteca della Facoltà di Architettura dell'Università degli studi di Roma "La Sapienza"* 53 (1995), 68.

115 Letter from Marcello Piacentini to Mari, 19 September 1938, in AMP, issue 52.1. See also Elisabetta Susani, "La resistenza al moderno: L'architettura maggiore," in *Milano dietro le quinte: Luigi Lorenzo Secchi*, ed. Elisabetta Susani (Milan: Electa, 1999), 78.

116 Report of 18 June 1938 quoted in Dario Matteoni, "Città e architettura: Dalla 'Livorno scomparsa' alla ricostruzione," in Francesca Cagianelli and Dario Matteoni, *Livorno, la costruzione di un'immagine: Tradizione e modernità nel Novecento* (Cinisello Balsamo: Silvana, 2003), 54–7; to the document is useful in reconstructing the whole event.

117 Pascoletti was Piacentini's main collaborator in Turin, where he had graduated and where he moved back during the construction.

118 Arnaldo Toffali, "Cronache urbanistiche: Piani e monumenti a Bolzano (1927–1943)," in Ugo Soragni, *Il monumento alla vittoria di Bolzano: Architettura e scultura per la città italiana (1926–1938)* (Vicenza: Neri Pozza, 1993), 101–15.

119 Galeazzo Ciano, *Diario 1937–1943*, ed. Renzo De Felice (Milan: Rizzoli, 1990), 206 (1 November 1938).

120 "Direttive del Duce al Prefetto e al Podestà di Bologna," *Il Popolo d'Italia*, 10 May 1939. On the events regarding the competition, see Federica Legnani, "Via Roma, 1936–1937," in *Norma e arbitrio: Architetti e ingegneri a Bologna. 1850–1950*, ed. Giuliano Gresleri and Pier Giorgio Massarenti (Venice: Marsilio, 2001), 287–97.

121 Lupano, *Marcello Piacentini*, 198.

122 Ibid., 199.

123 Luigi Lagomarsino, "Lo sviluppo urbanistico di Genova nel periodo 1925–1955," in *Architetture in Liguria dagli anni Venti agli anni Cinquanta*, ed. Silvia Barisione, Matteo Fochessati, Gianni Franzone, and Andrea Canziani (Milan: Abitare Segesta, 2004), 37–42.

124 Besides the Banco di Napoli, Piacentini designed the central headquarters of the Banco Nazionale di Lavoro, whose directors, Giuseppe Frignani and Arturo Osio, were divided by bitter arguments. See Valerio Castronovo, *Storia di una banca: La Banca Nazionale del Lavoro nell'economia italiana, 1913–2003* (Turin: Einaudi, 2003), 163–4, 212–13.

125 Letter from Marcello Piacentini to Feliciano Lepori, 18 June 1938; letter from Camillo Guerra to Marcello Piacentini, 3 July 1938, both in AMP, issue 52.1. See also Paolo Giordano, ed., *Napoli* (Rome: Officina, 1994), 24.

126 "Come sarà sistemata la stazione di Venezia," *Il Popolo d'Italia*, 4 February 1939.

127 Riccardo Domenichini, "I progetti di Mazzoni per la stazione ferroviaria di Venezia Santa Lucia," in *Angiolo Mazzoni: Architetto, ingegnere del Ministero delle Comunicazioni*, ed. Mauro Cozzi, Ezio Godoli, and Paola Pettenella (Milan: Skira, 2003), 194.

128 Massimo De Sabbata, "L'università," in *Trieste 1918–1954*, ed. Paolo Nicoloso and Federica Rovello (Trieste: Mgs Press, 2005), 227–34.

129 "Il piano regolatore di Udine: Nostra intervista con il Podestà," *Il Popolo del Friuli*, 25 April 1939.

130 Letter from Marcello Piacentini to Gino Cipriani, 13 November 1939, in AMP, issue 102.
131 "Protagonisti: Filiberto Guala e Renato Bonelli." Interviews edited by Paola Di Biagi and Paolo Nicoloso, *La grande ricostruzione: Il piano Ina-Casa e l'Italia degli anni cinquanta*, ed. Paola Di Biagi (Rome: Donzelli, 2001), 145.
132 Information, 20 April 1938, ACS, MI, PS, Pol. Polit., issue Personali, 1926–44, issue 1051, s. issue Marcello Piacentini.
133 Paolo Nicoloso, "I concorsi di architettura durante il fascismo," *Casabella* 683 (November 2000), 4–7. For more on the competitions, see Maristella Casciato, "I concorsi per gli edifici pubblici: 1927–1936," in *Storia dell'architettura italiana: Il primo Novecento*, ed. Giorgio Ciucci and Giorgio Muratore (Milan: Electa, 2004), 208–33. Giovannoni, who was one of the most assiduous members of the commissions with his 43 appointments, had a more independent position when compared to Piacentini, as demonstrated by the events related to the Aprilia city plan.
134 Gio Ponti, "La prossima Triennale e l'attrezzatura artistica italiana," *Corriere della Sera*, 4 May 1942.
135 See Fulvio Irace, *Gio Ponti* (Milan: Electa, 1988), 39; Giorgio Ciucci, "Gli architetti e la guerra," in *Storia dell'architettura italiana: Il primo Novecento*, ed. Ciucci and Muratore, 483–4; Renata Piccinetti, "Una rivista tra le due guerre: Da 'Architettura e arti decorative' ad 'Architettura,' 1921–1944," tesi di laurea (MA diss., Politecnico di Milano, a.a. 2005–6), 117, 154, 218.
136 Foschini suggested the names of the candidates to the management. Letter from Arnaldo Foschini to Marcello Piacentini, 15 October 1942, in AMP, b. 111.
137 GAIU, "Statuto," typescript, in AMP, issue 337. The enterprise failed in March 1943: "As you know, everything went up in smoke. The jealousies played out furiously!" Letter from Marcello Piacentini to Raffaello Fagnoni, 30 March 1943, in AMP, issue 337.
138 Letter from Marcello Piacentini to Vittorio Cini, 11 February 1943, in ACS, Fondo Cini, b. 1, issue 7.
139 Letter from Raffaello Fagnoni to Marcello Piacentini, 26 March 1943, in AMP, issue 337.

Epilogue

1 Renzo De Felice, *Mussolini l'alleato*, vol. 1, *L'Italia in guerra 1940–1943*, tomo 1, *Dalla guerra "breve" alla guerra lunga* (Turin: Einaudi, 1996), 97.
2 Alessandra Muntoni, "Il Palazzo della civiltà italiana," in *E42: Utopia e scenario del regime*, vol. 2, *Urbanistica, architettura, arte e decorazione*, ed. Maurizio Calvesi, Enrico Guidoni, and Simonetta Lux (Venice: Marsilio, 1987), 356; Antonella La Torre, "Il Palazzo dei ricevimenti e congressi," in *E42*, ed. Calvesi, Guidoni, and Lux, 2:324.

3 Massimiliano Savorra, *Enrico Agostino Griffini* (Naples: Electa Napoli, 2000), 132.

4 Massimo De Sabbata, "L'università," in *Trieste 1918–1954*, ed. Paolo Nicoloso and Federica Rovello (Trieste: Mgs Press, 2005), 233.

5 Alfredo Forti, "La Stazione principale di Roma," in *Angiolo Mazzoni (1884–1979): Architetto nell'Italia tra le due guerre* (Casalecchio di Reno: Grafis, 1984), 212.

6 ACS, SPD, CO, 1922–43, issue 203.426.

7 Renzo De Felice, *Mussolini l'alleato*, vol. 1, *L'Italia in guerra 1940–1943*, tomo 2, *Crisi e agonia del regime* (Turin: Einaudi, 1990), 975.

8 "Revisione del 'Programma di massima' del 1937," December 1940, in ACS, PCM, 1937–9, issue 14.1, n. 200/6.3. The document is quoted in its entirety in *E42: Utopia e scenario del regime*, vol. 1, *Ideologia e programma dell'Olimpiade delle Civiltà*, ed. Tullio Gregory and Achille Tartaro (Venice: Marsilio, 1987), 166–70.

9 Letter from Marcello Piacentini to Vittorio Cini, 25 August 1940, in Riccardo Mariani, *E42: Un progetto per l' "Ordine Nuovo"* (Milan: Comunità, 1987), 140–2.

10 "A giant Roman arch will dominate." Benito Mussolini, *Opera omnia*, ed. Edoardo Susmel and Duilio Susmel (Florence: La Fenice, 1951–80), 29:266. Mussolini gave this speech on 20 April 1939. The idea of building an arch made of aluminium with a span of 300 metres and a height of 170 metres, despite economic and construction difficulties, was still supported in March 1941. Antonella La Torre, "Arco monumentale," *E42*, ed. Calvesi, Guidoni, and Lux, 2:467–70.

11 Letter from Vittorio Cini to Mussolini, 4 January 1941, in Mariani, *E42*, 142–3. The sketch of the Ara Pacis was presented by Sandro Scarrocchia, *Albert Speer e Marcello Piacentini: L'architettura del totalitarismo negli anni trenta* (Milan: Skira, 1999), 115. See also Paolo Ostilio Rossi, "L'esposizione del 1942 e le Olimpiadi del 1944: L'E42 e il Foro Mussolini come porte urbane della Terza Roma," *MdiR* 1–2 (January–December 2004), 24–5.

12 Marcello Piacentini, "Onore all'architettura italiana," *Architettura* 7 (July 1941), 263–73; reprinted in Mario Pisani, ed., *Marcello Piacentini: Architettura moderna* (Venice: Marsilio, 1996), 255–63.

13 Information, 8 January 1943, ACS, MI, PS, Pol. Polit., issue Personali, 1926–44, issue 1051, s. issue Marcello Piacentini. See also Giuseppe Bottai, *Diario 1935–1944*, ed. Giordano Bruno Guerri (Milan: Rizzoli, 1994), 352 (16 January 1943).

14 Ugo Ojetti, *Taccuini, 1914–1943* (Florence: Sansoni, 1954), 562 (22 June 1921).

15 Information, 8 January 1943, ACS, MI, PS, Pol. Polit., issue Personali, 1926–44, issue 1051, s. issue Marcello Piacentini.

16 The list continued with 12 post offices, 3 maritime stations, 1 airport, 4 ministry headquarters, 8 hospitals, 5 war memorials, 2 nursery schools, 3 Case del Balilla, 4 Case della GIL, 5 Case del Fascio, 12 marine sun therapy camps, 7 lyceums, 3 war schools, 5 stadiums, and 5 lots of social housing.

17 The names of the architects appeared only in the pictures which illustrated the article.

18 Piacentini, "Onore all'architettura italiana," 263.

19 Ibid., 266, 273.

20 De Felice, *Mussolini l'alleato*, 1/2:975.

21 MacGregor Knox, *Destino comune: Dittatura, politica estera e guerra nell'Italia fascista e nella Germania nazista* (Turin: Einaudi, 2000), 84.

22 Joachim Fest, *Speer: Una biografia* (Milan: Garzanti, 2000), 88–9, 105.

23 Albert Speer, *Memorie del Terzo Reich* (Milan: Mondadori, 1995 [1969]), 214–15, 218. For more on the climax of the consensus achieved by Hitler during the War, see Ian Kershaw, *Il "mito di Hitler": Immagine e realtà nel Terzo Reich* (Turin: Bollati Boringhieri, 1998), 153–62.

24 De Felice, *Mussolini l'alleato*, 1/1: 398–400.

25 Marcello Piacentini, "Architettura romana nel mondo," *Augustea* 23–4 (December 1942), 791–6.

26 Information, 4 December 1942 and 8 January 1943, ACS, MI, PS, Pol. Polit., issue Personali, 1926–44, issue 1051, s. issue Marcello Piacentini.

27 Emil Ludwig, *Colloqui con Mussolini* (Milan: Mondadori, 1970 [1932]), 209; Renzo De Felice, *Mussolini il duce*, vol. 2, *Lo Stato totalitario 1936–1940* (Turin: Einaudi, 1981), 274–5.

28 "Memoria del prof. Marcello Piacentini al Presidente della Commissione di epurazione del personale universitario," typescript, undated (confirmed later than 3 February 1945), in AMP, issue 112.2.

29 "Architettura," in *Dizionario di Politica*, ed. PNF (Rome: Istituto dell'Enciclopedia Italiana, 1940), 1:159.

30 See Sergio Luzzatto, *Il corpo del duce* (Turin: Einaudi, 1998), 98–206.

31 The decision to transform the Palazzo del Littorio into the Foreign Ministry headquarters had already been made under the fascist regime. See Vittorio Vidotto, "Il mito di Mussolini e le memorie nazionali: Le trasformazioni del Foro Italico, in Roma,"in *Roma: Architettura e città negli anni della seconda guerra mondiale*, ed. Pietro Scoppola, Lucio V. Barbera, and Paolo Ostilio Rossi (Rome: Gangemi, 2004), 115.

32 For more on the relationship between national identity and cultural heritage, see Salvatore Settis, *Italia S.p.A.* (Turin: Einaudi, 2002), 3–29. For more on the difference between history and memory, see Sergio Luzzatto, *La crisi dell'antifascismo* (Turin: Einaudi, 2004).

33 For more on the history of the different ideas of the nation in Italy during the twentieth century, see Emilio Gentile, *La Grande Italia: Il mito della nazione nel XX secolo* (Rome-Bari: Laterza, 2006).

Index of Names and Subjects

Piazza della Vittoria in Genoa,
228; Piazza Duomo in Milan,
222; redevelopment of Parma,
227; Santa Lucia Station in
Venice, 228; Stazione Termini
in Rome, 228; Via Cavour in
Novara, 229
projects: Ara Pacis at the E42,
234–5, 235ff, 298n11; avenue
from Via del Corso to Ponte
Umberto I in Rome, 206;
Città Universitaria in Rome,
13, 56, 85, 153, 161, 164, 172,
174–7, 179, 179ff, 180, 203, 205,
279n32; connection between
Città Universitaria and Termini
Station, 178; Mole Littoria
in Rome, 155f, 162; Palazzo
della Confederazione Fascista
degli Industriali in Rome, 161;
Piazza della Vittoria in Bolzano,
226–7, 227ff; Piazza Diaz in
Milan, 165, 167, 223, 226,
295n105; university campus in
Rio de Janeiro, 172, 282n66
proposal to relocate government
headquarters to the
Campidoglio, 154
rebirth of Italian architecture, 204,
224–5
relationship with Fascist Party,
162
relationship with Hitler, 219
relationship with Mussolini, 13,
158–9, 160, 162–3, 165–7, 172,
182, 187–8, 238–40
role of "building dictator,"
204, 216
Società Nazionale di
Progettazione, 232
Stadio del Partito Fascista in Rome,
162

tomb for Bruno Mussolini, 13,
238
Torre dei Caduti in Bergamo, 154
totalitarian turnaround, 203–4, 224
urban development plans: city
centre in Livorno, 124, 226;
E42, 73f, 77, 95, 163, 167, 180–2,
185, 186ff, 187, 188ff, 200, 208;
Ethiopia, 163; "la Grande Roma"
1925, 46, 154, 155ff; Rome
(1929), 158; Rome (1931), 55,
158–9, 167; Rome, revised in
1941 ("Variante del 1941"), 48,
168, 207, 220, 239
Via Barberini in Rome, 56, 167
Via Bissolati in Rome, 101, 162
Via Conciliazione in Rome, 28, 55,
64, 66, 70, 78, 150, 164f, 167,
205, 241, 242, 258n109
Piacentini, Pio
Palazzo delle Esposizioni in Rome,
162
proposal to relocate government
headquarters to the
Campidoglio, 154
Piccinato, Luigi, 12, 39, 89, 189, 211,
232, 237, 286n81
town hall tower in Sabaudia,
131–2, 138
urban development plan for the
E42, 182, 186ff, 188ff, 200
urban plan for Sabaudia, 86–7,
122, 131, 148ff, 171
Pierro, Mariano, 281n62
Pini, Giorgio, 105, 138
Pinna Berchet, Federico, 191,
287n95
Pirelli, Alberto, 181, 182
Pius XI (Achille Ratti), 70
Pollaci, Antonino: Caserma del Vigili
del Fuoco in Palermo, 27
Pollini, Gino, 12, 260n1, 263n31

Index of Places